Your Options Handbook

Your Options Handbook

The Practical Reference and Strategy Guide to Trading Options

JARED A. LEVY

WILEY

John Wiley & Sons, Inc.

Published by John Wiley & Sons, Inc., Hoboken, New Jersey.
Published simultaneously in Canada.

For general information on our other products and services or for technical support, please contact our Customer Care Department within the United States at (800) 762–2974, outside the United States at (317) 572–3993 or fax (317) 572–4002.

Wiley also publishes its books in a variety of electronic formats. Some content that appears in print may not be available in electronic books. For more information about Wiley products, visit our web site at www.wiley.com.

Library of Congress Cataloging-in-Publication Data:

Levy, Jared, 1976–
    Your options handbook : the practical reference and strategy guide to trading options / Jared Levy.
        p. cm. – (Wiley trading series)
    Includes index.
    ISBN 978-0-470-60362-8 (hardback); ISBN 978-1-118-04118-5 (ebk);
    ISBN 978-1-118-04119-2 (ebk); ISBN 978-1-118-04120-8 (ebk)
    1. Options (Finance) I. Title.
    HG6024.A3L485 2011
    332.64′53–dc22

                                                                        2010049287

Printed in the United States of America

10 9 8 7 6 5 4 3 2 1

This book is dedicated to those who lost their lives in the attacks of September 11, 2001, and to all those who have been innocent victims as the human race struggles for peace.

Contents

Foreword

When the first Treasury Bond option contracts were introduced in 1982, I was working as a retail commodities broker for Merrill Lynch at their Chicago Board of Trade office. At the time, options on futures were relatively new products, so Merrill sent a team of experts to each of their offices to instruct us (the brokers) on how to use them and of course how to sell them to our customer base.

During this presentation, one of the experts explained that there were over eight billion possible spread combinations between the new Treasury Bond options, bond futures, and cash bonds. That number, eight billion, really surprised me. But at the same time I was immediately fascinated with the idea that it could take years for traders to discover even a small percentage of the various ways that options could be used to make money.

Now for those of you who are new to options, the implications are really exciting. Even though it is almost 30 years later, options still represent an arena of vast untapped potential for creative expression. In other words, there are still countless ways of using options that no one else has thought of yet.

But there's more; besides the seemingly endless possibilities to make money, trading certain types of options strategies can also have a beneficial effect on helping you develop into a "consistently" successful trader. You can be the kind of trader whose equity curve rises at a nice steady angle, free of inordinately large drawdowns, and, most importantly, engenders a sense of confidence that causes one to believe he can actually make a living as a trader.

Here's what I mean.

If you're going to be in this business for any length of time, you will eventually come to the realization that there's more to developing into the kind of trader that has the ability to produce a consistent, reliable income than finding a good trading method or strategy. You also have to develop the ability to utilize that strategy to its maximum potential. Meaning there's a performance component to trading that people typically take for granted by assuming that if they get the right method or do the right market analysis, everything else about their trading will just take care of itself.

This assumption couldn't be further from the truth. The only way you can transform good analysis or a good trading method into consistent profits is if you can execute your trades properly. Flawless execution is not something that can be taken for granted because it requires the ability to achieve an objective state of mind and stay positively focused on doing exactly what you need to do, when you need to do it, without fear, hesitation, second thoughts or any other negative encumbrances that would cause you to make a trading error.

The consequences of not being able to properly implement your analysis or method will eventually create what I call a profit gap. A profit gap is the difference between what your method or analysis made available in the way of potential profits over a series of trades and the reality of what you actually ended up with, which in virtually all cases, except for a professional trader, will be less. To say the least, unrealized potential is something that most people find very painful and therefore would like to avoid.

So how do you go about learning to implement your analysis or method as it was designed to be traded? Not exactly a simple task when you consider there are several psychological factors that can cause people to "get in their own way," so to speak. However, there is one performance factor in particular that has a negative effect on nearly everyone who decides to step into the process of trying to become a successful trader.

Most of the difficulties that people experience performing as needed to properly trade their analysis or follow the rules of their trading methodology stem from not fully "accepting the risk that anything can happen." What do I mean by "accepting the risk that anything can happen"?

It's believing at the very core of your trading personality that the market is capable of doing anything, for any reason, at any moment. It means that regardless of how good your analysis or method has been in the past or the extent to which you may go to convince yourself the next trade you are about to put on will be a winner, the risk of losing is *always* present, it *never* goes away—*ever*. And, regardless of how it may seem, there's no method or form of market analysis that can prevent experiencing a losing trade.

As much as traders like to think of themselves as risk takers, the reality is that only the very best have truly accepted the inherent risks of trading at a deep enough level that would allow them to achieve an objective state of mind and stay confidently focused on performing flawlessly.

Which brings us to the point where I can explain why trading options can be so beneficial to your overall development, as well as why I like this book.

One of the most distinctive characteristics of an options contract is that you can genuinely limit the risk of your trade. When you buy an option contract you are not putting up margin. What you pay is the actual cost of the contract. And what you are buying is the opportunity to profit, if the value of the contact increases. But since the contract is paid for, you can't lose more than what it cost no matter what the market does.

This is blatantly not the case with trading stocks on margin, trading futures, and Forex contracts where the risk of how much money you can lose is virtually unlimited. When you are putting up margin to trade stocks, futures or, Forex, nothing is paid for. As a result, if the market moves against your position, there's nothing to limit the amount of money you could lose except whatever psychological resources you have to get out of a losing trade.

One of the most common mistakes traders make is not predefining the risk of a trade. Which means determining in advance of getting into a trade the dollar value of how far the market has to move against your position to tell you the trade isn't working and therefore not worth spending any more money to find out if it will. If you haven't considered or don't know in advance of getting into a trade what the market has to do or not do to tell you the trade isn't working, then you are setting yourself up to experience a catastrophic type of loss.

Think of it like this: If you find yourself in an unanticipated situation where you're losing, to get out of the trade will require admitting that you're wrong and of course taking a loss. Not exactly a desirable or easy thing to do, especially when it's far easier and more appealing to talk yourself into believing you're not really in a losing trade. Certainly the market could come back and make you whole. But if it doesn't, choosing not to get out could result in a loss far greater than anything you could have ever imagined possible.

Unfortunately for many people, it only takes just one of these catastrophic type drawdowns and for all intents and purposes their trading career is over. Because even though most people will recover financially, only a small percentage find their way to a full emotional recovery. To be more specific, the kind of recovery that allows one to eventually develop into a consistently successful trader, someone who has a profitable trading method and the ability to stay positively focused on executing that method flawlessly. In other words, no "profit gap" because she's no longer to susceptible to fear-based trading errors.

What makes options so attractive is there are plenty of strategies available that make money and at the same time automatically compensate for the fact that "anything can happen." So, if you can accept the cost of an option, at least to the extent that you can "get your wallet out" so to speak and actually pay for it, then from a psychological perspective you'll be in a much better state of mind to trade properly than anyone trading on margin who hasn't fully integrated the "anything can happen" principle into their trading regime.

The reason why I like Jared's book is because he champions limited risk options strategies. He is going to teach several limited risk strategies that not only have a high percentage for success, they also have excellent profit potential. And more importantly, at least with respect to your long-term success, his strategies will help you naturally ease into a complete acceptance that really "anything can happen."

I know many of you reading this book want your success to be "right now." But if you cultivate a genuine appreciation for the process of becoming a successful trader, and study Jared's book, the journey will be a lot less arduous and definitely more fun.

MARK DOUGLAS

Author of *The Disciplined Trader*^{TM}: *Developing Winning Attitudes* and *Trading in the Zone*^{TM}: *Master the Market with Confidence, Discipline, and a Winning Attitude*

February 2011

Preface

In 22 years, from modest beginnings and even after leaving school without a degree I found myself responsible for millions of dollars and making decisions about money and risk that most people would never experience in their lifetimes. It was extremely humbling, although I didn't realize or understand that emotion at first—I guess I couldn't. What I did realize was that I didn't have the gift of an Ivy League education, nor did I have the risk capital to throw into too many ideas that might not work. What I did possess was an extreme focus and obsession for the markets and, most importantly, derivatives. I was also following my passion without a real mentor or guide, which led to inevitable, but tolerable mistakes.

I realized as I became successful that there was *no* specific guru, method, or model you need to follow per se, and there was not even a perfect personality suited to being a trader (although some may be better suited than others). I also realized that there were literally hundreds of ways to make money (and lose it) in the markets and many of them seemed so logical and some of them realistically ascertainable. Unfortunately, all of these possible paths seem to lead to confusion and failure for many, partially because there is not really one concise guide to becoming a successful trader or investor, and once you start down one path you may pick up a book or listen to a speech that sends you down another.

I believe that what most of us really need is someone to help cut through the tangled web of information, nonsense, and hype to develop a method that works for you as an individual. Now, of course, that method needs to have some sort of basis, credence, and consistency and should be tested. You can't just arbitrarily choose a way to invest and hope it works or coat-tail someone else's. (You can, but it's a tough course to take).

In this book I offer you the indicators, methods, and data that I examine and use. I'll explain what I look for in them as well as the technique I use to find stocks to trade, and finally teach you the options strategies I use to trade them in simplified, specific, and practical detail.

Much of these methods are interpretations and combinations of all my mentors' teachings and my own personal experiences over the years. There is no perfect system and every person rationalizes data, situations, risk, and problems differently. My goal is to level the peaks and valleys, styles, and formats, and offer a real options trader's handbook, which I hope can make you some extra money, save you from losing more money than you would have, or just offer some cool insight to our little world of derivatives.

In this book are the most of the tools and knowledge that you must know to become a consistent, successful trader or to start your own trading business.

My approach is not perfect, but the methods and suggestions that you find in this book not only have worked for me in the past, they enabled me to make my living as a trader, both on and off the floor. I can't promise that everyone who picks up this book will walk away an expert options trader, but what I can promise is that you will get your money's worth. I left behind $70,000 to my first trading partners because they taught me the craft—that was my *options training tuition*. I think the cost of this book is a much better deal! But in all sincerity, teaching, along with trading, are my passions and this book is packed with tips, suggestions, and tricks of the trade from a professional market maker's perspective, I know that some of the data contained within this book will help you become a better trader, at least on some level.

I tried my best to write in plain language and do my best to ensure your complete understanding of any unique verbiage or nomenclature that is used.

Don't be discouraged if it all doesn't make sense at first. The seeds of information that you sow today will germinate into the wisdom that will carry you through your trading journey.

At the end of the day, it is my belief that the understanding of human behavior as well as recognizing your own, in conjunction with the detailed knowledge of a stock or sector, its typical behavior, and the management of your personal risk will lead you to success.

I know that's a ton to handle, but be patient.

The subtle nuances and "intuition" that it takes to be a successful trader *cannot* be taught in a book or a series of books, much like reading your state's driving laws and studying the mechanics of the automobile won't make you the world's top Formula 1 driver. You must get in the driver's seat. Like racing, there are risks and rewards, and this book teaches you how to minimize the risks and reap the most consistent reward.

I do want to give thanks to the great traders, risk managers, game theorists, and so many other brilliant minds out there that have influenced me directly or indirectly over the years. There have been many great books written, which I am sure have found their way into my head in bits and pieces and formed the amalgamation of styles, beliefs, systems, and techniques that I have made my own and made me successful.

HOW AND WHY I BECAME A MARKET MAKER

I now realize that growing up in a middle class diverse neighborhood in Philadelphia gave me just about everything I needed to be a successful trader. My preteen friends were probably the most assorted circle that you could imagine—from trouble makers to trust fund babies and everyone in between. Being around this group allowed me to observe the different rationales of extremely different minds at close range and at a time when I was most impressionable. For many of us, we have this intuition; sometimes we just ignore or don't trust it or maybe just don't require those intuitive skills later on in life so much, so we let them fade.

My hyperactive personality gave me a propensity to get bored easily in class and goof off. Luckily, there were some amazing and tolerant teachers in the Philadelphia public school system, in addition to my parents, who stimulated and motivated me to do bigger and better things with my life.

But it was finance that became my passion early on after an exercise in elementary school where we picked stocks in a mock portfolio.

After my first trip to visit the New York Stock Exchange (NYSE), at about 12 years old, I wanted to be a trader. I was hooked. I became obsessed with the stock exchange system and the traders standing on the floor. At first, the lure was the cool jackets, the frenetic energy that fit my persona, the excitement of all that money passing from person to person, not to mention the ability for me to go to work and yell at people I worked with. I guess from a preteen's eyes that was nirvana.

This was a kid's dream for sure, albeit a closet geeky kid, who from a young age was exposed to just about everything a kid shouldn't be exposed to. My parents, who were complete polar opposites of each other, did everything they could to make me feel so not middle class, even though the situation was tense between them most of the time.

My mother, who was a high school English teacher in an inner-city Philadelphia school, encouraged me to let my mind to run free, and to dream and follow whatever dream or vision I had. My father, who was the rational, realist of the two, tried to help me think before acting, which was definitely not my strong suit.

Most of the time I had too much freedom and for a prepubescent kid that was a problem.

I remember taking apart my new Adam computer in 1983, which probably cost my mom a month's salary. I dissected and labeled the more than 400 components on the living room floor, because I really wanted to know exactly how it worked, but that didn't go over too well.

My father, who was an electrician by trade, instilled more of my practical, logical, and realistic thought processes. We would assemble complex electronic components, go to military surplus stores to purchase gas masks and hazmat suits so we could compare the combustibility of ether versus different types of alcohol, and played with liquid mercury, definitely not typical. (Child protective services would have had a field day.)

WWF wrestlers and G.I. Joe action figures seldom found their way into my playpen. By the time I was in my teens, I had an insatiable desire for knowledge, but more importantly I broke down seemingly complex problems by using rational, practical solutions—this desire was partially blurred by chasing girls, of course.

Most humans just don't want to be bothered with the inner workings of everything around them. It's much easier to look at a device and say, "That is a clock; it tells us the time. That is a computer; it allows me to surf the net," or a process like buying a stock and think, "I am buying this stock from my stock broker so I can hopefully make money." That was never good enough for me. I wanted to know every part of every process, device, and object around me, be it man-made or organic.

My theory is that many assumptions and beliefs are only partially correct and that many of us believe certain things because a trustworthy source told us so, not because we have researched the facts. I have found that many people share these traits and it's not necessarily a bad thing.

Teachers, which include our parents and friends, are typically there to provide us with guidance or opinions on various topics and help us in our decision-making process. The problem is that the answers we receive are sometimes based on that person's specific belief system or observations, which may affect the outcome of the answer. But more importantly, an answer to a question may not give you all of the reasoning, which I always believed was the key to true understanding. I guess my strange way of viewing the world and my obsessive-compulsive nature drove me through some major twists and turns growing up, both good and bad, but that desire to be a trader was still in the back of my mind all through my teenage years.

In my late teens that dream began to manifest itself into reality when I broke into the industry. I started in retail brokerage and off-floor trading, which I loved. But I soon found out a couple things about being a stock broker:

My clients loved and hated me all at the same time, which drove me up a wall.
They were never really 100% happy with my performance, which gave me feelings of inadequacy.
I was an awful salesperson, which made it really hard to raise money.
Options and the jargon associated with them scared most people, which made business even harder.

Discount brokers and regulation were reducing commission rates drastically.

I just wanted to trade on the floor and control my own life and risk.

So with that, I made my graceful exit from the money management business and down to the floor of the Philadelphia Stock Exchange to start my options trading career on a wing and a prayer. (There were a few other stops along the way.)

The first time I walked on to the floor of the exchange as a clerk, I realized that things were completely different, the regular rules didn't apply—you could be yourself, say what you want, make your own rules, and I knew that if I played my cards right, I could really make a ton of money and maybe change my life. I knew about guys and girls who were making millions of dollars, but had no idea how. I thought I could do the same but I didn't really know how or where to start, nor did I have a wealthy family to "loan" me money to trade. I was lucky to have friends on the floor and a passion for the game and that was enough to propel me to learn more.

Being a floor trader and an options market maker was the most wonderful, enlightening, and liberating (and scary at times) experience of my life—and I have done some extremely wild things over the years. While most stock jockeys were gambling on the wrong side of the table, I had a chance to be the house. I could make the rules and I could control, to an extent, what my fate was going to be and not be a complete slave to the mysterious oscillations of the stock market that every MBA and quant from every Ivy League school has tried to master and control.

Options traders were a different breed. We took a statistical, mathematical, rational (most of the time) approach to the marketplace. We added another layer of probability and risk control that just could not be had with trading stocks alone. We made bets on things like volatility and didn't always care which way the stock went. Everything was at least partially hedged, which reduced the need for Maalox, Prozac, and heavy drinking, which many of my stock-trading brethren had to rely on more often.

We had our own rules, which many didn't understand, and, to be honest, we didn't want to in the beginning. It was pretty cool when no one really understood your business or the risks involved, but yet wanted to keep giving you money. This was in the early days of options trading and it is still true somewhat today. Most investors took long shots, buying options, and did not understand the first thing about how they derived their value or how they could consistently make money trading them. To most retail investors, they were viewed as cheap lottery tickets that, in an irrational marketplace, could be the ticket to pay dirt.

On my first day as a market maker I walked into the pits, no longer a humble clerk, but rather a (sort of) confident, combat-ready trader. I was extremely anxious, inexperienced, and frankly petrified. My heart raced as I walked into the pits as a new trader, wearing my brown badge proudly. They gave new traders brown badges to ensure that everyone knew that they were new and thus ensure that they would get extra abuse from other market makers, brokers, and surveillance there to make sure that all the rules of decorum were followed. As soon as I heard the loud, Rocky-like, open outcries of Philadelphia and New York tri-state-accented locals who obviously didn't grow up with a silver spoon, I knew that this was real. One part of me felt at home, and the other part was thinking of how tough I really needed to be. I did, however, know that this was the place for me and I was going to make this work at all costs! If I didn't, I would be doomed to failure, which was just not acceptable. I had blown off my parents' requests to be a doctor or an attorney in order to be a trader, so if I screwed this up, I would never live it down.

Most floor traders have been there awhile, some since 1973, when standard options began trading on an exchange. For many, this was all they knew and it was all they ever wanted to do—it was their home and they intended on defending it.

They were all in the same club and I was not a welcome guest. When I stood in the pit for the first time, most of the other traders looked at me like I had just repossessed their car and was having an affair with their wife, maybe at the same time. Others were friendlier, but most of them definitely looked like they had grown up hustling in the streets. Not that they weren't smart—each had his or her own unique gift and angle.

Now that's not to say we didn't have some of the white-shoe, Harvard-type guys down there, but for the most part, it was a diverse crowd of everything from professional gamblers and the world's best bridge and poker players, to the math geeks, suave neighborhood kids who had a knack for reading people, and the big oaky linebacker guys who were seven feet tall and muscled their way into trades. Heck, we even had guys who would just whine so much you had to put them on a trade to shut them up. It was awesome! It was my kind of place.

Once you're in the pit and breaking into the crowd, you're trying to figure out everyone's position and angle along with their strengths and weaknesses. It's kind of like the world's largest poker game and everyone is trying to call your bluff and find your weak spot and you theirs. It helped to be a comedian and to be loud; luckily, everyone in my family had a great sense of humor. My grandfather had told me enough dirty jokes over the years to keep the guys entertained till the Rapture. My mother was a teacher and cheerleading coach in one of the worst inner-city schools in Philly, so she could yell and hold her own, as could I. My dad was more of the quiet, intellectual type, who actually despised loud places, but his demeanor and teachings helped me relate to my inner geek and thus the other geeks and more mathematical types in the crowd.

So thankfully, it didn't take me long to become one of them and because I wasn't a complete moron, I think most of the guys respected me early on. Besides, they had more to worry about than some new kid from Northeast Philadelphia breaking into their crowd—the markets and exchanges were changing and although this change would be remarkable for the retail customer, it would be devastating for most of the independent floor traders and brokers.

In the early days, which were after the über-glory days of the late 1970s and 1980s, we all had to adapt to a changing landscape as pit traders. When I first started, there were no real computers or phones on the floor, other than the house phones to call your booth and a couple of personal computers around the floor to look at a chart and check quotes. Everything was done with paper sheets, hundreds of them, which displayed all the Greeks, prices, and volatility measurements, all printed in about a font size of one! It took a sharp mind, great math skills, and some serious options know-how to be a floor trader. The open-outcry pits were the central meeting places for all orders, and most stock options had one exchange that they traded on, which meant that if you wanted to trade the Nasdaq 100 (QQQ), you had to send your order to the American Stock Exchange.

Markets were wide and not nearly as liquid as today's marketplace, not because of open outcry, but because of less broad knowledge of options and relatively low overall options volume traded by retail customers and even professionals.

I remember trading Dell Computer stock, which traded only on the Philadelphia Stock Exchange. Our markets would be something like $1 half-bid to $2 ask, 20 up (yes, we still used fractions back then), which basically meant that you could buy or sell 20 contracts at those prices. If you wanted to trade more, the price might change. It wasn't that we were trying to steal from anyone wanting to trade options, we just had to have some extra edge in our trades because of the smaller amounts of liquidity and the lack of high-speed, real-time monster computers that figured and measured changes in risk, volatility, news, order flow, arbitrage opportunities, and so on. When an option is bought or sold by a customer, typically the market maker who trades on the other side will hedge that trade by buying or selling stock or another option. Without computers, we had to manually keep track of all of our positions and how they influenced one another.

At the time, most of our positions and risks were either in our head or written on little cards and sheets of paper that stuck out of the top pockets of our trading jackets. This made risk management a bit more difficult in the beginning. So at that time, because of the lack of computers and technology in general to assist me and for the fear of not being able to feed myself, let alone pay for my car and condo, I was generally willing to buy or sell 100 contracts on either side of the market if needed. This means the equivalent of 10,000 shares. Even though I was a market maker, I had to control risk. Limiting my contract size (to 100 max) and hedging just about every trade I participated in were some of the methods I employed. Because of the way I traded I didn't necessarily have stop losses or target profits. As a market maker, I was really just trying to capture edge and make bets on volatility here and there. What I could control was the exposure I had to certain market variations. In other words, I could control my "Greeks" by using different methods. Greeks are a series of variables that can tell traders how their option is going to move, based on a variety of influences (but more on those later). Suffice to say that I had to look for creative ways to gain an edge.

Remember, I had to know at every moment how a trade would affect my master position of potentially thousands of options contracts all at different strikes, months, calls, puts, long, and short.

If I knew that I was short a ton of Gamma (I will explain this later, but it is ultimately tied to the price of the stock) and there was a large order to buy some calls (which would mean I would have to sell them) I may go and buy some puts as a hedge as opposed to stock if I didn't want to exacerbate my already short Gamma position. There were literally dozens of different ways that I could and would hedge myself and amalgamate these new trades into my master position. I was forced to learn these intricacies quickly, and this is why I feel confident that I'll be able to teach them to you.

Keep in mind that for the most part, I had no real-time way to monitor my positions or risk (yes, I realize I sound like a grumpy grandfather telling a group of kids how he had to walk to school in the snow—uphill both ways).

The Internet and handheld computers brought increased efficiency to the options markets, which not only helped established traders increase our accuracy, risk management, and in turn size of trades, but they also enabled some traders to get fed theoretical values from traders off the floor onto a handheld computer we dubbed *the box*. These traders, typically from larger firms, could look at risk and hedging more dynamically and thus tighten their bid-ask spreads and take down sizable volume on average.

In the late 1990s we called them *box monkeys*. I know, the term sounds harsh, possibly because we felt cheated at the time and that was a childish attempt to make us feel better about our dying breed and the coming of a new age. Many of these traders really had minimal knowledge of the options marketplace or managing risk. It was just his or her job to buy for less than the value on the screen and sell for more than the value on the screen, period. Unfortunately for us, the box monkeys were the way of the future and in many cases were able to make markets faster and deeper than we were.

Right about the time the box monkeys were coming into vogue, the United States filed suit on September 11, 2000, against the options exchanges for failing to list the same stock options on multiple exchanges. The International Securities Exchange (ISE) was *not* named in the complaint; it had just begun trading options that year. Up until 1990, the Securities and Exchange Commission (SEC) prohibited, with a few exceptions, equity options from being traded on more than one exchange. From 1990 to 1999 few new stock options were traded on multiple exchanges, even though they could have been. The late 1990s and early 2000s brought big change to the way we did business and in the blink of an eye, many exclusive products began trading on three, four, and five different exchanges, opening up opportunities for competition and better prices for consumers. Advances in hardware and software functionality and complexity were making options markets more and more liquid. Moore's law seemed to apply directly to the capabilities of the big trading firms, leaving many of the independent traders behind as they struggled to adapt to the new markets.

Mergers and acquisitions of firms and exchanges also shaped the landscape, favoring the customer and increasing speed, liquidity, and execution costs.

In late 2000, I decided to become a box monkey of sorts, opting to move to a larger, more integrated firm that could help me take down more size and price trades quicker and reduce my personal risk. I jumped from trading up to 100 contracts a trade to sometimes 10,000, if the trade was right. The train was moving fast and every day something seemed to change, when it had remained the same for so long. At the time, I was one of the largest size (volume) market makers in the QQQ (Nasdaq 100) options pit on the AMEX and Philadelphia Stock Exchange (PHLX) for about two years combined.

It was an exhilarating experience; it took courage to trade the QQQs and everyone wanted in. Our pit swelled from a dozen or so to more than 80 traders in just a couple months in 2000. We were getting in at 5 A.M. just to get the best spots. There were about three specialists and six clerks managing the QQQ options book, when the norm was maybe one specialist and a clerk or two. But those heydays were numbered as well, as things were continuing to change.

In 2001 I left the AMEX to launch a new specialist operation on the floor of the PHLX and I remember how difficult it was to compete against the four other exchanges and how they would try to pick us off at every turn. The technology on the PHLX at the time was certainly not cutting edge. Krispy Kreme Doughnuts was one of the issues I was trading at the time. What a crème-filled mess that was! I could barely keep up with the pace at which the orders flew in. Complex spread orders were being fired down to the floor at lightning speed and obviously someone at the time thought my markets were out of line in this hard-to-borrow-and-trade issue. I knew it was the beginning of the end for me (and many of my kind) on the floor. It was just too hard to do it by yourself with the technology that we were using.

For customers the markets were improving by leaps and bounds, offering them lightning, fast execution and next-to-free pricing. Internet-based tools and analysis were getting cheaper and more accessible for the mainstream investor.

For floor traders, the climate is much different. Today the exchange floors are a ghost town—a shadow of what they once were. The screams and shouts of young, testosterone-fueled traders are now gone, replaced in large by the sound of keystrokes and ESPN on the TV screens. Many of the old-timers had made enough money to retire or start brokerage firms or go into other businesses. Some of the younger generation like me were trading off-floor or educating around the world.

This is a retail trader's paradise that we live in. There is no longer a real advantage to standing in a pit. The flow of information and the amount of competition among traders from around the world equates to a well-balanced, deep, accurate marketplace that represents known data extremely efficiently. The major difference now is that you must be in tune with the forces that push and pull the markets. They are no longer able to be observed physically or audibly in a crowd, but observed through the screen of an LCD monitor. This takes skill and adaptation.

You are at an extreme advantage due to the fact that you are not *forced* to make two-sided markets and make trades when you don't necessarily want to. You have the luxury of time and flexibility. If you control your mind and risk and completely understand the strategies that you are employing, you can control your own destiny (at least to a certain extent).

IT DOESN'T HAVE TO BE THAT COMPLICATED

I am sometimes amused at the myriad of complex indicators, correlations, techniques, and theories that some professional investors utilize and claim to be the answer. I also giggle at how some hedge fund managers who can barely beat the Standard & Poor's are viewed as glorified heroes because most of their extreme wealth is not due to the amazing steady returns they are able to attain, but to the gobs of fees and commissions that their investors and limited partners feed them. This is certainly not the case for all and please don't take that as total disdain for the fund community, because it is not. Rather, it is meant to be a confidence builder for you, knowing that just because people call themselves fund managers and are wealthy, doesn't mean that they are investing gurus and should be idolized. Follow your own path and trade what you know and are comfortable with. If it doesn't make sense, learn it or leave it alone.

With the techniques and the strategies contained within these pages, you have everything you need to beat any hedge fund manager. At first, some of the information may seem overwhelming, but go through it again if it doesn't make sense. It will come into focus over time.

A CHANGING LANDSCAPE

The tactics, mechanics, and business of trading are constantly evolving. The advent of advanced computers and the integration and centralization of these systems and exchanges has created an extremely efficient marketplace that digests data at the speed of light and captures arbitrage opportunities even faster. The edge that used to belong to the greatest minds in the industry who had the ability to compute without the aid of electronic devices and could visualize risk in a dynamic real-time environment in their heads or had special access to data or a team of researchers working for them gathering data used in their analysis is no longer the case. Although it may seem like some super genius has the edge with his mind, the Internet, tools, and readily available data to all has leveled the playing field. True, some have faster and more quality information than others, but the truth is that for most of us, not running multibillion dollar hedge funds, the speed and quality of the data we have access to is more than enough to enable us to make money. You might actually be surprised in knowing that the professionals, analysts, and traders you watch on television use the same exact tools that you do and are still able to achieve the respect of the masses and hopefully profits in their accounts at the same time.

That is not to say that there is not a plethora of poor or incorrect data floating around, but I will address this later and offer you tactics to help ensure data accuracy and timeliness.

In the 15 years I have been in the industry, one thing that has not changed is the behavior of man and the hysteria of crowds, especially surrounding news events (such as earnings reports) and new, unexplored businesses and technology. If you can learn to interpret those trends and recognize opportunities within them, while they are happening, you should be able to reap success in the marketplace. More importantly, you must have a system or method and good risk management, neither of which needs to be perfect, just something that gives you discipline and guidelines to follow.

The tools available to the average investor for free today dwarf the high-priced cutting-edge tools I used to be a successful market maker on the floor more than 10 years ago. Tools, such as price and probability calculators, advanced charting packages, risk analysis tools, and real-time blogs, news, Twitter, and so on, which all enable to gauge mass sentiment and risk in record time, certainly make life easier and faster for the home-gamer trader. Both Kathy and Dean go a bit more in depth on the methods, tools, tricks, and details on trading either from home or starting a trading business.

But before we get into how to trade, let's start at the beginning. When did trading begin? And what's it all about, anyway?

Acknowledgments

I t has always been a dream of mine to become an author and even with this work, I still don't feel worthy of the title. The fact that you are allowing my words, thoughts, and emotions into your mind is extremely humbling. For that, I thank you, whoever you are reading this. John Wiley & Sons has provided me with a unique opportunity and for that I am grateful.

Mark Douglas has been an amazing friend and advisor through this entire process and was kind enough to offer his words in the foreword. Thank you.

Dean Somes and Denise Shull, both of whom are good friends, were generous enough to take time out of their lives to contribute two amazing chapters for this book. Kathy Chaffee, who has been an inspiration and confidant over the years. Beth Moon has helped me keep my erratic and complex thought process, diction, and spelling in check. Darlene March, the public relations pit bull, and CNBC, for giving me an international stage to vocalize my opinions—I thank you all.

I would be remiss to not give thanks to my wonderful parents, family, friends, teachers, and colleagues who have provided me with love, support, patience, inspiration, and who have influenced me in so many ways throughout my life.

I could not possibly name everyone who deserves a thank you from me, as I believe just about everyone with whom I have interacted has helped me up the stairway of life in some way.

I am forever grateful just to have the chance to maybe help influence the way you think about the options markets and taking risks in the marketplace.

JARED A. LEVY
2011

CHAPTER 1

Market Basics and Market Mechanics

What Is Going On and How Does It All Work?

[New market] complexity suggests that there is no longer any room for the individual investor in today's institutionalized markets. Nothing could be further from the truth. You can do as well as the experts—perhaps even better.

—Burton G. Malkiel
A Random Walk Down Wall Street

As long as humans and cultures have been exchanging and trading goods, price has been at the center of that trade. This is true whether it took 10 bags of rice to purchase a goat or 150 U.S. dollars to buy a barrel of oil. Discovering a price or value of goods, commodities, housing, land, and so forth has been essential to cultural sustainability, global social and economic growth, and in the end, for some, prosperity. It has also led to the demise of great nations for that matter. This chapter explains the basic mechanics of the marketplace and offers insight as to how stocks are traded and valued.

THE MARKETS

Trading and speculating on prices is in our nature. It takes place every day around us. For most of us the forever changing price of gasoline is the first exposure we get to the marketplace, although many don't even realize it. The price you see at the pump is determined by supply and demand, along with people called *speculators* (folks who don't really want to own anything, but rather take risk on prices going up or down) and by our friends at the Organization of the Petroleum Exporting Countries (OPEC), who actually control supply (that's a topic for another book).

For something to increase in value there must either be high demand for that *widget* or a reason or motivation that one would pay a higher price than the masses are willing to pay at that moment in time.

So why would someone think something is going to rise in price?

Maybe that motivation is sentimental; maybe it is because you have done more research than most and you believe that the item is worth more or will be worth more to you or someone else either now or in the future. Maybe the value of that tangible item has not been realized yet (think back to the early days of the Internet or a company like Google or maybe Apple), because of the lack of a catalyst or a distribution channel. Maybe you know that if you bought this item in Europe for $10, you could ship it for $2 and sell it for $15 in the United States. This is a basic form of arbitrage and takes place every day in the marketplace (we discuss this later).

These theories (reversed) can work against the price of something as well, driving the price lower.

All of this unique reasoning applies to stocks in companies, (which are referred to as "intangibles") as well and this is why we actually have a (stock and option) marketplace, so people with varying opinions can come together in one place and exchange their assets. There are many reasons why prices are constantly changing; I offer you insight on stock price movement. But it's not just stocks. From gasoline to gallons of milk to sweaters, there is an exchange where people can trade just about anything. Farmers use the commodity markets to lock in prices of their crops or to speculate on the price of corn, wheat, or another commodity.

Many Varying Opinions

A wide array of reasoning, emotions, and other forces can actually help to stabilize the market, because buyers and sellers with varying opinions will create a more balanced and stable marketplace as opposed to everyone having one view and one directional opinion, which would create exaggerated moves in one direction or the other. This is why it is important to allow markets to trade freely and allow the traders of the world to continue to create their own systems, algorithms, strategies, and interpretations of the market with minimal regulatory influence. Some folks, in Washington particularly, have tried to change this and restrict free trade. Although it is obviously important to have rules and regulations when it comes to risk, we must be careful when regulating the rationale or reasoning behind the trades that are made. When you restrict what a person can trade and how they trade it, you may create unnatural price trends.

It's like being forced to buy fuel only from Exxon if you live in Texas. If Exxon knew that everyone in Texas was allowed to buy gas only from them, what do you think they would do with the price? Probably raise it a little bit. The beauty of the marketplace is the ability for anyone of legal age from anywhere in the world to buy and sell shares according to his or her own thesis. The stock exchanges centralize all this trading activity and allow for consistent and liquid (high volume) markets that are transparent. Think of the stock exchanges as the world's biggest flea market of stocks, one place where you know you can go to shop for the item (stock) that you want, knowing that there will be always be tons of buyers and sellers there to find the best value at that moment in time.

Unfortunately, there will be winners as well as losers when it comes to investing—it is the way the game has always been played.

I bring all this up because at times you may feel like the market makes no sense or you might hear things like "this market is cheap or expensive based on earnings" or the market is overbought or oversold. How can one make these assumptions? I know I have heard pundits en masse state the markets are overbought (too expensive) and yet they continued to rise another 10% and vice versa. Human emotion plays a large role in the behaviors and subsequent price actions of any marketplace. Get yourself in tune with mass sentiment, but don't be a slave to it. Use it to adjust what risks you are willing to take and how much profit you are looking to make. That tactic is developed as you read through this book.

What Exactly Is a Stock?

When you are long a share(s) of stock (meaning you have purchased that share), you actually own a part of the company, albeit a small one usually. You have certain rights as a shareholder, but they are minimal. You have the right to vote on certain corporate actions (not many) and you have the right to a dividend, if a company is offering one. If a company falters and declares bankruptcy, stockholders are on the bottom of the list when it comes to getting paid. Remember, you are *not* a creditor; you are theoretically an owner, with skin in the game. It's just as if you bought a lemonade stand with three of your friends, things are good for a while, but then take a turn for the worst—no one is buying lemonade and you decide to shut down for lack of profitability. Unfortunately, you only have $10 in the bank and you owe your lemon supplier $10; if the business shuts down and you pay your "lemon guy" what you owe him as a creditor, the four of you are each left with zilch. That can happen with a large company in bankruptcy as well, but generally not that often with major, well-established companies.

When a company "goes public" they sell a certain amount of shares to retail stock investors, typically through a process called an IPO, or *initial public offering*. The price at which stock is first sold for and subsequently trades for can be extremely subjective. Companies have many reasons for going public, but the most typical reason is to raise capital.

By offering shares of stock, a company is able to raise money to expand its business in a multitude of ways. Stock can also be used for employee bonuses, as a means to acquire other companies, and for many other uses during the lifetime of that company. Companies can buy and sell their shares in the open market as well after going public. These actions, respectively, are called a *stock buyback* and a *secondary offering*, but basically what you need to know is that if a company is acquiring shares in the open market, it may be a sign that the company is healthy, as it is reinvesting in itself.

If you are new to the marketplace or if you have limited knowledge of how the stock market functions, I encourage you to read more on this topic because it will be essential to perfecting your trading of options, which derive their prices from stocks.

How Stocks Get Priced

If I could tell you exactly what a stock should be trading for at any given time, I would most likely be the richest man on Earth, lounging on a tropical island somewhere sipping mojitos with little paper umbrellas in the glass, while the surf tickled my toes.

In reality, there is a fairly complex process that a company will undergo when offering shares to regular investors. Even more esoteric is the "value" that the markets assign to a stock at any given time once it has begun trading publicly.

Companies generally offer shares to the public to attain capital to expand their businesses. Shares can be offered in a couple ways. Prior to the stock even trading on an exchange, a company can sell its shares through a private placement offering, at which time the shares are typically illiquid. Those shares may never trade on a public exchange.

An IPO is when the company has decided to "bring its company public," allowing just about anyone to invest in its stock (these are the types of companies that I discuss). In an IPO, the issuing company and an underwriter will determine the initial offering price. From there, it is purely supply, demand, and the profitability of the company that drives the price of its stock.

The Initial Public Offering   When a company decides to list its stock on an exchange, this is called *taking the company public*. This process enables a company to sell some of its corporate shares to the public and allows it to raise capital in the process (the company usually retains a large amount of its shares initially). A company will hire an investment banking firm like Goldman Sachs to sell its shares to investors and structure the deal. Depending on the size of the deal, several firms may participate in the offering; this selling group is called a *syndicate*. There are also different types of commitments that the investment bank makes to the company going public. For the sake of brevity, there are essentially two points and prices that are important in an Initial Public Offering (IPO). Just before the company's shares begin trading on the open market, shares are distributed to investors at a price that is determined by the issuer and the underwriter (aka the investment bank).

Historically, on average, IPOs have been underpriced, meaning that the price for shares offered to investors directly from the issuer before they are traded publicly is cheaper than the price at which the general public pays for the shares in the open market once they begin trading on an exchange, which is the next step in the process for a newly trading company.

There is much more reading on this subject and I highly encourage you to learn about how companies come to the marketplace. As a beginner, realize that IPOs generally carry more risk than buying stock that has been established in the marketplace. Even if you are able to obtain shares of a company before it goes public, there is no guarantee of future appreciation, and sometimes buying a stock right after the IPO can be extremely risky because the hype surrounding the IPO temporarily inflates the price and when it comes back to a more realistic level, you may be left with a loser. Do your homework here and realize that purchasing an IPO just as it begins trading can be extremely risky!

Stock Value After the IPO   After a stock begins trading publicly on a major exchange, the issuing company is required to meet certain criteria, such as reporting their earnings and audited financials on a regular basis. If a company is listed on an exchange, the SEC (Securities and Exchange Commission) and the exchanges themselves require the company to disclose detailed financial information on a quarterly basis (earnings reports) as well as to provide investors with an annual report (10-K report). This not only helps us to value a company, but this data should be used by you (the investor) to decide whether to buy, sell, or hold the stock. This is why I encourage you to invest in stocks that are listed on major exchanges and be wary of foreign companies that may not be subject to our same accounting rules and regulations.

Because of the ever-changing demand for a company's products or services, it is next to impossible to predict with 100% accuracy the amount of goods or services that will be sold to the public over a given period of time.

This uncertainty, coupled with the fact that the stock market is also driven by the whims of its investors, makes it next to impossible to predict the future price of a company's stock (if it were easy, none of us would need day jobs). Although, I will offer you a set of guidelines and strategies to follow to put the odds on your side.

Speaking of day jobs, we do have analysts who crunch these numbers (sales, costs, economic trends, etc.) day in and day out, which can certainly help us gain future perspectives and create somewhat realistic expectations for a company's sales and revenue, which can help project future demand for the shares. But even analysts get it wrong. Once a stock begins trading publicly, the price is solely determined by the supply and demand of the marketplace. This is why it is extremely difficult to place a specific value on a stock. What you can do is compare a stock to its peers to find relative value and/or use the historical prices of the stock to help you assess its current value in comparison. Analyst reports can help you with your decision making; they are available from different brokerage firms, usually for a fee.

What Goes into Determining a Company's Worth?　　The input costs (like raw materials, commodities, etc.) that a company may use to produce its goods or services may be rising or falling, which would influence profit margins. Miners, oil producers and refiners, and agriculture and fertilizer companies are all examples of companies that are highly susceptible to this risk. Another example of how high raw material costs could affect a company (or another in a completely different space) would be the price of oil. We all remember the oil price spike of 2008. Although this was great for the companies getting oil out of the ground, we must always remember that necessity is the mother of invention. What I mean is that with oil above $125 and gasoline, heating oil, and natural gas getting extremely expensive, other businesses may become viable alternatives, like solar power and wind energy. Sustained high energy prices may have kept the price of solar and wind stocks high, so when oil prices fell, their prices fell as well. The lesson here is to fully understand how a company makes money and what their dependencies are, as their future may rely on another's. Other companies depend more on intellectual capital and/or patents and have minimal exposure to the ebbs and flows of commodities. Google is a good example of this sort of company.

Public sentiment about the company's business may also be shifting. For instance, a company may be in the coal business and as the green revolution continues, the masses may make a conscious effort to switch to alternative fuels, which may have an adverse effect on a company's earnings and thus their stock price. The reverse could obviously work in favor for a company as well.

Executive management also plays a large role in the vision of the company and its growth and/or its demise. Having an adaptable management team that has proven to evolve with an ever-changing market climate certainly helps. We can look in the past history of a company (or its CEO) to evaluate this; for newer companies, it may be more difficult. Apple computer is an example of a company that has changed with the times and continues to manufacture products that sell and are adopted by the masses. Xerox, on the other hand, struggled to roll with the punches as consumers shifted from the analog world to the highly integrated digital climate of the twenty-first century.

Economic, social, and geopolitical climate changes may also affect a company's success.

Recession, growth, housing values, unemployment rates, technology, societal shifts all can obviously play a role in a stock's value and the market's value for that matter. In tough times or when the United States or global economy is entering into a contraction phase, traders begin to sell certain stocks in anticipation of the global downturn, which eventually may decrease the amount of goods and services that companies are able to sell, which in turn may lower their revenue and thus their earnings per share or how much income (revenues–costs) a company brings in. Companies can cut costs by laying off employees or streamlining their businesses by consolidation, technology, reduction of expenses in marketing, bonuses, and so forth. This affects a company's bottom line or what it brought in total income. Some analysts and traders want to see "top-line" growth or an increase in real goods or services sold when a company is emerging from a downturn, as a company can only cut so many costs, which would increase their bottom line only. Know whether your investment tends to be more cyclical or defensive. I will discuss that in more depth shortly.

For the average investor, a knowledge of the different macro industries that stocks are categorized by and what stocks, industries, and sectors are currently in favor combined with a general knowledge of the current economic climate can help you understand why your company will continue to be in favor or fall out of favor. Don't worry if you don't understand it all, most people don't and that is where options theory and strategy can offer an edge.

When's the Right Time to Buy and Sell?

First off, when you look at a stock quote, you are viewing the best price at that moment in time. The guy who was willing to sell for the least and the guy who was willing to pay the most meet and determine price (for that millisecond). We all know how quickly that price can change.

Let's assume you like a company (for whatever reason) or its products and you want to buy its stock. That's the first step of the battle! But how do you know where or when to buy? Everyone has heard "buy low, sell high," but that is certainly easier said than done and is completely relative. The question of "fair price" has plagued investors forever, whether they are analyzing stocks, mutual funds, or even the latest fashion craze.

The wide span of investor opinions and motivations are what create fair value for the current trading price of a stock or other instrument. In fact, the many ways of determining value, coupled with the varying opinions toward risk and timing are just a couple of the factors that create the free marketplace, as I discussed earlier.

For example, what if you bought a home 15 years ago for you and your young family in a developing neighborhood for $50,000? Flash forward 15 years to 2010, when your home value has increased to $175,000. The neighborhood is now crowded with condos, traffic, and young urban professionals, and it is no longer desirable for you and your teenage kids who are about to enter high school. Now you want to move to the suburbs and upgrade your home, so you sell your single house for $175,000, which is a win for you (you made a profit and got what you wanted) and it is probably also a win for the twentysomething couple that bought it, because they are getting a relatively good deal on a home in a hip neighborhood that they believe will not only be a perfect living situation, but also will increase in value because of the density and demand in the neighborhood. A trade has been made!

This happens every day in the stock market as well, where traders who have owned a stock for some time (maybe at a much lower price) sell to other traders, who maybe just want to hold it for a week, day, or even an hour to see a little appreciation. Investors don't always sell because they think the stock is going to tank; there may be other motives involved, such as their need for money or having found another opportunity. And even if there isn't another reason, there is usually someone there to buy it because they believe there is value at that price.

One trader's trash may be another's treasure, as they could have completely different investment objectives.

Timing Your Entries into Stocks   Projecting the future direction in a stock or the market as a whole is everyone's goal and obviously an impossible task. I believe it's more realistic and statistically easier to bet on a "range" or an "area" of price that the market or stock will be at in the future and certain option strategies will allow you to do this.

There are a myriad of methods and techniques that are used by traders and investors around the world. They range from insanely complex to relatively simple. Some investors spend countless hours looking at dozens and dozens of different data points combined with economic theories and technical indicators before they even think about making a trade. Others maybe have one technical indicator or maybe just *read the tape*[1] to decide when to jump in and out. The interesting thing is that you have this huge gap in style and on both ends you have immensely successful traders and at the same time complete failures. There is no secret sauce! All I can tell you is that you should try to keep your analysis and tools relatively simple, but use the data consistently and with that you should at least improve your chances to succeed. You don't want to find yourself stuck in that cliché *paralysis by analysis*, where you are looking at so many different things you can't come to a decision, because the more data points you need to agree with one another, the lower probability you have of them doing so. In the coming chapters I give you the fundamental (data driven) and technical (chart driven) indicators and methods that I use to time my entries and exits. You need to test them in a "paper trading" environment until you create your plan and hone your own methods.

SECTORS AND INDUSTRIES

Stocks can be broken up and categorized into industries and sectors. Doing so will help you understand and target which sectors and companies are in favor. This can also help you choose which strategy to employ. Stocks are first broken up into two basic large groups: cyclical and noncyclical (or defensive). These designations define a stock's sensitivity to economic and broad market fluctuations. The main difference between the two is necessity versus luxury.

Cyclical names are companies that produce a luxury, or discretionary item (such as apparel or electronics). Noncyclical (defensive) companies are those that offer goods and services that humans need to maintain their basic health and home, things we *cannot* live without.

Noncyclical or defensive stocks will typically experience profit regardless of economic fluctuations because they produce or distribute goods and services humans need even when times are tough. Examples are food, energy, water, and some hygiene products (nondurable goods—toothpaste, soap, etc.).

Industry Groups

Stocks can be broken up into about 10 to 12 basic sectors and then further separated into microsectors. For example, within health care, companies like Johnson & Johnson and UnitedHealth are lumped together, but one is a health-care insurance provider and the other is a consumer goods manufacturer. Both may be considered defensive in nature. In my opinion, classifying your stock in its broad market classification is more important than figuring out which microsector it falls into, as I want to have an idea about its sensitivity to an economic gyration and where it lies in the sector rotation. I discuss this later.

Following are some examples of sectors and the stocks contained within. In times of plenty, when investors become less discerning, all stocks within a favored sector may rise together, with some unjustly because their business and earnings may not be as strong as their peers. This can also work in the opposite direction; make yourself aware of sectors that are in and out of favor and try to pinpoint the strongest and weakest stocks in each by examining earnings growth, price and earnings, popularity, and so on. Within each broad sector there are subsectors. For example, within the energy space you could have oil stocks, wind, and solar.

Sector Examples

Consumer Goods	Consumer Services	Industrial	Energy	Financial	Tech
PG	WMT	BA	XTO	GS	GOOG
PEP	DIS	LUK	DVN	BAC	IBM
PM	UPS	HON	HAL	JPM	AAPL
KO	HD	CAT	XOM	C	AKAM

When Is it Time to Get In (or Out of) the "Broad" Market?

Use the market as a primary gauge for the health of our economy.

If we are emerging from a recessionary phase, the stock market is typically the first to rally, with the other indicators falling in line eventually. The stock market is the über leading indicator of economic growth (or the perception thereof) for many investors and economists (there are several others, such as building permits and the money supply). When the equity market begins its march higher, market participants look to coincident indicators like personal spending, consumer confidence, gross domestic product (GDP), retail sales, and so on, as well as earnings for confirmation, justification, and acceptance of the higher stock prices. Finally, economists and investors want to see the lagging indicators such as the unemployment rate and consumer price index come in line with other indicators, in addition to performance based on historical observations. Generally by this time, according to Econ 101, the economy may be well on its way to recovering. If the indicators remain stable, so should your bullish outlook. When they begin to change, you must re-examine just how bullish you want to be.

Don't Overreact to News or Data

Economists, like doctors, are constantly practicing what they were taught. Each day, as more and more data is observed and crunched, regression models created and articles written, they learn a bit more. Past observations and methods can indeed help all of us to understand the future, but as we evolve globally, certain theories may not hold like they once did. Relationships between indicators may become disconnected and once-normal occurrences or deviations that we look for may become exaggerated or muted.

The point is that economists (and analysts) are not predictors of the future. The amount of variables involved in the global economic equation is staggering. I believe it's impossible to relate some data points to one another, let alone to use this data to predict future momentum. What we *can* do is look at correlations over a certain period and conclude that two things are related—the reason *why* they are correlated may be unrelated to either, however, and disconnect may be unexplainable.

The average investor can review little pieces of economic news at a time and become aware of market catalysts. We can then follow trusted sources to help us form opinions about the outcome of those market catalysts and use options strategies to adjust our risk based on the confidence we have in our hypothesis.

The equity market was certainly in the lead in mid- to late 2009, when the major indexes rallied more than 50% without all of the economic indicators showing real strength. Where we may see corrections is when the stock market's anticipation of future earnings and economic growth overshoots reality; in other words, the estimates that traders and analysts projected that earnings are too aggressive. Basically, by inflating their expectations, they inflate the stock prices at the same time and when prices get too far ahead of themselves, the chances for disappointment increase.

Before you jump into any investment, just give it a quick checkup at least.

I use the P/E ratio (stock price divided by annual earnings) and not just earnings reports alone, because, remember, it is all about price. Compare a company's PE ratio to its peers. Does it seem really high or low? If so, dig a bit deeper and find out why.

If a company's stock price does not change and its earnings growth is even moderate, its P/E ratio should decrease, potentially making that stock a potential value compared to its peers. This can happen if there are other more exciting or more popular stocks in its sector that traders tend to favor.

ETFS—A DIFFERENT KIND OF INVESTMENT

Exchange Traded Funds (ETFs) are a new product that has seen meteoric growth over the past several years. They are similar to a mutual fund in that they typically hold a basket of assets that have some sort of a common trait, investment objective, or are all part of a specific index. The difference is that unlike mutual funds, ETFs are traded like stock and you can buy and sell them during market hours because many of them are listed on major exchanges. An ETF, like a mutual fund, may have fees associated with it (most do) that are in addition to any commissions your broker may charge you. The fee structure of a standard ETF is typically a flat annual percentage that is paid to the administrator of the fund. These operating costs are typically low because most ETFs are not actively managed.

ETFs provide investors with diversity and a potential hedge against a catastrophic move in an individual stock. The first ETF actually began its life in 1989 with the Index Participation Shares (IPS), which was created as an S&P 500 proxy that traded on the American Stock Exchange and the Philadelphia Stock Exchange. IPS did not last long because of a lawsuit filed by the Chicago Mercantile Exchange.

The Toronto Stock Exchange (TSE) created its version of the Index Participation Shares, which began trading in 1990. This ETF tracked the TSE 35 and later the TSE 100 stocks, and was extremely well received. The American Stock Exchange would follow in 1993 with the then-largest ETF in the world and still popular today, the SPY or 'Spiders," which allowed investors to trade the S&P 500 index like a stock at one-tenth of its cost.

The Pros and Cons of ETFs

Here are a couple key points you must understand about ETFs. For the most part, ETFs offer unique investment vehicles—just be sure that you read the fine print and understand exactly what you are buying when you are investing in an ETF.

- ETFs have changed the investing landscape, opening doors for novice retail investors to professional hedge fund managers to trade just about any commodity, sector, index, future, currency, or other complex investment vehicle like a stock.
- ETFs are much like mutual funds in that they can contain many different stocks or other securities, but unlike mutual funds that are only settled at the end of the day and are not easily tradable, ETFs trade like stocks—they have bids and offers and some have heavier volume than

others. Many ETFs, unlike mutual funds, are not actively managed. In other words, there is no fund manager who buys and sells positions within the fund trying to get the best return for you. That is not to say that the funds run themselves—depending on the ETF's objective it may require more active management. Check the prospectus to learn how and who runs the fund.

- These funds can buy anything from a basket of tech stocks to futures contracts in oil and gas. Some funds even purchase hard assets like gold (GLD).
- ETFs can offer investors a quick way to diversify their portfolios and mitigate certain risks. (Some ETFs can also increase risk.)
- Some ETFs may provide a slight buffer against volatility and risk in some cases, but add to one or both in others. Do your homework.
- Many ETFs are also optionable.
- ETFs come in all shapes, sizes, and flavors. From gold to oil to retail, if there is a need for it, an ETF can be created.

Commodity- and Futures-Based ETFs—Danger Sometimes Lurks

One of the more popular ETFs in the beginning of the twenty-first century was the United States Oil Fund NYSE: USO; it was never a favorite product of mine, for several reasons.

At times, the flattening of the crude oil forward (futures) price curve may actually provide a benefit for this unique ETF. The USO is a security that invests in and attempts to track the price of West Texas Intermediate Crude Oil by purchasing crude oil futures (and others) on the New York Mercantile Exchange (NYMEX). The USO charges a management fee of 45 basis points (back in 2010), which investors pay not in commissions, but in holding the ETF over time.

The USO does provide a vehicle for the average investor who does not trade futures to speculate or hedge themselves with or against the changes in price in crude oil.

One of my biggest sources of contention with the fund has to do with its monthly rolls, which are posted on its website for everyone to see. A "roll" is similar to what we do with the options trades we choose to extend to a later month. The USO only holds futures contracts in the front month, so that each month, it sells its front-month contracts and buys the next month. There are two issues here. The first is the fact that these dates are known and the market makers can take advantage of this immense order flow, which they know will always be the same: Sell the front month, buy the next month. This could be a detriment to the holders of the USO because they may not be getting the most advantageous pricing.

Now in the USO's defense, I am sure it has top-tier traders working those rolls and doing everything they can to make the best of it.

The word *contango* doesn't typically roll off the tongues of most retail investors; however, contango can have an effect on some of the products that retail traders may invest in.

Contango   Contango relates to the futures markets specifically and basically means that the forward curve or future price of that commodity is positive. This is considered a "normal" situation, especially with futures on commodities with a cost to carry, like oil. Oil costs money to store, transport, insure, and so on. All of these things are contributors to the future price of oil being higher than today's spot price (see Table 1.1).

When you think about it, if a trader were to buy oil on spot today and store it and insure it for delivery at a future date, that future price should reflect those costs. This is why it is a normal occurrence to see contango in the oil futures markets.

The second and even more important than the roll dates being a foregone conclusion is the "negative roll yield" that USO will experience each month in a contango situation (see Table 1.2).

Normally, each month the USO sells its thousands of contracts (22,000-plus in early 2010) for a certain price in the front month, and then has to go out and purchase more contracts at a slightly higher price the next month, meaning that the USO is able to buy fewer contracts, thus having a negative effect on yield.

Think about it like this (I'm oversimplifying here):

- *You have 10 contracts of crude in May that you can sell for $80—you net $800.*
- *You must buy $800 of the next month's contracts, which are trading at $85, which means you can only buy nine contracts. (Balance goes into cash, which is invested in short-term Treasuries.)*

TABLE 1.1   Crude Oil Futures Prices

Ticker	Month	Last
CJK0	Apr 10	↓79.81
CLK0	May 10	↓80.08
CLM0	Jun 10	↓80.45
CLN0	Jul 10	↓80.75
CLQ0	Aug 10	↓80.95
CLU0	Sep 10	↑81.28
CLV0	Oct 10	↓81.48
CLX0	Nov 10	82.30
CLZ0	Dec 10	↑82.21

TABLE 1.2 Roll Dates

Roll Start	Roll End
March 8, 2010	March 11, 2010
April 6, 2010	April 9, 2010
May 6, 2010	May 11, 2010
June 8, 2010	June 11, 2010
July 6, 2010	July 9, 2010
August 6, 2010	August 11, 2010
September 7, 2010	September 10, 2010
October 6, 2010	October 11, 2010
November 5, 2010	November 10, 2010
December 6, 2010	December 9, 2010

- *Now let's assume that crude rallies $10 to $95. You would make $90 (9 contracts × 10), whereas the month before you would have made $100 on the same price advance.*

This does also mean that you would lose less if it dropped.

Although the roll doesn't make you "lose" money necessarily—it may slow the rate at which the USO responds to movements in the long term in crude oil; this is the key to this chapter.

Some traders may become frustrated that their investments in USO did not grow as fast as the underlying futures contracts.

The lesson here is that you must always research and understand the nuances of the products you invest in. It may not just be the fees that could potentially cost you money.

The opposite of contango is called backwardation. Let's explore an example.

What Happens in Backwardation?   In early 2010, gas and oil futures in Europe flipped into backwardation mode—the opposite of contango—where the forward price of a commodity is *less* than the spot price. In this case, you are able to potentially buy *more* contracts during each roll, thus potentially increasing yield.

I pulled the futures strip for West Texas Intermediate Crude (WTI) futures and it looks like the curve has flattened a bit, but is not in backwardation yet, in any month. The good news is that this flattening helps USO, but certainly does not eliminate risk or costs associated with trading in this product. Be sure you check on the futures prices of WTI as well as the roll dates of the USO before investing.

Leveraged ETFs—Risk Amplified

Leveraged ETFs use complex financial instruments like total return swaps along with derivatives and other techniques to gain leverage (amplified movement) in a certain sector or underlying security but are more commonly based on a group of securities, or index. They can also be contrary and move opposite to the index in price.

Basically, although a 3:1 leveraged ETF may provide you with 300% of the return of an underlying index in a day's time (if the index moves 1%, the ETF might move 3% during the trading day), they will *not* provide you with this return over time. This means that if an index moved up 5% over a year's time, there is no telling where the ETF would be; in fact, there is a possibility the ETF has actually lost money or is flat. This is partially due to daily rebalancing of the ETF, amongst other things.

Many are optionable, but it may be best to steer clear of these products unless you are extremely advanced. They are *not* meant to be long-term instruments!

Also keep in mind that although these ETFs can provide amplified returns, they can also amplify losses.

Most importantly, to gain this leverage, these ETFs often have costs that may make them even more disadvantageous to hold over a long period of time and some can be quite costly, so read your prospectus.

If you have no clue what a total return swap is, let alone how they work, you should probably steer clear of leveraged ETFs such as some of the products offered by companies like ProShares, Rydex, Direxion Shares, and Horizon. Not that these firms are bad or have ill intent, but these products were developed for sophisticated investors and typically are meant to be extremely short-term trading instruments.

FINAL THOUGHTS

The markets can seem extremely complex and overwhelming at times, so remember the simple principles that govern their behavior. They are simply interpretations of human emotions—mainly greed and fear. The successful trader is able to interpret the *tone* (sentiment) of the market and then choose the best vehicle to invest in.

As you progress in your trading journey, make it a priority to specialize! No one understands everything about every product and process. The real winners find a niche and exploit it.

Do your homework and read as much of the fine print as possible. Don't deviate from investing in what you know.

CHAPTER 2

Data That Moves the Markets

The First Step in Your Analysis

Leading [economic] indicators are like brake lights on a car ahead of you on a highway. When they light up, you don't know whether the other driver is tapping his brakes or slamming them! You have to be extra careful when putting on trades using solely leading indicators.

—Alexander Elder
Trading for a Living

You might be thinking that this is supposed to be an options book, so why are we worried about data that moves the equity and debt markets?

Remember that before you choose which option strategy you are going to apply, you must first form a thesis on the underlying security; to that end, you must be aware of any other (economic) forces that might be pushing and pulling on the marketplace, beyond what is going on with the security (stock) itself. Every option *derives* its price from a security, so if you are going to trade options, you *must* understand and have an opinion on the security first.

This chapter explores the larger macro forces that influence the markets. From the information you gather from macro data, you are better able to form your individual stock thesis and strategy. Having knowledge of upcoming events will help you tailor your risk more appropriately.

I like to work from the outside in, meaning that I want to get a gauge for the macro climate, then work my way into the company fundamentals, and

17

technical, and finally make a decision on a strategy once I have completed my research.

The good thing about macroeconomic data trend is that it tends to move a little slower, which is why I get it out of the way first, before digging into entries and exits on a potentially fast-moving stock.

This chapter won't teach you everything you need to know about the intricacies and behaviors of these indicators because you can probably read through a slew of books for that. I am simply going to talk about the basics and offer you some practical situations that may help you to better understand what they are and how they work. Believe it or not, just having the awareness of the event and the typical market reaction is a large part of the work.

The following chapter outlines a few of the indicators that I pay close attention to as well as the general economic cycle. They are also some of the indicators that the media tends to focus on.

DATA AND SENTIMENT

It is important when interpreting data to not only get the tone of what the majority of analysts and pundits are expecting, but the context in which these indicators are being analyzed. At different moments in time the economic cycle and market cycles may dictate how data is interpreted and acted on in the marketplace, investors may look for very different behaviors from each indicator at different times, which can not only vary greatly, but can be extremely confusing. There is a pattern to these reactions that develops over time.

For example, in a market that is overheating and if there is a threat of inflation, consumer prices and producer prices should remain at bay, whereas in times of potential deflation, the opposite may be true.

It will take time for you to associate market reactions to certain data points, but over time, you will notice that there is a rhythm and pattern to how the market responds to data at different points in the economic cycle.

ECONOMISTS, PREDICTIONS, AND INDICATORS

I have a great respect for economists and analysts. These brilliant individuals spend countless hours poring through mounds of complex data from multiple sources to form a thesis on everything from the fiscal health of an individual city or state to predicting the gross domestic product (GDP) of an entire country. They strive to do this with data and events that are ever changing, sometimes on a daily basis. As I said in Chapter 1, they are constantly "practicing" what they were taught as well as what they learned from experience.

Each day, as more and more data is observed and crunched, regression models created and analyzed, and events unfold, as time moves forward and more data is collected, economists and analysts are hopefully able to refine their theories with conviction and in turn attempt to predict the future path of that trend or another. Much of the predictions made in the markets and the economy are based on historical data. Past observations and methods can indeed help us to understand the future, but as we evolve globally, certain economic theories may not hold like they once did. Relationships between economic indicators may become disconnected and once-normal occurrences or deviations that economists look for may become exaggerated or muted, thus creating a potential deficit in the analysis and theory.

Does the Harvard or MIT Grad Really Have All the Answers?

Economists and analysts are not predictors of the future. The amount of variables involved in the global economic equation is staggering, even predicting the sales of a single company can be a daunting task. They are good, however, at backing up their theories with data and you should do the same.

Be careful with correlations. Many experts look at correlations between two or more data sets to help predict one or the other's move. Even when you look at correlations over a certain period and conclude that two things are related—the reason *why* they are correlated may be unrelated to either and any disconnect may be unexplainable, they just happened to move together or opposite for a certain period of time while no real relationship between the two ever existed. This is my opinion and obviously some may disagree.

I certainly don't pretend to be an economist; I simply examine the words that they and other "experts" offer and use their sentiments to adjust my risk tolerance accordingly. Basically, if the majority of prominent analysts and economists are saying that things are going to be okay and we are in a strong recovery mode, I may be more apt to take on more risky strategies and get a bit greedier with my target profits. If the opposite is true and the majority sentiment is negative, I will be more conservative in my overall risk. Money can be made (and lost) in any economic environment.

The average investor should review little pieces of economic news at a time and become aware of market catalysts. From there, you can then follow trusted sources to help you form an opinion about the outcome of those market catalysts and use options strategies to adjust your risk based on the confidence you have in your hypothesis.

Try to Simplify the Headlines and Look Around You

When it comes to my own investing, I like to look out of my proverbial window to make predictions in my little world. I look for trends that I see and concepts I comprehend. If I don't fully understand something, I tend to either learn everything I can about it or stay away from anything I feel may be influenced by it. This is key if you are a newbie or unfamiliar with certain concepts or economic data.

TRADER TIP

If you read that someone was recommending buying a new ETF tied to the TED spread, but you didn't understand exactly what influences the TED spread value or what the heck the TED spread even is, would you invest in it? You say no, but every day, people invest in either products they don't fully understand (the FAS, FAZ ETFs, for example) or they employ options strategies they don't fully grasp. Don't fall into this trap—do your research.

Because the stock market generally leads into and out of economic cycles, you need to put its movements into context. The movements need to be supported by something. Think of economic data and corporate earnings as the "legs" of a table, which represents the stock market. The less support you have from your different indicators and earnings reports, the less sturdy the table. As stocks move higher and higher the table becomes heavier and heavier, requiring more support. If the market has been rallying for some time and seems overbought, the failure of one or more of these legs can be catastrophic. This is why your initial macro foundation is paramount when deciphering the amount of risk you are willing to put on that table.

If you have been around the market for some time, your gut can help you, but you should try to back up your thesis with something concrete (let the economists do their work and hopefully the majority gets it at least partially right).

In the next section, I share the indicators that I pay attention to and the basic functions of them. Again, the most important nugget to get out of this section is to make you aware of when these data sets are released and what the expectations are for them. It is also important to get an idea of how they have been affecting the market over the past several months.

ECONOMIC INDICATORS

You can find a calendar of economic data on many financial websites or possibly on your broker's website. It may look like something similar to Figure 2.1.

The data in Figure 2.1 is from www.forexfactory.com; it displays all of the upcoming events along with consensus estimates from analysts as well as what the last data point was for comparison. What I specifically find helpful on the site is the *color coding* applied to each data point. Red for the most important, then orange, yellow, and white for the least; obviously. This book is printed in black and white, but the site itself is in color. Keep tabs on the "Red" ones.

Steps to Analyze Data

Follow these steps as you are learning the impacts of economic data. Keep a journal! If you have a record of market reactions, you can gauge the amount of risk you are willing to take ahead of each event.

- **Get prepared.** Make yourself aware of the upcoming week's data that is on tap and what the media and others are anticipating. Do this by finding the data—estimates as well as opinions—to help form your own. Does the media seem to be making a big deal of this data? If so, then you may want to dig deeper.
- **Check the past.** How has this data impacted the markets in the recent past (use price charts and note the dates)? How might it affect your positions? Is the potential volatility or downside acceptable to you? Use Google to check news articles, blogs, and so on. The most credible and popular ones should come to the top of the search, but not always.
- **Adjust your position.** Modify your position if needed. If the masses are saying things like, "this number could be nasty," or "the market really needs this number to be X" and you feel it may not be, you may want to reduce risk or change your strategy from a higher-risk trade to a more moderate one. You learn how to do this in the strategy section.
- **Journal what happened.** After the event, it's preferred that you write the results down, until you get a feel for it. For example, if people expected unemployment to come in at 9%, but it was at 9.2% and the

Date	Time	Currency	Impact	Event	Detail	Actual	Forecast	Previous	Chart
Sun Jun 27	Day 2	ALL		G20 Meetings					
Mon Jun 28	8:30am	USD		Core PCE Price Index m/m		0.2%	0.1%	0.1%	
	8:30am	USD		Personal Spending m/m		0.2%	0.1%	0.0%	
	8:30am	USD		Personal Income m/m		0.4%	0.5%	0.5%	
	12:45pm	USD		FOMC Member Warsh Speaks					
Tue Jun 29	9:00am	USD		S&P/CS Composite-20 HPI y/y		3.8%	3.5%	2.3%	
	10:00am	USD		CB Consumer Confidence		52.9	62.8	62.7	
Wed Jun 30	8:15am	USD		ADP Non-Farm Employment Change		13K	59K	57K	
	9:00am	USD		FOMC Member Duke Speaks					
	9:45am	USD		Chicago PMI		59.1	59.1	59.7	
	10:30am	USD		Crude Oil Inventories		-2.0M	-0.9M	2.0M	
Thu Jul 1	7:30am	USD		Challenger Job Cuts y/y		-47.1%		-65.1%	
	8:30am	USD		Unemployment Claims		472K	454K	459K	
	10:00am	USD		ISM Manufacturing PMI		56.2	58.9	59.7	
	10:00am	USD		Pending Home Sales m/m		-30.0%	-7.4%	6.0%	
	10:00am	USD		Construction Spending m/m		-0.2%	-0.7%	2.3%	
	10:00am	USD		ISM Manufacturing Prices		57.0	72.2	77.5	
	10:30am	USD		Natural Gas Storage		60B	65B	81B	
	All Day	USD		Total Vehicle Sales		11.1M	11.4M	11.6M	
Fri Jul 2	8:30am	USD		Non-Farm Employment Change		-125K	-106K	433K	
	8:30am	USD		Unemployment Rate		9.5%	9.8%	9.7%	
	8:30am	USD		Average Hourly Earnings m/m		-0.1%	0.1%	0.2%	
	10:00am	USD		Factory Orders m/m		-1.4%	-0.5%	1.0%	

FIGURE 2.1 Economic Data Calendar forexfactory.com
Source: www.forexfactory.com.

market sold off 5%, write that down. Also be sure to include general market sentiment as well as your own personal feelings and what happened in your trade.

Three Types of Economic Indicators and Their Timing

A common rookie mistake is to see a positive data point, for example, and form the thesis that the data is a glimmer of hope for the economy; unfortunately, that data may be coming from a lagging indicator at a time when all the leading and coincident indicators are moving lower. Some lagging indicators can take months to see the effect of a change in the state of the economy; you need to know whether the indicator you're analyzing is leading, lagging, or coincident.

- **Leading.** Leading economic indicators are indicators that tend to change before the economy changes.

  The stock market itself is generally a leading indicator, as it usually begins to decline before the economy declines and it improves before the economy begins to pull out of a recession. Building permits and money supply also are considered leading indicators. Leading economic indicators are the most important type for investors as they help predict what the economy will be like in the future.
- **Lagging.** A lagging economic indicator is one that may not change direction until a few quarters after the economy does or has shown improvement in the other leading indicators. The unemployment rate is a lagging economic indicator, as the unemployment rate may take several quarters to reflect improvement after the economy really starts to improve. The prime rate is also a lagging indicator.
- **Coincident.** A coincident economic indicator is one that simply moves at the same time the economy does. The gross domestic product, retail sales, and consumer confidence and sentiment are all coincident indicators (see Figure 2.2).

The Bigger Economic Picture

Part of figuring out just exactly how bullish or bearish you really are may depend on the state of the economy. All of the research and analysis we do can sometime be for naught if the economy is headed in the opposite direction and the stock market is moving with it. I can't stress enough how important it is to stack the odds in your favor because there are no guarantees in this market. Ask questions and get a consensus of where we are in the economic cycle at the present moment!

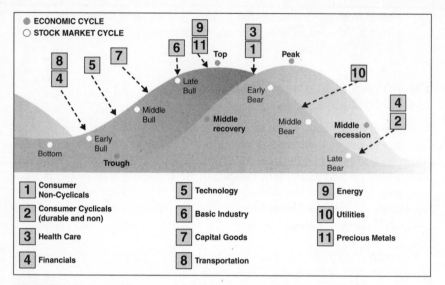

FIGURE 2.2 The Economic Cycle and the Stock Market
Source: www.fxwords.com.

It is important to be mindful of domestic and global concerns even if you plan on trading stocks in a particular sector that might seem immune (for example, technology). It is also important to be cognizant of historical market cycles, which some call *seasonality*.

Take a look below at the chart of the economic cycle and compare it to what is happening in the market around you—do you know where we stand in the cycle?

Here are some statistics and characteristics about economic cycles to help you identify where in the cycle we are (see Figure 2.3).

Economic Cycles

- From 1854 to 2001 there were 32 cycles with the average (peak to peak) being 56 months.
- The average cycle from trough to peak (bottom to top) was 38 months.
- The longest cycle in duration, peaking March 2001, was 128 months.
- The shortest cycle was 17 months, peaking January 1920.
- The current cycle, measured from the previous peak in March 2001, is more than 80 months in duration, making it the fourth longest (out of 32 cycles) since 1854.

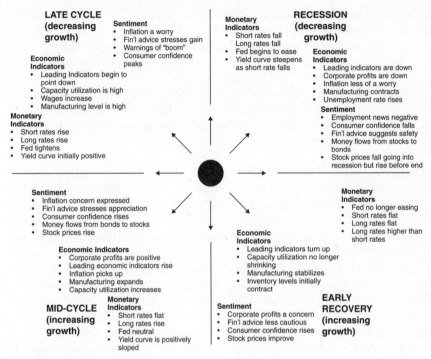

FIGURE 2.3 Economic Cycle Detail
Source: www.fxwords.com.

Booms and Expansions: Typical Characteristics

- Above-trend GDP growth.
- Higher disposable incomes—Data and trends can be found at www.bea.gov/newsreleases/national/pi/pinewsrelease.htm.
- Less unemployment at www.bls.gov/.
- Increased consumer spending at www.bls.gov/.

Recessions and Contractions: Typical Characteristics

Key features of a recession:
- Below-average GDP growth. The textbook definition of a recession is when the economy has two consecutive quarters of negative growth. If you look back to 2008, the market has already priced in the recession. Most recessions have a time span of 18 to 24 months.

- Lower disposable incomes.
- Higher unemployment rates.
- Decreased consumer spending is caused by the conditions mentioned earlier, lower disposable income from inflationary pressures, higher commodity prices such as oil or food sources. Less spending can lead to higher unemployment. Many times this first shows up in the retail sector. The three items mentioned, basically, will manifest itself on the other and snowball into a recessionary period.

Charting GDP   Figure 2.4 shows us the growth of U.S. GDP in dollars from 1960 to early 2010; note the increase in slope after the 1980s, but don't be fooled—this chart is *not* logarithmic, which means the view is in dollar change, not percentage. As the dollar amount increases, so should the slope of a chart like the one in Figure 2.5. This chart obviously does *not* account for our spending.

Figure 2.5 gives us a different picture of that same data. Here we can see annualized percentage growth, which looks much more volatile. Although the broader dollar growth example in Figure 2.4 shows a smooth rise in growth, Figure 2.5 gives us the real picture. When analyzing data, try to look at it from different angles and always get a couple opinions.

It is always a good idea to know where we are at the economic cycle and adjust your risk and allocations accordingly.

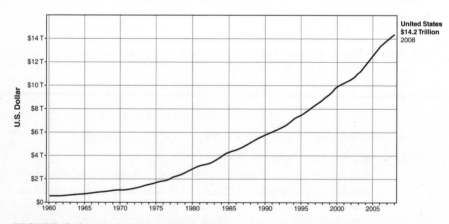

FIGURE 2.4 U.S. GDP Growth Over Time
Source: Google.
Note: GDP not adjusted for inflation.

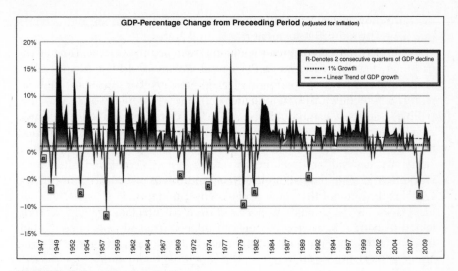

FIGURE 2.5 GDP Annualized
Source: Bureau of Economic Analysis.

KEY INDICATORS TO WATCH

Following are some other indicators that every trader should know and follow to gauge both growth and inflation trends. They are by no means all of them, but they are the data points that I tend to focus on in my day-to-day trading.

Consumer Price Index (CPI)

Release date:	Second or third week of the month—Thursday or Friday
Release time:	8:30 A.M. Eastern Standard Time
Data set released:	Previous month
Released by:	Bureau of Labor Statistics (BLS)
Where to find:	www.bls.gov/cpi/

What Is the CPI Index? The Consumer Price Index (CPI) is released every month by the Bureau of Labor Statistics (BLS). It is a complex compilation of thousands of points of data from all the states. The CPI is a measure of the average change in prices over time of goods and services purchased by households across the United States.

The BLS actually releases CPIs for two population groups: (1) the CPI for Urban Wage Earners and Clerical Workers (CPI-W), which covers households of wage earners and clerical workers that compose approximately 32% of the total population; and (2) the CPI for All Urban Consumers (CPI-U) and the Chained CPI for All Urban Consumers (C-CPIU), which cover approximately 87% of the total population and include (in addition to wage earners and clerical worker households) groups such as professional, managerial, and technical workers, the self-employed, short-term workers, the unemployed, and retirees and others not in the labor force. CPI-U is the number that most of the media publicizes.

Prices for the goods and services used to calculate the CPI are collected from 87 urban areas throughout the country and from about 23,000 unique retail and service establishments. Data on rents are collected from about 50,000 landlords or tenants. The weighting for an item within the CPI numbers is derived from reported expenditures on that item as estimated by the Consumer Expenditure Survey.

What Does CPI Data Tell You?   The CPI can be an efficient indicator of inflation (or deflation) and is a common statistic among market participants. Its high profile and investor following also will allow you to research estimates fairly easily. Large increases in CPI over a brief time period may denote inflation and large decreases in CPI over shorter periods generally indicate deflationary trends.

How Can CPI Data Be Used?   CPI data can be used:

- As an economic indicator. Typically, the CPI is regarded as the most widely used measure of inflation.
- As an indicator of the effectiveness of government policy. In addition, business executives, labor leaders, and other private citizens use the index as a guide for making economic decisions.
- As a deflator of other economic series. The CPI and its components are used to adjust other economic series for price change and to translate these series into inflation-free dollars.
- As a means for adjusting income payments (adjusting Social Security for inflation, for example).

The markets interpret this data in many different ways depending on the current economic cycle and what the majority of market participants feel is the biggest risk. For instance, if inflation is a concern and the economy has been expanding, market participants would most likely want to see more moderate increases or no change in CPI. On the flip side, if we are looking for signals of a bottom during a contraction period, seeing increased spending, coupled with consumer price increases, may offer a positive indication of growth and confidence.

The CPI data used in conjunction with other data as well as an awareness of the economic cycle and current market sentiment will help you determine the effects and interpretation of the monthly CPI data being released.

Table 2.1 shows the full data from the BLS on the most recent CPI-U data. You can see energy being the driver of most of the positive change in the total CPI number. If you look at core CPI (sans food and energy) you will note the 0.1% change for August. Funny, but it is food and energy that are always the most volatile, and I would have to believe that we all have to eat and most of us tend to use energy in some way.

On a seasonally adjusted basis, the Consumer Price Index for all Urban Consumers (CPI-U) rose 0.4% in August, the Bureau of Labor Statistics reported today. The index has decreased 1.5% over the past 12 months on a seasonally adjusted basis.

The 0.4% seasonally adjusted increase in the CPI-U was driven by a 9.1% rise in the gasoline index. This increase accounted for almost the entire advance in the energy index and more than 80% of the overall increase. Despite the August increase, the gasoline index has fallen 30% over the past 12 months.

Producer Price Index (PPI)

Release date:	Second or third week of the month
Release time:	8:30 A.M. Eastern Standard Time
Data set released:	Previous month
Released by:	Bureau of Labor Statistics (BLS)
Where to find:	www.bls.gov/ppi/

What Is the PPI Index? The Producer Price Index (PPI) is a family of indexes only in the United States that measures the average change over time in selling prices received by domestic producers of goods and services. PPIs measure price change from the perspective of the seller. In other words, what are manufacturers of the products able to sell their goods for?

This data is compiled and released monthly and is the sum of more than 10,000 separate PPIs for individual products and groups of products.

TABLE 2.1 Sample CPI Data Table from the BLS—September 12, 2009

Percent changes in CPI for all Urban Consumers (CPI-U): U.S. city average

	2/09	3/09	4/09	5/09	6/09	7/09	8/09	Unadjusted 12 months ended 8/09
All items	0.4	−0.1	0.0	0.1	0.7	0.0	0.4	−1.5
Food	−0.1	−0.1	−0.2	−0.2	0.0	−0.3	0.1	0.4
Food at home	−0.4	−0.4	−0.6	−0.5	0.0	−0.5	0.0	−1.6
Food away from home	0.3	0.1	0.3	0.1	0.1	0.1	0.1	3.0
Energy	3.3	−3.0	−2.4	0.2	7.4	−0.4	4.6	−23.0
Energy commodities	6.9	−4.7	−2.6	2.3	16.2	−0.4	8.5	−30.8
Gasoline (all types)	8.3	−4.0	−2.8	3.1	17.3	−0.8	9.1	−30.0
Fuel oil	−3.8	−8.5	−0.3	−3.3	4.8	−1.5	6.2	−39.9
Energy services	0.0	−1.4	−2.2	−1.7	−1.2	−0.3	0.0	−10.6
Electricity	0.5	−0.2	−0.6	−0.4	−1.9	−0.6	−0.1	−1.2
Utility (piped) gas	−1.6	−4.8	−7.0	−5.7	1.3	0.9	0.4	−32.7
All items less food and energy	0.2	0.2	0.3	0.1	0.2	0.1	0.1	1.4
Commodities less good and energy commodities	0.4	0.4	0.5	0.2	0.3	0.2	−0.3	1.1
New vehicles	0.8	0.6	0.4	0.5	0.7	0.5	−1.3	0.5
Used cars and trucks	−1.7	−1.7	−0.1	1.0	0.9	0.0	1.9	−5.4
Apparel	1.3	−0.2	−0.2	−0.2	0.7	0.6	−0.1	0.6
Medical care commodities	0.6	0.2	0.3	0.3	0.1	−0.1	0.5	3.7
Services less energy services	0.1	0.1	0.2	0.2	0.1	0.0	0.2	1.6
Shelter	0.0	0.0	0.2	0.2	0.1	−0.2	0.1	0.9
Transportation services	0.4	−0.1	0.3	0.3	−0.1	0.5	0.6	1.4
Medical care services	0.3	0.2	0.4	0.4	0.2	0.3	0.2	3.2

Seasonally adjusted changes from preceding month.

PPIs are available for the products of virtually every industry in the mining and manufacturing sectors of the U.S. economy, and according to the BLS, new PPIs are gradually being introduced for the products of industries in the transportation, utilities, trade, finance, and services sectors of the economy. The PPI index will account for all prices from the seller's perspective no matter to whom he is selling.

This is different from the Consumer Price Index (CPI), which measures price change from the purchaser's (consumer's) perspective. Sellers' and purchasers' prices may differ due to government subsidies, sales and excise taxes, and distribution costs. Basically, the PPI does *not* factor in sales or tax data and the CPI does. The CPI also will take imported goods into its calculation.

What Does PPI Data Tell You?   The PPI's most important role is that it gives you a "sneak peek" at the CPI number. Obviously, if costs are rising on the seller side, the consumer most likely will end up paying more, and this is reflected in the CPI number. You can also get detailed with the data and look for trends and correlations back in time, as the PPI has been around for a while. PPI can be a market mover.

PPI Facts   Following are useful facts and information about PPI data:

The three main PPI publication structures

1. Industry-based.

   The PPI publishes more than 600 industry price indexes in combination with more than 5,000 specific product line and product category subindexes.

2. Commodity-based.

   The PPI publishes more than 2,000 commodity price indexes organized by type of product and end use.

3. Stage-of-processing based.

   The PPI publishes aggregate price indexes organized by commodity-based processing stage. The three stages of processing include Finished Goods; Intermediate Materials, Supplies, and Components; and Crude Materials for Further Processing.

Coverage

- The PPI tracks price change for practically the entire output of domestic goods-producing sectors: agriculture, forestry, fisheries, mining, scrap, and manufacturing.
- In recent years, the PPI has extended coverage to many of the nongoods-producing sectors of the economy, including transportation, retail trade, insurance, real estate, health, legal, and professional services.
- The PPI continues to increase coverage of several other nongoods-producing sectors of the economy. New PPIs are gradually being introduced for the products of industries in the utilities, finance, business services, and construction sectors of the economy.

Data source

* The PPI sample includes more than 25,000 establishments providing approximately 100,000 price quotations per month.
* Participating establishments report price data primarily through the mail.
* Goods and services included in the PPI are weighted by value-of-shipments data contained in the 1997 economic censuses.
* Industries and products are systematically resampled as needed.
* Selected PPI indexes are published in the BLS *Monthly Labor Review*.
* A limited amount of historical data is made available through the *Handbook of Labor Statistics*.
* Additional data can be found at: www.usinflationcalculator.com/inflation/consumer-price-index-release-schedule/.

Personal Income and Outlays

Release date:	Second or third week of the month
Release time:	8:30 A.M. Eastern Standard Time
Data set released:	Previous month—1 month lag
Released by:	Bureau of Economic Analysis /U.S. Dept. of Commerce
Where to find:	www.bea.gov/newsreleases/rels.htm

What Are Personal Income and Outlays?   Personal income and outlays data consist of housing data, building permits, data on housing starts, data on existing and new home sales, and home prices.

What Does Personal Income and Outlays Tell You?   Personal income and outlays data is focused on the consumer income and spending habits on a macro level. Where PPI and CPI are tracking prices of goods and services, personal income and outlays data is the actual dollar amounts consumers are spending and the income that they are receiving. This gives us insight into the consumer's "balance sheet." The report will highlight changes in percentage terms month to month as well as offer details into where and how much U.S. citizens are spending and saving their money. It also is a gauge of the fiscal health of the consumer and ties in with employment and consumer prices. This report also shows supplemental income like rents. It is subject to revisions.

Housing Data

Residential housing data comes in many forms from several different sources, including the U.S. Census Bureau, Standard & Poor's

(Case-Shiller) and even the homebuilders themselves in their statements and earnings releases, The home is the largest purchase that most Americans make and we all need shelter, so housing data is considered a crucial measurement of the health of the consumer and the economy as housing prices and growth (contraction) can have a tremendous impact on the consumer's confidence, spending habits, and ability to borrow money. Educate yourself of the past and current trends in both sales and prices of housing and what experts are predicting for the future. Interest rates also play a large role in the health of this sector for obvious reasons. Different housing data can be construed as coincident (permits, starts) and lagging (existing homes sales), so use caution when analyzing. Most would classify this as lagging data, because in a bad economy, the first sign of a recovery isn't the purchase of a home. Also note that the future direction of interest rates can have a dramatic effect on housing and in periods of historically low rates, buying a home will be economical, but if rates begin to rise, home prices will come under pressure, and have a negative effect on not only the consumer, but the homebuilders as well.

Building Permits—U.S. Census Bureau   Building permits are the starting point in the construction of a new home. The monthly numbers that are disseminated by the U.S. Census Bureau are actually estimates that are generated through a mail survey of permit offices around the country. They can differ greatly from the actual number of permits applied for and even more so from the actual number of homes that are built. They are what I like to call a sort of *free look* into the actual housing starts data. These numbers can influence the markets.

Housing Starts—U.S. Census Bureau   Building permits, housing starts, and housing completions are contained within the same report from the U.S. Census Bureau. Once the permit process has started there is much that can change before construction actually starts. Even with those variables, the market looks at this number as a sign of an "increasing pipeline" of homes being built, which is a sign of perceived strength both for the economy and homebuilders. See Permit & Housing Start data found at www.bls.gov. A complete explanation of permits, starts, and completions can be found at www.census.gov/const/www/nrcdatarelationships.html.

Existing Home Sales—National Association of Realtors   This is a monthly report on both the sales and prices of existing homes. They offer quite a bit of commentary on the site as to the change and projections of the data. Data can be found at www.realtor.org/research/research/ehsdata.

New Home Sales—U.S. Census Bureau/HUD   This is also a simple monthly report that tracks the amount of new homes that actually sold as well as the average home price in that period. The report also highlights the amount of homes currently on the market and how long of a supply that represents. The longer the supply, the less perceived demand and perhaps that may mean downward price pressure on the market. There are many factors that play a role in the price of housing, interest rates, and the general health and optimism of the economy. This data is watched closely by market participants. You can google "new home sales" in the news search section to get a feel for what experts are expecting out of the report.[1]

Home Prices—U.S. Census Bureau/HUD/Case-Shiller/N.A.R. Both the new and existing home price sales reports offer us the ability to see the average price of homes sold across the United States. From that data alone you can get a general idea of price trends. Case-Shiller indexes (Standard & Poor's) aggregates and computes existing home sale/price data to offer an even more specific and even tradable index. Case-Shiller has a 20 and 10 city index and will also track individual cities contained within those 20 large metropolitan areas. The Case-Shiller data is considered a reliable real estate pricing benchmark, which can be used to analyze trends.[2] Standard & Poor's will also offer commentary and analysis on the data it finds when reports are released.

Federal Meetings and Rate Decisions

The federal open market committee (FOMC) meets eight times per year and will add meetings if necessary. Once a meeting has occurred, the minutes of those regularly scheduled meetings are released to the public three weeks after the date of the policy decision, which is where we can get grainy details of the meeting aside from the statement that the chairman makes at the end of each session. The FOMC's main function is to essentially dictate monetary policy or the supply of money, mainly through the adjustment of several interest rates. *Monetary policy is not to be confused with fiscal policy, which is the dictation of taxes and expenditures.*

For the average investor, it is important to keep yourself abreast of FOMC meetings on interest rates as well as the commentary (minutes) and the summary of the current economic condition (Beige Book), which will help you gain a better understanding of pending changes in policy and/or interest rates, which may have an effect on not only the stock market, but the rate at which you can borrow money.

A calendar of meetings is available at the Federal Reserve Bank website at www.federalreserve.gov/monetarypolicy/fomccalendars.htm.

The Beige Book is available at: www.federalreserve.gov/FOMC/BeigeBook/.

Durable Goods

Release date:	Advance report released in last week of month
Release time:	8:30 A.M. Eastern Standard Time
Data set released:	Previous month—1 month lag
Released by:	U.S. Census Bureau
Where to find:	www.census.gov/manufacturing/m3/

What Is the Durable Goods Report? The durable goods report can be considered a leading indicator as we may see orders increasing and inventories dropping before profits are released by public companies; this increase in business would most likely precede growth in the economy and may influence the stock market. Of course, faltering durable goods numbers could be a sign of weakness. Typically durable goods include many *non*staple items, meaning that in a sluggish economy, most people wouldn't be going out and buying cars, computers, and so forth.

What Does the Durable Goods Report Tell You? The monthly *Advance Durable Goods Report* contains data on new orders received as well as shipments, inventory, and order backlogs from more than 4,000 manufacturers of durable goods. A durable good is essentially something that will typically have a useful life of three years or more, such as washing machines, computers, cars, airplanes, and heavy machinery. Capital goods and noncapital goods are included. Generally speaking, durable goods are also higher-priced nonfood items. The monthly survey is quite diverse in its representation of industry, with more than 85 unique sectors included.

In the report, you will see actual dollar amounts along with percentage changes from the prior month and prior year for new orders, total shipments, total unfilled orders (orders that have been booked but not filled as of month-end) and inventories. Any revisions are also included in the report.

Retail Sales

Release date:	Released Monthly—Mid-month
Release time:	8:30 A.M. Eastern Standard Time
Data set released:	Previous month—1 month lag
Released by:	U.S. Census Bureau
Where to find:	www.census.gov/retail/marts/www/ marts_current.html

What Are Retail Sales?   The retail and automotive sales data is compiled by the U.S. Census Bureau and measures sales data derived by using
a complex model that extracts the records for all employer establishments
located in the United States and classified in the Retail Trade and Accommodation and Food Services sectors as defined by the 2002 North American Product Classification System (NAPCS). For these establishments, the
Census Bureau extracts sales, payroll, employment, name and address information, as well as primary identifiers from IRS data directly. You can
find the census data at: www.census.gov/retail/
   Individual retailers will report their monthly sales numbers as well.
This is in addition to the detailed feedback that they will also offer on their
earnings report conference calls, which you can and should listen to as
much as possible if you are trying to really learn about a company. Sometimes a retailer's sales data will be in direct contrast to what the Census
Bureau is showing in terms of growth or contraction. That is your cue to
find out why because there might be a trade there.
   Automotive sales are released by individual companies as well as the
National Automobile Dealers Association (NADA) and U.S. Census Bureau. You can contact auto companies or go to their websites to find out
when they report sales. You can visit the NADA site at www.nada.org/
publications/nadadata/default.html.

What Does the Retail Sales Data Tell You?   The U.S. Census Bureau data set will offer you both actual sales dollar amounts as well as
comparisons to prior months and years. Use the data to spot trends or to
confirm/deny your thesis about not only the health of the retail sector but
of the consumer's spending habits. You will want to dig into these numbers a bit because the Census Bureau includes both discretionary (cars,
furniture, clothing, etc.) as well as nondiscretionary (food). The census
site contains a plethora of data. Watch the "Advance Monthly Sales for
Retail and Food Services." They do an excellent job of breaking the data
down and offering monthly and yearly comparisons in the different major areas. When you are looking at the data, use a Google search to check
out what analysts and pundits are looking for in the numbers. Also read
the news, especially headlines see what is happening around the country.
I try to look for local papers in cities across the United States for clues
as to the health of the consumer. If you notice that there seems to be a
large number of stores closing and it's making the papers, maybe retail isn't
the best place to be. The most important thing that you want to get from
this data is a trend as well as make yourself aware of when future reports
are due out.

ISM Purchasing Managers Index—Manufacturing and Nonmanufacturing

Release date:	PMI manufacture on first business day after month end Nonmanu on third business day after month end
Release time:	8:30 A.M. Eastern Standard Time
Data set released:	Previous month
Released by:	Institute of Supply Management
Where to find:	www.ism.ws/

What Is the PMI Index?   The PMI (Purchasing Managers Index) manufacturing data is considered a leading indicator of economic health because businesses react quickly to market conditions, and their purchasing managers' habits are real-time reactions to current conditions. This data is extremely relevant and can give great insight into manufacturers' views of the economy. The data is gathered and disseminated by the Institute for Supply Management (ISM).

The data is derived by a survey of about 400 purchasing managers. Researchers ask respondents to rate the relative level of business conditions including employment, production, new orders, prices, supplier deliveries, and inventories. The survey began in 1948 and gives a fast but rather vague indication of growth or the lack thereof. It basically measured from zero to 100. A PMI over 50 indicates that the economy is expanding while anything below 50 suggests that the economy is contracting. The monthly latest PMI data reports can be found at www.ism.ws/ISMReport/MfgROB.cfm.

Nonmanufacturing PMI   There is also a Nonmanufacturing Business Activity Index, which is measured on the same scale, but excludes manufacturers of goods. A reading over 50 indicates that the economy is expanding while anything below 50 suggests that the economy is contracting. Individual industries are broken down in the report.

Sectors (industries) represented here include Arts, Entertainment & Recreation; Construction; Real Estate, Rental & Leasing; Educational Services; Transportation & Warehousing; Finance & Insurance; Accommodation & Food Services; Information; Wholesale Trade; Agriculture, Forestry, Fishing & Hunting; Mining; Professional, Scientific & Technical Services; Management of Companies & Support Services; Utilities; Retail Trade; Health Care & Social Assistance; and Public Administration. The monthly latest nonmanu PMI data reports can be found at www.ism.ws/ISMReport/NonMfgROB.cfm.

Consumer Confidence (CCI)

Release date:	Released monthly on the last Tuesday of the month
Release time:	10:00 A.M. Eastern Standard Time
Data set released:	Previous month
Released by:	The Conference Board
Where to find:	www.conference-board.org/data/ consumerconfidence.cfm

What Is Consumer Confidence? This data essentially measures the level of confidence consumers have. It is derived from a survey of about 5,000 households across the United States. The survey (given by a company called TNS) asks participants to rate the relative level of current and future economic conditions including labor availability, business conditions, and overall economic situation. The index is a composite based on surveyed households.

The index was launched in 1967 and was benchmarked in 1985 at 100 and varies in measurement from zero to 100. The report can have an immediate impact on market movement and is broken down by many publications to offer detailed explanations as well as changes in the index from month to month and year to year.

I consider consumer confidence a leading/coincident indicator.

What Does the Consumer Confidence Tell You? The key here is that consumer confidence is vital to spending and is a leading indicator of such. Remember that the bulk of our GDP is derived from consumer spending (coupled with government health-care spending). This report can give us a look into where the consumer sees strength and weakness forward in time with the expectations that are contained in the reports. I like to think of consumer confidence as a quick confirmation or denial of other data being released. Consumer confidence and sentiment can change rapidly. Large changes (plus or minus 5%) are considered major possible changes in our economy or at least the consumer's economic view. Do not use this data in a vacuum.

Consumer Sentiment (ICS—MCSI)

Release date:	Released monthly—Mid-month
Release time:	9:55 A.M. Eastern Standard Time
Data set released:	Current month (preliminary)
Released by:	University of Michigan/Reuters
Where to find:	www.isr.umich.edu/home/news/

What Is Consumer Sentiment? Like the data supplied by the Conference Board the consumer sentiment index attempts to gauge consumer attitudes and expectations in real time (slightly delayed). The index is normalized to have a value of 100 in 1964 (it began in the 1940s) and fluctuates in value from zero to 100. This survey is one-tenth the size of the Conference Board's with 500 telephone interviews conducted in the contiguous United States.

I consider consumer sentiment a leading/coincident indicator.

What Does Consumer Sentiment Tell You? The reports generally offer detailed, easy-to-read commentary based on the interviews conducted. I find it helpful to read the entire report as it's usually about a page long. Look for major changes from month to month. Also note that the report contains specific data on consumer income and job prospects, which can be used to help gauge the results of other reports that are broader, such as nonfarm payroll and consumer spending. You can also glean insight on housing and mortgage data.[3]

The Reuters/UofM reports can be found at https://customers.reuters.com/community/university/default.aspx.

Miscellaneous Economic Data

For those of you who are thirsty for more information, don't overload, but if you want to get a detailed snapshot of many economic indicators, check out the U.S. Census Bureau's website at www.census.gov/cgi-bin/briefroom/BriefRm.

GDP data is available on the Bureau of Economic Analysis (BEA) site at www.bea.gov/newsreleases/rels.htm.

The Unemployment Rate

In some ways, the market is much like a large, stretchy rubber band attached to the unemployment rate, as it is a lagging indicator. If the market begins to rally like it did from 2009 to April 2010, it can do so for a while without jobs (unemployment rate) following in lockstep. But if the market begins to move higher and the unemployment rate remains high or climbs higher, there has historically been a downward force applied to equity prices. That was the situation from May 2010 until July 2010, especially when high unemployment was combined with factors like European economic weakness, China demand worries, consumer confidence, and other coincident indicators, which were stalling a sustainable rise in the marketplace. Of course, if earnings growth is sustained, the market may continue to increase in value.

The following are some facts about the unemployment rate:

- Nonfarm payroll data is released on the first Friday of every month by the Bureau of Labor Statistics; it is broken down into several categories.
- Nonfarm workers account for approximately 80% of the workers who produce the entire gross domestic product of the United States.
- Workers *not* included in nonfarm payroll are:
  - General government employees.
  - Private household employees.
  - Employees of nonprofit organizations that provide assistance to
  - individuals.
  - Farm employees.

Always Look Deeper into the Numbers   Sometimes headlines can be deceptive. As a trader or investor, be careful when acting on a headline alone; remember that what the bold print giveth, the fine print taketh away. I'll use an unemployment report as an example. Back in February 2010 (though the date isn't important), I took a look into the ever-important jobs number, which even though may be a lagging indicator, can sometimes begin to dictate market direction, especially if strong jobs are needed to validate a recent rally in the stock market. Following is what I wrote:

Evaluation Example: My Nonfarm Payroll Analysis from Friday, February 5, 2010   This morning, the Bureau of Labor Statistics (BLS) released the monthly unemployment report that so many of us traders and investment professionals examine with great care. Frankly, the unemployment number will most likely be splashed all over nightly news broadcasts around the country (and the world for that matter).

We lost more jobs than was expected, and gave back another 65,000 jobs in December with the most recent revision. Maybe some market participants were focusing on the 3% sell-off we experienced yesterday and were thinking a bounce was in order and since at first glance the jobs number didn't seem all that bad, maybe it seemed like the right thing to do. That sentiment may have been their reasoning for leaning bullish right after the number was announced this morning, but I don't buy it. Don't forget that this is an estimation folks; we need to look a bit deeper into this survey.

The bigger headline though, was that the overall unemployment rate dropped unexpectedly, again. This could be the "bullish nugget" that traders are focusing on. Regardless, the major index futures changed direction in a big way when this data was released this morning, from being way down, rallying to flat. The market is still having a tough time as we have begun the session.

Here were the BLS results:

- January Nonfarm Payrolls –20K versus +15K consensus, December revised to –150K from –85K
- January Unemployment Rate 9.7% versus 10.0% consensus, December 10.0%
- January Average Hourly Earnings Y/Y +2.5% versus +2.2% consensus
- January Average Hourly Earnings M/M +0.3% versus +0.2% consensus

So we lost 20,000 more jobs, when many analysts were expecting us to *gain* more than 10,000–20,000. We also lost an additional 65,000 jobs in December. Take a look at the chart in Figure 2.6 (courtesy of Forex Factory) showing the trend for the past two years. It has been moderating as of late, but is certainly *not* strong—we are still losing jobs! But miraculously, the unemployment rate is less? I have some issues with the validity of that number.

Let's take a look at some other figures.

Table 2.2 comes from the Bureau of Labor Statistics (BLS) and shows the specifics on the actual employment and workforce data collected in the month of January 2010, as well the months of December, November, and January of 2009 for comparison. Draw your attention to several data points, the first being the *participation rate*. This is basically the ratio of people working versus the number of people who are "in the labor force."

The *labor force* does *not* include students, retirees, stay-at-home parents, people who are incarcerated or in similar institutions, people who work "under the table" or who do not report their income, as well as discouraged workers (basically anyone who is not looking or having luck finding a job or is disabled) who cannot find work.

It is the participation rate that skews the real unemployment rate; take a look at Figure 2.7 (see p. 43).

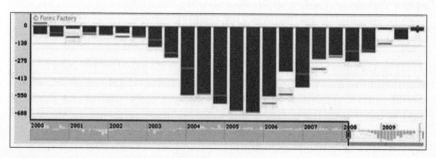

FIGURE 2.6 Monthly Change in Employment
Source: www.forexfactory.com.

TABLE 2.2 Household Employment Data Sample

HOUSEHOLD DATA

Summary table A. Household data, seasonally adjusted numbers in thousands

Category	Jan. 2009	Nov. 2009	Dec. 2009	Jan. 2010	Change from: Dec. 2009–Jan. 2010
Employment status					
Civilian non-institutional population	234,739	236,743	236,924	236,832	–
Civilian labor force	154,140	153,720	153,059	153,170	–
Participation rate	65.7	65.9	64.6	64.7	0.1
Employed	142,221	138,381	137,792	138,333	–
Unemployed	11,919	15,340	15,267	14,837	–
Unemployment rate	7.7	10.0	10.0	9.7	−0.3
Not in labor force	80,599	83,022	83,865	83,663	–

These figures also do not include military jobs, and remember all the numbers are estimates, hence the revisions.
Source: BLS.gov.

Although the historically low participation rate has helped make our current picture look a bit better, a rising participation rate would actually cause the unemployment number to rise. In all fairness, there was not a large month-to-month change (decrease) in the "participation rate," which would lower the unemployment rate.

The *civilian noninstitutional population* consists of persons 16 years of age and older residing in the 50 states and the District of Columbia who are not inmates of institutions (for example, penal and mental facilities and homes for the aged) and who are not on active duty in the Armed Forces—according to the BLS.

If you take the "employed" number and divide that by the "civilian noninstitutional population," you get an employment rate of 58.4%, which would equal a rate of 41.6% of the eligible populace that is *not* working. This is not cause for a panic, but more to keep us aware of the whole picture—the fine print, and not just the headlines.

Things that make you go hmm....

Maybe I am just skeptical by nature, but I think I have proved my point that we are *not* out of the woods just yet with respect to employment.

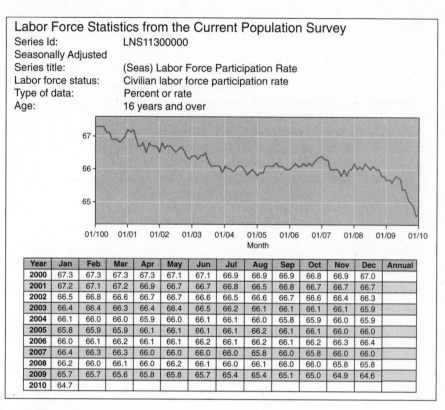

Labor Force Statistics from the Current Population Survey
Series Id: LNS11300000
Seasonally Adjusted
Series title: (Seas) Labor Force Participation Rate
Labor force status: Civilian labor force participation rate
Type of data: Percent or rate
Age: 16 years and over

Year	Jan	Feb	Mar	Apr	May	Jun	Jul	Aug	Sep	Oct	Nov	Dec	Annual
2000	67.3	67.3	67.3	67.3	67.1	67.1	66.9	66.9	66.9	66.8	66.9	67.0	
2001	67.2	67.1	67.2	66.9	66.7	66.7	66.8	66.5	66.8	66.7	66.7	66.7	
2002	66.5	66.8	66.6	66.7	66.7	66.6	66.5	66.6	66.7	66.6	66.4	66.3	
2003	66.4	66.4	66.3	66.4	66.4	66.5	66.2	66.1	66.1	66.1	66.1	65.9	
2004	66.1	66.0	66.0	65.9	66.0	66.1	66.1	66.0	65.8	65.9	66.0	65.9	
2005	65.8	65.9	65.9	66.1	66.1	66.1	66.1	66.2	66.1	66.1	66.0	66.0	
2006	66.0	66.1	66.2	66.1	66.1	66.2	66.1	66.2	66.1	66.2	66.3	66.4	
2007	66.4	66.3	66.3	66.0	66.0	66.0	66.0	65.8	66.0	65.8	66.0	66.0	
2008	66.2	66.0	66.1	66.0	66.2	66.1	66.0	66.1	66.0	66.0	65.8	65.8	
2009	65.7	65.7	65.6	65.8	65.8	65.7	65.4	65.4	65.1	65.0	64.9	64.6	
2010	64.7												

FIGURE 2.7 Labor Force Participation Rate BLS.gov

I think we are now seeing the markets examine this data a little deeper as the major indexes continue to slip on a day when we may have seen a bit of a bullish reversion to the mean.

Obviously, the market pays attention to the headline number as well, but you can arm yourself with just a bit more ammunition and confidence, if you get the whole picture. It never hurts to take a deeper look and question everything you hear.

FINAL THOUGHTS

I know it seems like an overwhelming amount of data to keep track of; however, with time, once you know what the data means, gauging the overall health of the U.S. economy by using the data points I discussed becomes fairly easy. Use reputable sources for commentary and accurate data, such as the *Wall Street Journal, IBD, Barron's,* and so on, for commentary and interpretation of the data. They can also help keep you informed about important upcoming data.

It is paramount that you have a macro opinion as well as an opinion about an individual stock, because many of the companies we invest in are dependent on U.S. (and global) consumers spending their money.

If the overall picture seems to be improving, then you can choose to be more risky with your bullish sentiment trades and perhaps more aggressive with your allocation of riskier trades. On the contrary, if the outlook is murky and or negative, use caution and scale back the amount of risk you are willing to take. In the next chapter we explore analyzing individual stocks.

CHAPTER 3

Fundamental and Technical Stock Analysis and Tools

The Second Step in Your Analysis

The attempt to predict accurately the future course of stock prices and thus the appropriate time to buy or sell a stock must rank as one of investors' most persistent endeavors. This search for the golden egg has spawned a variety of methods ranging from the scientific to the occult. There are many people today who forecast the future stock prices by measuring sunspots, phases of the moon, or measuring the vibrations along the San Andreas Fault. Most, however, opt for one of two methods: technical or fundamental analysis.

—Burton G. Malkiel
A Random Walk Down Wall Street

Once you have formed your macro market thesis, it's time to drill down to the individual company itself and decide if there is a potential trade there and then what strategy you will employ based on your research and opinion.

In this chapter I explore some basic fundamental data points I look for as well as get into depth on the technical formations and indicators I use to trade. I tend to focus more heavily on technical and statistical analyses for my trades and back them up with a basic fundamental and macro thesis. In addition to all that, risk is always a consideration and how much risk I want to assume will be dictated both by strategy and by amount invested.

Fundamental analysis is the examination of a company's past, current, and future financial health. There are many data points to examine

45

when assessing a company's financial condition and just as many opinions on which are most important. Reading analysts' reports and ratings can usually provide us with enough logical insight into a company's revenue, spending, and future earnings outlook for us to form an educated opinion about the stock's future earnings prospects. It doesn't hurt for there to be a logical reason to buy the stock! The fundamental data points that I outline are only a small part of the gamut of information, statistics, and points that financial analysts and investors look at. You don't need to read every analyst's report to be a successful trader or investor.

As long as I believe in what a company does and it meets my minimum fundamental criteria, that company passes my litmus test and allows me to move on to the next part of my analysis, which are technicals and strategy selection. This is my method, which has allowed me a great deal of success over the past 15 years. I do this not only because I tend to focus more on technical analysis and options strategies, but because I believe that predicting a company's success with the regression models that many analysts use is not going to tell you if the public is going to continue to buy its products or services, let alone its stock.

Market behavior seems to be a constant conundrum. I have found that I can find direction better with a chart, headlines and basic relative fundamental comparisons as opposed to examining a balance sheet and earnings models.

With that said, I do want to stress the importance of having a sound fundamental thesis if you are a longer-term investor.

INTRODUCTION TO FUNDAMENTAL ANALYSIS

We've reviewed some of the big data points that can impact the entire market. But sometimes your favorite stock's price might be dropping even while the market rallies (or vice versa!). There are plenty of reasons, at the stock level, why shares might move dramatically. At the very least, there should be some factors by which you measure a company's fiscal health before you decide to invest. Some super-active traders may know nothing or little about what a company does let alone its financial specifics. This is acceptable as long as you are trading the company intraday and not holding your position over night. If you're placing a swing trade (1 to 3 day hold) and you are basing your entries and exits on technical analysis or momentum, at the very least make yourself aware of any corporate events, earnings reports, or economic data that could influence your trade in a negative (or positive) way.

I am more of a technical and statistical-type trader, so my focus will be more on technical analysis. If you want to learn more about balance sheet analysis, there are a multitude of books and classes out there that will teach you. That is not my forte. I prefer to form a macro thesis based on what a company does (or produces) and the sector's strength and then I simply check the following data points and read what the analysts have to say about its overall health to confirm or deny my thesis. Next, I apply the appropriate strategy once my technicals have given me the appropriate signals.

Frequently I will trade the same stocks over and over again. I tend to keep a list of stocks that I have become familiar with—that way my pretrade research can be reduced and expedited if need be.

Finding Value

In the long run, earnings are what should drive a stock's price. Over time, a company is expected to be profitable and return those profits to shareholders through appreciation in the value of their shares or dividends. There are many ways a trader may examine a stock's value and stocks typically trade at a certain multiple of their earnings. This "multiple" varies from sector to sector and even from company to company. A company that is growing fast and has the potential to continue to grow may have a higher multiple than its peers and vice versa. We examine this a bit later in this chapter.

To simplify, there are two basic ways to look at a stock's earnings. You can look back at the past, which would be a stock's trailing earnings, or look to the future, which would be its forward earnings (or predictions thereof). There are a multitude of ways that analysts and stockpickers try to project future earnings values. That would take an entire separate book to discuss.

P/E as a Means to Measure Price   Price-to-earnings (P/E) is typically expressed in the media as a forward-looking number, although many of the P/E numbers you may see published on popular websites are "trailing" (looking back at the past year's earnings and offering a ratio).

In Figure 3.1, you can see the P/E marked "TTM." Trailing or historical P/E ratios are typically identified with TTM following the number and forward earnings are typically identified by a future date. Here is an example from Yahoo Finance, for IBM stock.

If a company, XYZ, has earned $5 per share, per quarter and the stock is trading at $200, then it is trading at 10 times trailing earnings ($5 per quarter × 4 quarters in a year = 20; then take the $200 stock price and divide by the annual earnings number 20 = 10 P/E). If the company is projected to earn an average of $6 per quarter for the next four quarters, now they should earn $24 a share and are trading on an 8 P/E. If the average P/E for that sector is 12, plus XYZ normally trades at a 10–11 P/E, plus you are

Key Statistics

Data provided by Capital IQ, except where noted.

VALUATION MEASURES

Market Cap (intraday)[5]:	164.09B
Enterprise Value (Jul 11, 2010)[3]:	176.43B
Trailing P/E (ttm, intraday):	12.44
Forward P/E (fye Dec 31, 2011)[1]:	10.39
PEG Ratio (5 yr expected):	1.05
Price/Sales (ttm):	1.69
Price/Book (mrq):	7.45
Enterprise Value/Revenue (ttm)[3]:	1.82
Enterprise Value/EBITDA (ttm)[3]:	7.34

FIGURE 3.1 Fundamental Measurements
Source: Courtesy of Yahoo! Finance.

confident that XYZ Corporation will meet or exceed its expectations for the next year, you may be inclined to buy the company here at $200, which is only eight times the forward earnings price. If XYZ returns to "normal" P/E values or 10 in this case, it should be trading for at least $240 in a year's time ($6 quarterly earnings $\times 4 = 24 \times 10$ normal P/E = $240).

This is *not* a guarantee and much can happen in a year's time; it is simply one of the ways to rationalize buying or selling a stock based on its current and future value.

P/Es will often be lower if we are headed into a contraction cycle in anticipation of rough times ahead. Conversely, P/Es may seem elevated when we are emerging from a recessionary period.

In Figure 3.2, we see a chart of the collective P/E ratio of the S&P 500, which is a broad index. This illustration shows how the trailing P/E was getting very high, above 25 times earnings on average, but as companies began to report stronger earnings, that multiple came down to around 18. Remember, in trailing P/E ratios, we are looking back at actual historical data. Future earnings are making assumptions. If companies in the S&P 500 were making less money on average, the overall P/E would be increasing.

Using Charts to Track P/E There are ways to chart not only stock price growth, but both their earnings and their P/E ratio. Several data providers and brokers allow you to perform these types of analyses. Bloomberg is my selected source here and is an industry standard because of the quality and timeliness of its data. Be sure that you check not only

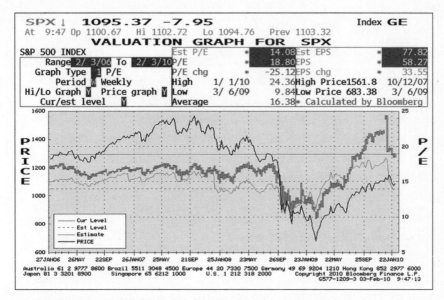

FIGURE 3.2 Current and Forward P/E of the S&P 500 Index 2/2010
Source: www.Bloomberg.com.

the credibility of the sources that you use, but the timeliness of the data because some free packages have delayed or incomplete data.

Figure 3.2 is a chart of the S&P 500 total P/E ratio, compared with its price and the estimate of where the P/E would be a year from that moment in time

The illustration in Figure 3.3 shows the average growth of the individual sectors in the S&P 500 compared to the same quarter one year ago.

For example, the materials sector earnings grew 1,101.85% in a year.

This chart helps us to visualize not only the overall growth picture but also the positive and negative surprises. This can be of great assistance when trying to determine the future earnings potential of all the companies in the S&P 500.

As you can see, 142 out of the 242 companies reported that they have experienced positive growth, whereas 93 of them experienced negative growth at the end of earnings season. When all 500 companies have reported their growth, we will get a really clear picture as to the current earnings trajectory. We will also be able to see which sectors are growing at faster rates and which are growing at slower rates. We can then analyze those sector growth rates and see if there are any valuable opportunities or potential overpricing situations with regard to the companies' price to earnings ratios. If you again look at the materials sector you'll notice that

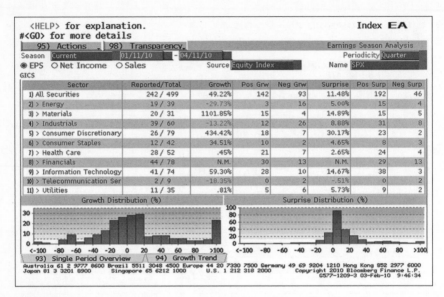

FIGURE 3.3 Fourth-Quarter Earnings Results and Year-Over-Year Change
Source: www.Bloomberg.com.

the growth rate was more than 1,100%, which looks excessive. In early 2010 the materials sector took quite a hit. The materials sector realized the great boom with the continued growth anticipated in China. But when the fears of global recession and weakening in the European Union, not to mention potential trade and commodity demand issues with China began to become apparent, most of that extra future value was taken out, resulting in a drop in many of the materials stocks. The faster a stock rises, the more it is expected to perform when it reports earnings and perhaps the higher the chance of a disappointment and subsequent sell-off.

You should understand that P/E multiples vary for several reasons. Figure 3.4 shows volatility around earnings, when looking at the S&P 500 index as a whole during the earnings months of January, April, July and October.[1]

P/E of the S&P 500   In early February 2010, the S&P 500 index (SPX) was trading at 1,133 and the SPDR S&P 500 (SPY), which is an ETF representing one-tenth of the SPX, trading at $113. According to *Bloomberg*, on that date (not important), the average trailing price-to-earnings[2] (P/E) ratio was about 18 (average) for the S&P 500. This means the index's market value ($113) divided by collective earnings per share was 18x, a fairly high number for the index (the average since 1900 was about 15x). It was the end-of-earnings season and after the most recent quarter of earnings, the

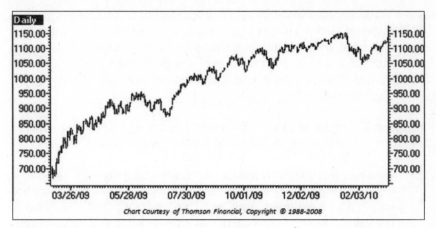

FIGURE 3.4 Daily Chart of the SPX 3/2009–3/2010
Source: Thomson Financial.

forward P/E, looking one year out, was about 14, which is much more in line, maybe even on the low side, when compared with the historical P/E ratios of the S&P 500. In other words, analysts were expecting the ratio to drop from $18 to $14 over the course of a year so something in the formula (the numerator—the market value or the denominator—the earnings) would have to change.

For most investors, earnings are the end-all, be-all, when it comes to the decision to buy, sell, or hold a company. The trailing P/E ratio of the S&P 500 is historically in a range between the 14 and 17 level—lower if we are going into a recessionary period and higher when we are emerging from one. Remember that the markets are forward-looking, so if the market perceives danger ahead of time, prices may drop, which would lower the trailing P/E. If the market perceives recovery and stock prices rise, on the other hand, the trailing P/E may appear high in anticipation of a higher earnings number.

The latter scenario is the case back in early 2010. The key is how aggressive analysts and companies are forecasting earnings, combined with the prices investors are paying for stocks today. Then obviously there is the economy as a whole, which hopefully is figured into the base cases of most analysts. In early 2010, based on forward valuations and the many opinions of analysts and professionals, it appeared as though there was still some value in the S&P 500 moving into the latter half of the year. Many of us professionals doubted the aggressive expectations because we just were not seeing it in the economic data and out our front door. If you see P/E ratios relatively high and lackluster economic data, combined with your friends, family, and neighbors still struggling and complaining about how tough times are, be cautious when buying into a market that has been on a tear to the upside. Don't forget, however, to take a stock's sector into consideration, as some may be in or out of favor and command relatively high or low earnings multiples.

Judging Value in Sectors   Depending on the sector that a stock is in, that sector may, in particular, warrant a higher or lower multiple.

- Tech or high-growth companies may command a higher P/E multiple because of their ability to grow their earnings. With high-earnings expectations and multiples come high expectations, which may lead to large disappointments and sharp stock price declines if that company fails to live up to its expectations. Higher P/Es may lead to higher volatility, especially over earnings.
- Utilities or older established companies may have a lower multiple, because they are less likely to grow as fast. These companies, although they may not grow as quickly, typically are more stable and may offer less volatility as well. They also are more likely to pay higher dividend yields on average.
- The P/E ratio and has been a longtime accepted practice and is what many analysts and traders use to rationalize their trading decisions and judge whether a stock's value is appropriate.

Although the P/E ratio is arguably one of the more popular so-called *fundamental indicators* of a company or a sector's help, it is merely one arrow in the quiver of stock analysts. The next chapter explores some of the more macro data sets that motivate the markets.

Earnings Announcements   For fundamentalists, making predictions for a company's earnings is paramount to their reasoning for buying or selling a stock.

Remember, the market is forward-looking, and buying and selling is typically done in anticipation of an event or perceived change in market values, be it positive or negative.

Because of this forward-looking nature, it is typical that the market must make certain assumptions. These assumptions are a blend of both past occurrences, volatility, earnings, seasonal variables, and pro forma models used to make predictions about a company's growth as well as economic growth. These models can be quite advanced, taking into account dozens of variables that could influence the future earnings potential of a corporation. These models are how analysts are able to "predict" or at least try to predict a company's earnings per share. This is where they get the "analysts' expectations" from. These expectations are absorbed by Wall Street traders and investors around the globe. Traders and investors then buy or sell that stock accordingly. Certain investors may disagree with analysts and take a more positive thesis and pay up for the stock, or vice versa.

TRADER TIP

Earnings can be an excellent way to search for potential trade candidates for certain options strategies (usually less risky, more neutral spreads). In other words, go to a site like www.earnings.com or similar and look for upcoming earnings events on a company that you may be familiar with, then research analysts' reports and use your own analysis to create a thesis and to build a trade around. If you are looking for opportunities, earnings announcements can be a quick way to find stocks on the move (or that will be on the move). Use caution with this method, as earnings are typically catalysts for high volatility.

During earnings announcements, you frequently hear the term *whisper number* mentioned in the media. This number is a certain earnings expectation that some big traders and Wall Street firms place on a company's earnings announcement. If the company fails to meet this whisper number, sometimes you'll see traders sell shares of that company driving the price lower (whisper numbers may be slightly higher than the *consensus estimate*). Consequently, if a company exceeds that whisper number you may see shares of that company being bought, driving the price higher.

Basically, analysts and investors put certain expectations on the company's earnings if those expectations are exceeded or if the P/E is lower than expected. Because the company earned more, traders may buy that stock to normalize the P/E ratio or, if they don't meet that company's expectation, traders may sell shares to normalize the P/E ratio. (The P/E is not the only measurement of a company's health or the value of its shares. I am focusing on P/E, because it is common and used frequently when discussing the relative price of a stock.)

So how do you know if a company is going to exceed, fall in line with, or miss its earnings expectations? This requires a bit more skill. It involves looking back at the history of the company in certain seasons, economic conditions as well as reading a bit into the news and looking for clues as to recent strength or weakness. Preferably, news that is *not* specific to your stock because that will have a more profound effect on expectations.

For example, if you are wondering if Neiman Marcus's earnings are going to beat analysts' estimates, but you notice articles in major publications about the dismal shopping season and how malls have been empty, chances are poor that high-end retail is going to stun investors with a bullish report.

You might also need to examine what sort of guidance that company gave for the current quarter. Guidance usually occurs during the earnings call from the previous quarter. Earnings conference calls typically occur shortly after the actual earnings announcement.

If you're more of a longer-term trader, look for companies that have products or services that are in demand and are likely to stay in demand for a long time. Also look for lower relative P/Es both trailing and forward to help ensure that a company's stock price is a decent relative value—*relative* being the operative word.

At the end of the day if you look at the long-term performance (one year or more) of the stock, chances are that if the stock has been increasing in value it has also been increasing its earnings per share. If the stock has been decreasing in value chances are that it has decreased its earnings per share.

In the short term, there are other variables that can influence a stock, causing fluctuations that may seem disconnected with your long-term outlook.

Other Influences on Price　　The reasons for these fluctuations vary. They can include economic data that is favorable or unfavorable; they can include good or bad news by a company's peer or peers; or it can be that the stock is moving too slow or too fast compared to the rest of the market. Because there are so many market participants with so many unique opinions and strategies, trading in the short term may be difficult for the pure fundamentalist-type trader, meaning that traders who focus solely on earnings per share may find themselves disappointed with a stock's short-term downward oscillations. This is where technical analysis and statistical trading may come in handy when striving to identify shorter-term trends (less than a year). I believe that blending both a good fundamental understanding of a company along with a decent grasp of technical analysis and finally overlaying an option strategy on top of that can help improve your chances of success. We will discuss technical analysis in a later chapter and obviously offer you a myriad of options strategies to have at your fingertips for specific situations that present themselves in the marketplace.

How Do You Trade with So Much Uncertainty?　　In Burton G. Malkiel's book *A Random Walk Down Wall Street,* he pointed out three potential flaws in fundamental analysis:

1. Information and analysis may be incorrect. In gathering objective data, we may rely on many different sources to aggregate, sort, or help us interpret data. During this process, data points may be bad, misinterpreted, or miscategorized.

2. Analysts' forward estimates of value may be incorrect. Analysts *must* make certain assumptions. Even with quality, organized, objective data, the analyst must make a subjective forecast that is dependent on a multitude of factors, none of which have to come to fruition and even if they do, the market may have already priced in that data.

3. The market doesn't have to "find" estimated value. So let's assume that your thesis and the analyst's thesis is correct and that all of your assumptions become reality—your stock of choice may still decline in value. Perhaps because the "market" wants more from the company, maybe where value today is a P/E of 15, six months from now, the market thinks 10 is the right number (that would equal either a drop in price or a substantial jump in earnings).

This is not to discourage you or make you think that all fundamental analysis is bunk, because you surely want to have a strong fundamental foundation if you are going long and vice versa if you are positioning yourself short. More importantly, these flaws are the precise reason I became an options trader.

You do not have to be a visionary or have an immense wealth of knowledge to trade the markets; in fact, sometimes overthinking can prevent you from not only making a trade, but also exiting a winning or losing trade that you are in, which can have catastrophic consequences either way.

Investing in companies that you have faith in or know really well and believe will thrive is certainly a method that has been proven to be *somewhat* successful over the longer term (10 or more years). This is one of Warren Buffett's mantras and has made him successful, although historically, he is actually not a great market timer. His investments do work out, but I remember during the crisis of 2008, Mr. Buffett made a $5 billion investment in Goldman Sachs. The price of Goldman Sachs that day hit a high of about $126 and did go higher for a couple days before plummeting all the way down to $47.41. It was seven months before Goldman returned to the $126 level.

So obviously there are certainly exceptions and caveats to buy-and-hold success. Think about this: If you bought just about any major stock in the Nasdaq 100 in 1999 or went long the entire index (QQQQ, which is and ETF that tracks the Nasdaq 100), in 2009, 10 years later, you would have been losing money. I am a believer in investing and I do believe that investing in quality companies that have demonstrated not only growth, but adaptability and viability over the long term with good future prospects can be candidates at the right price for longer-term investments.

I also believe that I don't want to leave everything to chance and would use options to not only enhance my returns and give me a possible statistical edge, but also to protect my profit if I have one or at least offer me reduced risk if the situation seems much less predictable or volatile.

Don't Believe the Hype—Well, Not All of the Time   I am intrigued and amused at the same time when I listen to analysts make extremely specific calls. How can a single individual accurately predict the emotions and actions of millions of people? What I believe is more feasible is making an estimation and taking or giving odds where appropriate. I am guilty of this as well. For example, in many of my appearances on CNBC, Bloomberg, Fox, and so on, I speak with such conviction, not because I am trying to mislead anyone, but rather because I want to offer a firm, believable rationale that is the basis for my method of investing and risk management, without it, I would never make a trade myself. You see, no rationale, theory, or method is flawless or without error. In playing the market game, the key is having a method that you can follow and rules that you can adhere to and that make sense to you. The rules can be bent and sometimes must be bent, but your method and plan should tell you precisely how much they will bend.

The difficulty is finding the perfect balance between understanding the beliefs and behavior of market participants and combining that with the fundamental story of the individual stock. In other words, does the fundamental story and predictions coincide with the value the market has given to the company (price/earnings)?

Then before entering a trade, you must decide for how long you believe you will maintain that opinion and what will cause you to change it.

Then once you are in the trade, you should be able, at any given moment in time, to act on a signal (in profit or loss) to exit that trade. If you compound those opinions with global economic ebbs and flows and the extremely contradictory media judgments, things can get quite confusing, practice will help, but will never make perfect.

TRADER TIP

One of the ways I have been able to mitigate the negative effect of the slew of sometimes conflicting data is to use the fundamental and economic data to give me an overall bullish or bearish basic sentiment, then use technical indicators to time, monitor, and exit my trades. On top of that, I will use certain options strategies, which may give me statistical advantage, such as vertical spreads or condors if I think the stock will be range-bound. I will teach you the intricacies of those strategies later on in the book.

What I find to be the most common issue with retail investors is that they are often either too late to finally make their trades or they lack conviction in that trade to maintain their position and stick to their guns and plans.

DIGESTING THE NEWS

Another challenge in the "hyper information age" that we live in, aside from sifting through tons of often useless or repetitive data, is determining whether the market has over- or underpriced a news story into a stock. An important step in your analysis is to play the role of a crime scene investigator. You may have to look back in time, up to six months in some cases, to help rationalize movements or lack of movements in a stock. In other words, if a chart looks really out of step with the broad market, it's your job to find out why.

Is News Already "Baked In"?

Often you will hear analysts, experts, and traders use the term *baked in*, meaning that the stock is already trading at a premium or discount based on an upcoming news event, product release, or earnings surprise or disappointment. This most often happens with companies that are in the "limelight" so to speak; that is companies with heavy analyst coverage and tons of media attention. You will typically recognize these companies' names and or products and if you watch major financial networks like CNBC, Bloomberg, or Fox Business, the names of these companies can be heard multiple times throughout the day, sometimes ad nauseam.

This overexposure is actually one of the reasons a stock may have already seen its stock react prior to the event. This move is amplified as coverage increases or high-profile analysts or personalities like Jim Cramer (on CNBC) or an Abby Cohen (Goldman Sachs) begins to recommend or shun a particular stock. When examining a potential investment candidate, try to correlate the news releases with a stock's movement. The Internet is a great resource for this. You can check blogs, Google, Yahoo!, and other news aggregators for "buzz" stories.

If the masses are saying that the news has been baked in and the stock has rallied abnormally based on these news stories (not the actual event itself) then it may be time to:

- Take a contrarian position.
- Take less risk than first desired.
- Avoid the trade altogether.

A perfect example of this was Apple (AAPL). In early January 2010, with the smartphone and tablet PC wars in full blast, the CES show in Vegas swirling with Goggle's Nexus one, MSFT's tablet, and others, AAPL had all eyes on its iPad, which no one had even seen or heard of. The stock had rallied 30% in a couple weeks and the firm had not even reported earnings yet. Remember what I said earlier about earnings being the end-all and be-all for many analysts? Their models try to predict what a company will *earn* in the future. When the company drops a "wild card" like a new, unique product that has never been sold before, investors (and analysts) can go bonkers and bid the stock up. Watch for abnormal movements. Use the ATR, Bollinger bands, and charts to help you determine this. Apple's stock did drop from a high of $215 in January 2010 down to $190 before resuming its run higher.

Buy the Rumor, Sell the News

You will often hear this phrase; it refers to what I just discussed. Buy on the rumor and sell on the news essentially means to get long on a stock when the rumor mill is churning, but no concrete data has been released yet and then either right before or during the actual news release, sell your shares.

This method may be advantageous because market participants tend to get overexcited ahead of a perceived event like a takeover or product release, but once the actual event takes place, stocks often sell off because the details of the event are known.

As easy as it is to say, it can be difficult to determine if a stock has been unjustly bid up or sold off on rumor, hearsay, or anticipation of an event, news story, or product release. This is where is helps to look at the past performance of a stock during certain situations. From 2008 to 2010 Apple earned a reputation for bidding up ahead of a product launch and then selling off or at least plateauing after it released a new product. The bottom line is that if you are in stock that is being bid up on rumor and you have a profit on the table, don't be afraid to take it. No reason to "test the theory" with your account as a guinea pig. Often, if the market seems to be overreacting, it probably is. Of course, if you are intimate with a company's products or services and think that the release of a certain product or anticipated event is underrealized, you can certainly speculate if you choose.

Correlations

I am enthralled and still amazed with how the masses interpret statistics and data. Investors love old adages like "the January effect" and "Santa

Claus rally." Get to know them by reading the *Stock Traders Almanac* by Jeffery Hirsch (John Wiley & Sons). This will help give you insight to some of the more common theories and correlations in the marketplace. I have spent many years watching the markets and the people who watch the markets. I am fascinated with the behavior of the markets and, by extension, the behavior of crowds.

What I have found is that people will try to correlate just about anything with something else to try to find relationships that lead, lag, hedge, or leverage the other. Caution must be used when "finding" correlations. The problem, I think, really, is with the word *correlation*, to begin with, as I think that most investors should not be looking for correlation, but rather for causation.

Many correlations that are discussed or even used as indicators may be complete happenstance and may easily lose any evidence of the high correlation that may be observed at that moment in time.

This phenomenon is actually talked about frequently. Investment experts will talk about how the correlation between certain securities has ceased to exist. The question is—did it ever exist at all? With the effects of the Internet, Twitter, online chat rooms, Facebook, CNBC, Bloomberg, Fox Business, and others, data, news, and opinions can spread quite quickly, as can "perceived correlations."

The equity market is especially susceptible to bouts of crowd hysteria, where a "high-profile expert" may begin discussing a correlation and then the news spreads like wildfire, potentially exacerbating a *correlation* that maybe was never a true correlation to begin with, but because of the perceived connection between the two, traders and investors can actually increase the correlation rate.

I do feel some correlations are semi-dependable. One example of this may be that extreme movements in the dollar may cause inverse price action in oil or perhaps more so in gold. Because oil is denominated in U.S. dollars, as the dollar weakens versus other global currencies, it requires more U.S. dollars to buy oil, therefore the price rises, and so on.

The question is: Which is independent and which is dependent? Which is the leader/follower? For that matter, when and will they disconnect?

I would like to think that the more liquid, more fundamental, less manipulatable issues, such as currency, tend to be independent, whereas smaller issues may tend to be dependent. However, I do not have the research to prove this is correct.

What many fail to realize is that this becomes even more difficult when there may be another force moving one or both of the securities you are trying to correlate.

Aside from the fact that you might think that I am crazy at this point (the worst part is that this is what I dream about at night), hopefully this opened up your eyes a bit and maybe you will take pause next time you want to jump on a correlation trade.

The bottom line is that unless you have studied the correlations extensively and feel absolutely comfortable with them, don't place all your bets on correlations or expect them to get you out of trouble.

Oil Correlations—A Practical Example   When you see the price of oil go up or down and think about filling your gas tank, you're not the only one watching intently. The ever-changing price of oil has ramifications far beyond the cost of petrol for you and me.

Back in late April 2010, the price of oil had dropped more than 21% from $87 to $68 in a couple of weeks, This new lower price may have meant lower prices at the pump, which would be a good thing for all of us, but there are stocks that may be negatively affected by the change.

There are publicly traded companies that are involved in the entire process of getting the oil from the earth to the consumer—from drilling and production names to transporters, to refiners, and finally to the sellers of oil and distillate products. They all have their place in the proverbial *crude food chain* and all are sensitive to changes in oil prices.

If we start first with getting the oil from the earth, you have different ways of harvesting it. The most expensive and not as common method is the Canadian oil sands production, which may cost up to and about $70 to $80 per barrel (as of early 2010) just to produce. Deepwater drilling—the process used in the British Petroleum (BP) Deepwater Horizon rig disaster in April 2010—costs about $50 to $60 per barrel. The shallow water drillers using jack-up type rigs can get oil out of the ground for cheaper still.

Then there are the oil-producing countries, pulling directly from the ground on land. In the Middle East, the raw cost to produce a barrel of oil is around $20 to $30, but many of these countries (other than the United States) subsidize social programs and offer other benefits to citizens, directly from production, so their "real" cost is likely closer to $55 per barrel.

As the price of oil drops, programs like oil sand refining and deepwater drilling become less viable, which is part of the reason companies like Suncor Energy (NYSE: SU), which develops and mines the Canadian oils, and Transocean LTD (NYSE: RIG), which has large exposure to deepwater rigs, may see their stock prices drop as well. The Deepwater Horizon platform was leased by BP from RIG.

Viability of alternative energy sources like solar power and wind power may also negatively affect the prices of stocks in those sectors. Some publicly traded companies in this arena include First Solar (NASDAQ: FSLR), which manufactures solar panels, and Vestas Wind Systems (PINK: VWDRY), the largest global supplier of wind turbines in 2010.

So remember that even though you *might* save a couple of cents at the pump, stocks in your portfolio could be experiencing losses due to the same drivers. Be sure that you are aware of any correlations your stocks may have to the price of crude oil and other commodities.

CHEAP VERSUS VALUE

These words are probably two of the most mixed up and misused adjectives in the market today. As an investor or trader, you must know the difference between both, not to mention their advantages and disadvantages. When we say a stock is cheap, we could either be referring to price or to its price relative to its earnings. The problem is that just because a stock is cheap both in price and even from a price-to-earnings standpoint, it is not always valuable.

I'm sure that somewhere along the line, someone has told you that things are cheap for a reason—this applies to stocks as well!

Relative Value

One of the quickest ways to determine if a stock is cheap or if it is a good value is to compare it to something, maybe its past price/valuations or other similar companies. You could first look at the prices at which the stock has traded in the past and assume that because it's trading for 30% lower than it's been in 10 years, the price seems cheap. But is it cheap for a reason? Are similar stocks in its sector also trading for a discount as well and if so, why? Is it a sector or industry that is maturing or dying out? Or is there real *value* there?

To find value, you must dig a little deeper. From a high level, a quick way to determine the overall "cost" of the S&P 500 is to take a look at the P/E of the SPX itself, I went through this exercise earlier in this chapter. This simple data point can give you something to compare to when you drill deeper into the stocks within.

If the P/E of the market is 14, which is on the low side, you can gather that stocks are relatively cheap based on what they are earning. Of course, in that case you have to make sure that the future is looking brighter, not dimmer, for business. If the opposite were true and the P/E of the SPX was elevated, you might assume stocks were relatively expensive.

Assuming the overall P/E is relatively low, you can begin looking at those cheap (dollar) stocks and see if you can uncover some value.

The price-to-earnings ratio is just one data set, which can offer a good starting point, but is by no means the only way to spot value.

Other Guidelines for Finding Value

Many value investors also consider dividends, book value, cash flow, Price/Earnings to Growth ratio (PEG), and Debt to Equity Ratios. (And more!)

There are some general guidelines that value investors follow. An Investopedia article titled *5 Must-Have Metrics For Value Investors*[3] outlines them:

- Price-to-Earnings Ratio
- Price-to-Book Ratio
- Debt-Equity
- Free Cash Flow
- PEG Ratio

Of course, you also need to know what you're looking for in each of these figures. Some standard guidelines say the P/E ratio of a "value" company should be at the lowest 10% of all equity securities. Another guideline is that the PEG should be less than one, as should the Debt-to-Equity ratio.

There are investors who talk about share prices being no more than two-thirds of the company's intrinsic worth, assets at two times current liabilities, and earnings growth at least 7% a year over the past decade.

There are a lot of parameters, and applying them all in today's market really narrows your possibilities of finding the perfect candidate. Sometimes you just have to choose a limited number of data points to analyze; if not, you may have a hard time making a trade, because rarely is everything perfect.

Diving into the Markets   Let's take a look at two well-known tech companies in order to find out which is a better value. The following shows the data (from 2010) side by side:

	Apple, Inc (AAPL: Nasdaq)	Microsoft (MSFT: Nasdaq)
1. Price/Earnings	18.33	11.20
2. Price/Book	5.14	4.44
3. Debt/Equity	2.31	2.13
4. Free Cash Flow	$7.66 billion	$16.34 billion
5. PEG Ratio	0.88	0.97

Microsoft has a lower P/E ratio and a lower debt ratio. MSFT also has a higher Free Cash Flow, and a PEG that's still below one.

But let's take a closer look at the Price-to-Book ratio, and what it means for these two companies.

This ratio tells you how much investors are willing to pay for a company's assets. It's calculated by dividing the share price by the company's net assets, which don't include intangible things like patents or proprietary technology.[4]

In both Apple and Microsoft, this value is high. A guideline for value stocks is a price/book ratio below 1.5.

That said, in our comparison, Microsoft is a better value and compared to the personal computer industry, whose price-to-book value is 6.09 with an average P/E ratio of 20, it's comparatively undervalued.

MSFT was still about 2% lower than prices were a year prior, but we hadn't seen a true bottom yet after the swift rise through last year and the rounding over of this year. Which company would you have wanted to buy? It's not just about ratios! Apple was the market's darling and MSFT was an aging has-been in many ways. Don't forget common sense!

Here's another comparison of two stocks in a different sector (remember that certain sectors may command higher multiples, because of higher expected growth). Their numbers as of September 2010:

	Exxon Mobil, Inc. (XOM: NYSE)	ConocoPhillips (COP: NYSE)
1. Price/Earnings	11.41	8.32
2. Price/Book	2.14	1.20
3. Debt/Equity	1.08	1.04
4. Free Cash Flow	$11.11 billion	$9.21 billion
5. PEG Ratio	0.65	0.49

ConocoPhillips clearly trumped Exxon across the board even with PEG, which is short for price/earnings to growth. Take the P/E ratio and divide it by annual earnings per share growth. Like P/E ratios, the lower the number, the more undervalued the company could be.

We see that Exxon had a higher free cash flow, which is good. . . . But with COP's figure well positive, that's not a concern. The free cash flow accounts for how much money a company has left after any capital investments. Had COP's free cash flow figure been in the millions instead of billions, we might have had some cause for concern.

Compared to the major integrated oil and gas industry, which at the time had an average P/E ratio of 10.20 and price/book value of 1.55, ConocoPhillips is undervalued.

ConocoPhillips had seen a significant pullback in the stock since May 2010's high of $60.53. A dip below $52 makes COP a buy in my book.[5]

Comparing the fundamentals of companies within a certain sector is an excellent way to weed out the "worst in breed" stocks and find the strongest relative performers. With that said, there are some companies within certain sectors that may now look bad on paper but have high future growth potential or an excellent product that will propel their stock higher. Netflix in 2009–2010 was an example of this. If you choose to just buy a cheap stock or ignore certain fundamentals, be sure it is for good reason and that you have a concrete thesis that you can really back up.

MERGERS AND ACQUISITIONS FOR THE EVERYDAY OPTIONS TRADER

Mergers, acquisitions, or *consolidation*, as it is often called, is a part of the normal overall market day to day and something you need to be aware of, but not obsess over unless you want to specialize in it. Merger and/or acquisition activity is not typically taking place every day, so changes in normal patterns of this activity can have positive or negative effects on your investments. When merger and acquisition activity is relatively high, market participants tend to view this as positive. This makes sense for several reasons, the first being that if one company is laying out cash, stock, or leverage (borrowing money) they believe that the value of the target company may be undervalued (the stock may be cheap). If more companies are able to do more deals, chances are that their businesses are strong, which is always a good thing. It could also mean that the acquiring company (or both) believes that a combination of the two companies will make for a stronger whole or maybe the purchaser is simply removing some competition because it wants to reap more rewards in a growing space. All these reasons can be construed as bullish.

Think about it on the most basic level: If you had a lemonade stand and you thought the lemonade business was going to stagnate or drop, would you even entertain any of those reasons for purchasing another lemonade stand down the street? Maybe to combine forces and hopefully lower costs and make a better lemonade, but if business was really bad, chances are you wouldn't be looking to expand it.

Try Not to Buy a Company That Is Being Acquired

Once a company has been acquired (announced the acquisition) its behavior will often drastically change and if it is bought for cash, it will usually move to the buyout price and stay there, which is not where you want to be.

After an acquisition or merger has been announced and both stocks make their initial moves, most deals take months to complete and often, after the news and hype dies down, you may find yourself in a trade that involves the acquiring company or the target company, without having knowledge or intention of doing so. In other words, you may have bought a company not knowing that it is being acquired. This is why looking back on past news stories is paramount.

I will sometimes go six months or more back in time to get an accurate reading on the climate of a company that I'm not familiar with; sometimes a past news story can help explain anomalies in options prices, volatility readings, or odd behavior. By "odd" behavior, I am talking about a stock that is unusually flat (could be a cash takeover target) or a stock that is moving in lockstep with another company (this might be an example of a stock-for-stock takeover).

Option Prices in a Possible Takeover Target

Sometimes you will notice that the upside calls (bullish option bets) are unusually expensive compared to downside puts (bearish option bets), which means that implied volatility of those options has a positive *skew* (I will talk more about skew in Chapter 4). This positive skew can be a tell-tale sign of a company that is rumored to be taken over or there might be takeover chatter within the sector. Use caution though, because some products (indexes, ETFs, gold) naturally have a very high skew, which can be misleading as they are generally not takeover targets. There are arbitrageurs who focus solely on trading the two or more stocks that are involved in a merger or takeover deal; it's very precise business and potentially risky for the novice. They will even trade the company that is being acquired. I would leave that sort of trading to the pros. If you do find yourself positioned in a stock *after* a deal has been announced, try to be sure it's the stock doing the acquiring, not the one being acquired, as it has most likely reached its zenith in price.

THE WISDOM (OR LACK THEREOF) OF CROWDS

In Gustave Le Bon's book, *The Crowd*,[6] he noted that, "The memorable events of history are the visible effects of the invisible changes of human thought." He was referring to major events in human record, such as the fall of the Roman Empire and the foundation of the Arabian Empire.

These concepts are applicable to the marketplace as well, although the sometimes extraordinary price movements of an individual stock or an index may not be memorable to all of society, to the participants (crowd members), they certainly can be. Short-term price fluctuations are, in my opinion, great manifestations of human emotion, which when part of the crowd create characteristics that are often exaggerated and may even completely disconnect from the underlying company's financial health. These price fluctuations may seem odd when you step back and just look at the stock in a vacuum, ignoring all the news, chatter, and hype surrounding it. Price fluctuations driven by the "crowd" can sometimes be guided by chart patterns.

Le Bon defined crowds as:

> *From the psychological point of view, the expression the "crowd" assumes quite a different signification. Under certain given circumstances, and only under those circumstances, an agglomeration of men presents new characteristics very different from those of the individuals composing it. The sentiments and ideas of all the persons in the gathering take one and the same direction, and their conscious personality vanishes. A collective mind is formed, doubtless transitory, but presenting very clearly defined characteristics. The gathering has thus become what, in the absence of a better expression, I will call an organized crowd, or, if the term is considered preferable, a psychological crowd. It forms a single being, and is subjected to the law of the mental unity of crowds.*

Basically, when like-minded people are united together and begin to feed off each other—usually under the direction of either a leader or guru—or maybe if the crowd simply has similar passions, techniques, beliefs, or goals, they may lose their individual rationality and thus begin to assimilate more of the collective crowd's behavior, which may be in complete contrast to the rational conduct of the individual if they were in isolation. That deviation from normal rationale may benefit that individual temporarily, but at some point there is bound to be a realization or a reversion to the mean or normal set of behaviors. If individuals make an irrational decision involving the stock market, it could possibly cause individuals either to make a trade that didn't fit their profile or take more risk than needed or worse.

Possessing a crowd mentality doesn't necessarily mean that you are gathered shoulder to shoulder with other like-minded individuals in a field somewhere, but rather bound by a similar belief system that is fueled by media hype, technical formations, and the like. Many of us want to be part of the crowd, we want to play on the same team as the Wall Street heavy hitters that we see every day on television and we want to emulate their every move, because we believe that if they can do it, so can we. What many of us fail to miss are the often subtle but sometimes drastic differences between each of our trading skills, risk tolerance, and what I like to call *uncontrollable influences*, like a spouse, children, and a regular job, for example. This uncontrollable pressure can cause you to make decisions that will never be the same as the guy or gal next door, and in trading, timing and pricing are everything.

I say all this because I base much of my thesis on what the crowd will most likely do and how I can exploit the crowd without being sucked into it. I try to measure crowd or popular behavior combined with elements of past reactions to similar news or occurrences in a stock and the stock's financial health now and in the future when determining what strategy I will employ. Obviously this involves balancing my risk and reward with both the statistical and emotional probability that I gather from my research. Understanding, preparing for, and ultimately accepting sometimes irrational market (crowd) behavior in addition to your own will help you limit risk and react without hesitation.

There have been many excellent books written on crowd theory, which will be able to take this subject into more depth.

It doesn't take a PhD to come up with these conclusions, although some people are inherently better at it than others. Over time, you will begin to see certain patterns and movements associated with certain types of stocks and news. If everyone and her mother is talking about a certain stock, be extra cautious and closely evaluate its recent movements and current and future valuations, as it may have recently been overbought or oversold. I recommend testing your theories and journaling what went right and what went wrong with your thesis.

TRADING TACTICS AND TECHNICAL ANALYSIS

It is the subtle nuances that may make the difference between a successful trade and a losing trade and maybe even make or break a trader's career altogether. Over the years, I have observed many tactics that traders employ. I have wanted to share the methods that I apply as well as some unique insight on money management, crowds, and abnormalities in addition to how I use technical analysis to trade.

There are a multitude of books that can teach you technical analysis and I have suggested a couple in the recommended reading section, but like fundamental analysis, keep it as simple and effective as possible.

I suggest that you focus on some of the most commonly used technical analysis techniques as the basis of your strategy, because I believe that more common basic indicators that are followed by many have a better chance of becoming self-fulfilling prophecies as opposed to the more obscure methods. You can add in a specialized indicator that may offer a bit of a unique edge or confirmation for you to enter and exit your trades, along with helping you to monitor trades, but don't ignore the common indicators.

When you are ready to apply technical analysis on an individual stock, make sure that basic fundamental and macroeconomic data supports your thesis. Once you have determined the technical signals you are going to follow, you will apply the appropriate options strategy based on what is found both in the charts as well as the relative volatility of the options, which I discuss later.

Take Kibbles and Bits, Not the Whole Pie

It's hard to turn on any financial network, read any paper, or browse any finance website without feeling compelled to make a trade in one direction or the other. Not to mention that greed sometimes or most of the time gets the best of us, forcing us to ignore our natural instincts or our trading rules. When you hear someone else (or many others) getting excited about a trade or making money, it may be difficult to control your urges to jump in as well.

There will *always* be opportunities in the marketplace. Don't get the "once in a lifetime trade" syndrome, because it's bull. Also remember that the market does not care about you, nor does it know at what price you are long or short. Most of us are just along for a fairly random ride trying to make logical sense of the bucking bronco that is the equity markets.

Most retail traders and investors are still searching for that special sauce, that indicator, or method that will work like an ATM machine. Unfortunately, that Holy Grail tool or method does not exist for any of us. The market is a truly random series of occurrences, with patterns and beliefs that allow us to harness opportunity. There are no absolute rules of movement, anything can happen, and you must always keep that in the back of your mind.

The good news is that with some solid basic knowledge of options, some fundamental data, and a working knowledge of charts and the technical indicators of your choice, that's about 40% of what is needed to succeed. For most traders, money management, controlling greed and fear, and finding the right "happy place" when it comes to trading is the real challenge, which in my opinion is the majority of the battle. Your happy place is the amount of money that you are satisfied making (or losing) in each trade. This is easier said than done. We all know that once you're in the trade and it's moving in your direction, even if you are happy with the money you're making, that little voice in the back of your head (greed/emotion) sees the brass ring and tells your logical voice to shut up and let it ride. You need to learn to suppress that voice or tendency, as the adverse effects from your lack of control may be more devastating than just one or two losing trades. Denise Shull will discuss psychology of trading in depth in Chapter 10.

As a trader, controlling your greed cannot only help preserve your regular capital, but your mental capital as well. Let's assume you bought Williams-Sonoma (WSM) at $12 on May 27, 2009; one week later, the stock was trading at $14.70. You could take some profit off the table, either by selling some of your shares or selling your in-the-money calls to purchase some cheaper out-of-the-money calls with the profit you have made (hopefully leaving some extra in your account), or by even selling the position altogether. Not only would you have a winning trade that would increase the size of your account, but you would also have a sense of accomplishment and feel more confident when entering your next trade. Not to mention that you would have the capital freed up to do so.

Now let's look at the flip side and assume you don't sell because you had no profit goal established when you initiated the trade and your greedy side saw the possibility of a large reward. So you hold your long stock and WSM reports earnings, which turn out to be not so good. In addition, the market is a bit overbought and coincidentally sells off and WSM trades down to $11.50. Now you're beating yourself up for not exiting, stressed because your opinion of the stock may have changed and your account is in the red, and you have 20% of your account tied up in this trade, which could have been used to buy a different company that may have better prospects.

All of a sudden, hoping, wishing, and praying become your strategy of choice. You may be reluctant to enter another trade for fear of repeating what you just did. This is where the vicious cycle sometimes begins. Each trade you make after this loser becomes a revenge trade to get back at the markets for what "they" did to you. Frustration and a low reserve of *psychological capital* will cause mistakes; I can almost assure you of that.

Obviously this is an extreme example, but not out of the ordinary. In fact, I have seen this type of situation for years. The point is to have a trade plan, target goal, and acceptable loss level in place before making the trade. Think about the best poker players, how even against all odds (literally) they keep their cool and evaluate the situation through techniques like bluffing and money management (folding). The randomness of the deck (which you can equate to the markets) can be somewhat controlled through good money-management techniques, psychological control, and, of course, a strategy.

When things are good and the profits are in your hands, do something to protect them! It's *much* more difficult to sell when a market is tumbling and you are under duress.

Using Charts, Technical Analysis, and Tools

There are people who are for and against technical analysis. I tend to be heavily focused on the technical side or the analysis of charts and patterns for one simple reason. There really are no rules when it comes to the stock market. There is no fundamentally based guideline that says where a stock should trade. All the analysts in the world who crunch a company's fundamental data and use complex models to try determine what a stock value should be at any moment in time are only hypothesizing.

Sometimes I agree with them, sometimes I don't, because I don't really see how they can predict the minds of millions of investors.

Technical Analysis—A Self-Fulfilling Prophecy?

Technical analysis, on the other hand, more or less offers guidelines and rationales for the marketplace, based on less esoteric observations. Support and resistance levels give us specific prices at which to enter or exit. Average True Range (ATR) and volatility help us to quantify how a stock "normally" moves and if it is behaving oddly and presenting us with an opportunity or cautioning us that there might be an underlying problem. There are dozens of different indicators to choose from—some are better than others.

I also believe that technical analysis only works because so many people believe in it and use it that it almost becomes a self-fulfilling prophecy. It has been used in some form or fashion for thousands of years, dating all the way back to 18th century Japanese rice farmers. The patterns and indicators sometimes seem so esoteric, but amazingly they still manage to manifest themselves in a stock's price. . . . I mean, how else would the Fibonacci sequence appear in the marketplace? (Read more about Fibonacci in Chapter 9.)

We humans have a complex and sometimes funny way of responding to uncertainty. In Leonard Mlodinow's book, *The Drunkard's Walk*,[7] he describes this and many other interesting points about the randomness in our lives and how we deal with it every day. (I encourage you to read his book.)

TRADER TIP

In nature, there are numerous examples of Fibonacci's golden ratio in everything from the number of petals on flowers, to pineapples to pine cones and snail shells. Even the ratio and proportion of our facial features; but how do they appear in the stock market? Perhaps it is as simple as having an idea of where those levels are that (Fibonacci and others) drives market participants to buy or sell up or down to that level. This can even happen subconsciously. (It happens to me frequently.)

I guess that I give the average human mind much more credit that most probably would and believe that our subconscious looks for patterns in the market even if they do not exist. Those patterns can manifest themselves through previous training, reading, or just randomly in the trader's mind. I find this frequently; traders, without referencing a specific indicator, seem to arbitrarily pick a target to sell or a level to buy that coincide with a widely known technical indicator.

My hypothesis is that most market participants heard or saw a certain chart, price level, or recommendation to buy or sell at a certain level on television, read it in a paper, or observed that price level while looking at a chart without even realizing it and stored it away in their subconscious and acted on it later. Or maybe that level just looked nice on the chart they were viewing for some reason. I just don't believe that humans (especially market participants) are that random, even though we think we are.

Many of the books published about the markets, including the one you are reading now, instruct you to act a certain way in response to a news or data occurrence, indicator, or pattern. These teachings, along with common statistics, share many commonalities and thus encourage the masses to act together in a certain way, creating at least some sort of typical response. (The reason we can't really predict the market is because we don't know what those occurrences will be.)

So if the conscious technical traders buy and sell based on certain chart patterns, along with the fundamentalists who are trying to time their trades a bit better, use those same indicators along with newer traders who just store what they hear in their subconscious. I feel pretty confident about the validity of technical analysis.

Know Your Indicators

Technical indicators are often misused; make sure you understand exactly what it is that you are looking at and what the signal is supposed to look

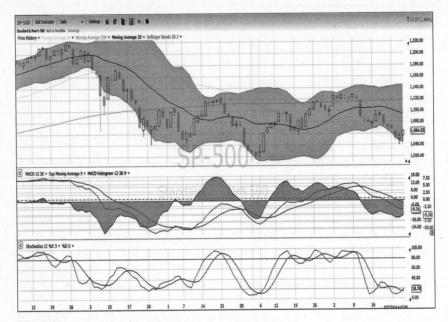

FIGURE 3.5 Example of My Basic Chart Screen Setup
Courtesy of www.freestockcharts.com.

like. More importantly, be sure that you understand how the masses are using the indicator.

I find it helpful to know how the indicator derives its value. That way, you will be more accurately able to interpret the data and utilize it most efficiently. I always say you can add your own spin on using an indicator, just make sure that the logic of your usage fits with what the indicator is attempting to measure.

Figure 3.5 shows my typical technical chart setup.[8]

Technical Analysis, Options, and How I Trade with Them

At the end of the day, I want an edge or an advantage in the trades that I do. Casinos have an edge in *every* game that they offer and they certainly do allow players to win occasionally, just like you should be prepared to lose occasionally. What the casino is good at is mitigating their losses through very specific rules and regulations, which prevent them from disabling themselves (their cash reserves) beyond repair and not collecting their edge, which they do over a longer series of games. One of these rules is the table limits at roulette, which stop the outside bet layers from doubling their bets until they win back what they have lost. Roulette is also the perfect example of the casino's edge. Options can offer this edge.

Speculating on the increase or decrease in the price of all things goes back a long time. In fact, there is record of civilizations using options going back thousands of years, even to Greek and Roman times. Options and the laws of put-call parity specifically (which you will learn later) were also used to bypass usury laws; there are actually options strategies in which one market participant can lend or borrow money to another and so much more.

Technical analysis can help you visualize and rationalize price movements of a stock. They can offer us entry and exit signals and alert us to abnormal movements, but they, too, like fundamental analysis are flawed.

Throughout my lifetime I have encountered just about every market theory and type of trade style known to man. Of course, there will be many, many more as time progresses. Build your own method and test it and try to keep your system and risk consistent without being swayed by the latest and greatest methods that will purportedly make you exceptional returns.

Remember, it is not all about how you look at the market or an individual stock, but more so how the masses will perceive the current situation now and in the future. What will drive that stock higher or lower—what has done so in the past? These questions can be answered by using the charts and technicals.

Indicators

Following is a discussion of the indicators I use to trade.

TRADER TIP

Pattern recognition. When setting up your charts, make it easy on your brain and use *logarithmic* scaling to keep the changes in price visually equal and keep the percentage change in price over time consistent.

Moving Averages   Moving averages are an extremely common technical analysis tool that I use along with many other traders. Some experts say that moving averages are losing their ability to help time the markets. I partially disagree. Moving averages create smooth lines from otherwise noisy, sometimes choppy data (prices). A moving average is a dynamic, rolling indicator that takes the closing prices of the period chosen and averages that data. As new days, weeks, or months are added, they are automatically averaged in with the existing data, which allows the moving average to continue on. I tend to use simple moving averages (SMA), which only average closing prices and ignore volume. Exponential moving averages (EMA) give more weight to the most recent price action in the average. In other words, the current day's price movement will have a bigger part of the average than yesterday's price movement. In a stock that has recently experienced large moves, the EMA would tend to skew the average, but it also diminishes changes to today's average due to "tail" data dropping off. There are arguments for and against SMA and EMA. I just tend to favor SMA. Moving averages are also used as part of other indicators I favor as well.

I use the 10-, 20-, 50-, and 200-day simple moving averages in a couple different ways.

Long-Term Trend—Longer-Term Traders Tend to Hold Positions for More Than Two Months and Sometimes Much Longer   The 200-day moving average, which will tend to be the smoothest line compared to the other three I use, with the least amount of variation over time and can be a simple indicator of whether the stock is in a long-term bullish or bearish trend. If the stock is above the 200-day SMA, it can be considered to be in a bullish trend and the 200-day SMA can be considered a level of support (where you might want to buy the stock). At the same time, if a stock closes below its 200-day SMA and does not immediately recover, the stock might be changing its trend and it could be a time to examine exiting any bullish trades you are in. If the stock has been below the 200-day SMA and breaks through it coinciding with overall bullish fundamental data, that could be a time to buy the stock.

Intermediate Trends—Intermediate Traders Tend to Hold Positions for One to Five Weeks   For the intermediate trade you can use the 50-day SMA and following the same rules as above. The 20-day SMA can also be used in conjunction with or in place of the 50-day SMA to offer an "early indication"—for example, if you are in a bullish trade and the stock breaks below the 20, but hasn't broken the 50, you might want to be on high alert, as it could be a sign that the bullish trend is breaking down.

Shorter-Term Trends—Short-Term Traders Hold Positions for One to Four Days   Swing traders will most likely focus on the 10- and 20-day SMAs as a means of identifying shorter-term trends. Keep in mind that the long-term trend can still be bullish, with the short-term trend in a bearish formation. As a short-term trader, you must be nimble, and because the moving averages are only accounting for 10 or 20 days of data, you will see more movement in these averages. In addition to the increased movement, you might also get some false signals, so be sure to stay on your toes.

When Moving Averages Cross Each Other *Technical analysts also use points of intersection between moving averages as a means to signal an entry or an exit.* Selecting which moving average to use is a matter of preference; typically it's when a shorter duration moving average like a 20- or 10-period moving average crosses above or below a longer duration such as the 100- or 200-period moving average.

20-Day Jumps Above 200-Day SMA This is one of the most simple bullish entry signals for me, for an intermediate- to longer-term trade. I will exit the trade either if I meet my profit target, stop loss, or when the 20-day falls back below 200. Use caution with this technique because the stock may have to fall quite a bit before the 20 falls below the 200, at which point you could be losing quite a bit of money. Consider placing a stop loss just below your point of entry to prevent this. You can always get back in.

The Death Cross Although the name sounds ominous, it merely means that a shorter-term moving average (50-day SMA or EMA) has moved below the longer-term moving average (200-day). Some analysts use different periods. I stick with the 200 and 50. According to Marketwatch.com, in the past 114 years, there have been 85 death crosses—an average of one every 16 months or so. They also noted that the track record has not been that great. If you look at the cross in the SPX in June of 2010 (see Figure 3.6), the index had already lost a ton of ground, but it did eventually continue lower. The death cross, I believe, should be more of a general confirmation of a change in trend, not a "sell now" indicator.

MACD Oscillator—Moving Average Convergence/Divergence

This indicator is one of my favorites because it tends to act more like a leading indicator as opposed to a guideline based on past observations. The MACD is simple to use and is great for monitoring momentum in a trade. It consists of two basic parts, the MACD line itself, which is measuring the convergence or divergence of two moving averages along with a "Signal" line, which is simply a moving average of the MACD itself. Don't worry, it sounds much more complicated than it is.

This signal line smoothes the movements and allows you to spot crossover points, which could signal a change in trend. Your charting package may also allow you see a histogram, which is a set of bars that measures the distance between the signal line and the MACD and gives you a visual indication of increasing or diminishing strength. Being an oscillator, the lines move above and below a zero line indicating bearish momentum or

FIGURE 3.6   SPX Daily Chart—June to August 2010—50- and 200-Moving Average
Source: www.freestockcharts.com.

bullish momentum, the MACD and signal can flatten out above, below, or at the zero line, which would indicate no real momentum. Figure 3.7 shows both the signal and the MACD itself. Your platform will allow you to customize settings to your liking.

How I Use MACD   I like to combine the MACD with other indicators or sentiment, but the MACD can signal an entry or exit for me all by itself. I use the standard 12, 26 period configuration when setting up my MACD and I always want to view the histogram so I can more accurately monitor momentum.

Bullish   Once the MACD crosses over (above) the signal line, I am looking to get long. I will frequently wait for good separation in the lines as indicated by the histogram. While in the trade, I will monitor the histogram for decreasing momentum in addition to monitoring the price of the underlying security. I will exit once my target profit has been obtained, my options strategy is expiring, or if the MACD touches the signal line again. I don't have to have them cross for an exit.

Bearish   Everything is the same on the bearish side; only the MACD will cross *under* the signal line. I will still monitor momentum as well as other support points in the charts. I will exit using similar criteria as before.

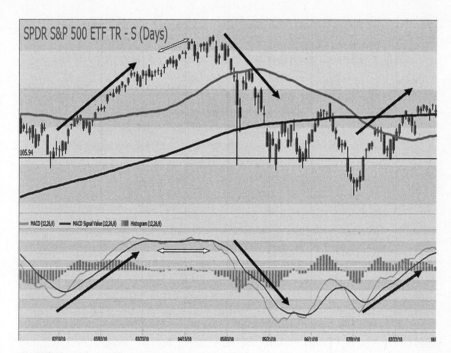

FIGURE 3.7 Daily MACD and SPX Price Chart
Courtesy of Lightwave.

TRADER TIP

Remember that MACD can be applied to *any* time frame from minutes to days and even months. Be aware of the trend and the chart in which you are following and make sure it coincides with your trade plan.

Stochastic Oscillator   Another one of my preferred indicators is the stochastic. I use it in conjunction with my price chart studies as well as the MACD indicator. The stochastic has its own panel in my standard chart screen setup, positioned under the MACD lines.

The definition for the stochastic oscillator is:

$$\%K = [(\text{Close} - \text{Low } n)/(\text{High } n - \text{Low } n)] * 100$$
$$\text{Low } n = \text{The Lowest Low within } n \text{ periods}$$
$$\text{High } n = \text{The Highest High within } n \text{ periods}$$

This gives you the fast stochastic

$\%D$ = The moving average of $\%K$ (typically 3 days or periods)

Where   Price is the last closing price
         $LOW_N(Price)$ is the lowest price over the last N periods
         $HIGH_N(Price)$ is the highest price over the last N periods
         $EMA_3(\%D)$ is a 3-period exponential moving average of $\%K$
         $EMA_3(\%D - Slow)$ is a 3-period exponential moving average
         of $\%D$

The stochastic oscillator is another indicator of trend momentum, but also identifies overbought and oversold conditions, although one of the flaws of this indicator is that in a strong, sharp, and sustained uptrend, the stochastic will be stuck above the overbought line, and if the trend is sustained to the downside, it may be stuck in the oversold area, at which time I tend to focus on other indicators like MACD and price for changes in trend. There are multitudes of ways you can use this indicator. I tend to stick to the basics of identifying overbought, sold conditions and reversals of trends, but I will look for certain diverging patterns as well, which I will explain. This indicator is also frequently misinterpreted, so use caution when buying or selling just based on the oscillator's position.

Just like the MACD, it has two lines, a fast line $\%K$ and a slow line $\%D$. (Don't concern yourself too much with those names.) Also like the MACD, the stochastic simple moves between an upper and lower level. In this case 100 and 0 are the top and bottom of the range, respectively. The key reasons I use stochastic are to identify overbought and oversold conditions as well as a confirmation of price movement and avoidance of price capitulation either to the upside or downside.

When the stochastic is above 80, the stock is considered to be in an overbought state; when the stochastic is below 20, the stock is considered to be in an oversold state. If you notice a stochastic move into these areas, it might be a cue to reduce some of your exposure, as a retracement or reversal of trend might be coming, although keep in mind that even with the stochastic in an *overbought* or *oversold* area, the stock can still continue in its current trend higher or lower, so be cautious of *false signals*. This behavior is shown in Figure 3.8 where the price of the S&P 500 continues to rise, even with the stochastic in an overbought area.

When examining the trend of the stochastic oscillator compared to the price trend of the stock, it may be beneficial to see a divergence. If you are noticing higher highs in the price trend, but at the same time noticing lower lows in the stochastic, this is actually preferred and is an example of

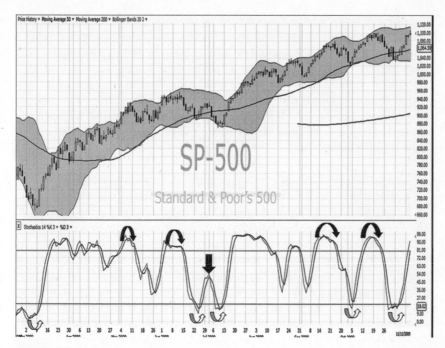

FIGURE 3.8 Basic Overbought/Sold Indications—Note the Overall Trend of the S&P 500 Is Up in this Period
Source: www.freestockcharts.com.

the convergence/divergence method of the oscillator that traders use when examining broader trends in a security in an effort to reduce noise.

- Note that a possible entry or setup is present when the %*D* line is in an extreme area and diverging from the price action of the underlying security.
- Stochastics work best in *non*trending markets that are fluctuating up and down and are especially useful in volatile markets.
- The shorter the time period, the more actively you will be buying and selling.
- It may be a signal to exit your position when stochastic %*D* crosses %*K* in reverse direction used to open trade.

Bollinger Bands In 1983 John Bollinger published one of the more popular indicators of the late twentieth century.[9] According to Mr. Bollinger, they are extremely simple and are meant to help determine relative price levels over a given period of time. Placing bands around stock is a way to find rational areas where a stock may be overbought or oversold within a channel; it could also be used to spot changes in trend. One way to create a band around a stock price could be to use the beta of a stock (its volatility compared to the overall market) or maybe even a fixed band based on a percentage. Both of these methods would not offer the dynamic adaptability that Bollinger bands do.

Bollinger bands use observed actual volatility to set the width of the bands. Here is the formula if you care to dig deeper (you don't have to know it to trade with bands).

- Middle band = Moving average (usually 20 periods in length)
- Upper band = middle band + width (usually 2 sd) * volatility
- Lower band = middle band – width (usually 2 sd) * volatility
- Where volatility = standard deviation of the moving average data

How Do You Use Them? Bands tend to capture really high and low relative movements of stock by using two standard deviations as a statistical gauge of price distribution, basically 90% to 95% of the time. Normal stock movements should stay within the bands. If they travel outside, it could indicate a possible mean reversion (reversal) or trend change. I find them very accurate in daily charts. Can you find the reversions in Figure 3.9?

Bands define possible extreme high and low points on a relative basis and indicate if:

- Prices are high at the upper band—may be a short-term sell.
- Prices are low at the lower band—may be a short-term buy.

John has always used 20-period (day) moving average as a good sample of short- to intermediate-term data to find the trend. You can adjust this up or down depending on what moving averages you tend to use to signal your entries and exits. If you don't have this, stick to 20.

There are in-depth classes and books on using his tools and he also integrates other related indicators such as %b and bandwidth, which are available with many advanced charting systems.

Bandwidth As a standalone indicator, it can be plotted and compared across time and from stock to stock, bandwidth would most likely coincide with volatility in the markets and the stock itself. Bands can bulge, which tend to occur at the end of a trend or a chaotic sell-off or pinch (squeeze), which would indicate a consistent, low relative volatility trend. It can also be used to identify periods of high and low volatility when considering options trades.

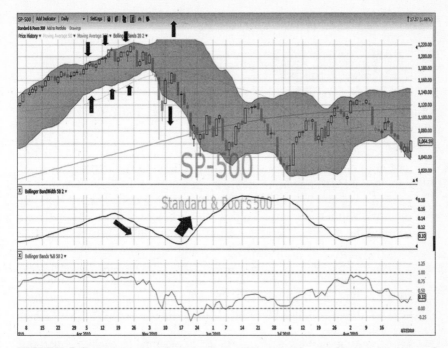

FIGURE 3.9 Bollinger Bands Around the SPX—Note the Pinching and Bulging of the Bands, Indicating Low and High Periods of Volatility, Respectively
Source: www.freestockcharts.com.

%B This tells you exactly where the stock is in relation to the bands, basically confirming your visual of the stock in relation to the band. Note *%b* drifting slightly lower as the price of the stock moved higher on the left-hand side of the chart in Figure 3.9.

Volume Without volume, nothing would happen in the stock market. A price doesn't necessarily move without an action or indication of intent, both of which would require either a certain amount of shares to be bought or sold or the signal of a certain amount of shares that are going to be bid for or offer to the marketplace. I am not going to spend too much time here, but I will offer a few basic guidelines when it comes to volume:

- Volume is the cause and price change is the effect; the more volume the better.
- High volume ensures liquidity. Make sure your stock, index, or ETF trades adequate volume. I personally look for 1 million shares average daily volume, but will go as low as 600k average daily volume as long

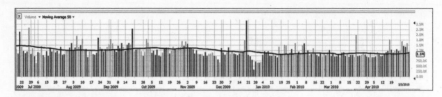

FIGURE 3.10 Volume with 50-Day Moving Average—You Can See the Spikes Above and Troughs Below the Moving Average

as I am familiar with the stock. Thin volume in the underlying stock usually equals thin volume and low open interest in the options.

- Look for volume trends. In addition to spotting trends in price and indicators, volume can offer a quick and dirty look into the strength of a trend. If the price has been rising but volume continues to decline, that may be a sign that fewer and fewer real buyers are buying and it may simply be the sellers moving out of the way and letting the price move higher so they can sell into the thin buying. This works the same way to the downside. If volume is increasing into a trend, that could be a sign that the trend may continue. Don't forget to look for confirmation elsewhere.
- Use a volume moving average, 10 or 20 periods, to easily spot trends and smooth the noise. The shorter the duration, the less smooth the line will be but if you are a short-term trader, you may want to see the short-term increases or decreases, whereas the 40 period really offers a more normalized view of volatility trends (see Figure 3.10).
- **Watch for spikes.** A volume spike to the downside coupled with a sharp sell-off outside of the lower Bollinger band could mean capitulation and spark a sharp, quick reversal. Also use volume spikes to identify abnormal trading and check for news or insider trading (legal).

TRADER TIP

If your chart package has the capability, you can view "normalized volume," which will basically show you the 50-day average in the center of the chart (which would be represented as 100%) as a straight line and the volume deviations away from that average will be more pronounced, allowing you to make better judgments in real percentage terms on trends relative to the "normal" behavior of the volume.

*The formula is Volume/50-day SMA of volume *100/SMA. SMA stands for simple moving average.

Gaps Gaps are an everyday occurrence in the marketplace. A gap simply means that there is a pronounced gap or difference in between the closing price and opening price of a security. Gaps carry not only different interpretations and meanings, but strategies to trade them. Here are a couple I tend to trade.

- **Filling a gap.** A popular strategy is to fill or fade a gap that occurs on a positive or negative news story or market event. When the stock opens sharply higher or lower, a trader may sell into that strength or buy into the weakness on hopes that prices will normalize in the short term.
- **Breakaway gap.** When a stock has been in a sideways consolidation pattern with clearly defined support and resistance levels and gaps above or below those levels with volume, which may be a cue that the stock could begin a breakout, which can either be traded actively or longer term, depending on which chart the pattern appears (see Figure 3.11). Volume should remain strong after the breakout, indicating strength in the trend.

FIGURE 3.11 Extreme Breakaway Gaps and Filling a Gap in ABK during 2010
Source: www.freestockcharts.com.

Head and Shoulders and Reverse Head and Shoulders   Traders
use terms like *head and shoulders, cup and handle, flag (pennant)* and
others to describe formations that appear when analyzing a chart. Understanding this jargon is unfortunately a necessary evil, at least to an extent,
if you are planning on using technicals as part of your trade plan (which I
recommend you do). These patterns along with others are used to describe
the *look* and characteristics of a trend, but more importantly may determine
if that trend will continue, strengthen, or reverse. Some technical patterns
help predict channels, support, resistance, and breakouts (when a stock
makes a sharp move out of its current range). I encourage you to educate
yourself at least on the basics of the patterns that I mentioned for nothing
more than to prevent yourself from making a trade that completely contra-
dicts a major formation in the charts.

Head and Shoulders—Bearish/Reversal of Trend   This pattern can
be found in any time-frame chart and is most effective when the stock is in
an overall uptrend. The chart duration (minutes, days, weeks, etc.) will dictate how long and how strong of an effect the formation may have on your
underlying stock. So if you saw a head and shoulders (H&S) in a minute
chart, you might expect a quick small drop in the stock price and you would
trade it accordingly, exiting within minutes, whereas in a monthly chart, a
H&S pattern there might signal a longer-term short position, which could
be held for a month or more.

Characteristics   Typically you will have to wait until the left shoulder
and head have been formed before the pattern comes into view, albeit
partially. The head and shoulders formation is created from modest buying, then a moderate sell-off forming the left shoulder. Buyers will look
strong when the first shoulder is formed; then, once the stock retraces and
a support level (neck line) has been found, the stock will make a bullish
run even higher than the previous high—this forms the head. Most likely
(and preferably) the buying volume will be diminishing as the stock makes
new relative highs, indicating failing strength and tired, scarce buyers. The
downside volume should be increasing preferably as well. If the stock finds
support around the prior support level and confirms the neckline, the next
bounce higher will most likely be less pronounced and probably have even
less volume; this will be the creation of the right shoulder and will complete the formation. After the stock rallies to form the last shoulder and
the sell-off ensues, the point at which the stock breaks below the neckline
could create a short-term breakout to the downside. Although this may be
an opportunity to take a quick short position, it is *not* confirmation of a
reversal of trend and extremely bearish signal. This will happen only if the
stock (once below the neckline) fails to break back above it as indicated

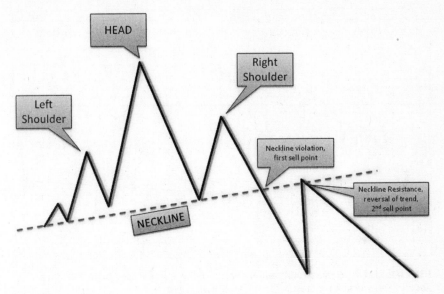

FIGURE 3.12 Proper Head and Shoulders Formation

in Figure 3.12. Figure 3.13 is an example of a stock (SPX) that did *not* fail (fall below) at the neckline, and therefore held its trend.

Reverse Head and Shoulders—Bullish/Reversal of Trend This pattern can be found in any time-frame chart and is most effective when the stock is in an overall downtrend. Like the regular head and shoulders, the chart duration (minutes, days, weeks, etc.) will dictate how long and how strong of an effect the formation may have on your underlying stock. So if you saw a head and shoulders in a minute chart, you might expect a quick small rally in the stock price and you would trade it accordingly, exiting within minutes, whereas in a monthly chart, a reverse H&S pattern might signal a longer-term long position, which could be held for a month or more.

Characteristics Basically, just turn the head and shoulders pattern upside down. The price and volume characteristics will be the same, but price movement will be in reverse. After the final right shoulder, the stock will have to break *above* the neckline resistance and then hold its support level (neckline) to confirm the change in trend. You can buy on the first breakout, but the stronger buy signal will be after the stock confirms final support at the neckline as indicated in Figure 3.14.

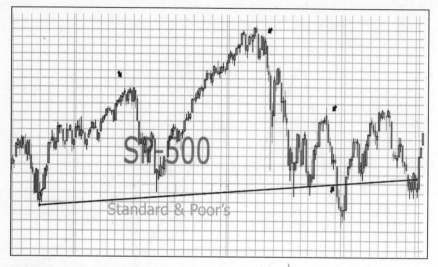

FIGURE 3.13 Head and Shoulders Formed, But Came Back Above Neckline
Source: freestockcharts.com.

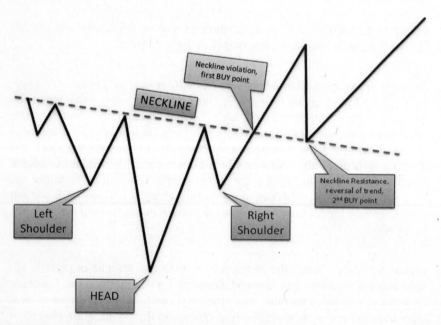

FIGURE 3.14 Reverse Head and Shoulders Formation

Average True Range (ATR)   ATR can be used to find a normal price range of an underlying asset within a certain period of time. It can be used to place stop losses outside of normal oscillations to mitigate premature exits due to regular intra period movements as well as set realistic targets that are attainable in a certain time frame based on normal movements. It can be displayed in chart form or simply as a dynamic number that coincides with the time period that you select.

Concept and Calculation Example   The concept of ATR was developed by J. Welles Wilder in his book, *New Concepts in Technical Trading Systems*, back in the late 1970s.

Wilder started with a concept he called *True Range* (TR), which is defined as the greatest of the following:

- The current High less the current Low.
- The absolute value of the current High less the previous Close.
- The absolute value of the current Low less the previous Close.

This method was able to capture the gaps of a stock (or future, which is what his focus was).

The Average True Range (ATR) generally is based on 14 periods and can be calculated on an intraday, daily, weekly, or monthly basis. To begin his calculation, the first TR value in a series is simply the High minus the Low, and the first 14-day ATR is the average of the daily ATR values for the last 14 days. To further smooth the data set, he incorporated the previous period's ATR value. The second and subsequent 14-day ATR value would be calculated with the following steps:

- Multiply the previous 14-day ATR by 13.
- Add the most recent day's TR value.
- Divide by 14.

The nice part is that you don't have to figure all this out yourself; many charting packages offer it as a study that you can add to any chart. You can see an example of this in Figure 3.15. Note the correlation with the BBands (Wide BBands = Elevated ATR).

Using ATR to Find Stops and Targets   If you know what the ATR of a stock is, you can get a good idea about how it has been moving. Use caution here—remember that ATR is only looking back 14 periods and if you are looking at the daily ATR (daily chart) you are only looking about two weeks back, so if the stock has been extra-volatile, your ATR may look a bit high. If the stock and the market as a whole have been trending

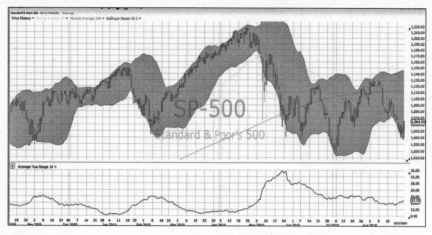

FIGURE 3.15 ATR Displayed as a Line Chart Below Price Chart with BBands

extremely sideways, the ATR may be a bit low compared to normal. Both could be a detriment to placing your stops or targets.

I help to minimize miscalculation by placing Bollinger bands (technical measures that gauge trends) on my chart and looking at the current space between them, looking to ensure that they are not abnormally wide or abnormally narrow compared to the rest of the chart. The good thing is that the 14-period look back is usually enough to get a good idea of a stock's behavior over that time frame.

I then take the ATR of the time frame that I want to be in the trade and use that as my starting point to figure out stops and targets.

- Daily Chart—Swing Trade (1–5 days)
- Weekly Chart—Intermediate-term trade (1–4 weeks)
- Monthly Chart—Position trade (+1 month)

Swing Trade Stock Example—Using ATR If the stock has a daily ATR of $1, I would multiply that number by 1.2 to find my profit goal in the stock, which would mean I would look to make $1.20 in my trade.

For a stop loss, I multiply the ATR times 1.5, which would mean I am willing to lose $1.50 in the trade.

These calculations are based on the way that I trade and because I have a high rate of success when it comes to my swing trades. Test out different multiples in your account to find a good balance. The goal here is to use ATR to find realistic price movements.

Options Example For buying in the money calls and puts, the calculations are somewhat similar, except that I account for delta. (These methods may not work well for other options strategies because of other factors.)[10]

When setting your long call or put's stop loss, take the ATR from the appropriate time frame for your trade (daily, weekly or monthly chart), multiply it by 1.5 and then multiply by the delta (if trading options).

- Let's assume the option costs $15.
- So if the daily ATR is $3 and the option has a 0.70 delta, the math looks like this:
  - [Entry Price] $15 − (3.00[ATR] ∗ 1.5) ∗ 0.70 [DELTA] = stop loss of $11.85.

The stop-loss order would be placed at $11.85, which is $3.15 below the purchase price of $15 in this case. This loss may seem steep, but remember that you were willing to originally tolerate even more in the stock and with the option; you always have only the premium paid at risk, which was $1,500 in this case.

TRADER TIP

I have found that if you are a trader who tends to stay in a position for a month to three months, using the monthly ATR as your stop-loss gauge tends to give you a realistic cushion in the stock's normal movement, because of a stock's propensity to revert to the mean or to oscillate in a range as it is in a trend. If the stock breaks this normal trend, you would most likely want to exit anyway.

Finding Technical Patterns

If you are trying to locate patterns without having to sift through hundreds of charts, the website www.finviz.com is a great resource for scanning the markets for both technical patterns as well as fundamental data. For the best-looking and most dynamic charting package, www.freestockcharts.com also includes the ability to scan the markets for technical patterns as well as to offer the ability to set alerts based on trend lines and other indicators. The Wordon family started in the charting business in the 1980s and they provide a terrific free charting package system as well as premium services that are moderately priced and powerful. They also offer a software version of their program, which is much more robust.

The Fear Factor—Panic Selling and Stops

Although investors and traders may have differing strategies or outlooks, there are times when this group moves in one fell swoop (call it the *herd mentality*). This frequently occurs among well-publicized fundamental changes with a company itself or in the overall stock market. Changes like these can spark a panic, and investors may begin to sell their shares to "get out while the getting is good." Recognizing the type of panic selling that is going on is not an easy task, and does require skill and knowledge of not only the markets as a whole, but of the stocks themselves. One of the easiest ways to look for panic buying or selling is a spike in stock volume, which is easy to see on any stock chart.

Remember that for a trade to take place, there has to be two willing participants—one buyer and one seller. When a stock is in a bearish panic mode, the sellers are in a frenzy to sell and the professional buyers know this, so they simply keep lowering their prices, taking small long positions along the way as they average down.[11] Falling prices are feared by the majority of retail investors because most are long the market. Learn to recognize panic by abnormal volumes and price changes outside of the Bollinger bands.

In addition, as a stock price drops, this drop may trigger existing stop orders and other trigger orders to sell, which can further exacerbate the sell-off and increase the panic selling. Remember, when you purchase a stock, if you place a stop-loss order to sell, usually somewhere below where you bought the stock at, and that stock is dropping sharply, it may be triggering potentially thousands of sell orders, which trigger further sell orders and so on, creating exponential bearish pressure.

A historical example of panic selling happened on May 6, 2010, when the Dow Jones dropped almost 1,000 points (or more than 10%) in a matter of minutes. Panic sell-offs like this are often characterized by abnormal volume spikes and abnormal price movements (stocks actually do have somewhat "normal" variations and behaviors; we discuss that later). Often, after an abnormal occurrence like this, a stock's price will tend to revert to the mean or rally from the panic sell-off price levels, barring a complete breakdown in fundamentals, such as a bankruptcy (resulting in a sharp decline) or, conversely, a takeover bid (sparking a rally). Projecting this reversion to the mean is the basis for the "filling the gap" strategy.

If we look at an intraday chart of the Dow on May 6, you can see the reversion to the mean came swiftly, within about 30 minutes, then within a day it went back to where it was the day before the "flash crash" (see Figure 3.16). This, of course, was a short-term occurrence and the index actually moved much lower in the weeks to follow.

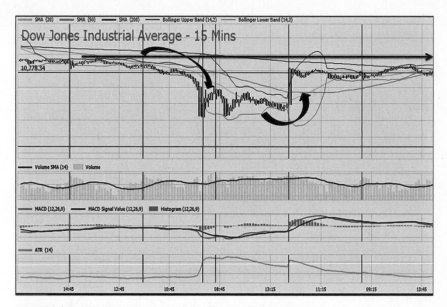

FIGURE 3.16 Reversion to the Mean in the "Flash Crash"
Source: Lightwave.

By 2010, markets were almost completely electronic and the products that tied them all together were complex. High frequency trading (HFT), automated algorithms and nonhuman initiated trades accounted for a large part of the daily trading stock volume, which I believe exacerbated the sell-off and sent the markets much lower than they should have, triggering panic selling and stop losses among the human market participants. During this period, it would have been advantageous to buy stock or long calls when the market was selling off, as it quickly recovered.

Unfortunately, the reality for many investors was that their stops were triggered and they were forced to exit their trades, potentially at a loss, when the market recovered the next day. There is no way to prepare for this sort of occurrence, but if you do notice the market's volatility increasing or abnormal behavior, it is okay to temporarily remove your physical stop loss and execute it manually. Just make sure you write it down and replace it if you are going to be away from your computer for an extended period.

Identifying Abnormalities in the Marketplace

For most of us, being hyperaware of an extremely overbought or oversold condition that may be unwarranted is most likely the first way to target

irrational behavior of market participants. Some quick techniques to identify this sort of situation are:

- Stock has moved more than 150% of its ATR in the given time frame.
- A stock's Bollinger bands have widened to abnormal levels and the
  stock is outside one of the bands.
  - Bollinger bands are trend lines that measure historical volatility
    (standard deviation, which I discuss later). A so-called *widening*
    of the bands indicates increased movement in the stock, but if this
    movement has been uni-directional, it may be unwarranted and the
    stock may experience a short-term reversal of that trend.
- The stock is a target of bias (bullish or bearish) commentary/analysis
  in the mass media (TV, radio, Internet) and has seen abnormal short-
  term movements as of late with no real justification for such a change
  in price.
  - Apple stock, ahead of a major release of a new product such as the
    iPad, saw a meteoric rise of $190 to $238 (April 1, 2010) in less than
    two months, a 25% gain, adding $43.5 billion in market capitaliza-
    tion (the stock market value of the company). It eclipsed Walmart in
    market cap in that time. Does the iPad add $43 billion in value to the
    company, when it has not even been released yet?
  - In reality, it is hard to determine the exact future value of a product
    like the iPad to a company's bottom line. What I can say is that in the
    past there has been a run-up in the stock ahead of a release like this
    and then a sell-off once it hits the market; once Apple stock sold off,
    I might use an spread strategy to limit my risk.

The bottom line is that if you're at the local McDonald's and the person behind the counter is talking about how much Apple's stock has risen,
it may be time to sell. The euphoria may have become so widespread
for so long that the reality of the situation may begin to surface and the
stock in question or the market for that matter may be due for a reduction
in price.

This can be true in the opposite direction as well, so if a stock has
been the target of negative publicity by the majority of participants, it
may be unfairly sold off, but I urge you to exercise caution when trying
to buy companies that are dropping sharply, as it may be like catching a
falling knife.

The broad market can be perceived by some to be overbought or oversold even if the target stock is fairly priced according to their earnings and
expectations; unfortunately, when the masses begin selling (or buying) the
broad market, it may affect your individual stock just because it is a part
of that index.

ETFs on indexes, such as the SPY, may buy or sell actual shares in the companies held within them, and by the purchase and/or sale of that ETF, there may be an influence on the stock prices themselves.

PLANS OF ATTACK

Having a plan of attack that includes both an outline for success as well as a contingency plan in case of failure is essential in trading and investing. What one has to realize is that the creation of a plan or strategy is simply an outline of methods, expectations, and contingencies, not a perfect roadmap that will lead you to success. Turning the human mind into a thoughtless machine is extremely difficult if not impossible, especially given that fact that each day brings unique emotional changes both in the market and in your home life. To completely disconnect yourself from your emotions, in my view, is impossible. Instead, learn your tendencies and control your impulses or lack thereof.

Seldom is a trading plan followed to the tee. This is completely acceptable; one must leave room for adaptation and adjustments for the unknowns. The most crucial part of the trading plan should be the money spent on each trade and the strategies that one is going to apply for each specific situation. This includes rough estimates for adjustments when things go both according to plan and completely wrong.

Creating and Sticking to Your Plan

One of the toughest things a trader can do is admit defeat and just exit a losing trade, especially when others look to that trader for advice. Another problem many of us face is not listening to what our gut is telling us. From the time I started trading, I have tried my hardest to stay in tune with myself and my money management and risk principles, and to not let positions run away from me.

From time to time, I certainly break the rules. I have never been a big risk taker and part of the reasoning behind that is that I recognize my faults and realize I am human and I have certainly allowed greed to sometimes control me. In hindsight, I needed to be able to control *myself*, when my back is against the wall. I needed to be able to just stop the bleeding, take the loss, and move on.

Taking Losses With large positions and big risk, you have so much on the line, you bet big with the intentions of the big win. And when it goes against you, the loss may be too immense to stomach or accept, forcing you to hold on. So it gets worse and worse until you *have* to exit to salvage what is left of your account, or you leave the position untouched until it expires worthless. Either way, you are left with a fraction of your starting account value, but what might be worse is your shattered confidence. After that mental and monetary injury, you may be reluctant to continue following your investment plan for fear of a recurrence.

Having a manageable position also comes in handy when you need to hold on to a position that may be oversold and likely to recover.

Very seldom does one walk into a trade thinking how much he will lose. Why would investors do that? It would seem like they would be setting themselves up for failure right from the start. But on the contrary, it may be the thing that saves your life (or at least your dollars and sense). I was pondering these thoughts when I was writing this book, fueled by an investment property that I was buying. In my due diligence prior to entering a bid for the home, I put the investment through a stress test of sorts and I thought it fit well with these concepts.

I looked at worse-case scenarios like major plumbing or electrical damage, structural damage, the life expectancy and age of the systems in the building, the condo board's management style and history, budget, taxes, the possibility of going months without rent, and so forth. All these possible occurrences and data were entered into my own little regression model of sorts and from that I came up with an acceptable price to bid for the home given my findings.

This sounds rather complicated and in reality, placing an options trade is much, much more simple and there are many more realistic opportunities. The regression model that you use for gauging an options trade could be something like the profit/loss and probability calculators at your brokerage house or other tools that allow you to model possible situations and outcomes. I encourage you to play out different profit and loss scenarios before you place a trade with real money.

Once you have narrowed down your strategy, you must decide on how much risk you want to take. This would depend on other positions in your account, macro market sentiment, earnings, and so forth. Adjusting your contract size or modifying the width of your spread are both simple risk adjustment measures you will learn in the strategy section.

Options and Investment Properties

Trading options, in many ways, is similar to my only being committed to a property I am buying for only a year's time and having the option to renew if I wish. For that exposure, I risk much less than the full price of the home. If things are going my way and I believe that they will continue, I may take another option on the home or just buy it outright, but having reduced risk is the name of the game.

We should trade the market the same way, but often traders do not. Options are frequently misused and losing positions that should be cut are held, typically because of the fear of being wrong and giving up some potential profit. Another problem I see frequently is the abuse of leverage, where a trader buys as many option contracts as he would shares of stock, hoping to amplify return.

The problem is that many times, leverage works both ways: You can lose money just as fast as you can gain it.

Just pulling the plug on a profitable investment and locking in profit before it deteriorates should happen more often, but here is another situation many traders find themselves in today, as markets have recovered. They stay in and watch a once-profitable trade turn negative.

Maybe it is the desire to earn back losses from a prior year, or maybe you think you are "on a roll." The market does not know who you are, it doesn't care whether you make or lose money, and it certainly does not owe you anything. Take your bits and pieces while you can and keep your risk minimal. If something seems too good to be true or you think the market needs a break, chances are that many people are thinking the same thing. Perception often becomes reality in the marketplace, as all market participants are human like you and me.

Options strategies will play heavily into your plan, and depending on what strategy you are employing, may completely alter your plan of attack. So once you have read this chapter and get the gist of it, go through the strategy chapter, ensure that you understand whatever strategies you are choosing to use (probability and risk and reward characteristics specifically), then reread this chapter and adjust your plan accordingly.

Questions You Need to Ask Yourself   Money management involves understanding how much risk you are willing to take for your account per trade while using your system or method for entries and exits. However, after checking these for a valid entry, the question then is how many shares, contracts, or spreads you should purchase to keep your risk in any given trade less than 5% of your total account (or whatever level you choose). *How much should you invest in any given trade?*

The question of exactly how much risk you are going to take in each trade depends on several factors:

- What is the probability of success?
- How aligned are your indicators? Very bullish, very bearish, mixed?
- Where is support and resistance in the stock?

- When is the next earnings report?
- What is my time horizon for the trade?
- What is the overall macroeconomic situation?
- What is the current market tone?
- Is the market oversold/overbought? (Bollinger bands can help here.)
- How much is your account up or down?
- What is the status of your psychological capital?
- How many trades have you won/lost in the past three months?
- What is your typical winning trade percentage gain/losing trade loss?

All of these factors and more should go into your decision-making process. I know it seems like a ton of questions to answer just to find your risk in each trade, but they usually can be answered within seconds or minutes. This is where students I have taught in the past become frustrated, because they want me to give specific answers to each and the reality is that *you* must assess your own individual situations and results. I can offer you techniques and ways to both realize what you need to do as well as offer some psychological tactics to help, but the rest is on you. Use common sense and if something feels a bit risky or you don't completely understand the ramifications of a trade's potential outcome, either stay away, paper trade it, or use an extremely small relative investment amount.

How Much Should You Lose on an Investment that Goes Wrong?
Evaluating the real risk of a trade in addition to the potential reward is not common and the lack of doing this usually thwarts many traders' attempts to succeed. It's just one of those things that none of us want to do. No one makes a trade and expects to lose. It's just not how our brains are programmed, and I mean why in the heck would I place the risk if I didn't think that there would be a payoff? The point is not to teach yourself to be a loser, but rather to get into the habit of truly evaluating all the potential risks of a trade and using a truly quantifiable loss amount in every trade. Depending on the trade that you make, you may be able to control risk by using a certain strategy combined with appropriate allocation of assets. In more basic, less statistically advantaged trades such as long or short stock, or long calls or puts, the only real loss prevention can be with metering the amount of stock or options that you buy combined with an actual stop-loss level either based on the stock or on the investment amount.

Look at Your History   Your past success rate and patterns of trading can offer priceless advice and a free look into your future trading patterns. For example, let's assume that you are typically a swing trader and on average you risk about 10% of your account on each trade that you make. Look back over the past six months; you find that your success rate averages about 70%, meaning that out of a series of 20 trades, six of them turned out to be losers on average. Of course, there will be exceptions—you may have long winning streaks of 20 or more trades with no losers, but then maybe experience a much higher than average losing streak. The bottom line is that if you are following the same methods of analyzing, trading, and exiting positions (using the similar strategies), you will most likely develop some sort of pattern. For some of you, that pattern may be a ton of losing trades and therefore you might need to reevaluate the methods that you are using or your money management. The bottom line is that you *must* look for patterns of both success and failure to help you to determine where your strengths and weaknesses lie, as well as get an idea of your success rate in trades. Make minute adjustments and then test. Do not make multiple changes to your plan, because you won't know which ones are affecting your outcome.

Money Management   It is critical to your success that you understand that entry and exit rules are only a fraction of what makes a trader successful. The misnomer is that if you have an extremely high success rate, you are guaranteed success. This is not true. Even with 90% success, you can still fail if you don't manage your losers (and winners) appropriately.

Let's assume that you make nine trades, risking 100% of your account on each (bad money management, by the way) and each trade you make 5%. At the end of that nine trade series you have a 45% rate of return in your account. Your account just went from $1,000 to $1,450 (for simplicity). Now let's assume that you risk the $1,450 in your next trade, which turns out to be your 1 in 10 loser; you lose 50% of your money invested, or $725. Your account is now worth $725; you have lost 27.5% of your original account value. This was with a 90% success rate, but with the one loser, you not only lost an excessive amount in percentage terms, but with each trade you were risking more and more money. You were stepping up your risk each time. If you just adjusted the amount of money down to maybe your starting account value, you would have been down only $50 net on that series of trades. Obviously something also should have been done to control the 50% loss, when you were only typically making 5% on your other trades.

One of the most misunderstood and misused rudiments in any trading plan is money management. It is more frequent that a trader just sets a basic stop loss if at all, but what many fail to realize is that money management encompasses so many things, not just setting a stop loss. Knowing how much you can purchase or short is critical to seeing consistent success because it determines how much you are presently risking in a given trade, which ultimately impacts your reward. Additionally, knowing how much real risk you are presently exposed to in the market can give you both confidence and discipline to follow your trading rules regardless of the circumstances. The intricate and delicate balance of winning trades to losing trades (on a percentage basis) combined with the amount that you win or lose on each will dictate a net gain or loss over time.

Don't be afraid or think that you won't have losing trades—I promise you will.

TRADER TIP

Risk can be fine-tuned and controlled with more precision by using spreads, which you will learn later.

Profit and Loss Extremes If you notice that your account seems to grow and shrink in massive waves, you are probably doing something wrong. If you have found yourself extremely uncomfortable with the size of a loss that you are taking and then once that loss is realized you do everything you can to make it up, maybe you need to risk less, change your strategy or take profits sooner, thereby cutting your losses before they grow out of control. Just the realization of this tendency is at least a start to remedying a potentially dangerous habit. For some people, those boom-and-bust cycles are perfectly acceptable, and if that's the case, you don't have to change. But at least try to identify a pattern to your trades. If it is hard for you to find a pattern to your trades and you are not fond of the booms and busts, it may be time to refine the techniques that you are using to locate, analyze, and trade your stocks and strategies or maybe use a spread strategy like selling an out-of-the-money vertical spread (which you will learn later) instead of just buying stock or calls and puts. This may help you to minimize the profit-and-loss (P&L) roller coaster.

Examples and Techniques to Control Your Allocations Following are some scenarios that might help you to better understand how to allocate funds to certain trades given specific trade probabilities and trade history. Asset allocation based on risk, probability of success, and historical observations is a crucial part of money management and should be incorporated into your trade plan. Controlling the percentage or dollars that you risk in each trade can prevent catastrophe in your whole account. The allocation amounts and percentages can apply to both stock and options. If you don't understand options strategies yet, you can refer back to this section.

Basic Risk Analysis Example—Trader A Trader A is considering purchasing a January 20 call option (which has 60 days until expiration and a delta of .70) on Microsoft (MSFT) (trading at $23) at $4 a contract after his methodology/tool is indicating a bullish entry signal. The trade outcome seems probable based on his knowledge of the stock and the analysis he has done. In the past year, using the long call he has had about a 70% success rate by using this method of analysis and timing. Statistically speaking, the long-call strategy has a reduced probability of success because the breakeven for the long call is higher than the current stock price. (Other strategies may actually increase probability.) Trader A plans on being in the trade for about one to four weeks.

He currently has an account of $10,000. He has determined that he will invest 20% of his account in the trade, which means putting $2,000 into the $20 calls on MSFT.

- $10,000 account × 20% = $2,000 (total investment allocation).
- Since the option is trading at $4 a contract, he is looking to purchase 5 contracts.
- $2,000 (total allocation)/$2 a contract = 5 contracts.

After deciding on purchasing five contracts, Trader A decides to enter a stop loss of 40% ($1.60 loss). He feels that if the options were to fall 40% in price, it would constitute a miscalculation in timing and he would prefer to exit.

This 40% stop loss needs to also coincide with several factors that are specific to each strategy. In the case of the call option, using the ATR as a cross-reference point to decide whether you have placed a realistic stop-loss point is a good start. In this case the weekly ATR is about $1.50, so trader A feels his stop loss of $1.60 is acceptable and realistic.

TRADER TIP

If the stock's ATR is greater than the stop loss that you have in mind, you may be stopped out prematurely!

When you purchase a call option, for example, you are already risking much less than if you purchased 100 shares of stock, or in this case, five contracts would be the equivalent of 500 shares, or about $11,500, if you were to buy the stock at $23.

He is looking to use 40% as his stop percentage, so the amount per contract would be $160. This means that his total dollar risk in this trade is about $800 ($160 × 5 contracts).

By trading the option, not the stock, the trader has not only lessened his total exposure if something were to go terribly wrong, he reduced his risk even further by not allowing his entire call investment to go worthless. In reality, Trader A really wants to risk only 8% of his total account on this trade. But it was a dollar amount that Trader A originally set.

- $4 per contract × 40% = $1.60 per contract stop loss.
- $1.60 ($160) per contract × 5 contracts = $800.
- Entry at $4.
- Stop loss order placed at $2.40.
- Risk per share = $1.60.
- Risk per contract = $160.

The total potential risk Trader A has exposed to his account is approximately 8%. If the stock doesn't gap or move abnormally, he is likely to lose no more than $800.

- $160 per contract × 5 contracts = $800 risk.
- $800/$10,000 (account size) = 8% *total risk*.

Is this acceptable to you?

Basic Risk Analysis Example—Trader B   Trader B is also considering the $20 call options on Microsoft (MSFT) at $4 a contract, which fits her rules for a longer-term position trade (1–4 months).

She is not interested in taking a loss of more than 12% in her account, which is currently also sitting at $10,000. Based on her risk tolerance, she will not risk more than $1,200 per trade.

$$\$10,000 \text{ account} \times 12\% = \$1,200 \text{ (total risk)}$$

There are a couple ways that she can trade this. If she feels that she wants to stay in the money, because her trade plan (and I) recommend it, those same contracts will cost her $4, the same as Trader A.

She can choose to risk all $1,200 and buy three contracts and just use the entire investment amount as her stop loss.

$$3 \times \$400 \text{ (cost of option)} = \$1,200.$$

By doing this, she is reducing her leverage because she owns fewer contracts, but also will not have to worry about a stop loss, as the entire option premium is her stop. This might be advisable if the stock is more volatile.

But in this case, with MSFT, she feels that according to her trading rules and with how MSFT test to behave (ATR, etc.) a 50% stop loss on her option trade would be acceptable and it will allow her to purchase more contracts. Based on a 50% stop loss, she will be able to purchase six contracts and will need to enter a stop at $2 a share for a total risk of $200 a contract × 6, which is her original risk allocation for the trade.[12]

> Stop-loss math: $4a contract × 50%
> = $2 per contract-total acceptable risk.[13]

Entry at $4
Stop at $2.
Max risk $200 per contract.

Since Trader B knows her portfolio risk and her trade risk, she needs to determine how many contracts to trade. In the following example, she has taken her portfolio risk of $1,200 and divided by $200 a contract to determine the right number of contracts to trade.

$1,200 Portfolio Risk/$200 Trade Risk = 6 contracts.
6 contracts × $400 = $2,400 invested (risk controlled with stop.)
$2,400/$10,000 = 24% invested (higher *potential* risk if stops,
    not contracts, are used for control.)

NEW TRADER TIPS

Following are eight tips for new traders:

1. **Understand the equity markets.** Options are derivatives, meaning that they derive their prices from the prices of the stocks, ETFs, and indexes they are listed on. Although options strategies can limit risk or even change the risk you take, you should have some sort of opinion of the general direction and timing of the particular security you are trading. Additionally, it's probably good if you previously traded in the equity market. Market mechanics also play a role in how the options markets behave. Know where and how your stock trades, its volume patterns, and any relevant fundamental data. Be aware of upcoming economic data being released, as macro data may also impact your trades. Also important to note is that options have multipliers; one options contract represents the right/obligation to buy or sell 100 shares of the underlying. Additionally, an option's price also has a multiple of 100, so an option priced at $1.50 will in actuality cost $150 in your account.

2. **Know your broker's platform, commissions, and important phone numbers.** Before you even click the buy or sell button, make sure you know exactly how your broker's platform works. This includes understanding all the different order types (market, limit, stop, trailing, target, all or none, fill or kill, etc.). It is easy as a beginner and even as an experienced trader to make a simple mistake unrelated to the direction of the stock or the strategy you choose and put yourself in a pickle.

Hitting "buy" as opposed to "sell" and vice versa is a common error, and using a market order in a fast-moving market (resulting in a disadvantageous fill) is another. There are a multitude of other common pitfalls. Practice entering spreads and making sure you get them right. OptionsHouse, for example, will let you know the total commissions before you enter the trade, which is a nice feature, but be sure you check breakpoints on commissions if your broker offers any.

The option chain layout is one screen that is essential to all option traders, as it lists the strike prices, expiration dates, and Greeks of all available calls or puts for any particular security. An option chain also includes the most current prices paid for the calls and puts, as well as the daily changes in these prices. You should be able to access the option chains for the stocks in your portfolio via your brokerage platform or on websites specializing in option trading information. Note that option chains are only available on stocks, ETFs, and indexes on which options are traded.

Finally, it might be a good idea to write down your trades in a notebook along with your account numbers and the important phone numbers for your brokerage firm(s). In the event that your computer fails or your power goes out, you will be prepared. These are all real possibilities.

3. **Know your strategy in and out and *test* it!** Many brokers offer virtual trading and tools for you to simulate different stock and options strategies and experiment before you put your real money at work. One of the most common mistakes new traders make is to only look at the best-case scenario. When you are learning and testing a strategy, simulate what will happen if the stock and/or volatility and time move in your favor *and* what happens if these factors move against you. What would you do then? How will your strategy behave if volatility makes a large move in either direction? What happens if the stock goes nowhere for two months? Do you have an exit strategy in place other than taking profits?

Running simulations and understanding your strategy and its behavior in the real marketplace will not only increase your confidence, but it will allow you to set exit parameters more accurately. This also includes any technical data or patterns that you are looking at and specific trigger points on the charts that you will be using to enter and exit.

4. **Be aware of key facts about your company's fundamentals.** While most of us are not certified financial analysts, those analysts who are accredited (as well as major publications and reputable websites) can offer us plenty of data when it comes to researching potential stocks to trade. Whatever parameters or financial data points you look at, make a checklist. Many professionals focus on the ability of a company to earn and grow its earnings over time. They also look at the ratio of a stock's price compared to its earnings per share. This data point is only one of many, but you should have several fundamental points you check before entering a trade, bullish or bearish.

5. **Be aware of earnings and expectations.** Earnings can be a catalyst for a stock to move up or down violently (or maybe even not at all). Make yourself familiar with how a stock has moved in the past and what analysts are expecting for the upcoming report. These dates are published by the companies themselves and are available on many sites and are generally available through most brokerage platforms. You may also find it helpful to research peer data and earnings dates, which may have an effect on the company you are trading.

6. **Before you enter your trade, have a plan. Once you're in the trade, follow that plan.** The key point here is that you manage your money and your trades in line with the risk of each individual trade and your account as a whole. What that means is that you are in control of your account and your risk at all times. If you have a $10,000 account, it may not be sound money management to put 50% in a startup tech stock and the other 50% in another extremely volatile tech stock that might be a little more mature.

In that case, you would have 100% of your capital invested in two potentially risky assets. The ultimate decisions is yours, so allocate your trades with tact and thought and consider diversifying your account so your risk exposure isn't focused on one sector. No matter what your investment goals are, have a stop loss and a target in mind when placing your trades. Some traders may use the amount of contracts they buy as a stop loss (that is, they are willing to lose their entire premium paid). Others may set a maximum risk for each investment, which can be either a percentage or an absolute dollar amount.

7. **When trading options, keep an eye on the calendar.** Unlike stocks, options have expiration dates. On the third Friday of each month (with some rare exceptions, such as certain Good Fridays) that month's options cease to exist. This adds a variable to options trading that stocks

do not have—the element of time. Options will lose "time value" as expiration approaches, making money management that much more critical. Investors can exercise or be assigned U.S.-style options at any point between execution and expiration. European-style options may be exercised or assigned only on expiration day.

8. **Journal your trades.** Once you have exited the trade, record what happened, everything from your rationale and mood when entering to your money management plan to your reason for exit. Make this journal as detailed as possible. The more you record, the better you will be able to evaluate what went right and wrong in your trades. Hopefully, over time, this diligence will help you increase consistency in your trading.

TOP 10 THINGS PROFESSIONALS DO THAT THE AVERAGE RETAIL TRADER DOESN'T

I assembled 10 of the most important techniques and mantras you should use as well as some of the mistakes to avoid if you want to take your trading and investments to the next level.

No. 10. Hedge Your Bets/Diversify
- If you are an options trader, you can use spreads to reduce your investment's exposure to the overall market. Some option spreads cannot only greatly reduce how volatile your account is, but they actually can put the probability of success on your side.
- Diversify your investment portfolio not only with stocks in different sectors, but also with *beta*! Beta tells you how your stock will typically react to the market. If all your stocks have high betas, your account may be susceptible to just as much if not *more* volatility than the market, even if you bought stocks in different sectors.

No. 9. Plan Your Risk Ahead of the Trade
- Have a maximum downside dollar and/or percentage risk spelled out ahead of your investment, not after the fact.
- Use stop losses, put options or spreads to solidify your plan if you understand how to use them.
- Don't exceed your comfort zone; this may cause irrational decisions in your trade. In other words, don't make your investments too large in any one security.

No. 8. Be a Contrarian
- It's usually better to buy on rumour, sell on news.
- By the time everyone is talking about it, it might be too late.
- Don't be scared to think "outside the box."

No. 7. Sell or Protect While the Trend Is Still Strong
- It's much easier to sell when a stock is rising in value versus when it's in free fall.
- Remember, insurance is cheaper before you have an accident, so if you are an options trader, buy your puts when the market is complacent, not panicking.
- Think of a climber who is 30 yards from the summit of a mountain and runs out of oxygen. He may touch the top, but he won't get down. This is analogous to a stock that has been rallying for a long time and you take no action to exit. Although you may see the top in the stock, stocks can change direction frequently, and most investors don't get to sell the highest high!

No. 6. Learn from Your Losses, *Not* Only Your Profits
- Your losses can tell you just as much if not more about your trading personality.
- Sometimes just limiting losses can turn an unsuccessful trader into a thriving one, or at the very least, allow you to live to trade another day.

No. 5. Be Consistent in the Types of Issues You Trade
- Look for similarities in the behaviors of your securities; this will help you to find the patterns you are looking for and will help minimize errors. These attributes include ATR, price, volatility, sector, and chart patterns.
- Remember that most professionals are specialists in a certain group of stocks or sectors.
- If it feels uncomfortable in a trade, it is probably not for you.

No. 4. Think Three Steps Ahead
- Have a game plan for all possible outcomes in a trade (most retail investors just focus on the best outcome) and have alternatives for a flat investment as well as one that begins to go against you!
- The analogy here is to pretend that you're playing chess or poker; in both games you are thinking about what you might have to do if your opponent (the market) makes a move that puts you in danger. Investing is no different.

No. 3. Trust Yourself
- Professionals are confident in their abilities and their plan.
- *No one* knows exactly what you are thinking; only you can control your emotions.

- Your risk tolerance and views on the trade are completely unique; therefore, even though we can offer trade ideas and theses, you must execute them in your own way and use your individual money management to find how much of your account you will invest.

No. 2. Be Adaptable, Yet Adept in Your Strategy
- Be able to admit you're wrong and change direction when needed.
- Don't apply a strategy you are *not completely* comfortable with.

No. 1. Ask Questions
- If there is something you don't know, always ask.
- If there is any piece of the trade that didn't make sense, don't trade it with real money until you are able to quantify it. (Many brokers offer paper-trading platforms to test out new strategies.)
- The only stupid question is the one that is not asked.
- Professionals were not born that way; they too had to learn just like you!

TRADER TIP

Remember that at the end of the day, you are in control. In trading and investing, just like in many other areas of your life, it's the little things that usually make the biggest difference.

FINAL THOUGHTS

Before placing any trade, make sure that you have done your homework. Make a checklist of data points (both fundamental and technical) that you will examine, similar to what a mechanic performing an inspection on your car would do. Mechanics, pilots, and engineers all share this "checklist" method; start to think like they would. If the brakes on your car were completely worn out, is the car safe to drive? If the stock's technical formations are looking shaky, do you go long?

Each data point that you examine should have either a pass or fail rating, perhaps with a minimal "tolerance" or maximum variation you are willing to accept. If the stock does *not* pass your checklist, there is no reason to move on to the next step and trade. Find the next stock that meets your criteria. There will always be trades out there; don't force anything when it comes to your money.

CHAPTER 4

Options Basics

Techniques and Fundamentals to Master Before Applying Any Options Strategy

Learning about options is like learning how to use tools—and everyone applies tools in different ways. For example, if somebody teaches you how to use a saw, your first question becomes, "What can I do with this saw?"

Depending on how well you've learned your lesson, either you can make a beautiful piece of furniture—or you can cut off your hand.

Your Goal Is Not to Cut Off Your Hand.

—Sheldon Natenberg,
Options Volatility Trading Strategies

Now that you have gotten to the point where you have an opinion of the economy, the market, and you have found a stock to trade, you have a decision to make. Before you go and fire off an option strategy, you need to know the basics and mechanics of the options markets. This chapter explores both of those.

I sometimes look at non-options traders as absolutely foolish. Of course, not all of them are, but if I told you that you could make a 30% return on your risk and that the stock you wanted to invest in could go up, down, or sideways, wouldn't you want to trade options?

Of course, there are risks and tradeoffs, but you will learn that when used properly, options (derivatives) trump stock any day of the week. This chapter elucidates the rationale behind that claim.

TRADER TIP

Options traders do *not* view the markets as binary (long and short). An options trader determines not only his or her specific level of bullishness or bearishness (which cannot be done with stock alone), but also chooses a specific probability and risk tolerance in each and every trade.

Why Options Are Necessary

Some things never change. Although the news stories, players, politicians, bubbles, and correlations may change, much of the human element remains the same. We still tend to react the same way and move in waves and crowds. Sigmund Freud, Gustave Le Bon, Wilfred Trotter, Gabriel Tarde, and Elias Canetti and other great thinkers saw that people in a "crowd" act differently from those "thinking individually." With the lightning-fast flow of information, crowds are much easier to form and move, and crowds can change direction much faster, potentially creating more volatility.

The world is obviously much more connected and dependent on one another now more than ever and I would suspect this trend to become more prevalent (BRIC thesis). Global commerce, emerging and developing countries' consumption, and currency relationships play a larger role now more than ever in the profitability of many companies that we invest in, as the resources, imports, and exports shift.

The way we do business is forever changing and the ways that some companies make money are also evolving and becoming more and more complex. Even though individual traders have these great tools at their disposal, the forces that are pulling on market prices are becoming harder and harder to predict and measure.

The United States, unfortunately, no longer shares its far superior lead as the world's richest and most productive country and role as the dictator or barometer of the global economy. Most companies that we now trade are globally connected and the increasing importance of global economic relationships as well as shifts in social structure and resources can make it more difficult to make accurate directional investment bets, simply because of all the added influences. Many options strategies allow you to be "partially" correct in your thesis and still attain exceptional returns.

Data Overload   In August 2010, Eric Schmidt, CEO of Google, stated that "humans on the net create as much information in **two days** now as we did from the dawn of man through 2003."

I also believe that a good portion of investing difficulty stems from the overload of unqualified, unchecked, perhaps erroneous information that has to be digested by the mind in a short period of time, which may prohibit the individual from verifying facts, sources, dates, and so on. The blogosphere has helped create this problem. Just about anyone with a little tech savvy and marketing skill can tweet themselves into popularity and thus create a following.

Although the Internet has been instrumental in vastly improving the rate at which data travels and the amount of data, period, the amount of false, misleading, or opinion-type data that looks factual has increased at the same rate or worse. It becomes hard to decipher the good from the bad at times.

If you compound this with the countless unique opinions that are being expressed at any given moment, it's quite easy for investors to become confused or to latch on to someone who agrees with their own thesis even if it's completely misguided, leading them down a path of potential destruction.

Halos and delusions, which were outlined superbly in Phil Rosenzweig's book, *The Halo Effect,* can further blur the correlations and explanations of the attributes and reasons behind some of the most successful businesses. More importantly, what makes for a profitable company in the future? There is no perfect answer to this, but many theories.

I feel that because of this randomness and coincidence, in many cases, people who are completely mistaken in their rationale for a trade or investment, but end up making money because of some other force, are rewarded and perhaps doomed to failure over the long term, because luck won't last forever.

So if stock movements and market occurrences are so random, aren't we all at an extreme disadvantage? Not if you trade options.

Stock versus Options

What I find amazing is that randomness, coincidence, and the chance that you might make it big all adds to the great magnetism of the market—that belief that anyone from any background can be successful and make tons of money. Of course, there are a plethora of folks who fail miserably. What's worse is that stock-only traders are at a complete disadvantage, because they have no way to "trade the randomness."

I am *not* a believer that all trading and investing is a zero-sum game, meaning that there has to be a loser for every winner, as the game is perpetual and has many variables, although there are many losers, mainly due to greed and lack of a plan or capital after a series of inevitable losing trades. In the case of equities, the zero-sum argument could theoretically be upheld, as many of my quant friends will agree with. But with options, because most professionals are hedging their initial trades with other stock or options positions and taking risks other than direction, the zero-sum thesis becomes much harder to prove, although I know some will also argue my opinion here.

The bottom line is that I think stock traders are truly at a disadvantage. (Maybe I am a bit biased.)

Stock investors really only have one, maybe two choices when it comes to investing direction: Buy a stock long or go short (shorting stock can be extremely risky and not suitable or tolerable for some).

Another characteristic that stocks have (I think it's a partial detriment, but many would call it an advantage) is that they don't have an expiration date like options do. I know, I know, I am crazy. How could something that expires be better than something that will live in perpetuity (or bankruptcy)? Well, many stock traders become married to their positions, they don't have an end to the trade, they just buy it, it goes up, then they hold it, then it drops down, hold it, it becomes a horrible losing trade and they continue to hold it some more (in some cases until the stock dwindles to a fraction of what they bought it at).

The missed opportunities alone are enough to drive me mad! The thing is that when used properly, options force traders into thinking about the future in more details; they are also forced to think about risk and reward and set a true time horizon to their trades. This means that there will be a beginning, middle, and end to their trades, hopefully compelling them to have a superior plan, which is a good thing.

When you buy a stock, you have 100% of that stock's price times the number of shares at risk at all times! In certain options strategies, you might have one-tenth of that or less. Granted, some traders are foolish and risk just as much on one options position as they would in one stock position. Leverage can be a wonderful thing, but when abused, it can really hurt.

Options Can Control Risk

With options, you can control with precision the amount of risk and type of risk, for that matter, you wish to take in any given trade in any situation. One of my favorite strategies is the bull-put spread (I will go into depth later on the definition and mechanics of the trade).

If a stock trader is bullish on a stock and buys a stock for $100 and at the same time I sell a 90/80 bull-put spread (which is an option strategy that bets the stock to stay above 90) for $1.50 ($8.50 is max risk) and the stock rises to $105 by the expiration of the spread (maybe in 30 days), the stock trader makes $5 or 5%, but I would have made 18% in my spread.

If the stock stays at $100, the stock trader makes nothing and I would have made 18%.

If the stock drops to $90, the stock trader loses $10 or 10% and I would make 18% still, all while only risking $8.50 of my investment dollars.

As you can see my "probability of success is greater," but I cap my return at 18%. This may seem like a large sacrifice, but think about it—an 18% move in a $100 stock is $18 and chances are the stock may not get there in 30 days or you'll sell out when it hits $115 because of fear. You will learn about the bull-put spread strategy in Chapter 7.

The bottom line is that options get a bad rap, mostly because they are vastly misunderstood and usually misused by inexperienced traders. In some cases, with certain strategies, the inherent greed of most investors deters them from capping their profits and using a spread strategy; even if it increases their chances of success by tenfold, they are still reluctant because there is always that chance of striking it filthy rich on one trade. I will detail all of this in later chapters and compare the different strategies and their applications.

My game is to hit a ton of singles and doubles with a high rate of success. From time to time, the home run will inevitably happen, but I hardly ever swing for the fences. The harder you swing, the less accuracy you will have.

THE ORACLE OF OMAHA DID IT, WHY CAN'T I?

Historically, a large group of stocks (in major companies) have been shown to appreciate over time. Investors like Warren Buffett buy quality companies when they feel they are valuable and hold them indefinitely. Even though some of the holdings may never appreciate in value in a big way, on average, major market indexes have shown positive returns if held for at least 10 years. (Of course, there are exceptions.) Mr. Buffett also invests in companies in ways that most of us cannot. A perfect example was his monetary injection into Goldman Sachs in late 2008 when he got $5 billion in senior preferred stock paying 10% (Warren also forced Goldman Sachs to make the preferreds callable at a 10% premium, when most preferreds are callable at par). In addition to that, Buffett got $5 billion worth of stock (warrants) at $115 per share for a "sweetener." Think of getting 435,000 Goldman Sachs $115 call options for free, just for buying a stock.

There are several flaws in this investment technique. The first is time, which many of us do not have the patience for or the luxury of "waiting it out." Some investors just throw in the towel before their stocks finally return to profitability, and obviously there are some stocks that never do. The other issue is stop losses, which might boot you out of a trade early and

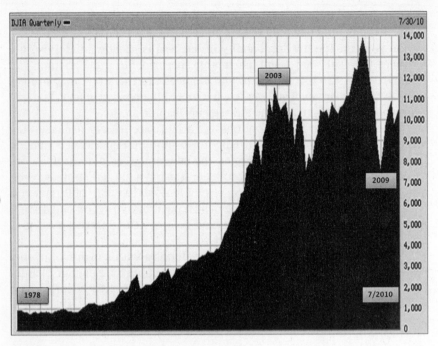

FIGURE 4.1   Dow Jones 1978 until Mid-2010

end your long holding game. Then if you hold on and forgo the stop loss, dealing with potentially losing more than 40% of your account value can have effects not only on your wallet, but also on your mental well-being.

It's all about your timing and tolerance. Take a look at Figure 4.1.

Figure 4.1 is a quarterly chart of the Dow Jones from 1978 to mid-2010; each line represents a year. There are periods of extreme growth (mid-1990s until 2000) and again from 2003 until 2007. But what if you bought in 2003 and waited until 2009?

Looking at the chart in Figure 4.1, it's fairly safe to say that if you bought the Dow Jones index and held it for 10 years, you would have some sort of profit in your account. The question is not only how much, but also the amount of anxiety you may have had to endure to get to the end of that 10 years.

Again, this is why trading stocks can be difficult and frustrating for many of us. At what point do you cut the cord on an investment you are in? How long is too long to stay in an investment? Long spans of time tend to be hard for the average mind to comprehend.

Think about how many things in your life will change in 10 years—your career, your likes and dislikes, music, possessions, weather, location ...

and more. The average person stays in a home for seven years, but you should be expected to hold the same stock investment for longer? This is obviously not always a bad thing, especially when things are going well, but what happens when they are not?

And besides, if it's that easy, then why isn't everyone rich beyond their wildest dreams from investing? One reason may be that stocks really have an unlimited horizon and most traders fail to place time horizons on their investments, along with profit goals and stop losses. I feel personally that this is a detriment, not a benefit, to most investors.

Adding More Precision and Advantages to Investing

Options, unlike stocks, can allow traders to really set up their time horizons, reduce risk, and make bets/investments with odds better than 1:1 and probability better than 50/50. There goes that casino analogy again, but you know, if I can place a bet (a certain option strategy) with an 80% statistical probability of winning on a company that has great fundamentals, all the while limiting my risk to 10% of what I could potentially lose in the stock to achieve the same return, I would take that any day over just buying stock.

You will learn shortly that when you buy a call or a put, the most you can lose is the premium that you pay, which usually costs much less than the equivalent amount of stock that one option controls.

If you follow my methods when trading long-call or long-put options, generally your cost will be about 10–15% of what you would have to pay for the stock. Even selling a put or a put spread at a level at which you would not mind owning the stock is a method you can employ to lower your risk. (You will learn these terms and strategies more in the upcoming chapters.)

What drew me to options is the fact that I can basically trade them on any company I choose, not to mention apply a strategy with a set risk, reward, and probability, without having to spend an entire day researching the company and at the same time still have a major advantage over the regular stock trader.

Options strategies are universal investment instruments and can be used to place bets on direction, time, volatility, interest rates, and so, on just about any security in any market anytime, anywhere, no matter the situation. With them, I have much more control over the position than if I just went long or short the underlying instrument.

You can choose to not be as much of a slave to the irrational crowd behavior that is often seen in the stock market, as many options strategies reduce volatility in your portfolio. You will be able to create your own odds, which is not only empowering, but the only way you should want to trade.

Try to think outside your normal "box," because once you learn options, you can trade just about anything that is presented to you and choose the appropriate strategy that not only truly matches your opinion on that stock but offers you a hedge against the sometimes irrational world we live in.

THE BASICS

Before we get into the more advanced concepts, let's be sure we understand the basic fundamentals and laws surrounding options.

TRADER TIP

Equity options, like what I am discussing in this book are completely different from a stock option that you might hear about on the news or even receive from the company you work for. There are some similarities, but generally speaking stock options given by a company are illiquid and not tradable or standardized like the equity options listed on exchanges.

History

Options in different forms have been trading for thousands of years. From olives to tulip bulb crazes, options have been a part of many cultures. Options were not standardized until 1973, but could be bought and sold, albeit at your own risk, from dealers since the early 1900s and are traced all the way back in some form or fashion to biblical times.

Options began exchange trading in 1973 in Chicago at the Chicago Board of Trade (CBOT), eventually moving across the street to the Chicago Board Options Exchange (CBOE). From there, options exchanges sprang up all across the country, attracting local companies to trade their options on a specific exchange.

In the early days, a company's stock was listed on one exchange, while its options were most likely listed on another.

For example, Dell Computer's stock may have been listed on the Nasdaq, while its options were listed only on the Philadelphia Exchange. This single listing method had been the typical method since the dawn of standardized options.

At the end of the twentieth century, the options markets began to change again with the introduction of multiple listings, where a company's options were now listed on more than one exchange, which enabled investors to trade options just about anywhere they wanted, but more importantly created competition among exchanges to earn business through cheaper transaction prices and tighter bid-ask spreads. Initially, it was a war that involved technology and liquidity, who could provide the fastest, most liquid markets with the best price. The National Market System, as it's called, continues to evolve to this day. As I am writing this, there are still multiple exchanges open trading and flourishing, although many exchanges have either closed for good or have changed the way they conduct business to keep up with the times. There are currently eight exchanges where options can be traded, all of which are fighting for your business.

The Options Exchanges

Since the dawn of exchange-traded options there has been growth and consolidation in the options exchanges. In October 2010 there were exchanges trading options both electronically and open-outcry. You can see their volumes traded and subsequent market share. Your broker will typically route your order to the best priced exchange, or that exchange will match the best price.

Following is the list of the U.S. options exchanges as of October 2010. In Figure 4.2 you can see a sample amount of contracts that were traded on

Exchange	Equity		Index/Other		Exchange Total	
	Volume	Market Share	Volume	Market Share	Volume	Market Share
AMEX	33,159,671	12.65%	148,777	0.70%	33,308,448	11.75%
ARCA	32,975,099	12.57%	80,715	0.38%	33,055,814	11.66%
BATS	1,260,860	0.48%	0	0.00%	1,260,860	0.44%
BOX	7,710,803	2.94%	10,468	0.05%	7,721,271	2.72%
CBOE	57,080,630	21.77%	19,953,245	93.88%	77,033,875	27.17%
ISE	50,986,802	19.44%	782,270	3.68%	51,769,072	18.26%
NSDQ	13,062,950	4.98%	7,803	0.04%	13,070,753	4.61%
PHLX	65,996,075	25.17%	269,725	1.27%	66,265,800	23.38%
OCC Totals	262,232,890	100.00%	21,253,003	100.00%	283,485,893	100.00%

FIGURE 4.2 Options Volume Data Provided by the Options Clearing Corporation (Monthly Options Volume August 2010)

these exchanges in August 2010. Keep in mind that volumes can and will change month to month and ebb and flow from exchange to exchange.

AMEX	The American Stock Exchange, housed on the NYSE
BOX	The Boston Stock Exchange
CBOE	The Chicago Board Options Exchange
ISE	The International Stock Exchange
BATS	The BATS Exchange, founded in June 2005 as an ECN
PCST	The Pacific Coast Stock Exchange, absorbed by NYSE
PHLX	The Philadelphia Stock Exchange, part of Nasdaq OMX
NASDAQ OMX	The Nasdaq Options Market

Options Are Standardized   Options are contracts. They are standardized, meaning that the trading rules and strike prices are guaranteed by the Options Clearing Corporation (www.occ.com). This doesn't mean you're guaranteed to make a profit; it simply means that if you are buying or selling an option, the Options Clearing Corporation ensures that your counterparty will perform their obligations.

I've always gotten questions about this, such as the following: If I were a trader who bought a put option and the stock went in my favor and actually fell to zero, what happens to the original trader who sold me the option? What if he ran out of cash to cover his position?

This is where the Options Clearing Corporation comes into play. When you trade an option, you usually don't trade with the same person who originally sold you that put because he probably bought it back when the stock started to drop from someone else, or he was short stock and was selling puts to collect some extra income. The bottom line is that as long as the stock is still trading on a major exchange, the options should be trading as well, which means you can enter or exit your position as you see fit. I will get into what happens during expiration later.

There are only two types of options: puts and calls. All the spreads and strategies that you hear of and can trade are combinations of two or more of these options. We explore them in depth later in this book.

Puts and Calls

Both puts and calls can either be bought or sold, just like stocks.

When you buy (to open) an option (paying a debit) you are said to be long that option and have rights as the owner.

When you sell (to open) an option (collecting a credit), you have a short position on or be "short that option," and in that case, you have obligations, not rights, and typically higher risk.

Most beginners start by just buying a call or buying a put.

Calls   A call gives the owner (long-call buyer) the right, but not the obligation to **buy** 100 shares of a stock at a specified price on or before a specified date.

A call buyer is bullish on the stock and may realize a profit if the stock rises in value.

Puts   A put gives the owner (long-put buyer) the right, but not the obligation to **sell** 100 shares of a stock at a specified price on or before a specified date.

A put buyer is bearish on the stock and may realize a profit if the stock falls in value.

Every option, both a call and a put, must have several components that go into determining its value, which actually make it an option.

Buyers of calls and puts generally *need* the stock to move in order to make a profit. All options must have a strike price, expiration date, and premium (cost).

TRADER TIP

Shorting options is not always as risky as shorting stock, because remember that there are two types of options. For example, selling a put is not as risky as selling a call; however, if you do short an option naked (by itself) you are generally taking on more risk than if you had bought that same option.

Strike Price   Strike price is the price at which the option owner can either buy (call) or sell (put) the underlying stock as well as the price at which the seller of the option is obligated to do the opposite of the owner.

If you break it down, it's the price at which the owner of an option can purchase (in the case of a call), or sell (in the case of a put), the underlying security or commodity as long as that option has not expired.

Option Sellers

The call seller must *sell* 100 shares of stock (or other security) at the strike price for every contract that is sold on or sometime before expiration. The put seller *must* buy 100 shares of stock (or other security) at the strike price for every contract that is sold on or sometime before expiration.

The strike price is also called the exercise price.

Expiration Date   Quite simply, the expiration date is the date at which that option ceases to trade or exist. After an option expires, it will either have value (intrinsic value) or be worth zero. The value of an option at expiration is determined by the amount it is in the money. Most options expire on the third Friday of the month and typically the option that is a "June" option would expire the third Friday of June; if it were an October option, then it would cease to exist on the third Friday of October, and so on. When an option expires, it is said to be at "parity," which is essentially what it is really worth, or its intrinsic value.

Premium (Cost)   In essence, an option's premium can be broken down into two separate values: intrinsic (aka parity, or real value, related to the price of the underlying stock, index, or ETF), and time (aka volatility) value. Both of these make up the total price you pay.

Intrinsic Value (Also Called *Moneyness*)

Intrinsic value is the real value of that option, so only "in-the-money" options have intrinsic value. The amount of intrinsic value in an option is determined by the strike price of the option and the movement of the underlying stock price only, plus or minus any dividends until expiration.

Nothing else can influence intrinsic value. So if you have a call option with a strike price of $50 and the stock is at $52, you would have $2 of intrinsic value. Whereas the $50 strike price put with the stock at $52 would have *no* intrinsic value.

The following example demonstrates the concept of intrinsic value, comparing different strike prices of calls and puts. Keep in mind that an option generally must trade for at least its intrinsic value and just because an option doesn't have any intrinsic value, it can still have a time value component to it.

Example

ABC Trading at $50

40 call	– has $10 Intrinsic	–	40 put has?
45 call	– has $5 Intrinsic	–	45 put has $0 Intrinsic
50 call	– has $0 Intrinsic	–	50 put has $0 Intrinsic
55 call	– has $0 Intrinsic	–	55 put has $5 Intrinsic
60 call	– has?	–	60 put has $10 Intrinsic

- If there were 45 days until these options expired, the options with no intrinsic value would most likely not be trading for $0. They would have some value to them; this value is basically the volatility, or time value, of the option. The more time an option has until expiration, the greater the chance it will move (and the greater its time value).
- If you have a stock in a more volatile sector or one that has had a history of being more volatile, its options will typically cost more when compared to a similar price stock in a less volatile sector.

TRADER TIP

An option will typically trade for its intrinsic value, plus an amount of time value. Some options are composed of completely time value (have no real value) and some may only be trading for only their intrinsic value (typically these options are very deep in the money and close to expiration).

Time Value

The time value of an option is determined obviously by how much time it has until expiration, but also it is determined by a volatility input. We discuss this later. All options are losing time value as they approach expiration. To find an option's time value, you must first determine if it is in or out of the money.

Any out-of-the-money options are *completely* composed of time value (which will eventually dwindle to zero by expiration). These options can become profitable if the stock moves in a favorable direction (higher for calls, lower for puts) and the option gains intrinsic value.

In-the-money options prices are typically a combination of both intrinsic value plus time value. To find the amount of time value for an in-the-money option, you simply subtract the amount the option is in the money from the total value of the option.

In the following example, with ABC stock at $50, we see actual options prices and how much is intrinsic value and how much is time value.

Example

ABC Stock Is $50

Calls	Puts
40 call costs $11.50—**$1.50 time** + **$10 intrinsic**	40 put costs $1.40—all time value

ABC Stock Is $50 (*Continued*)

Calls   **Puts**

50 call costs $4—all time value   50 put costs $3.75—all time value

60 call costs $2—all time value   60 put costs **$11.80—$1.80 time**
                                        + $10 intrinsic

In–At–Out of the Money

In the money, at the money, and *out of the money* are terms that options traders use to express where the option strike price is in relation to the stock price. To find whether an option is in or out of the money you simply need to know if that option has intrinsic value or not. If a put is in the money the same strike call *must* be out of the money. A put and a call with the same strike can never both be in and out of the money, but they can be at the money, which basically means that the strike price is equal to the stock price.

- In the money—Has intrinsic value.
- Out of the money—Does *not* have intrinsic value.
- At the money—Strike price is at or very close to the stock price (may have a little intrinsic value or not).
- In the money *calls* have a *strike price* that is *below* the *stock* price.
  - If the call strike price is above the stock price, it's always out of the money.
- In the money *puts* have a *strike price* that is *above* the *stock* price.
  - If the put strike price is below the stock price, it's always out of the money.

TRADER TIP

Remember that calls and puts with the same strike can never both be in or out, it's one or the other and if the call is in the put it is out and vice versa (of course, both can be at the money if the strikes are equal to the stock price).

Example Here I will use the same example as I used earlier to determine time value.

ABC stock is $50

Calls   **Puts**

60 call $2—Out of the money   60 put—In the money

50 call $4—At the money   50 put $3.75—At the money

40 call $11.50—In the money   40 put $1.40—Out of the money

Who Says What an Option Should Be Worth at Any Given Moment?

Professional traders use mathematical models to price an option at a certain moment in time given certain parameters. Models like Black-Scholes, Cox-Ross, binomial, and the like (you don't have to know these models to trade options) offer professional traders a theoretical value that they can buy and sell around. The thing that you must remember is that market makers (professionals) are *not* generally taking bets on where the stock is headed, nor do they typically trade something unhedged, meaning that for every action a market maker takes, he typically does something else (another trade) to try to lock in a small amount of profit. This is very different from the way that you and I trade in the retail world and, frankly, for most of you, having a dynamic theoretical pricing model will do you little good because a simple change in a stock's price will completely change an option's value from being a good deal to a very bad one. Stick to the basics and follow my guidelines in the strategy section. Don't get suckered into paying high dollars for a model that tells you what an option is worth right now, because I can almost guarantee that the value you see will change from minute to minute when the market is open.

Option Pricing Fact   Stocks that are more expensive also typically have more expensive options, even if they are similar in their volatility. For example, if you want to buy a $50 delta call with 40 days until expiration in a stock like GOOG, which is trading at $530 per share and has been moving at roughly a 26% annualized volatility, you are going to pay $20. For YHOO (Yahoo!) on the other hand, which has been slightly more volatile than GOOG (it's moving at about a 28% volatility) but has much cheaper options, the $50 delta call with 40 days until expiration will cost you only about 82 cents.

TRADER TIP

New traders can increase the amount of intrinsic value to mitigate the effects of "the Greeks," which are mathematical measures that indicate an option's vulnerability to time decay, movement in the underlying stock, and other factors. By purchasing an option that is deep in the money (put or call) the option will behave more like the stock and allow the trader to make a pure stock-based directional bet. In other words, deep-in-the-money options are more likely to move dollar for dollar with the stock itself. This concept is discussed in depth later.

TRADING OPTIONS—ORDER TYPES

Because there are a myriad of options strategies and because options can be a bit more complex than stock, you must not only understand the strategies themselves, but also how those strategies should be best executed in the marketplace by using the appropriate order type. Many of the order types that stock traders use are applicable in the options markets and the concepts are the same.

Trade Management and Order Types

Using the right order type can definitely make a difference in the outcome of your trade. It can mean the difference between disaster and profit, not to mention all the possible outcomes in between. Test the behavior of different order types in a practice trading account before you use them with real money.

Basic Options Order Types

These orders will function basically the same as they do with stock trades. Keep in mind that options will tend to have wider bid-ask spreads than stocks, which can sometimes prevent orders from being filled or triggered at the price you specify. Also be sure to clarify functionality and treatment of order types with your broker.

Market Order Market order means to execute my order as soon as possible at the current market price. These order types guarantee a fill, but *not* a price.

Limit Order Limited order means to execute my order as a price that I specify and this can be a buy or sell order. Limit orders guarantee a price, but *not* a fill. There are variations of limit orders, such as "fill or kill" and "all or none"; check out your broker's website for definitions and order types available to you.

Trigger Order Trigger order means that an order is triggered based on a particular price or variation of a specified stock, option, or even at a specific time. A trigger order can activate an entry or exit of a position, usually with your choice of order type (market, limit, etc.). You can use the underlying stock price to trigger an action in an option order as well.

Trigger Example One form of a trigger order is if you want to buy 10 GOOG $450 calls at the market when the bid (ask or last) price of AAPL hit $300, for example. Some traders use trigger orders as a means of jumping into a momentum type trade. Others use triggers in options positions based on technical levels in the underlying stock. Triggers offer a great degree of flexibility; check with your broker for what is available to you.

Because of all of the various trading styles, objectives, and risk tolerances out there, traders must really experiment with what order types are appropriate for their particular goals. Be careful when using market orders in fast-moving markets, as the price that you are filled at may not be what you anticipated.

Stop-Loss Orders The word *stop*, in essence, means *trigger* and the word *loss* means *at the market*. A stop loss, then, is a trigger order to exit your position at the market. Typically a trader would qualify this by identifying the order as a buy stop, which would trigger a market buy (to close) order for a short position and a sell stop, which would trigger a market sell (to close) order for a long position.

Stops can also be used to enter a position by triggering a buy or sell order for a nonexistent position. In other words, if I want to buy the SPDR S&P 500 ETF (SPY) if it breaks above a certain level, such as $100, I may set a buy-stop at $100. So even if I do not have an existing position, this would trigger a market buy order at $100. If, however, SPY is running higher, I may end up paying a higher price. Sell-stop orders can also be used for entering short positions to the downside. There are also "limit" stop orders, which can trigger a limit order. Remember that if you use these types of orders, you have no guarantee of getting filled, as the stock or option may blow past your stop.

Stop losses should be used to prevent catastrophe. They can be frustrating, but also can put an end to a trade that has gone terribly wrong from getting even worse. Be sure that your stop prices are not only in line with what you can tolerate, but *outside* the normal variations of the stock. This is where understanding volatility can really help you.

Trailing-Stop Orders I think it would be safe to say that I would not use trailing-stop orders unless I were already in profitable territory for a trade. I personally believe that a trailing stop is best used to retain profit and mechanize the trade.

Trailing stops are orders to buy or sell a security that "trail" or follow the market price of your security as it moves in a profitable direction, but locks in place if the underlying security changes direction.

Example: I bought an option for $5 and set a trailing stop at $4.50 (trail amount is $0.50). If the option moves higher to $6, our trailing stop is now at $5.50; if the option then trades down to $5.50, the trail will become active and take us out of our position.

Typically, trailing stops are placed tighter than regular stop orders as they are a ratcheting type of order that will let the stop price move higher but not lower (in the case of a long position). Placing a tight-trailing stop at the onset may prematurely force you out of the trade. It really boils down to your ability to time your entries into positions, the volatility of the stock, and your own personal risk tolerance and greed (err . . . "trading goals").

If you are a longer-term trader, placing a trailing stop just outside of one monthly standard deviation in your underlying stock might be a technique you can explore.

Shorter-term traders (intending to spend less than one week in a trade) might use a tight (0.10–0.40) trailing stop once their trades become profitable to try to capture momentum in the stock or option.

Be sure to paper trade any of these methods before attempting to apply them in the real market.

OCO Orders   OCO, or "One Cancels the Other," orders allow you flexibility and freedom in setting or orders. Where a trigger order would make an order active, an OCO order will cancel another order, preventing potential catastrophe.

Basically, it is an order stipulating that if one part of a multipart order is executed, then another part is automatically canceled. Where this might make sense is if you are bracketing a position with a stop-loss order below your entry price and a limit order above your entry price as your profit target.

OCO Example   You are long ABC stock, which is currently trading at $50, you want to capture potential gains by selling your shares of ABC if the stock goes up to $52. But at the same time you want to limit your potential losses by setting a stop loss at $47, because you bought the shares at $45.

This is where an OCO order would fit and here is what it would look like:

- A limit order to sell at a price of $52, plus
- A top-loss order @ $47

Both orders are "good till canceled" (GTC) and marked OCO. OCO ensures that if one of those orders is executed, the other is not still in place.

Without an OCO designation, if the stock dropped sharply and your stop loss was executed and you were unavailable to remove the limit sell order, the stock could rise again, hit your limit, and now you would have a short position at $52, which has unlimited risk. OCOs can be used with trailing stops in the same way, where the stop loss to the downside is actually a trailing stop and the upside target remains steady. You can also use OCO orders with completely different stocks or investment instruments.

OCO Usage For example, let's say you are looking to make an investment on a day where the market is volatile, but you have limited buying power. You set a limit order to buy two different stocks, one in tech and one in telecom. You can afford to buy one, but not both, so you can set the OCO order and walk away. If your limit order is hit, the other is canceled. Talk to your broker about other uses for OCOs.

Practical Stop Loss Tip Finding the appropriate place to enter your stop loss or limit price is always a challenge. It is nearly impossible to pick the best level that will protect you when the "trend changes" as opposed to forcing you out of your trade or investment prematurely.

There are many techniques that traders can employ to help them find an acceptable level. What I recommend is having a checklist of several factors and criteria that help determine the appropriate level. Combine all of the factors together to form a specific plan to place your stops.

If you are long, first start by examining the appropriate support levels in your stock. Appropriate in this case refers to the proper time-frame chart. For example, if you are a longer-term trader and are going to be potentially holding your position for several months, looking at support levels in a daily chart will most likely lead to a premature exit.

So if you are holding for a period of months, use a monthly chart; if you are holding for a period of weeks, obviously look at the weekly chart; swing traders should focus on the daily charts, and super-active traders on some sort of intraday chart (maybe using 10-minute or 5-minute bars).

Using the proper time frame for reference in your trade is paramount—what may look like strong support in a daily chart may not even be apparent in a weekly or monthly chart.

Once you have targeted support or resistance points in your appropriate chart, you must then rationalize your intended stock's movement over the period of time you anticipate being in the trade. This is where options traders excel, because we base many of our trading decisions on a stock's volatility alone.

To simplify things a bit, you can use the ATR (average true range) of a stock to get an idea of its normal movement over a period of time. This can be a quick-and-dirty way to target stop losses as well as set realistic targets.

Note that ATR is basically measuring volatility, or more specifically, the average greatest movement of a stock, over the last 14 periods.

OPTIONS EXPIRATION IN DETAIL

An option would not be an option without an expiration date. The expiration date is crucial in determining the theoretical value of an option. It is also one of the more difficult things for new options traders to deal with because stocks, unlike options, don't come with an expiration date, although some do go bankrupt from time to time.

Options are wasting assets, meaning that part of their value will naturally decay as expiration approaches, even if the underlying stock itself is performing according to plan. Time decay is nonlinear, so as expiration Friday draws closer, the amount of time value an option will lose with each passing day increases (this is measured by the Greek theta, which you will learn in Chapter 5).

Typically, option contracts expire according to a predetermined calendar. For instance, for U.S. exchange-listed equity option contracts, the expiration date is always on the Saturday that follows the third Friday of the month, unless that Friday is a market holiday, in which case the final day of trading is Thursday (and expiration is still on Saturday). The market is not open on Saturday, so that Friday is called options expiration day, because it is the last day that you can trade out of that option and typically the day you are making the decision to exercise your long options or get prepared to be assigned on your short options.

There are two types of options expiration.

1. **American**—Can be exercised any time up until expiration; most equity options that trade on U.S. exchanges are U.S. expiration.

2. **European**—Can be exercised only on expiration day (the last trading day); many cash-settled indexes are European expiration.

Equity Options

Most standard options that are traded on individual equities in the United States on U.S. exchanges are U.S. expiration, meaning that you can exercise them at any time up until expiration. (You can also be assigned if you are short.)

Index Options

Most cash index options (not ETFs) are European expiration, meaning that you can exercise them only on expiration day, which, by the way, may *not* be the third Friday. Some indexes actually cease trading the third Thursday of the month and are marked to the opening price of the stocks contained in that index on Friday.

ETFs Exchange Traded Funds (ETFs) generally expire the same way U.S. equity options do, on the third Friday of their expiration month. Check the prospectus or website of the ETF for specifics.

Binary Options Binary options will only be worth $1 or $0 at expiration. There are binary options listed on certain select stocks and indexes but they are not exercisable into stock or cash other than their final value on expiration. They are obviously not exercisable into stock and have very unique characteristics. More about these later in this chapter.

Expiration Cycles

Each and every set of options has its own expiration cycle. Essentially, the cycle sets the months that the stock will have options offered. This is in addition to every stock, index, and ETF having the first two months of options available to trade at all times.

There are some exceptions to this cycle, as some options will have contracts in every month and some products have additional quarterly and even weekly options. Most equity options trade with expiration months in one of the following three expiration cycles:

1. January cycle: Expirations in January, April, July, October (the first month of each quarter).
2. February cycle: Expirations in February, May, August, November (second month).
3. March cycle: Expirations in March, June, September, December (third month).
4. Weeklys: Weekly options begin trading the Thursday before the following Friday, allowing about 7 days to trade them before they expire. These options are listed on a handful of equities and indexes. Check www.cboe.com for details.

LEAPS—Long-Term Equity Anticipation Securities

LEAPS have a fancy name and there may be some subtle nuances to trading them, but in essence they are just longer-dated options, sometimes expiring three years in the future. Because of their longer duration, they tend to be more expensive than shorter-dated options. LEAPS can offer longer-term investors the chance to use options. They can also be combined with other LEAPS and regular options to make spreads. LEAPS always expire in January and will become regular options around May of the year before they expire. (Nothing really changes when that happens, by the way.)

Time Decay and Expiration

Expiration can sometimes work in your favor if you are short options. Remember that all options are losing time value as they approach expiration. If you are short an option that remains out of the money, its value is approaching zero as it moves closer to expiration. This is a good thing if you are short the call or put that is out of the money because the shorted option will likely expire worthless and you will keep the premium collected for selling the option (and won't have to pay exit commissions, to boot).

If you are long an out-of-the-money option on expiration Friday, hopefully you are not still holding an option that is virtually worthless, unless that was your intention or if it is part of a spread. At 4:00 P.M. Eastern (for equity options), that long option will have a value of zero (and chances are you paid more than that originally).

Remember that an option is a contract; the expiration date is the date on which that contract expires. The option holder (owner) must elect to exercise the option or allow it to expire worthless.

As the owner, this does *not* mean that you have to. You do have the right to contact your broker and ask her not to exercise your options, or only exercise a certain number of contracts.

If you don't have the funds to cover the purchase of shares upon exercising your call or put contracts—contact your broker or close the position!

Some brokers will exercise your call options and then automatically sell your shares for you in the open market come Monday (this is not a good thing, as you will have market fluctuation risk and *no* control over the price they sell your shares).

Other brokers may force you to sell your contracts back to the market on expiration day to avoid any risk over the weekend.

This works the same for puts typically, but remember that if you own a put and exercise that right, you will end up with *short* stock in your account come Monday, which could be much more risky than being long.

The bottom line is that you must contact your broker and make exercise/assignment part of your trade plan.

EXERCISE AND ASSIGNMENT

What is scary is that I have found that many relatively new options traders have never been through an exercise or assignment, where they were actually long or short an option after the close of trading on the third Friday of an options expiration month. Typically, most traders close out their positions before an option expires (which is not a bad thing). But expiration is an important time and how you treat it could have serious consequences on your portfolio and risk.

The term *exercise* is used to describe that action that the owner of a call or put takes to exercise his right to convert that option into stock. In other words, if you bought one call with a strike price of $50, you can exercise that call and you will be the proud owner of 100 shares of stock at $50 per share. Of course, you have to have the money to do so.

If you bought one put with a strike price of $50 and chose to exercise your option, you would end up short 100 shares at a price of $50.

Typically, most investors who are buying calls and puts do not hold their positions until expiration and therefore many do *not* end up exercising them.[1]

Assignment

Remember that for every buyer there is a seller. Some traders may sell an option or be "short" that option. Basically, *assignment* is the term used for the person who is *forced* to buy or sell shares of stock when the "owner" chooses to exercise.

Assignment works the opposite of exercise, in that a trader who is short one call with a strike price of $50 will be forced to *sell* 100 shares of stock at $50. Now those can be shares that you already may own, or you may have to assume a short position, the latter potentially having much more risk.

If you are short one put with a strike price of $50 and you are assigned, you will be forced to *buy* 100 shares of stock at $50. Again, depending on your investment objective and risk tolerance that may be good or bad.

What is even more important to know is that the OCC (Options Clearing Corporation) specifies that any equity option that is $0.01 or more in-the-money will be automatically exercised, so if you are long a call that is 0.01 or more in the money at 4 P.M. Eastern Standard Time on expiration Friday, you may end up with 100 shares of stock in your account come Monday. This works the same way if you are long a put, only you may end up with 100 shares short in your account on Monday.

TRADER TIP

You can actually request *not* to exercise your option. You would most likely do this if your option is just at the money and you are not sure whether you will be automatically exercised. If your option is in the money and you don't have the money to take on the stock position or if you don't want to have a stock position, just *sell* the option before the market closes!

If you are short, and that option is in the money by a cent or more, you will most likely have to either sell stock if you are short a call or buy stock if you are short a put, so be aware that automatic exercise will cause an automatic assignment as well.

Dangers

If you have that money or margin in your account to cover the exercise or assignment transaction, you may be just fine with either being automatically exercised if you are long or assigned if you are short, but what if the market makes a drastic move against you over the weekend. The option may have cost you $5,000, but now that you are long or short stock come Monday morning, you may have $50,000 or more at risk. This is why it is imperative to talk to your broker ahead of expiration or have a plan to exit or convert into stock, if that is what you chose to do.

How Many Options Expire Unexercised? How Many Are Exercised?

There are many myths surrounding options. Some say that 80% of options expire worthless and this is completely false; in fact, according to OCC statistics for year 2008 (for activity in customer and firm accounts), the breakdown is as follows:

Closing sales—69.4%
Exercised—11.6%
Unexercised at expiration—19%

So, in 2008, 19% of all options positions in customer and firm accounts expired unexercised; 11.6% of these positions were exercised; and 69.4% of these positions were closed out through sales.

Advanced Education on Early Exercise

Most novice retail traders will not be exercising options early, for in many cases there is no need to do so. Furthermore, realize that when you exercise an option you forfeit any remaining time value left in that option. There are, however, exceptions to this rule and certain instances where an early exercise is warranted. This next section is for the more advanced options traders.

Early assignment is something you need to be aware of in addition to possible assignment of your short options positions on expiration day. If you are short an option (put or call) that is deep in the money, you run a much higher risk of being assigned early because these options may be devoid of any time value and, depending on the situation, may be candidates for early exercise, as they would be better dead than alive. Dead means that the trader who is long those options would prefer to be long or short stock versus having that option sitting in his account, which may not entitle that trader to certain benefits that I outline later.

Furthermore, if you are short options as part of a spread, getting assigned on one or more of your short positions can potentially throw a monkey wrench into your risk management, or change the dynamics of your entire trade and even force you to realize the maximum loss in the trade.

This would apply to short vertical spreads, (bear call and bull put). First, if you have to worry about getting assigned in your short vertical spread, you have probably done something wrong all along because that would mean that the stock has moved through both your short strike and potentially your long. Don't let yourself get to this point! I discuss exit strategies in the strategy section. Regardless, if you are assigned in a short vertical spread, you will realize the max loss in that trade, which is the difference in strikes—minus the premium received.

Early exercise could also occur in a short straddle that has gone wrong, where the stock has moved way beyond your short strikes and if there is a dividend on the way.

But more common would be if you were long a time spread (horizontal/calendar) and the stock made a sharp move and put your short option (which is the one that is expiring first) deep in the money.

Early assignment would most likely be rare if you were handling your money management and risk properly.

TRADER TIP

If you are long a vertical spread (call or put) in the same month, early exercise is actually a blessing, because the early exercise of your short option would force you to just exercise your long strike and realize maximum gain the trade! I discuss this in depth in the strategy section.

Of course, if there was a dividend, and you had a deep in-the-money call spread long, it may behoove you to exercise your long call right ahead of the pay date to capture the dividend.

WHEN SHOULD YOU EXERCISE AN OPTION EARLY?

Typically, there are only two basic reasons to exercise an option early. As a retail trader, if you own a call option that has *no* time value (deep in the money) and there is a large dividend coming up, you would want to exercise your call to capture the dividend. Because most of you do not receive a credit for being short stock, you will generally never exercise a put that is deep in the money.

TRADER TIP

Dividends lower the price of the call by the amount of the dividend and raise the price of the put by the amount of the dividend.

Dividends (Call Exercise)

Call options should be exercised in advance of expiration if the dividend amount is greater than the time-value amount. Typically this is an option that is very deep in the money or close to expiring. In many cases, if an option has time value left, it would behoove you to sell it in the open market, capture the time value, and then just purchase the stock in order to collect the dividend (remember that options do not pay dividends like stocks do).

Here is the basic call value formula:

Call value = Intrinsic value + Interest rate value + Volatility value
$\qquad$ − Dividend value

To simplify, if you have a deep in-the-money call that is trading for close to parity and there is a dividend on the horizon, you may want to exercise that option (because you can't sell it for a premium over parity) and collect the dividend, rather than hold on to it.

Let's assume the market in the 45 call is $4.90–$5.20 (99 delta) and the stock is trading $50 with five days to go until expiration, the stock goes ex-dividend 30 cents tomorrow.

You should exercise that call, (you can only sell it in this case for less than parity) to capture 30 cents in dividend. Of course, you may have risk in the stock moving, but you would have that regardless if you stayed in the call position.[2]

If a trader can sell a deep in-the-money call for more than parity, it would be best to sell that call, capture the excess premium, then substitute the 100 delta call with stock and capture the dividend with stock, but this is next to impossible for the retail trader.

Remember that because the call is so deep in the money, it has lost its "optionality" and is behaving much like the stock, so the trader is simply substituting the 100 delta call with 100 shares of stock.

Capturing dividends can also be done by using deep-in-the-money call spreads; a trader might buy 10,000 deep call spreads for parity or a little bit under hoping to capture a dividend by taking advantage of the random assignment methods of the OCC. This usually requires that the traders have low commissions and exercise costs, otherwise the trade would cost too much and carry too much risk.

Calls are **not** an early exercise other than right before the stock goes ex-dividend!

Call Spread Example   A trader buys the 45/50 call spread for $5 10,000 times with the stock at $55, in the front month. The stock goes ex-dividend 0.30 tomorrow; the trader then exercises all the long calls and hopes that he does not get assigned on all of his short calls; therefore he is able to capture the dividend. Assuming that 500 of his short calls go unexercised, the trader can potentially capture ([500contract*100shares]*0.30), or $15,000, in dividends. Again, the trader is susceptible to market risk if he is unhedged.

Interest (Put Exercise Reasoning)

For the put, it may be slightly more complicated. Remember, for the put, the dividend is a positive, meaning that it adds to its value. An increase in volatility also adds to a put's value. Interest rates, however, are a negative for put values, so as interest rates rise, put values will decrease (increasing interest rates raise the forward price of a stock or index).

So if you have a deep in-the-money put that is trading close to parity (U.S. put options will *never* trade for less than parity) and you realize that by exercising this put you can get a short stock rebate that is greater than the time value of that put and it's right after a dividend (puts are not subject to paying dividend), the put may be an exercise. Remember that when you are short stock, professionals receive a rebate, but if that stock becomes hard to borrow or interest rates drop, that put exercise may have been a bad decision because the interest money that was supposed to be collected ceases to be paid or is reduced. Not to mention that the trader may even be forced to cover her short position, potentially having to buy another put at a premium to remain delta neutral.

TRADER TIP

Early exercise may be more common in lower volatility stocks versus higher ones because of the reduced risk of the stock blowing through the exercised call or put. Put exercise would also be more common in a rising interest rate environment and in options listed on a relatively stable stock that is liquid and has minimal risk of becoming hard to borrow.

For most retail traders, early exercise is *not* a typical occurrence. Retail traders should focus on their risk going into and coming out of expiration day, particularly if they have a spread on and the stock is in between strikes or near its short or long strike, as there is uncertainty whether it will be assigned or you have to exercise your options. Sometimes it is best to just sell or buy your position back to the marketplace, rather than take a chance on expiration and run the risk of coming in Monday with long or short stock that is moving against you.

This also goes for a covered call that is close to where the stock is closing on Friday; if you want to keep the stock, just buy the call back to remove your risk of being assigned.

The OCC will automatically exercise an option that is one cent in the money, unless the trader instructs otherwise, so your chances of being assigned are certainly high.

WHAT IS TRIPLE WITCHING? (OR QUADRUPLE WITCHING)

You should all know that on every third Friday of the month, equity options expire for that monthly series. And on the third Friday of every March, June, September, and December, we get triple (quadruple if you count stock futures) witching. The word *triple* in triple witching denotes the expiration of three kinds of securities bolded here:

1. **Stock market index futures**
2. **Stock market index options**
3. **Stock options**
4. Stock futures (quadruple witching)

I have always received tons of questions about what exactly happens before, during, and after the expiration process and how it affects the markets and adds volatility. I remember my first triple witching expiration as a rookie market maker in the mid 1990s on the floor of the PHLX. The floor was packed—probably about 40% more traders than on a typical day—the energy was frenetic . . . and for good reason!

Front-month options were expiring and most of the traders were trying not only to reduce their risk, but were also frantically absorbing orders that were flying in from customers and other traders around the world, who were closing or rolling positions out to the next month or perhaps just letting their options expire. Contrary to what some may think, options expiration is a time of massive liquidity, a flood of orders in both directions, buying and selling, puts and calls.

At that moment, I didn't realize the enormity of what was going on or how this simple monthly occurrence could potentially have such a major impact on a trader. The risks of expiration vary from trader to trader; retail and professional traders both may have issues to deal with on expiration day.

For the average retail investor, this may be the end of a "hope and pray" trade that never worked out as they find their options moving closer to worthlessness. Other traders may be elated that the covered calls they wrote on stocks they owned are finishing just out of the money, allowing them to keep the premiums they sold them for and hold on to the stocks as well.

For the market maker on the floor, expiration (even triple witching) usually means something different, *risk reduction*. For *most* of us market makers, we are there providing liquidity and buying and selling options that *others* want to trade. Because we are there to take the other side of everyone else's trades, we may sometimes be forced into positions we may not want and we also have to be aware of what those positions might morph into when we come in Monday following expiration. Whether it is a regular expiration or quadruple witching, you need to focus on risk reduction. I will discuss this in more depth in later chapters.

Remember Exercise and Assignment?

For the sake of brevity, I am not going into all the possible scenarios, but let's just examine one situation that a trader may find himself in. Let's assume I am a market maker in Google (GOOG) and I am short 10,000 at the money ($400) straddles on expiration Friday in GOOG (meaning that I am expecting limited volatility, or movement in Google shares themselves). Even if I have been profitable in the overall trade, I still have some issues on Friday. At 3:55, Google is trading right around $399.95 and remember that at 4:00 P.M. Eastern, either my call or my put will have a delta of one and the other will have zero. Meaning that one will be long stock, the other short stock—the question is what is it going to be.

Another way to think about it is that depending on where Google stock closes, I will be assigned on either my call or put and come in Monday with either 1,000,000 shares long or short. Right now, if Google stays put, my put will be in the money if I have no other position in my account.

Come Monday, I will have no options position and be long 1,000,000 shares of stock. The question really is: Which is it going to be? What if I come in Monday long and the stock is gapping down on economic data? Or what if GOOG closes at $400.25, then I come in short stock on Monday and the shares rally on a brokerage upgrade? Should I sell 1,000,000 shares to flatten out my position, but what if I don't get assigned on my puts?

The bottom line is that I don't know the future of GOOG and probably don't want that exposure at all, so I am going to be selling or buying stock and options accordingly to level out my position; here is where part of the volatility comes from.

So again, if the stock looks like it is going to stay below $400, I may be selling some shares to neutralize my delta. But then if it rallies, I may have to buy some shares to neutralize my delta. This is called *negative gamma scalping* and it can further contribute to a stock "pinning" at a strike price.

Gamma, the Greek that measures the amount by which delta affects an option's price, is greatest in an at-the-money option on expiration day, because that option's delta will either be one or zero by 4 P.M. All this buying and selling can create added volatility in both the stock and options.

Some traders will look to trade with each other to get out of their positions. For instance, I may trade with someone else in the pit who has the opposite position as I do (they would be long the straddle). Traders are also rolling their positions out and up (or down) or possibly repositioning a trade they may want to stay on. With the advent of advanced computers and more efficient markets, expiration Friday has become less of an event, although it is still paramount that you understand how expiration will affect your positions.

A Few Words on Binary Options

Binary options are just another product to trade; they are nothing new and there are pros and cons to just about every vehicle that investors can trade. I can offer you my opinion on these options and how you might go about trading them.

First off, you must understand the product to trade it most effectively and safely.

Binary options, also called *all-or-nothing options*, *digital options*, or *fixed return options* (FROs), are offered and traded across many markets.

Second, there is not much open interest and so the spreads are fairly wide. On the outside, when you examine the valuation of binary options, they really begin to look much like N(d2), the probability that the option finishes in the money (the other delta).

Using the Black-Scholes model, you can interpret the premium of the binary option in the risk-neutral world as the expected value = probability of being in-the-money * unit, discounted to the present value.

To take volatility skew into account, a more sophisticated analysis based on call spreads can be used.

A binary call option is, at long expirations, similar to a tight call spread using two vanilla options. One can model the value of a binary cash-or-nothing option.

I have to tell you that I have not had much time to study or trade them. I think that the best use of them for a retail trader would be as a substitute for verticals, both credit and debit. There are obviously other ways you can put them to work, but let's say spot is 50 and the 40/45 put spread is $0.50 bid with 30 days until expiration.

In this trade, you have $4.50 at risk for a $0.50 credit, or an 11% return on risk (ROR). Even with that ROR, you can still lose much more money than you brought in—nine times as much.

Now let's assume we can sell the 45 put binary for $0.15. That option will only be worth zero or one at expiry, so we risk $0.75 on a $0.15 credit, or 20% ROR. You still risk five times what you stand to make. But also remember that there is no middle ground . . . this is either going to be one or zero.

Your breakeven on the put spread is $44.50 and you gradually lose money as the stock drops.

Your *absolute* breakeven on the binary is $45 in the stock.

So there is much to consider. It certainly is a niche product that has its place. Be sure that you use limit orders if you are trading them.

As of the time of this writing, binary options for the most part are thinly traded and relatively new. For some, they may be a cheap and easy-to-understand alternative to trading regular options.

You can learn more about them at www.cboe.com/micro/binaries/introduction.aspx.

FINAL THOUGHTS

Think about options strategies as the vehicle of choice that you use to carry your trade out. Some trades need a race car, others maybe a tank. The problem is that without the basic knowledge of options, you may not know how your vehicle is going to react to certain market conditions.

Understanding the mechanics of options can be thought of like understanding the specific components that make that vehicle run. More importantly, when you have a comprehensive understanding of those components, you can better understand what may be going wrong when you are driving through some rough terrain or when you encounter a major breakdown in your strategy.

CHAPTER 5

The Greeks

The Forces That Influence Options' Prices

Trading often appeals to impulsive people, to gamblers, and to those who feel that the world owes them a living. If you trade for the excitement, you are liable to take trades with bad odds and accept unnecessary risks. The markets are unforgiving, and emotional trading always results in losses.

—Alexander Elder
Trading for a Living

Now that you have learned the basics, I will explain the Greeks. The Greeks give you an explanation for the changes in the prices of options and can help you make profit-and-loss forecasts moving forward in time and price in the underlying stock. Some are more important than others, but all should be understood, at least on a basic level before you begin to trade with real money.

This chapter not only defines what they are and how to use them in simple terms, but offers you a view of the Greeks from a professional's eyes. After reading this chapter, you should understand what market forces influence option prices, and it allows you to grasp the behavior of all the strategies we discuss in Chapter 6 and helps you select the most appropriate one to utilize.

DELTA

For the beginner options trader, delta is probably the most important Greek to understand. Delta is the Greek letter that options traders use to symbolize and measure the change in the price of an option for a $1 change in the price of the underlying security (stock, ETF, index, etc.). There are other ways to use delta, which we discuss later.

All Options Have a Delta

Calls have a positive delta because of their positive correlations or relationships to the underlying stock; in other words, when stock prices go up, call prices should be rising, when stocks drop, call prices should be decreasing. Because of this, the call option is assigned a positive delta.

Puts, on the other hand have a negative delta, because of the negative or opposite correlation they have with the underlying stock. When a stock price rises, puts should *decrease* in value, and when stocks drop, put prices should be on the rise. This opposite relationship is why puts are assigned a negative delta.

Whether you are examining puts or calls, the theory and relationship is basically the same; you will just stick a (−) minus sign in front of a put's delta.

Delta Is Measured in Dollars

For example, if a call option has a *delta* of positive 0.60 and the option is worth $1 when the stock is trading $20, then that means that if the stock goes up $1 to $21, the option should be worth about $1.60 at this higher stock price, which we got by adding the delta to the original option price, $1 plus 60 cents. This also means that if stock were to instead drop by a dollar, we would *subtract* the delta from the option price to determine the expected new price, $1 dollar minus 60 cents, which is 40 cents.

Since calls profit from upward movements in stock, it makes sense that they have a positive delta, but how about puts? Since puts increase in value as stock *drops*, they would have a negative delta. In other words, you subtract the delta amount from the put price as stock goes *up* and *add* it as stock goes *down*.

For example, if a put option has a delta of negative 0.60 and the option is worth $1 when the stock is trading $20, then that means that if the stock goes up $1 to $21, the option should be worth about 40 cents at this higher stock price, which we got by subtracting the delta to the original option price, $1 minus 60 cents. This also means that if stock were to instead drop by a dollar, we would *add* the delta from the option price to determine the expected new price, $1 dollar plus 60 cents, which is $1.60.

Can you see the relationship here? If this were the same stock and we were looking at both the 0.60 delta call option and the 0.60 put option, and the stock moved $1, they both would change prices by the same amount, just one would increase and the other decrease, depending on which way the stock moved. There is a relationship that exists between calls and puts and believe it or not, if I know what the price of the call is, I can tell you what the put should be trading for and vice versa. This is called put-call parity and is discussed later.

Another characteristic of delta is that the more that an option is in the money, the higher the delta is. This makes intuitive sense because the more in the money an option is, the more likely it is to be exercised and, therefore, change in value exactly as the stock does. As an example, if stock XYZ trades for $54 per share, then the June 55 calls will have a higher delta than the June 60 calls because the June 55 calls are more in the money or, in this case, less out of the money and more likely to eventually be an exercise. For the puts, this would be reversed—the June 60 puts would have a higher delta than the June 55 puts because the 60 puts are more in the money and, therefore, more likely to be an exercise.

Let's get you speaking about delta like a pro trader. Although technically delta is measured in cents because it is change per dollar and, therefore, can take any value from zero to a dollar, the convention for traders is to speak of deltas as whole numbers from zero to 100. It wouldn't be referred to as a 50 cent delta call, but rather a 50 delta call. Also, even though puts have negative delta, we wouldn't say, "That's a minus point 30 delta put" or a "negative 30 delta put," it would just be a 30 delta put and it's implicitly understood among traders that puts have negative delta and calls have positive delta.

Delta's Other Functions

In addition to telling us how much an option's value will change for every one dollar move in the stock, delta also has some other unique functions that you should understand.

Probability of Being in the Money Delta (to an extent) also tells us the percentage chance that the option will be worth *anything* at expiration (that it will expire in the money). You can also think about delta as the probability of that option being worth more than zero at expiry. It does *not* tell you the percentage chance that you will be profitable. The models that are used to figure delta would assume that .000001 is still positive value, but isn't much money, so keep that in mind.

Here's what that means. Assume a call has a 0.15 delta; this means, given the current inputs of stock price, volatility, days until expiration, and so on, that option has a 15% chance of being in the money (by any amount) at expiration. Think about it as a horse that is a long shot. Hopefully, you're not going to bet the farm on that one, but you can bet a little bit—if he wins, the payoff may be substantial.

That call option (like the long shot) is cheap for a reason—the odds are against you; in other words, the probability is low, because there is a lower chance of that option winning or even being in the money. But always keep in mind that if that call had a strike price of 100 and the stock expired at 100.01, that option would be in the money, but you may have paid .60 for it, thus resulting in a loss.

This concept applies to puts as well. Even though deltas are expressed as negative numbers, the probability concept still applies.

Textbook mathematicians would argue that there is another measurement for probability, but most of us professional traders use delta as a quick and dirty way to forecast this.

Percentage Exposure to the Underlying stock   Professional traders use delta to find their total exposure to a stock's movement and how their P&L will change as the stock changes. Remember that 100 shares of long stock will have a delta of 100. One hundred shares of short stock will have a delta of –100. Being long or short stock one for one is the most bullish or bearish you can be when you think about it compared to options. If you were to buy a call with a delta of 0.70, for example, you would only be exposed to 70% of that stock's movement, participating in 0.70 of profit or loss for every dollar that stock moved. So if the stock jumped $1, you would make 0.70 and vice versa to the downside.

Another characteristic of delta is that it is *not* static. When you purchase a call with a delta of 0.70 and the stock drops $1, your new delta might drop as well to 0.60 (for example)—in essence, slowing how much money you have lost. This works in the other direction as well. If you bought a call with a delta of 0.70 and the stock rose $1, your call may then have a delta of 0.80, accelerating your profits. This rate of change is called *Gamma*; the "Greek" and I explore that next. But getting back to delta as a percentage of exposure to a stock's movement . . . this concept becomes important when you are managing your risk. Many brokers offer a risk management tool to offer a graphical representation of this data.

How much will your profit and loss (P&L) change with a $1 move in the stock?

If you bought 10 call options with a delta of about 54 each, your total position would be long about 540 delta (in total) as shown further on. This means that at this moment in time, if the stock were to rise $1, you would make about $540 and if it were to drop a dollar, you would lose about $540. Delta is extremely important in money and position management.

In Figure 5.1, you can see your "position" or total delta if you bought 10 call options. Delta can and will change and if this stock were to continue

Total position				
Bid: 3.80		Mid: 3.82		Ask: 3.85
Delta:	540.27	Gamma:		40.37
Theta:	-40.01	Vega:		184.28

FIGURE 5.1   Example of the "Greeks" If You Bought 10 Call Options

to rise, your postion delta would continue to increase eventually to 1,000, which would mean the delta of the calls you bought had increased to 100. When an option has a delta of 1 (100) it is moving 1 to 1 with the underlying stock.

Delta for the new trader is most important when trading long calls and long puts. It offers a quick way to find options that meet certain risk parameters or to identify whether an option is in, at, or out of the money.

If I am buying a long call or long put and trying to simply use an option as a proxy for long or short stock, I want that option to behave as much like the stock as possible, meaning I will choose an option that is in the money, with a delta of .70–.90. Leverage is my motivation for the purchase of the option, while paying minimal time value.

Gamma and Theta

For new option investors or those who trade only long calls, puts, and covered calls, being short or long gamma may not have much significance in the establishment of their trading lives. Most retail traders are more concerned with the ultimate outlook they have for the underlying instrument they are trading; in other words, they know they need the stock to get to X for them to make money.

Many retail traders tend to use different options strategies based on their risk and reward characteristics as well as their bullishness or bearishness. This moderate amount of ignorance is okay, as long as it is successful and repeatable. But as you progress further and further into the options universe, understanding the second derivative, gamma, becomes more and more important as you monitor your trading. Understanding gamma completely is not necessary to trade basic options, but it should be learned.

Theta, I believe, should hold a bit more precedence and at least be examined before a trade is made. Theta is simply the dollar amount the option will decay each day, so it's not a bad idea to keep your eye on how much you are paying (or collecting) in your trade. Think of theta as rent—you'll either be paying it or collecting it.

Gamma   Gamma, which measures the rate of change of the delta, can play a large part of the change in behavior of your single option trade or spread trade. Gamma, like delta, can and will change as the option moves closer to expiration and as the underlying stock and volatility change. Gamma specifically measures the rate of change in an option's **delta** for every one-point move in the underlying stock. Gamma is greatest in the at-the-money options and gets lower as you go away from that strike price, whether in or out of the money. Gamma will help you know what your delta will become as the stock moves around. Gamma is also displayed in most professional option trading platforms. Before going deeper into Gamma, I wanted to introduce Theta to you, because in many ways they go hand in hand.

Theta   Theta is the amount of value your option will lose each day. Because all options are decaying assets, they are all losing some amount of money each and every day, including weekends. When you look at an option chain and see the theta column, the values displayed there are in "dollars per day." So an option with a theta of 0.10 means that the option will decrease in value approximately 0.10 ($10) each and every day. Theta can help or hurt you. If you sell options (or trade a spread with positive theta) your P&L will benefit from the passage of time. Remember that when you sell something first, you want to buy it back cheaper at a later date, and because options are always decaying, theta is helping you!

When you purchase options, theta is costing you money because when you buy something first, you want to be able to sell it for a greater price later. Usually, the only way to overcome theta is to buy delta, or have the stock move in your desired direction!

Why They Are Related   Generally speaking, when you _buy_ options or are net long options in a spread, you are long gamma (you want the stock to move) and paying theta (losing money each day you hold the position).

When you _sell_ options or are net short options in a spread, you are typically short gamma (you want the stock to remain fairly still in your profitable zone) and you are collecting theta (making money each day from the passage of time).

Professionals use these two Greeks in conjunction with one another. Unless you intend on taking trading to the next level, you're okay to just understand what they both mean for your position.

Buying Options = Long Gamma   When you purchase an option, whether it is a call or a put, you are getting long gamma, which means that delta is changing in the direction you would want it to. In other words, when you purchase a call with a delta of 0.60 and a gamma of 0.05 and the stock moves up a dollar, your new delta might be something like 0.65, which means that essentially you are getting "more bullish" (making more money) as the stock rises, which is a good thing. If that same stock were to drop $1, the new delta might be something like 0.55, making your option position less bullish (losing less money) and thus having less relation to the stock's movement.

By the way, when you buy *any* option, you are typically paying theta, which means that it costs you money each day to be in that position.

Advanced Concept   In the professional market-making world, one of our objectives was to remain relatively delta neutral, which meant that we had to buy or sell stock (or something else) against our trades to mitigate our exposure to the underlying stock's movement. So if we bought a call with a 0.50 delta, we might sell 50 shares of stock to delta-neutralize our position. If that stock went even higher, I was forced to sell even more stock, because remember that my call delta was increasing. Then, if the stock came back down (like they often do) I could buy back those shares I sold as a hedge to make a profit. Hopefully, I made more money *scalping my stock*, as it is called, than I was paying in theta (or time decay) each day.

TRADER TIP

When a *professional* trader is long gamma, he or she has the ability to scalp stock (for a profit) against his position to help offset what that option's position is costing him. Being long gamma is warranted in some situations, typically if a stock is expected to be very volatile.

Selling Options = Short Gamma   Short gamma, on the other hand, means that you want that stock to stay perfectly still if at all possible and also most short gamma positions want to see a decrease in implied volatility once the position is put on. This is logical, because if buying options makes you long gamma, selling options makes you short gamma. A position that is short gamma can really behave oddly if you are not used to it.

Advanced Concept   Short gamma means that your position deltas are moving opposite to what the underlying stock is doing, so if you are short a call and the stock begins to move higher (not a good thing), you get shorter and shorter, which would mean you would have to buy stock to remain delta-neutral. Then, if the stock drops, you get positive delta, which means that you may have to sell stock to neutralize.

Some of you are scratching your heads, thinking that that situation makes *no* sense; buy high, sell low, how do I make money? Well, remember when you are short options you are *collecting* theta; time benefits your position. This is true for both calls and puts. Hopefully, when you are *short* gamma, those *losses* from your negative scalping will be less than the theta you are collecting.

As you begin to understand more and more about position behavior, think about what gamma situation you would like to find yourself in. There is no right answer, because there is a time to buy and a time to sell options. But I encourage you that the next time you make a trade—whether it is a single option or a spread—take a look at your gamma and watch how it behaves as you progress toward expiration.

Also remember that gamma is greatest in the at-the-money options, which means that you will see your biggest change in delta the closer the option is to the stock price. Gamma is also greatest in those options at the moments right before expiration (expiration Friday at 3:59 P.M. EST) because an option will either have a delta of one or zero after expiring and the gamma will help dictate how fast it will change.

Kevin Cook's Comments on Gamma   I had the pleasure of working with a fellow trader, Kevin Cook, for some time at PEAK6, which at the time of this writing, is one of the largest option trading firms in the United States. Not only does he have one of the sharpest minds I know, he has a great way of explaining certain concepts. The following are some of his thoughts on gamma.

Curvature and Acceleration   Gamma is one of the option trader's most important risk management tools (see Figure 5.2). The only second-order derivative of the option pricing model, it tells traders how sensitive their positions are to directional movement. Since most option pros tend to carry what we call *delta neutral* positions, it seems at first glance that they should not be worried about the market moving in either direction.

But because delta changes ever so slightly with moves in stock, professional options traders are forced to continuously adjust the hedges on their positions when those changes add up because of position size or big

$$\Gamma = \frac{\partial \Delta}{\partial \text{Price}} = \frac{\text{Change in delta}}{\text{Change in underlying price}}$$

FIGURE 5.2 Gamma Formula

percentage stock moves. They do this by either buying or selling the underlying stock to get the delta position back to neutral. This is often called *gamma scalping*, because in a relatively stable market, with no surprises like a big change in volatility, it is a profitable adjunct to the option trader's primary goal of volatility arbitrage.

There's a lot to learn about gamma that I cannot begin to explain here. We haven't even touched on how time and volatility figure into determining both delta and gamma, or how gamma changes. But I close with some simple descriptions that have helped me picture their power and usefulness as concepts and tools.

Delta is often called the *slope* of an option. And gamma is sometimes described as the *curvature* of the option because as the underlying price changes, the option delta also changes in a nonlinear way—sort of the way I used the "gearing" analogy. Engineers and other quantitative types should readily understand this stuff.

For us nonquant types, I like the way author Sheldon Natenberg once explained it to us in class at the Chicago Mercantile Exchange (CME) in the mid-1990s. He said that you can think of delta as the *speed* of the option and gamma as its *acceleration*. That I can relate to.

Practical Application of Long Gamma: Advanced Concept In the last quarter of 2009, Research in Motion, (RIMM) made a 12% move over earnings, which was greater than what the options markets were predicting. I took profits on bullish spreads and stock a bit early (not that I was disappointed), but how could you have profited from this move without knowing direction?

Professional options traders tend to approach the markets and options prices specifically in a different way. As a former market maker, my day-to-day activities consisted of trying to buy options for less than their theoretical value at that moment and sell them for more than that value thousands of times (contracts) daily. Whether it was a call or a put, it generally did not matter. I was more concerned with the movement or volatility of the underlying spot price in whatever security I was trading and, thus equally concerned with the volatility of the options that I was buying or selling were implying (this was determined by the price that the trades occurred at).

More often than not, I tended to end my trading day delta-neutral or not have a "directional bet" going into the next morning. We options traders tend to have an "if, then" attitude, as opposed to a regular stock trader's, which tends to be more rigid in predictions and theses. I certainly prefer the former versus the latter, because I still have yet to meet the person who knows exactly where a stock is going, not to mention, I always like contingency plans as well as having the choice of getting or giving odds, depending on the situation. So let's get back to the "if, then" thing. Most stock traders have a choice when it comes to investing: long or short. They will either begin to lose or gain money immediately once they have entered the trade. If the stock rallies, traders must sell to capture that profit, and if it falls, a long stockholder needs to sell at a loss or get the Bible out and hope it doesn't fall too far.

Options traders can use certain strategies to take a neutral position in a stock and either use gamma or their dollar breakevens to become profitable. There are, of course, ways that options traders can simulate the exact risk profile of a stock, but who would want to do that?

The gamma function can be quite intimidating to understand completely because it is an extension of the factorial function to numbers and has several definitions. We don't need to know all of the intricacies of gamma to be able to trade with it and know how your options position will be affected.

What you do need to know is that gamma tells us roughly how much our delta will change for every dollar move in the underlying spot price. Gamma is greatest in the at-the-money options, both calls and puts. When you buy an option (call or put), you are long gamma, and when you sell an option, you are short gamma.

Being long gamma enables you to scalp stock (which is your hedge) for a profit, while maintaining delta neutrality in your overall position. Typically you are paying theta to have long gamma, but there are some exceptions to this.

Scalping for Dollars   Ahead of RIMM's earnings, the December 65-straddle was trading for roughly $6 with five days until earnings and subsequent expiration the next business day. This means that the options markets were essentially betting on roughly an 8% move over earnings (I backed out the small amount of parity that was in the call options, as the stock was slightly above $65.20 at the time).

So, what if you bought that 65-straddle for $6? How can you make money? There are several ways that this trade can be profitable. The first, and probably the easiest way, would be for the stock to move away from the strike more than the amount you paid for the total straddle, so $71 or $59 would be your breakevens. The next effect would be an unexpected jump in volatility, which would need to be greater than the amount of theta that you are paying each day. You see, nothing in life is free, and options are no exception. The third way you might be able to get profitable would be to scalp your gamma. RIMM must not only move around for you to do this, but you must also time your entries and exits and be extremely proactive in monitoring and trading the position. The beauty of being long a

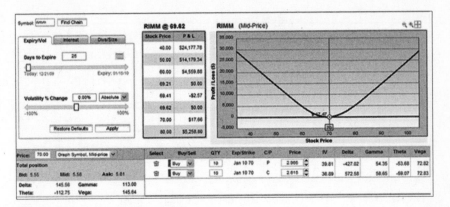

FIGURE 5.3 Greeks with RIMM at $70
Source: OptionsHouse.com.

straddle and having long gamma is that even if RIMM gaps up or down unpredictably, you may still stand to benefit.

Take a look at the profit-loss chart in Figure 5.3 of a January 70-straddle in RIMM with 25 days to expiration (DTE). Cost is about $5.50 (earnings just passed). Also take a look at your delta and gamma. In this chart, you see you have about 113 gamma and you are long 145 deltas, or the equivalent of 145 shares of stock. Using that gamma measurement, for every dollar that RIMM moves, your deltas will increase or decrease by about 113. You are paying approximately $112 per day (Theta) to be in this long straddle position (both based on 10 contracts); that is certainly something you cannot ignore.

So what if RIMM jumps to $73 today? What is your position now? (See Figure 5.4, price is displayed in lower right corner.)

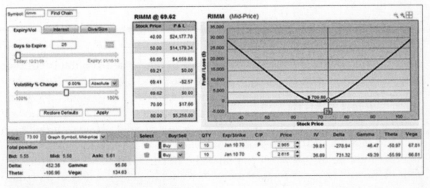

FIGURE 5.4 Greeks with RIMM at $73
Source: www.OptionsHouse.com.

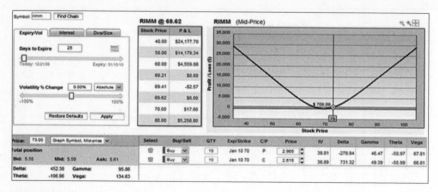

FIGURE 5.5   Greeks with RIMM Straddle + 450 Shares Short
Source: www.ivolatility.com.

As you can see, the deltas are 452.38, which means that if you wanted to neutralize this position, you might go and sell 450 shares of stock. We are now flat delta, which means we have no directional bias at this moment (see Figure 5.5).

Now if the stock drops back down to say $68 dollars tomorrow, we will most likely be short about 420 deltas. Remember that our gamma tells us how much the delta will change. Guess what we can do now? We buy back the 450 shares of stock that we sold and pocket $4 × 450 (shares) = $1,800 over two days. Did we pay for the $220 in theta? Yes! And chances are that if the stock made that big of a move, we might see a slight jump in implied volatility that would cause our spread to increase in value and maybe we could sell it back to the market for what we paid for it two days ago and keep the $1,580 in profits we made, minus any commissions, of course.

Short Gamma   When you net sell options, you are generally short gamma, which means basically that the delta (and often profitably) of the options or spread that you are positioned in will move *opposite of the stock*. When the stock rises, your deltas will decrease; when the stock falls, your deltas will increase.

A good example of this is if you were to sell a 50 put with a delta of 0.50 and gamma of 0.10 with the stock at $50. (This means that you are actually long delta, because you sold the put.) If the stock rises to $51, your delta will *decrease* by 0.10 and you would in this case see an increase in your P&L. This is the opposite if you had bought that same put—you would have been short deltas and seen a loss with that same move.

Some facts:

- When you sell an individual option, such as a call or a put, your position will always be short gamma—it will be greatest when the option is at the money.
- Spreads can go from being long gamma to short gamma and vice versa, depending on time and stock price.

Practical Application of Short Gamma—Advanced Concept I discussed how professional traders scalp gamma around a long options position. We used Research in Motion (RIMM) as an example ahead of earnings, and explained how traders could buy a straddle in RIMM and trade the movement in gamma to potentially profit after making up for the theta they were paying by owning that straddle.

Let us not forget that it is quite common for implied volatility to come in sharply after an earnings report. So holding a long straddle through a flat earnings report where the stock doesn't move can be quite disastrous, as your long straddle premium may quickly evaporate with the massive volatility crush that comes with the passing of earnings.

This is a dilemma for any average retail trader. Do I get long a straddle and hope for a big move and maybe I am able to scalp my stock out to overcome my theta and any reduction in implied volatility, or do I sell the straddle and pray that the stock stays within a range until expiration? Here lies the dichotomy of the straddle: One camp might be a seller of that straddle, thinking that there is no way that the stock moves greater than what the straddle is selling for and volatility is certain to come in; and then you have a another camp that believes the opposite—that either volatility will expand or that they will be able to positively scalp their gamma or maybe that the eventual parity of either the call or put will lead them to victory in the trade.

Short-gamma players certainly have their work cut out for them, or maybe it's better to say that they don't want to have their work cut out for them. As I have become a general premium seller in my life as an off-floor retail-type trader, I tend to favor being short credit spreads, which would thus lead me to the land of being short gamma. But also remember that the gamma of a credit vertical spread varies greatly from and has less risk than a short straddle. Selling an at-the-money straddle is the most efficient way to get short gamma and sell premium as at-the-money (ATM) options have the most time value (vega sensitivity) in real dollar terms and the most gamma. It is also a high-risk proposition when unhedged—this is why most professionals would look to buy or sell stock against that trade to even out their deltas at least most of the time.

In Chapter 6 you will learn about a strategy called a short straddle, which is the sale of a call and the sale of a put at the same strike in the same month. Your goal as a straddle seller is to have the stock right at the strike of the options you sold.

Remember the rules of assignment? Approaching expiration, if the stock is below your strike, your short put would eventually force you to buy shares at a higher price, which means that you need to sell stock to offset the risk of being long at a higher price. In essence, the farther your stock moves below strike, the longer your position delta gets—you have to sell stock when spot is low. What about when the stock rallies above your straddle strike? Then your short call starts to kick in, you get short more and more deltas the higher the stock goes, which means that you would have to buy stock to hedge.

Sell low and buy high? Something doesn't sound right! But this is a struggle that dynamic hedgers have to face every day. Unlike the long straddle that is costing you theta as each day passes, the short straddle is paying you theta every day, assuming nothing else changes (like volatility or the stock price). Remember, there is no such thing as a free lunch and because you chose to collect theta (cash) every day, you can't have your stock move, but if it does, you may be forced to negatively scalp your position, which means that you may lose money every time you have to buy or sell, but not always.

Some of you might be asking yourselves, why do I have to hedge, or who cares if I am a little short or a little long going into the close? Again, this all comes back to risk tolerance. Imagine that you sell 10 RIMM January 65-straddles for $5.50 and the stock closes up around $69. This leaves you short about 550 deltas going into the close, giving you a bearish bias.

In Figure 5.6 you can see the short straddle Greeks with RIMM, where I moved the price in the calculator to $69, note the negative 550 delta and negative 95 gamma.

You have a decision to make, At this point, if you think the stock will move lower, you might decide not to hedge (buy shares at $69). What if the next day the stock moves higher? If the stock gapped up to $73, for example, your position would then be short 830 deltas (we get that from the negative gamma). Not only are you now shorter, but you could have bought 550 shares at $69 and made $4 per share or $2,200 dollars to offset your losses, which now, without the hedge, would be totaling over $3,200.

This is where negative scalping can bite you, because now assume the opposite, that you bought 550 shares at $69, but the stock turned around and dropped to $66.

Figure 5.7 shows your Greeks with the same short straddle but with the purchase of 550 shares at $69 and then drops to $66. Note how the deltas are now getting longer!

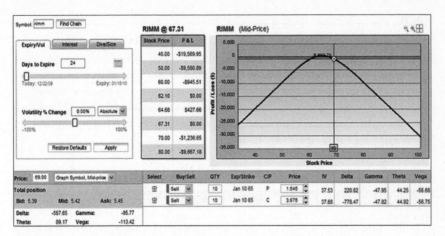

FIGURE 5.6 Short Straddle Risk Graph with RIMM Marked at $69

Take a look at your deltas now! You are now long 305 deltas, which means that in order to neutralize (hedge) you would have to sell 305 shares down here at $66 and take a $3 loss on 305 shares that you chose to buy at $69. Now what do you do?

Because you have long deltas, you want the stock to rise; if it drops more you will be hurting even more and if you hedge and it rallies, then you may feel equally as bad—what a spot to be in. As bad as this may seem, hedging is an art in itself. Overhedging and underhedging can equally be a problem. At the end of the day, having a strong knowledge of the stock that you are trading and its patterns of volatility, stock movement and news can help you not only select the appropriate strategy, but also adjust and hedge that position as you move forward in time.

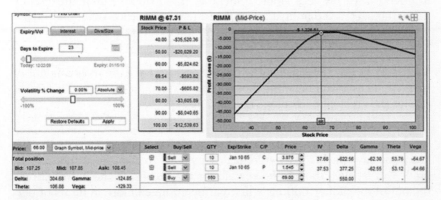

FIGURE 5.7 Risk Graph After RIMM Stock Drops to $66

Vega

Vega is the option's sensitivity to changes in implied volatility. If you look at an option chain and find an option with a vega of 0.20, this means that the value of the option will increase roughly 0.20 ($20) with a 1% *absolute* rise in volatility and will lose 0.20 with a 1% absolute decrease in volatility. Vega is *not* static and will change throughout an option's life. The more time an option has till expiration, the greater the vega when compared to the same strike in a nearer month.

TRADER TIP

Volatility going from 10% to 11% is a 1% absolute change as is volatility going from 99% to 100%. Absolute can be thought of as actual change, not percentage change.

Implied volatility in and of itself can be a complex concept to grasp and if you are a beginner, I don't expect you to completely get it, and that's okay!

Implied volatility is actually figured backward from an options price, so if people are paying more for options (which they tend to do in times of fear or when a stock starts to move around a lot) implied volatility will be on the rise. On the contrary, if there is no upcoming news and a stock seems like its settling into a range, implied volatility may be dropping.

So if the stock starts to move extremely fast (up or down) and implied volatility rises, the options with the greatest vega will have the most change in price (based on vega alone, remember they will also be influenced by delta, theta, etc.). Volatility affects the time-value portion of an option, but will cause the overall premium of that option to rise or fall.

Nominal Vega   Because at-the-money options have the most amount of time value, they will have the most nominal (amount) of vega. This is not always the greatest percentage change.

Vega as a Percentage of Price   Out-of-the-money options, both calls and puts, have the highest percentage sensitivity to changes in volatility. In other words, even though the vega looks the highest in the ATM options, the out-of-the-money options will be affected much more in terms of percentage change than the at- or in-the-money option.

Where Do You Find the Implied Volatility? Many brokers offer implied volatility (IV) right on their option chains, but better yet is to look at a graphical representation of IV over time. By doing this, you can get a better idea of where implied volatility is at present in relation to where it has been. This can help you adjust your risk. In other words, if IV seems relatively high and you are concerned that it might drop, maybe you might want to look at an option with a lower vega or just trade fewer contracts. On the flip side, if volatility seems cheap and you think it might rise, maybe you will look to purchase options with greater vega. In doing this, remember the other Greeks.

Every individual option has its own vega, but frequently professionals will reference the IV of the at-the-money options to gauge whether options in that month are relatively cheap or expensive as a whole.

Deep in-the-money options will have the least amount of vega in relation to their total price, and will therefore be least susceptible to changes in volatility in percentage terms.

TRADER TIP

If you are a beginner and just buying calls and puts, following my methods for long call and put will mitigate your vega risk. Certain vertical spreads will also neutralize your vega risk.

As shown in Figure 5.8, the darker line in the chart shows the IV of IBM at the money options. As you can see on the right side of the chart, the current IV reading doesn't seem extremely high or low relative to the rest of the chart, so at first glance a trader might have more of a neutral bias on volatility unless, of course, there is a slew of events on the horizon, which could be a catalyst for movement in IBM and thus an increase in volatility. Or perhaps, relative quiet is expected for a certain period of time, in which case a trader may be inclined to get short vega (sell options).

Rho

By definition, Rho is an option's sensitivity to changes in interest rates. Out of all the Greeks, Rho is the least important for most traders, especially those trading shorter-dated options. Rho is expressed in dollar terms and represents the change in the theoretical value of the option for a one percentage point (absolute) movement in interest rates.

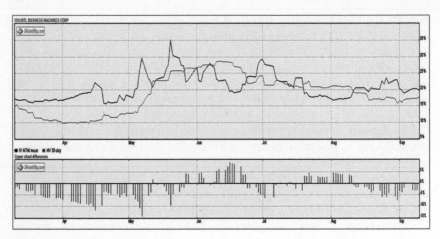

FIGURE 5.8   IBM IV and Historical Volatility Over the Past Six Months

Rho is greatest for *in-the-money* options with the furthest expiration date.

Interest rates affect the forward price of an underlying asset such as a stock or ETF. As interest rates increase, forwards rise, causing an increase in call values and a decrease in put values. Rho measures the amount of change.

Assume that you have a call with a theoretical value of $5, with a Rho value of 0.30. If the current interest rate of 3% increases to 4%, you should expect the value of the call to increase 30 cents to $5.30 (roughly).

In that same example, if it were a put with a Rho of −0.30 and a value of $5 (puts have negative Rho), that same change in interest rates would cause the put to drop 30 cents to $4.70.

Rho is generally the Greek you are going to be least concerned with if you are a retail investor/trader.

How interest rates affect options is discussed further in the advanced concepts in Chapter 8.

FINAL THOUGHTS

Greeks are similar to your driving and navigation instruments in your vehicle—they tell you exactly how your position (vehicle) is going to behave given certain changes in the marketplace. Delta tells you how fast your vehicle is going, gamma tells you whether that speed is accelerating or decelerating, and theta can be thought of as your cost of fuel to be in that trade. In some trades, you're actually collecting fuel to be in the trade. Vega tells you how much your position will get a push or pull from changes in the market around you. If you are long vega and the market or your stock is getting more volatile, that's good; if you are long vega and things are getting quiet in the markets, that's bad. The opposite is true if you are short. Remember, Rho has minimal impact for most of us. I find it helpful to associate complex concepts with things that Interact with every day. I encourage you to paper-trade all sorts of options before you trade with real money to observe and journal the Greeks in action.

CHAPTER 6

Strategy: The Basic Options Trades

Thus it is said that one who knows the enemy and knows himself will not be endangered in a hundred engagements. One who does not know the enemy but knows himself will sometimes be victorious, sometimes meet with defeat. One who knows neither the enemy nor himself will invariably be defeated in every engagement.

—Sun Tzu * Sun Pin
The Art of War

The ultimate goal of your options education should be to change your mind-set from "Should I buy or sell this stock?" to "What strategy would be appropriate for my thesis on this stock?"

You have now reached the point in your analysis where you should be ready to select a strategy. This will occur once you have found an underlying instrument to trade (stock, ETF, index, etc.) and done your homework both on that instrument as well as the overall markets.

Depending on how bullish, bearish, or indifferent you are, you will select the appropriate strategy to employ. Obviously, once you commit and make a trade, then money management, risk control, psychological control, and gut takes over.

In this chapter, I take you through the way I trade basic strategies and review them step by step from my perspective. My explanation of each strategy includes both factual characteristics as well as opinions of how I would personally use each strategy in addition to how I would position strikes, expiration dates, timing, premiums, and risks of each.

Sun Tzu's 2,500-year-old writings on strategy are not only applicable in politics, big business, organization, and even love, they are also extremely effective when it comes to trading tactics. Sun Tzu's wisdom on war offers many parallels to the markets. He discusses how people should react to certain scenarios on the battlefield and know their enemies. For just about every tactic the enemy throws at him, he has a counter-tactic. He also believed that defensive measures are equally as important and aggressive. In trading, sometimes a more defensive stance is the appropriate one. There are also times when you must walk away from a potential trade.

The plethora of options strategies are your tactics to act effectively against or in alliance with the market and its participants. Be sure you understand your tactic before employing it.

BASIC SINGLE OPTIONS STRATEGIES

Here I review the single options strategies for a long call, covered call (or buy-write), and long put. You will notice a great amount of detail in my explanation of the basics because these are the foundations for the more advanced strategies you learn later in Chapters 7 and 8, where I expect you to know the basic concepts.

THE LONG CALL

The characteristics, sentiment, and risk of a long call are:

- *Market sentiment.* Bullish
- *Risk.* Varies, but limited to premium paid
- *Potential reward.* Unlimited
- *Passage of time.* BAD
- *Probability characteristics.* Stock must rise in value, no statistical advantage, statistically you are at a disadvantage because you are paying time decay (or extrinsic value)
- *Time in trade.* Very short term (days) to very long term (a year or more)
- *When to apply this strategy.* You have a moderate to aggressive bullish opinion of the stock
- *How you will win.* Stock rises in value before expiration, greater than the amount of time value you paid
- *How you will get hurt.* Stock stays flat up to expiration; you will gradually lose your time value and retain your intrinsic value (if you had

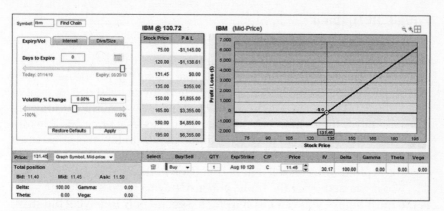

FIGURE 6.1 Long Call Risk Graph at Expiration

any to begin with). Stock drops; you will lose intrinsic value and you will gradually lose time value with no change in implied volatility

In Figure 6.1, you can see the risk graph for the long call. The horizontal line in the center is your breakeven point on expiration. Note the flat, limited risk as the stock moves lower and the unlimited profit indicated by the profit line at a 45-degree angle to the upside.

Long call Greek attributes are:

- Delta

  Positive—Delta can range from + 0.01 to + 1.00.

  The higher the delta purchased (> 0.65), the more the call will behave like the stock. A lower-delta call (< 0.30) will react minimally when the stock moves and will be extremely sensitive to changes in volatility on a percentage basis.

- Gamma

  Positive—Gamma is greatest at the money.

- Theta

  Short—You are paying theta; at-the-money options will pay the most theta.

- Vega

  Long—You are long vega, which means you want implied volatility to increase, which will benefit your trade. A decrease in implied volatility will hurt your position.

- Rho

  Long—You want interest rates to rise as a general rule, but they will have minimal impact on your position. This is the least worry you have in the trade.

Long Call Defined

The long call is typically the first option a retail investor will trade. Buying a call is a bullish act, in which the investor can choose a range of strike prices and deltas. There are multitudes of ways that a long call can be used. They can be day traded, swing traded, and even held for an extended amount of time using a LEAPS (a LEAPS is basically a long-term option). The long call gives the buyer the right to buy 100 shares at a specific price on or before a specific date. You do *not* have to have the money to buy the stock when you purchase a call option. As long as the stock is trading and your option has not expired, you can sell that option back to the market.

When you first enter the trade, you are "buying to open." Buying a call is the most bullish you can be on a stock, second only to buying the stock itself. I say this because when you buy a call, time is working against you and you *need* the stock to move higher to be profitable generally. (If the stock stays flat and volatility rises sharply, you can also get profitable.)

There are three basic types of call strike choices as discussed in Chapter 4.

1. **In the money.**

    In the money means that the call option has intrinsic, or real, value. In-the-money options have a strike price that is less than the current stock price. Deeper in-the-money calls (those with a delta of .70 or greater) tend to behave more like the stock, mimicking its moves with greater accuracy. These options will provide you with less leverage and will cost more than cheaper, lower delta options, but will tend to behave more like a stock. They are a good choice if you believe the stock will move higher, but are not thinking there will be a large, fast move in the stock. They also will be the least sensitive to changes in time and implied volatility on a percentage basis compared to at-the-money and out-of-the-money options. In-the-money calls will be more expensive than at- or out-of-the-money options.

2. **At the money.**

    These options have a strike price that is at or very close to the stock price. Typically, the delta of these options is around .40 to .60. At-the-money options have the most amount of time value relative to their overall price and are more expensive than out-of-the-money options. Because of their high level of time value, at-the-money options have the highest time decay, or theta, and the most sensitivity to volatility changes, or vega, as well as changes in time. They also have the most gamma, meaning that the delta will accelerate or decelerate the quickest. If you feel volatility is low and you believe that the stock is going to make a very fast, big move to the upside, at-the-money options can be considered; however, remember that you will be paying the most time value and thus losing the most theta with these options, so I do not typically recommend that traders buy at the money.

3. **Out of the money.**

The lottery tickets, out-of-the-money options, are the cheapest of the three. They have a strike price that is higher than the stock price. The analogy would be that you pay $500 for the right to buy (call) a $100,000 home for $110,000 (which is the strike price), which on the surface seems crazy, but what if the home value shot up to $120,000? The value of your call is now at least $10,000, a $9,500 premium to your $500 investment. This may sound far-fetched, but it also may entice you as a new options trader. This is one of the areas where options get their undeserved bad rap. Like the lottery tickets you buy in the store, these have a low probability of success, but, because of their price, have a high-profit potential and thus are a lure for some. If you remember the chapter on the Greeks and the delta discussion, you will remember that delta is also the percentage chance that an option will expire in the money. So if you buy a .15 delta call, you have a 15% shot, statistically, of that option being worth anything at expiration. Anything is the key word; .000001 is something and the delta is telling us that there is a 15% shot that this option will be worth less than zero. It is not very promising if you think about it like that. Out-of-the-money options can be used if you have a *very* strong belief that the stock will move very far, very fast. It helps to have a price target in mind and buy your call accordingly. In other words, if IBM is currently at $120 and you believe that it will be at $135 in two months, then buying the $130 call for .60 might be an option for you. However, remember that it is impossible for any person to predict a stock's movement with accuracy; just be sure that your price target is realistic based not only on the stock's volatility history, but also on an upcoming catalyst of some sort, especially if you are making a short-term trade.

The following is a step-by-step discussion of the basic checklist for buying a call.

Step 1. Locate a Potential Candidate   Finding potential stocks to trade can actually be quite easy; you can seek guidance from websites, TV, friends, workmates, family, and so on—you can even look around your home for ideas. Watch out for "Hot Tips," because it may be a surefire way to get burned and damage a friendship.

Be sure that once you have located a stock that you perform your due diligence. Remember, with a long call you *need* the stock to move higher, preferably quickly, during the trade. There are other options strategies that can be potentially profitable if you see a more moderate upside move.

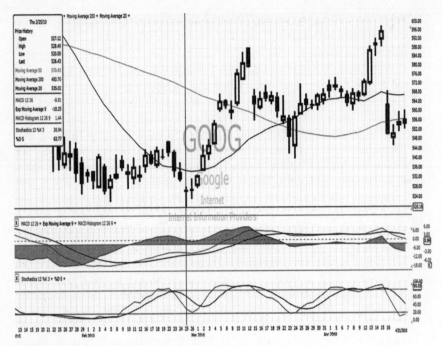

FIGURE 6.2 Monthly Chart in GOOG
Source: Lightwave.

When forming your trading plan, be sure to specify how you will go about locating potential trades. Many traders tend to focus on a group of stocks; this is acceptable, just be sure that you don't pigeonhole yourself into just one group that may not be performing well.

Practical Advice—Focus on the Same Group of Stocks/Sector I typically trade the same group of 15 stocks over and over. As a market maker, I became accustomed to trading the same issue all the time; therefore, I got extremely familiar with its earnings reports, trading patterns, volatility, and so on. One of the stocks I have traded over the years is Google (GOOG), which saw its stock price cut by 60% in less than six months back in November of 2008 (see Figure 6.2).

It took 2.5 years to get from its current price level to its all-time high previously, so I thought this move came rather quickly and put GOOG in a favorable P/E range compared to the past.

Fundamentally, I liked the stock. Aside from the financials, statistically Google is the world's largest search engine, on the cutting edge when it comes to technology and innovation, and they are always exploring new ways to make money.

Long call candidates are typically not stagnant stocks. Try to find a catalyst in upcoming news or in the marketplace. It is also never a bad thing to buy a call on weakness in your stock; however, use caution if a stock has dropped sharply because there may be a dramatic increase in implied volatility. One way to mitigate this volatility risk is to buy a deep in-the-money call.

Step 2: Fundamental Analysis   If you are a longer-term investor, you obviously want to invest in a company that will not only be around in a couple years, but will thrive. For day traders, fundamental analysis becomes less of an issue; in fact, there are some active traders who may trade a stock they know nothing about.

Fundamentals on GOOG   GOOG had a market cap of $92.5 billion and was one of the top performers in its sector back in late 2008. The company's after-tax profit margins were good compared to the rest of the sector, checking in at roughly 20% (as of the end of 2008) GOOG had been running at roughly a 25% profit margin over the past four years, on the average. This is only one indicator to consider; there are many other factors that can be used to evaluate a company's financial health and standing within its sector. Certainly GOOG was feeling some pain with the world in an economic downturn during that period.

I had noticed its ability to adapt in a changing marketplace. You may choose to go deeper into fundamentals, but I know that I am a shorter-term statistical trader and am satisfied with the small amount of research that I have done thus far.

TRADER TIP

Remember that my trading patterns and habits may not define your habits or patterns. What's important is that you remain consistent with your analysis points and know what analysts are projecting in the future for the company that you are trading.

Keep in mind that I had traded GOOG many times in the past and felt comfortable with the behavior of the stock and its volatility. One last thing I like to glance at—not that this is going to ensure success in a trade—is analyst recommendations. Out of the 21 major analysts that follow the stock, 16 rated it a "strong buy," 3 a "buy," and 2 a "hold." The mean 52-week price target for the stock is $475.

In reality, analysts give us their best guesses at the stock's direction based on certain factors that they deem important. They use models and make certain assumptions on trends. Even though I understand this risk, knowing that analysts are bullish makes me feel better about my trade.

GOOG Sentiment   GOOG hit $340 on January 6, 2009, and as of January 20, 2009, it has been hammered down to $295. The market has really been struggling with horrible employment numbers, foreclosures, and Bank of America asking for more TARP funds to help buffer the acquisition of Merrill Lynch. The situation seems bleak, but as a professional (and experiencing these types of situations before), I am deciding to take a calculated risk based on both historical valuations and the extremely oversold condition of the market at that time. Because of the lingering dangers, I would be much more apt to exit quickly with a smaller profit as opposed to taking more risk if the macro conditions were more favorable.

Step 3: Technical Analysis   I use technical analysis to confirm my bullish thinking and trigger my entry; the key to any market trading system is simplicity. You should have your stock, strategy, and money management plan in place before making any trade! The reason for the plan is to try to mitigate any surprises. However, even with the best planning, you can still be wrong in a trade at follow-up. Planning is also important in the mental preparation for your trade and to establish realistic expectations.

All trading systems are flawed; none will offer you perfect results. In fact, some don't offer any results at all. Look for a system or method that can offer you an edge, just a slight advantage when it comes to timing your entries and exits into and out of positions. The more complicated and longer trades take to analyze, the more difficult it will be for you to execute and be successful. I use a proprietary system that is easy for me to read and understand.

For my trades that I hold for less than a month, I look at 20-, 50-, and 200-day moving averages and look for where a stock is in relation to all of them. They help me to identify support and resistance points as well as determine trend.

A good rule of thumb is to look at the 200-day simple moving average (SMA) and look for your stock to be above it for a good long-term overall bullish trend. The 20 and 50 can offer you more short-term trend changes.

I also take a look at standard 20, two standard deviation Bollinger bands and look for oversold or overbought conditions. (This is an advanced technique that will require study; it is not intended for every trader.) But basically, I like to be a contrarian as a short-term trader. If a stock has breached the lower Bollinger band, but remains above its 200-SMA and let's say it's 20-, or 50-SMA, I would be a buyer on weakness.

Step 4: Selecting the Appropriate Option   Before clicking the buy button, be sure that the call you are selecting meets your trade-style objectives. Each and every trader will have a different pattern, different financial needs, and different goals and time frames to their trading. First and foremost, most traders have a hard time picking a stock that is going to move in the direction that they desire. In fact, it may be harder still to find an option with the best balance of leverage, probability of success, and enough time to expiry. Luckily, there are some simple guidelines that beginning traders can use to find the best potential call candidates.

If you want to trade an option that behaves the closest to the stock, look for a delta 0.70 to 0.90. This is my method and does not mean that every option with a 0.70 to 0.90 delta will behave exactly like the stock, nor does it mean that you will be successful trading this type of an option; it is purely a guideline. Trading a call with a high delta may solidify the relationship between stock and option (generally speaking, an option with a higher delta has a tendency to behave more like the stock). It will also help to ensure a high intrinsic-to-time ratio and will increase the chance that the option will move when the stock moves.

If you are still getting acquainted with the Greeks, a deep in-the-money call may be the best solution if you are just looking for leverage on your trades.

Buying a lower delta is not necessarily a bad thing; just understand that the relationship between stock and option will be more dependent on other factors, meaning that the stock may have to move further, faster for you to potentially profit. When placing a directional trade, in other words, if you are just buying a call because you feel the stock will increase in value, the delta that may *not* be desirable to purchase would be the 0.40 to 0.60 range, as the at-the-money options have the most amount of time value, relative to the other options. Remember, time value is the decaying part of the option (more time value means you must lose more per day to get to zero by expiration). Having the most amount of time value means the option is also the most sensitive to volatility changes.

Choosing the Right Delta For my GOOG example, I am staying in the money. I am executing this strategy for several reasons. As a rule, I like to buy a 0.70–0.90 delta option when I am making a single option directional bet. Here is my logic (usually it falls into line):

Delta and ATR: First, let's take a look at the average true range (ATR) of GOOG—the average deviation of GOOG over a recent month's time is $45. The ATR is a rolling 14-period average of a stock's greatest movement in that given time frame and can be used to measure minutes, days, weeks, months, and so on. ATR can be used not only to find your stop loss, but also to select the delta of your option, let me explain multiply the ATR of the time frame I think I will be in the trade times 1.2 to find a stop loss for my intended period. I do this to stay outside of the stock's normal variations.

To simplify the math: 45 (ATR) × 1.2 (my risk factor) = $54. This means that $54 would be my acceptable stop loss in the **stock**. This means that if the stock is trading at $300, I would subtract 54 from the current trading price to find where to place my stop order. In this case, $300 − $54 = $246. A friend of mine showed me a useful trick: You can subtract your stop-loss amount from the stock price and that's the strike that you buy. Again, this is just a formula that he uses and does not guarantee success in the trade. Using this formula, if GOOG is $300 and I subtract $54 (stop-loss amount) from it, I may purchase the 250 or 260 strike call, as long as it falls within the 0.70–0.90 delta range. The call I chose was the March 260 call for $51. If you're wondering why I chose March expiration, that is the next part in my checklist.

Choosing Expiration   Having enough time for your trade to work is a risk many options traders have to contend with. One of the ways to determine how much time to buy is to look back on your past trading history. If you have a history of being in trades for an average of a month, then maybe you should buy a minimum of 60 days to expiration (DTE). If you have never traded live before, you should practice trading your methods. Take a look at your practice trades in your virtual account and use those as a guide to how long you tend to be in trades. Before you begin to trade real money, be sure you understand all risks involved; as a general rule, you should place at least 25 or more trades in your virtual account and have a written trade plan before using real money.

I am typically an active-to-swing trader, meaning that I usually stay in my positions anywhere from a couple of minutes to about three days, maximum. Your time horizon is important to determine *before* you place your trade. It not only helps determine what strategy you employ, but also how much time you buy.

An Easy Formula   Because the long call has so much flexibility in the amount of time you can trade it, look back at your past two years of trading (or your total history if less than two years), then take all the trades you made and take the time you were in them and average them all. Then take your longest trade and average those two numbers (the average and the longest trade)—whatever number you come up with, add 30. The result is a good minimum days to expiration (DTE) to purchase when you are making trades. This is a formula that I have developed myself; it does not guarantee that you will always buy the right option, but it is a guideline to start with. I use this guideline because many traders that I have taught over the years have experienced a trade where they felt they needed to hold an option longer than expected. This situation is why I choose to add 30 (or more) days to my average trade length.

Obviously, purchasing more time for what you deem to be a more long-term investment is generally not a bad thing, although I would be careful buying less time, as we all know that sometimes things don't go exactly as planned in the market. Having more time in your trade may open some other options that you may not have had available to you if you were out of time. Most traders do not want to be long an option with 30 DTE or less, as time value begins to erode more exponentially the closer you get to expiry. Experienced traders who understand the more advanced behaviors of options may choose to trade front-month options.

Step 5: Monitoring the Trade   If the trade is going in your favor, you should be proactive in protecting your profits. In the beginning stages of the trade, you should have already either entered your stop loss or at least had a psychological stop level where you were going to exit the trade. As the stock moves higher, don't be afraid to move your stop loss higher as well. Trailing stops can also be used to lock in and protect your existing profits. Do *not* be greedy: Stick to your plan and execute it.

Setting Stops   I have found that if you are using the monthly ATR as your stop-loss gauge, it tends to put you in range of using the preceding method to find your delta. So the question is, now that I have chosen my option, do I set a stop loss or do I have to lose everything? Here is my method for the **option** stop loss: I take the ATR of the time frame that I want to be in the trade (monthly max); then I multiply it by 1.2 and then multiply by the delta.

So if my ATR is 45 and my option has a 0.70 delta, the math looks like this:

Entry Price [51] − ([45[ATR] ∗ 1.2] ∗ 0.70 DELTA) = stop loss amount of $37.80.

My stop-loss order would be placed at my entry price ([$51] − loss amount), or $16.20 in this case. This loss may seem steep, but remember that you were willing to originally tolerate a $54 loss in the stock, all the while having $300 per share tied up in the trade. You can obviously base your stop loss on the stock price if you wish; just test your method.

Moving Up Your Stops   If you buy a call you are obviously bullish and, hopefully, prior to getting into the trade, you have done your homework and have an understanding of the stock's ATR, normal volatility, earnings, news, and so on. In the practical application, I showed you how to use a stock's ATR to determine a realistic stop loss that won't get executed prematurely. Depending on the amount of time you plan on being in the trade, adjusting your stop losses higher may have a higher or lower priority. The shorter the duration of the trade, the more aggressive you may have to be in adjusting your stops.

For example, a short-term swing trader may buy a 75 delta call for $8 with the underlying stock at $50. His stop loss may be triggered by the stock if it drops to $45, based on his ATR and volatility assumptions. If the stock immediately rallies to $52, and moves the call to $9.50, the trader might want to move the stop up to $51 in the stock (trigger) or $8.50 in the call, ensuring a profit if the stock changes direction. This is a delicate science that cannot be mapped out in any book. The actions of the trader are predicated on his experience, risk tolerance, and trading history and patterns. In other words, if you are the type of trader that excels at the entry of the trade and typically find yourself in a profit right off the bat, but then giving it all back later, maybe you might employ the preceding method. Whereas, if you're typically stopped out prematurely, only to have the stock rally after you have exited, maybe you should be less aggressive with your stops or adjust the timing/methods you are using to enter your trades.

Repair versus Exit   Deciding to repair or completely abandon a trade has many determining factors. Some things to consider are:

- Has the fundamental picture changed in the stock?
- Have the charts broken down?
- Was there an earnings occurrence?
- Have you gone beyond your original stop-loss point?
- Is the trade consuming you?
- Do you really have enough time in your long call position to turn it into a spread?
- Will your repair not only be feasible, but dramatically improve the trade?
- If you extend the life of the trade, will the extra time for minimal loss recovery justify the capital committed to the trade?

TRADER TIP

If you have a profit, don't be afraid to take it or at least protect it with a trailing stop. Because of the nature of the call and its negative theta and sometimes close correlation with the stock, you are paying to be in the trade every day and if the stock moves drastically against you, your call may move drastically against you as well. Remember that because of leverage, your call costs much less than the stock and you need to focus on percentage returns in the option, not the dollar amount.

COVERED CALL (BUY-WRITE)

Each covered call (buy-write) is a combination of 100 shares of long stock and 1 short call sold against that long stock—it is still a bullish strategy.

- *Market sentiment.* Moderately bullish
- *Risk.* Long stock cost basis—Short call premium
- *Potential reward.* Limited, short call strike price minus net cost of stock (stock cost-call premium)
- *Passage of time.* Good
- *Probability characteristics.* Optimal situation would be for the stock to move to the call strike price and expire just a penny below (so you are not assigned). Because of the multitude of call strikes that you can sell and your original cost basis in the stock, the probability of profit in this trade varies.
- *Time in trade.* Typically covered calls are sold with less than 60 DTE, can be employed with more or less time, and are held until desired outcome is achieved or stock begins to plummet, in which case you may want to reevaluate the entire position.
- *When to apply this strategy.* You are overall bullish on a stock that you think may have a *temporary* pullback or will remain sideways (below the strike price that you sell).
- *How you will win.* Stock rises and stabilizes right at or just below the call strike that you sold on expiration. Or in some cases, the trader may desire that the stock be called away, meaning that the stock is above the short strike on expiration (breakeven at expiration = stock purchase price – call premium).
- *How you will get hurt.* Stock drops more than the amount of the call premium, which means that you are a net loser on the trade. If stock rises or stays flat, you will collect your theta and gain on your delta in the stock, which will always be greater than the delta in your call as long as the stock is *below* the strike price.[1]

Covered call Greek attributes are:

- Delta

  Positive. Delta can range from 0.01 to 0.99. You will always remain net long unless the stock moves up so high that the call delta rises to 1; if this has happened, you probably should have bought back the call a long time ago.

  The higher the delta purchased > -0.65, the more the put will behave like the stock. A lower delta put < -0.30 will react minimally when the stock moves and will be extremely sensitive to changes in volatility on a percentage basis.

- Gamma

  Negative, you are short a call option.

- Theta

  Long. You are collecting theta; at-the-money options will pay the most theta, and have the most time value; the goal in the covered call is to sell a call option with a high amount of time value at a strike that you believe the stock will stay **below** by the expiration date.

- Vega

  Short. You are short vega, which means that you want implied volatility to decrease; this will benefit your trade. An increase in implied volatility will hurt your position.

- Rho

  Short. You want interest rates to fall as a general rule, but they will have minimal impact on your position; this is the least worry you have in the trade.

In Figure 6.3, we see the Greeks in a covered call on Goldman Sachs, In this situation, the trader is long 100 shares of GS @140.00 and sell 1 June 150 call with 34 days till expiration for $4.42, reducing the cost basis of the stock down to $135.58, which would be the breakeven as well. Since the trader sold the 150 call, he has the potential to make $14.42 on the covered call and stock trade if it is left as is till expiration.

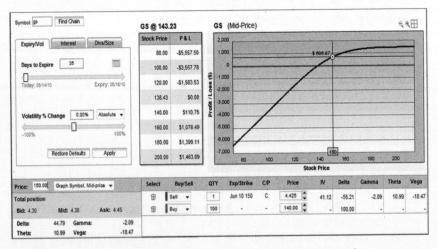

FIGURE 6.3 GS Buy-Write Risk Graph, with Greeks (Pre-Expiration)

Buy-Write/Covered Call Defined

Both the buy-write and covered call are similar; they both involve owning stock and selling a call against it. Remember that you must have 100 shares of stock long for every one call that you sell.

Both strategies are quasi-bullish strategies because at the end of the day you want the stock to move upward or at least remain stable, but not move lower. The basic difference between the two is really timing and intentions and I'll explain this later in detail.

Another important aspect of both strategies is that the sale of the call limits the stock's upside potential to the difference between the purchase price of the stock and the strike price plus the premium you receive for the call. This sacrifice to the upside allows the trader to reduce her cost basis and partially hedge against a pullback in the stock.

When a trader executes a buy-write (or a covered call) she should receive a premium for that call (not counting the cost of the stock). This premium, which can vary greatly depending on the stock price, its volatility, and which option is chosen, will be the total premium received in the trade (you can profit more than the premium received if the strike price is higher than the stock price).

If you were to purchase ABC stock for $50 and sell the 55 call for $1, the most you could make on this trade is $6, no matter how high the stock goes. Keep this in mind when choosing your call strike to sell.

TRADER TIP

A more advanced technique would be to buy back the call—potentially at a loss—if the stock began to rally, which would uncap the potential return.

Let's explore typical reasoning and application of the buy-write first. We will discuss the differences between it and the covered call shortly after.

A buy-write is the purchase of 100 shares of stock while simultaneously selling one call contract against it at the same time. Selling a call is a bearish act, and it may obligate the seller to deliver the stock at the strike price. This bearishness is offset by the purchase of the stock. Buy-write traders want to be long the stock, but may be concerned about a short-term pullback or they have a neutral view on the stock's direction and feel the yield they are collecting from the sale of the call is acceptable in the time they are in the trade. Buying a stock and selling a call may sound counterintuitive, but let's examine the components and see how they behave when combined.

Buying stock outright is one of the most bullish opinions and greatest downside risks you can have when compared to buying call options, which are lower in cost and thus lower in dollar risk.

Think about it—for every dollar the stock moves, if you own 100 shares of stock, you make $100 for every $1 the stock moves up (stock has 1 delta); same to the downside. If the stock falls a dollar, you lose $100.

The short call is extremely risky by itself; it is essentially as risky as shorting a stock. Don't forget that a stock can theoretically rise infinitely. A short call obligates the seller to deliver the shares of the underlying stock at a certain price (the strike price) on or potentially before expiration. A short call is also limited in profit, meaning that whatever a trader sells a call for is the maximum he can make in that trade—no matter how low the stock goes. When traders sell a call, it is most likely their intention to have the stock stay *below* the strike price they sell.

The short call benefits from the passage of time (positive theta), meaning that the trader will collect time decay (theta) each day. So why would a trader want to trade an option that seems so risky? There are a couple reasons why this may be viable. First, let's look back at a few statements: "A short call obligates the seller to deliver the shares of stock at a certain price (the strike price) on or potentially before expiration." The statement sounds a bit scary, but what if I added this statement: "The trader owns stock at a lower price than the strike price they sold"?

This statement means that if I own a stock for $50 and sell a 55 call for $1, I am obligated to sell the stock at $55, but I already own it at $50. Basically, I make a $5 profit, plus I still keep the $1 I originally brought in. Meaning that in this trade, I would have made $6, or 12% minus commissions.

The stock would have to be above $55 at expiration for me to be assigned (short call) on my option and forced to sell it. If, at expiration, the stock is below the strike price of the call I sold, I will retain the credit for selling the stock and I can repeat the process again. At this point, you may be thinking, this is a fantastic strategy, why doesn't everyone do it? Well, there is no such thing as a free lunch; and there are two important points. The first point is: If the stock falls, you *will* be at risk if the stock drops below your cost basis, all the way to zero.

You own the stock at $50 so you would suffer a $20 loss. The call you sold for a $1 might be worth nothing (if the trader wanted to buy back), which means you would make a $1 on the call, leaving you with a $19 net loss in the trade. Selling the call offers some income to offset costs in a trade, but it should not be construed as pure downside protection.

The second point is that selling a call against stock you own can potentially limit your upside potential. Keep that in mind if you believe that the stock is going to skyrocket to the upside. Buy-write traders tend to sell

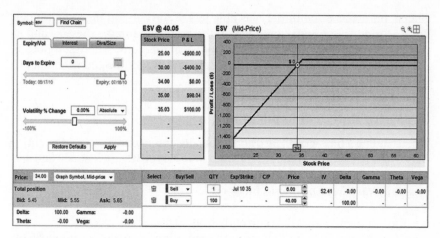

FIGURE 6.4 ESV Expiration Risk Graph

at the money options that have the most amount of time value so they can capture the highest yield.

TRADER TIP

Even though selling an in-the-money call seems tempting because of the higher premium received, remember that by selling the call you are *obligating* yourself to sell the stock at that strike. So if you bought stock at $40 and sold the 35 call for $6, you would make only $1 on the trade if the stock finished anywhere above 35 (your short call). That option had $5 of intrinsic, or parity, value, which you *lose* on expiration. What that in-the-money call did do was provide a hedge; it lowered your breakeven down to $34, which could be a hedge if you thought the stock would drop. Figure 6.4 is an example with ESV. Remember that if ESV finishes *anywhere* above 35 (short call strike) your stock will be called away.

BUY-WRITE VERSUS COVERED CALL

Let's now discuss the differences between the covered call and the buy-write. As I said earlier, it's really a question of timing and intention. The buy-write is just that—the simultaneous purchase of long stock and sale of a call. Generally the trader sells the at-the-money strike (if stock is $50, the trader may chose the 50 call). The intention is generally to have the stock called away from you, meaning that if the trader bought stock at $50, he would be forced to sell it at $50. That doesn't sound so great at first glance, but what if the trader was able to sell the call for $5? Even though the trader does not make anything on the stock, he retains the $5—and in this case would realize a 10% return less commissions. The issue here is that you have to be comfortable with only making $5; limited profit can in itself be a risk to some traders.

Buy-Write Practical Application

When trading a buy-write, the trader typically enters one price for the entire trade. In other words, if the trader wanted to buy ABC stock at $50 and sell the March 50 call for $5. The buy-write trade may be entered as follows (this may vary from broker to broker):

- Buy 100 shares of ABC (currently trading $50 at the ask).
- Sell 1 March 50 call (40 days until expiration) (currently trading $5 on the bid).
- Limit price of $45 (stock ask minus option bid = $45).

Note how the limit price is just one price, it does *not* specify the call or stock amounts individually.

There may be a variation in the prices of the stock and option when done this way, meaning that you might own stock at $50.50 and be short a call at $5.50, and so on. Generally speaking, the trade should take place within the market (between bid-ask spreads of both stock and option).[2]

TRADER TIP

Buy-writes are usually done with either the intention of being called out and capturing the yield of the call or they are a way to acquire stock for a lower cost basis. Remember that the covered call and the short put are identical in risk. Some traders use short puts to acquire stock at a cheaper price. The buy-write can work the same way, only you start off with the shares already in your account. If the stock stays below your strike price, you retain the credit you received for the call and keep your stock, now at a better price.

Covered Call Practical Application

The covered call is basically the same in principle, but typically the trader is selling a call against stock he already owns. Covered call writers may also have a tendency to want to keep their stock, meaning they may be slightly less aggressive in selling their calls opting to sell an out-of-the-money call versus at the money. This decision may be for sentimental value (stock has been gifted to them), general desire to hold the stock in the belief that it will continue to rise in value, or for tax reasons. Be sure to consult a qualified tax advisor for information.

Covered call writers sometimes use the term *renting* their stock out. This term is used because for both the buy-write and covered call the stock is used as collateral for the short call. The long stock is a hedge or an offset for the upside risk of a short call.

Both covered call and buy-write traders are generally bullish on their stocks, but the timing of their trades may vary slightly. Buy-write traders may enter a position after a recent retracement in the market, or at a time they deem appropriate for a bullish entry—meaning that they would want the stock to rally from that point because their main goal is to collect the premium from the short call and have the stock called away. Covered-call traders may actually do the exact opposite. Because covered-call traders typically want to hold on to their shares, they may actually time the selling of their call after a recent rally ahead of a retracement. By doing so, the traders are capturing more premium and potentially buying the call back after the stock retraces back down. This is only one technique; some traders prefer to let the option expire.

In closing, for both the covered call and buy-write, most want the stock to be moderately bullish.

Covered Call and the Short Put, A Love Story

The covered call/buy-write is similar in risk and reward to a naked short put (remember the synthetics). For traders who want similar risk/reward characteristics as the covered call, but don't yet own the stock, short puts may offer an alternative. Your broker will also only require a portion of the total risk of the short put as margin, which may be more cost-effective. When you sell a short put, you want the stock to just stay right above the strike that you sold. If that happens you will retain the credit you sold it for. If the stock falls below the put strike you sold on expiration, you may be forced to purchase the stock at the strike price of the put you sold. You will still retain the credit you sold it for, thus reducing your cost basis in the stock. Then you can begin to sell traditional covered calls on the stock now in your account!

Volatility and the Covered Call

Because we are selling options in the covered call and buy-write, you must be cognizant of volatility and use volatility to your advantage.

Many of us have opinions about where volatility is going, but for the retail investor, it's not just the direction of volatility, but what you should be doing with your trades given certain circumstances.

Volatility is all relative. When traders say, "Vol is expensive," typically they are making reference to the implied volatility of the options compared to how the underlying instrument is moving or its past observed (historical) volatility. Frankly, I have found that many new traders don't really know what that all means and even if they do, they are unsure exactly what to do. Most professional options market makers make most of their bets or assume a large portion of their risk based on volatility assumptions, so it's tough when you're a retail trader asking a professional what she thinks because most market makers try to have minimal bias when it comes to a stock's direction. They are typically hedging their positions, thus creating a delta-neutral net position, which is directionless.

What you should know is that options and volatility get more expensive for a reason, but those reasons may have less of an impact on you (or more) depending on the type of trader that you are. For longer-term traders, short-term bursts of volatility may offer opportunities and vice versa. For shorter-term traders, large variations in volatility may make it a bit harder to navigate and get it right, because they have less time to react and adjust.

Implied volatility rises because traders are willing or paying more for options because of increased underlying price oscillations or a shift in the future of the fundamentals of a stock or economy. Even Mother Nature can bring increased volatility; for example, hurricane season can increase the implied volatility of oil futures options. For covered call writers, this elevated volatility means increased premiums and higher potential returns (and risk).

Implied volatility can drop for the opposite reasons like slower moving stock, strong stable stock fundamentals (a no-leverage, larger cap blue chip–type company) or the end of a historically volatile weather season.

Most new options traders begin with the basic options strategies: long call, long put, covered call. Although all of these strategies are affected by volatility, the covered call is what I sometimes call the *bridge* strategy. I see it as the strategy that crosses stock traders to options traders. For covered call traders who own stock longer term, elevated volatility (high relative VIX) environments are a benefit (and sometimes a curse). Because many of these bridge options traders are inexperienced, it may be tougher for them to understand the volatility concepts.

Remember how I said earlier that options get more expensive in volatile markets? Well, yes, that means that you may be able to sell your covered call for more money, but that also means that stock may have a higher probability of moving lower or up through your short call, limiting your upside.

When you sell a call against long stock; your max profit is your strike + premium – cost basis in the stock. The key to this strategy is finding a stock that you know, that may have more expensive options due to things happening around it.

For example, let's assume that you are long JPM stock and you notice that IV is elevated. JPM does not necessarily have any news that is affecting it directly; however, GS is under investigation by the SEC. Obviously, JPM could be affected by a negative outcome in GS, and chances are that the effects won't be as severe, but you are still able to get a good amount of premium in JPM. This is one strategy that can be used, it certainly doesn't do away with risk, but it at least may mitigate it.

Also remember that you typically want to time the sale of a covered call when a stock is up but not selling off. Calls are more expensive when stocks are higher and you will be able to potentially collect a higher premium when a stock is up but beginning to weaken as opposed to it already falling off a cliff. Some traders use technical indicators such as MACD and momentum studies to target a weakening trend and sell their covered calls when they notice the beginning of a change in trend.

At the end of the day, if you are happy with the amount of premium that you are receiving, and you have set up the trade the way that you want with a plan in place, volatility may not be a huge concern. Just be aware of the effects it will have on your position and how you can maximize profit and limit loss using it.

Finding the Trade

Targeting a covered call candidate is a bit easier than a long call candidate. You are still bullish and you certainly don't want the stock to drop sharply, but in many situations, it's easy to find a stock that is in a range or you think will do nothing. Unlike the long call, you do *not* necessarily need the stock to move higher for you to make money As long as the stock stays at or just below your call strike, you're golden.

Delta In the covered call, focusing on delta is probably *not* the best way to go about targeting your short call. There are four things you need to figure out before selecting your option:

1. Resistance
   a. Find a resistance point that you think the stock will have trouble getting through. This could be a 52-week high, moving average, price level that it struggled at before, even a price target that analysts set. That is where you may consider selling the call.

2. Support
   a. If the stock were to drop, how far do you think it will go? This may be the level that you buy back your call (massaging the trade) or it may be the amount of hedge or protection you will want to sell the call for. This will be a balancing act, because if you are super bullish on the stock, you may move your strike price higher to allow appreciation in the stock and receive less premium, where if you think the stock could drop a large amount, you may reduce your short-call strike and get more premium as a hedge.

3. Premium
   a. The most important thing to look at is the amount of premium you are receiving for your short call. Selling a call for 20 cents or less may not be worth it (unless the stock is below $15). Make your trade worth it. If you have a $50 stock and you can only sell the $55 call for 0.25, is it worth it? If you think the stock is just going to rocket to $54.99 and stay there, then maybe, but if you think the stock could easily drop $2 or $3, maybe you need to lower your strike or even find another stock. The amount of premium you receive is predicated on time and volatility. The more time you have in your option, the more credit you should receive. This is again another balancing act, finding the perfect balance between time and premium received.

4. Timing
   a. I may have problems with commitment, but I also have a problem tying up my stock in a trade for a long period of time. If you remember our Greek discussions, theta tends to accelerate dramatically in the last 30 days of an option's life. With that said, covered calls and buy-writes, because they involve selling an option, should typically be done with less than 60 days until expiration. I find that this time frame allows you to get a decent amount of premium, good theta, and not tie yourself to the trade for too long. Remember that you can always sell another call if you choose. Also, in the last 30 days of an option's life, if the stock dips sharply, you may see that call drop to 0.05 or 10 cents, which you can buy it back and resell another call if the stock rallies.

Technical Analysis You are looking to sell calls with a strike price at or near resistance levels in the chart of the stock you are trading. Time the sale of the covered call when you notice momentum slowing down or a capitulation buy, which precedes a reversal. You will want to sell your call before the stock begins to sell off. Use overbought indicators as well as trend indicators such as MACD and stochastics to spot a slowing trend. The overall long-term trend of the stock should still be bullish.

Exiting Because the covered call is still a moderately bullish strategy with a large amount of potential downside (you will still own the stock), you must use similar risk management and exit strategies like you would if you bought stock alone. You can buy and sell the short call, as the stock fluctuates in a range (sell the call when stock is up and buy it back when stock falls). But if the stock seems like it may keep dropping, it might be time to cover your long stock position as well.

LONG PUT

Long puts can be a lower-risk alternative to shorting a stock. In fact, in some stocks that you cannot short, a put may be your only method of expressing a bearish opinion.

The characteristics, sentiment, and risk of a long put:

- *Market sentiment.* Very Bearish. You *need* stock to move lower.
- *Risk.* Varies, but limited to premium paid, less than shorting stock naked.
- *Potential reward.* Limited to strike value (a stock can fall only to zero).
- *Passage of time.* BAD.
- *Probability characteristics.* Stock *must* fall in value, no statistical advantage; statistically you are at a disadvantage because you are paying time decay and your breakeven is *lower* compared to short stock.
- *Time in trade.* Very short term (days) to very long term (year or more).
- *When to apply this strategy.* You have a moderate to extremely aggressive bearish opinion of the stock.
- *How you will win.* Stock falls in value before expiration, greater than the amount of time value you paid or below your breakeven by expiration.
- (*Breakeven at expiration* = *strike price – premium paid*)
- *How you will get hurt.*
  - *Stock stays flat up to expiration.* You will gradually lose your time value and retain your intrinsic value if you had any to begin with.
  - *Stock rises.* You will lose intrinsic value and you will gradually lose time value with no change in implied volatility.

Some long put Greek attributes:
- **Delta**
  Negative—Delta can range from $-.01$ to -1.

The higher the delta purchased > − 0.65, the more the put will behave like the stock. A lower delta put < − 0.30 will react minimally
when the stock moves and will be extremely sensitive to changes
in volatility on a percentage basis. Put deltas are *always* negative,
as they have an inverse P&L relationship to stock.

- **Gamma**

  Positive—Gamma is greatest at the money.

- **Theta**

  Short. You are paying theta, at the money options will pay the most
  theta, and have the most time value.

- **Vega**

  Long. You are long vega, which means that you want implied volatility to increase. This will benefit your trade. A decrease in implied
  volatility will hurt your position.

- **Rho**

  Short. You want interest rates to fall as a general rule, but they will
  have minimal impact on your position. This is the least worry you
  have in the trade.

In Figure 6.5 you can see the similar limited risk characteristics the
long put shares when compared to the long call, except the risk is now to
the upside. Of course, profitability is also reversed, because puts get more
expensive when stocks drop. Put profits are also limited, because a stock
can drop only to zero.

Long Put Defined

The long put is typically a bit more difficult to understand because of its
negative correlation with the underlying stock. The put rises in value as

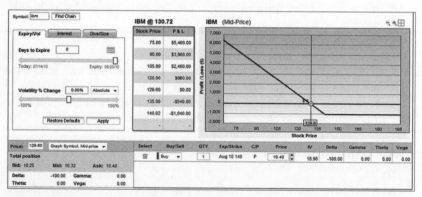

FIGURE 6.5 Long Put Expiration Risk Graph

the underlying stock drops and falls in value when it rises. This can be counterintuitive for the beginner. Buying a put is a bearish act in which the investor can choose a range of strike prices and deltas. It is an alternative to shorting a stock. Buying a put is limited in risk to the premium paid, similar to the long call. You do *not* have to have the cash or margin required to short stock when you purchase a put.

Choose an In-the-Money Put to Synthesize a Short Stock Position In the money means that the put option has intrinsic or real value. In-the-money options have a strike price that is higher than the current stock price. Deeper in-the-money puts (those with a delta of −0.65 to −1) tend to behave more like the stock, mimicking its moves with greater accuracy. Don't forget that puts will have an *inverse* relationship to the stock.

These options will provide you with less leverage and will cost more than cheaper, lower delta options, but will tend to behave more like a stock. They are a good choice if you believe the stock will move lower, but are not thinking there will be a large fast move in the stock. They also will be the least sensitive to changes in time and implied volatility on a percentage basis compared to at-the-money and out-of-the-money options. In-the-money puts will be more expensive than at- or out-of-the-money options.[3]

At-the-Money Put—Delta of −0.65 to −0.35 At- or near-the-money options have the highest amount of time value and thus the most sensitivity to changes in volatility, as well as the greatest theta, on a dollar basis than any other option. Unless you are making your bets on volatility, at-the-money options can be the worst choice, in that they may have more volatile profit and loss swings with changes in delta, volatility, and time all having great potential influence on the price of these options.

Out-of-the-Money Put—Delta of −0.35 to −0.01 They are the lottery tickets, as I like to call them. Out-of-the-money options are cheap for a reason. When you purchase an out-of-the-money put, be sure to examine its breakeven (put strike-premium) and make sure that level is where you think the stock can be below by expiration. Out-of-the-money options may require the stock to move fast and far down for you to be profitable. If you believe a stock is going to fall off a cliff and do so in a volatile manner, an out-of-the-money option can be used. These may also be used as inexpensive, protective insurance policies against long stock positions, if you want to protect against a catastrophic loss.

Short Stock versus Long Put

As an alternative to selling a stock short, options traders have the long put. In a short sale, the investor borrows the shares, sells them on the exchange, and delivers (buys back) the borrowed shares to complete the transaction. At some point in the future, the investor will buy the shares in the market at a lower price and return them to the party that loaned them. How hard is this to do? For shares that are fairly liquid, selling short can be accomplished through most brokers so long as you have a margin account. There will be requirements from your broker concerning how much cash you maintain in your account to be sure you can buy the shares back, particularly if the share price moves against you. There may be additional fees/interest charged for borrowing the shares in addition to possible commissions. Still, an investor who is determined to sell short will often be able to do so as long as the stock is not hard or impossible to borrow, which in that case, the long put is the only way to express a bearish opinion and profit from a subsequent drop in stock value.

TRADER TIP

Hard to borrow means that there are little or no shares in the float to borrow and thus the stock cannot be shorted any more than it already is. Some stocks are restricted from short selling altogether. If the short interest is really high in a stock and the stock becomes hard to borrow, there may be fees and costs associated with staying in a short stock position in addition to the possibility of being "bought in," which results in a potentially disadvantaged closing of the position by your broker buying shares in the open market. Your broker publishes a daily list of all stocks that are "hard to borrow."

However, from a risk point of view, the short stock investor is exposed to any increase in the share price. Increases can result in margin "calls," which are demands for additional margin to cover potential losses. Many investors are, rightly, reluctant to take on this form of risk.

If you believe that prices are going to drop it may behoove you to practice and master the long put strategy. Buying a put is a specialized form of investment that may not be suitable for every investor because of its unique behavior, but unlike short stock, risk is limited.

Following is a basic checklist for buying a put.

Step 1. Locate a Potential Candidate   Similar to finding a call candidate, finding potential stocks to trade puts on can be straightforward, but does require a shift in your thought process. Calls get more expensive as stocks rise, enabling you to take advantage of a stock's rise in value. Puts get more expensive as stocks fall in value, which is where investors can sometimes get confused.

Most investors tend to be bullish on stocks; that is, they tend to place trades in anticipation of a stock rising in value. When you think about it, investing in a company that you believe in, with hopes that it will become more and more profitable, is not only intuitive, it's a core social belief that many of us have; therefore, shorting stocks or buying puts seems strange to man.

You as an investor can take advantage of momentary or more prolonged downward trends in stocks by taking a short position in the stock, but shorting stock outright can be extremely risky. In fact, short stock has unlimited risk because a stock can theoretically rise to infinity. Conversely, the reward in shorting a stock is capped at the short sale price and will only reach maximum value if the stock price falls to zero.

Many seem to think, for some reason, that by taking a short position, they are "doing something wrong." What is scary is that regulators around the world took this view in September 2008 when the SEC banned short selling 799 financial companies, which was just absurd.

Then-SEC chairman Christopher Cox said, "The Commission is committed to using every weapon in its arsenal to combat market manipulation that threatens investors and capital markets. The emergency order temporarily banning short selling of financial stocks will restore equilibrium to markets. This action, which would not be necessary in a well-functioning market, is temporary in nature and part of the comprehensive set of steps being taken by the Federal Reserve, the Treasury, and the Congress."*

Didn't this restriction not qualify as "market manipulation"? But I digress.

It is my firm belief that without buyers and sellers together, a stock's true value in the marketplace would be hard to determine. Stocks can sometimes get relatively overpriced. If you disagree, take a look back at some of the dot-com companies of the mid- and late 1990s; some of these companies had little or no cash, no revenue, and maybe were in business for a couple months and yet were trading publicly at astronomic values. In my opinion, a company that is worth zero (or less) on paper with no history of revenue and no proven business model probably shouldn't have a market cap of $500 million. This is just an example; that is not to say there were not many great companies that emerged during that time. My point is that the market needs the buyer and the seller together to discover the best price, and it is not necessarily a bad thing if you think a stock is overpriced.

How to determine whether you want to buy a put on a stock is obviously a decision you must make for yourself. As you search for potential put candidates, keep in mind that you may be targeting companies that

---

*www.sec.gov/news/press/2008/2008-211.htm

do not have the strongest balance sheets, or may not be the best in their sector. Looking for the weaklings in a sector that have had their prices inflated based on the sector as a whole and not on their ability to earn and grow may be a trigger.

Increasing short interest in a stock may be a sign that more and more investors are beginning to express a negative sentiment in the stock is another way to sniff out potential upcoming weakness.

Be a Contrarian Of course, there is the contrarian strategy that looks for stocks that have been on a rocket to the upside and have been listed as a "strong buy" from the majority of analysts that follow them for some time. This sort of price action and hype can drive a stock price way beyond reasonable price to earnings levels and if the stock just falters slightly, shares can get slammed. This was the case with GOOG, which could do no wrong up until January 2010, when Google decided to quit China. Shares struggled for many months after. Ahead of that, Jim Cramer was jumping around with a Goggle $700 sign on his forehead. I was even caught up in the issue myself. Remember this stock was a long call trade a year earlier (see Figure 6.6).

The same tools and sources that are used to find long call candidates may also be used to search for a put (obviously you are looking for bearish sentiment).

Once you have located a stock you need to perform your due diligence. This process may include reading the analysts' reports, checking the news, indicators, past earnings dates and results, and noting upcoming earnings. Remember, you are looking for potential company weakness here.

FIGURE 6.6 GOOG Monthly Chart
Source: Courtesy of Lightwave.

Try to find news that you think will develop into something bigger. In other words, bad news isn't enough. Look for something that you feel leaves a large amount of uncertainty in the stock's future or something that may worsen as time goes on.

When forming your trading plan, be sure to specify how you will go about locating potential trades, in order to remain consistent. Many traders tend to focus on a group of stocks—this strategy is acceptable as well.

I have found in my trading that in many cases stocks tend to fall faster than they rise. If you look at broad-market indexes such as the Dow, Nasdaq, and S&P 500, you will notice that just about all three were at relative lows in early 2003; it took them all about four years to reach their five-year-high points, which came mid-2007 and less than a year and a half to return to their 2002–2003 levels.

The point I am making here is that greed can be a dominant factor in the marketplace. However, when fear takes hold, the corrections can come quickly and sharply.

Before I make any trade, I personally want to take note of how my stock has performed recently. For instance, each day a stock closes higher I have found that it becomes statistically less probable that the stock will continue to rise another day. Again, this is just my technique. It does not mean that this will work for everyone. Certainly a stock can drop after a single bullish day.

Step 2. Fundamental Analysis   Some traders look for certain characteristics in the companies in which they choose to take a short position. As with trading to the long side, fundamental analysis (which means analyzing a company's financial statements, management, and competitors) becomes much more important with regard to longer-term investing. When I buy a put, I look for potential future weakness in a company. For instance, maybe the company is dominated by another in its sector and is losing market share; possibly the company's products are not sustainable in the long term because of changes in technology. Eastman Kodak (EK) comes to mind.

Example: Eastman Kodak, A Company That Lost its Way   Kodak was known for its film and when I was young everyone needed film for all cameras, personal and professional. With the advent of digital image technology and the costs of that technology plunging, Eastman Kodak has tried to reinvent itself because mass demand for their film is now more of a niche demand. What was once an $80-per-share Dow component bellwether of corporate America has become a company with a $1 billion market cap trading around $4, in February 2009. This is only an example and I am by no means saying that Eastman Kodak is a short candidate or a bad company.

FIGURE 6.7 JPM Weekly Chart
Source: Courtesy of Lightwave.

This example was meant to illustrate how the fundamentals of a company can play a role. In Eastman Kodak's case, it was the potential of failing to adjust to a changing marketplace. Fast forward to July 2010—Eastman Kodak remained at about $4 to $5.

For day traders, short or long fundamental analysis generally becomes less of a concern. In fact, there are some active traders who may trade a stock they know nothing about. Personally, I feel that having knowledge and a level of familiarity with a company and its sector can only benefit you and increase your confidence in your trading decisions.

Fundamental Analysis Example JPM   For this example, I am going to use financial company JPMorgan Chase (JPM; see Figure 6.7). As many of you know, banks were under extreme pressure in late 2008 and most had seen their stock prices cut substantially. JPM is the largest in its sector in terms of market capitalization, which is something that I tend to read as bullish—but given the current circumstances I am bearish. Here is why. The potential creation of a "bad bank" that will aggregate all the toxic assets in our current banking system may help banks get back on their feet and enable them to resume lending. The issue with this "bad bank," in my mind, is that the banks selling the debt will have to assign a value. This value will probably be deeply discounted, even from current valuations. Remember, this bank is being formed along with private funds, which will most likely not want to pony up for these assets. In addition, in my opinion and based on many expert analysts' opinions, JPM's peers have been priced for nationalization. There is certainly no guarantee of this, and JPM, like

Goldman Sachs (GS) is a brokerage firm as well. The difference between the two is that JPM is also Chase Bank, which gives it added exposure. Goldman Sachs does not have the banking exposure because it has only recently become a bank holding company as of September 2008. I say this because it is important when you are comparing companies to be sure you're looking at apples to apples, not apples to oranges. (February 12, 2009: the market is down substantially, dragging JPM down as well. I will most likely wait until the market is rallying before placing my trade.)

This may be a trade that I will have for some time, as my goal for this trade is to make 10% to 20% in less than a month's time, with a stop loss of 40%. I will discuss these numbers later. Setting goals as well as stop losses in your account is key to good money management and potential success.

Step 3. What Type of Trade Will This Be? For this trade, I had chosen to commit myself in the trade up to a month because I feel that it may be some time before the trade works out, as the market is in a period of high volatility. It is important to determine your intended time frame *before* you place your trade, because this will influence the type of options strategy you employ as well as the expiry date you choose. In early 2009, the market had been struggling with horrible employment numbers, foreclosures, and many companies swinging to losses in the first quarter of 2009. Even with all this, I want to enter on a rally. I prefer to enter when the market is rallying because volatility typically comes in when the market is moving higher. When traders buy a put, they are long vega. In other words, they will benefit from a rise in volatility. Conversely, if implied volatility drops, long puts may lose some of their value.

Step 4. Technical Analysis I use technicals to confirm my bearish thinking and trigger my entries and exits; the key to any market-trading system is simplicity. Based on experience, you should have your stock, strategy, and money-management plan in place before making any trade! The reason for the plan is to try to mitigate any surprises. However, even with the best planning, you can still be wrong in a trade at follow-up. Planning is also important in the mental preparation for your trade, and to establish realistic expectations. My indicator is showing strong bearish trends over the long term, but suggesting a potential bounce from the 24.55 level (where JPM is currently trading), I am going to wait until my indicators show me a more advantageous entry. Again, this is only software; it cannot assure me a profitable trade, nor does it know exactly what a stock will do. I am only using it to interpret patterns.

Step 5. Selecting the Appropriate Put Option So you have already decided to trade a put. Before clicking the buy button, be sure that the trade you are selecting meets your trade-style objectives. Traders will have different patterns, different financial needs, and different goals and time frames to their trading. First and foremost, most traders have a hard enough time picking a stock that is going to move in the direction that they desire. In fact, it may be harder still to find an option with the best balance of leverage, probability of success, and enough time to expiry. Luckily there are some simple guidelines that beginning traders can use to find the best potential put candidates.

As a guideline, if you want to trade a put that behaves the closest to the stock, look for a delta −0.70 to −0.90. This is *my* method and does not mean that every option with a −0.70 to −0.90 delta will behave exactly like the stock, nor does it mean that you will be successful trading this type of an option. Trading a put with a higher delta may solidify the relationship between stock and option (generally speaking, an option with a higher delta +0.75 for calls and −0.75 for puts has a tendency to behave more like the stock). This could help ensure a higher intrinsic-to-time ratio and may increase the chance that the option will move when the stock moves. Buying a lower delta is not necessarily a bad thing; just understand that the relationship between stock and option will be more dependent on other factors, meaning that the stock may have to move further and faster for you to potentially profit. In other words, when placing a directional trade—if you are just buying a put because you feel the stock will decrease in value in my opinion—the undesirable delta to purchase would be the −0.40 to −0.60 range, as the at-the-money options have the most amount of time value relative to other options. Remember, time value is the decaying part of the option (more time value means that you must lose more per day to get to zero by expiration). Having the most amount of time value means that the option is also the most sensitive to volatility changes.

Strike Selection   For my JPM example, I stayed in the money. Remember that I executed this strategy for several reasons. As a rule, I like to buy a put with a −0.70 to −0.90 delta. Here is my logic (usually it falls into line): First, let's take a look at the monthly average true range (ATR) of JPM—the average deviation of JPM over a recent month's time is about $10. The ATR is a rolling 14-period average of a stock's greatest movement in that given time frame and can be used to measure minutes, days, weeks, and months. Just as I did with the call, I use ATR as a gauge to place my stop losses. I multiply the ATR by 1.2 to find a stop loss for my intended period. I use this formula to stay outside of the stock's normal variations. This is a personal preference. To simplify the math: 10 (ATR) × 1.2 (my risk factor) = $12. This means that $12 would be my acceptable stop loss in the stock. This means that if the stock is currently trading at $26, I would add (because we are going short) $12 from the current trading price to find where to place my stop order. In this case, $26 + $12 = $38. Remember our call delta trick? With puts, you can **add** your stop-loss amount from the stock price and that's the put strike that you buy. Again, this is just a formula that he uses and does not guarantee success in the trade. Using this formula, if JPM is $26 and I add $12 to it, I may purchase the $37.50 or $40 put, as long as it falls within the −0.70 to −0.90 delta range. The put I chose was the June $37.50 put for $13.50. If you're wondering why I chose a June expiration, see the next section in my checklist.

Now how do we set the stop loss for that option? Here is my method: I take the ATR of the time frame that I want to be in the trade (*monthly max*); then I multiply it by 1.2 and then multiply by the delta.

So, for example, if my monthly ATR is 10 and my option has a −0.71 delta the math looks like this:

Entry price [13.50 − (10[ATR] ∗ 1.2) ∗ 0.71[DELTA]) = stop loss at placed @$5, which would be a max loss of $8.50.

My stop-loss order would be placed at the entry price ([$13.50] + loss amount [$8.50]), or $5 in this case. Remember that puts go up in value as the underlying stock drops.

This loss may seem steep, but remember that you were willing to originally tolerate a $12 loss in the stock, all the while having $26 per share tied up in the trade.

Choosing the Right Expiration　　Having enough time for your trade to work is a risk that many options traders have to contend with. This is important whether you are trading puts or calls. One of the ways to determine how much time to buy is to look back on your past trading history. If you have a history of being in trades for an average of a month, then maybe you should buy a minimum of 60 days to expiration (DTE). If you have never traded live before, you should practice trading your methods before going live. Take a look at your practice trades in your virtual account and use those as a guide to how long you tend to be in trades. Before you begin to trade real money, be sure you understand all risks involved. As a general rule, you should place at least 25 or more trades in your virtual account and have a written trade plan before using real money.

Here is a straightforward formula that I have found useful.

Look back at your past two years of trading (or your total history if less than two years), then take all the trades you made and take the time you were in them and average them all out. Next, take your longest trade and average trade time and average those two numbers out (the average and the longest trade)—whatever number you come up with, add 30. The result is a good minimum DTE to purchase when you are making trades. This is a formula that I have developed myself; it does not guarantee that you will always buy the right option, but it is a guideline to start with. I use this guideline because many traders I have taught over the years have experienced a trade where they felt they needed to hold an option longer than expected. This situation is why I choose to add 30 (or more) days to my average trade length.

Obviously, purchasing more time for what you deem to be a more long-term investment is generally not a bad thing, although I would be careful buying less time, as we all know that sometimes things don't go exactly as planned in the market. Having more time in your trade may open some other alternatives that you may not have had available to you if you were out of time. In my opinion, most traders do not want to be long an option with 30 DTE or less, as time value begins to erode more exponentially the closer you get to expiry, and experienced traders who understand the more advanced behaviors of options may chose to trade front month options.

Buying Extra Time Is Okay   Even though I plan on being in the trade no more than a month, the market is quite turbulent and I know that I am human and make mistakes. This is where you need to be honest with yourself and assess your trading personality. If you are the type of person who has held on to trades for longer than you intended in the past, or if you know that you have a problem exiting trades in general—a good suggestion is to buy a longer-dated option. Although it may cost you a bit more, nothing is worse than owning an option in the last couple weeks of its life and the stock has not done what you need it to do. Of course, this is my opinion, but limited time is a factor that many new option traders have to learn to deal with. What's worse is holding an option to expiration and having the stock move in the direction you had picked the following Monday. For this trade I chose a June expiration, roughly 125 days out from the date this was written. This may seem like excess, but it gives me some peace of mind and the ability to turn this trade into a spread if need be.

Bid-Ask Spreads   I like to think of the spread as another commission—this one goes to the market makers. Typically you buy on the ask and sell on the bid and this goes for puts as well. You can always enter a limit order and get filled in between the market, but this is not a guarantee. Think about it like this: If you are trading a put with a bid-ask spread of $1 (yes, there are many of those out there) and you buy just 10 contracts, you are immediately marked at a $1,000 loss (excluding commission). Wow! Psychologically, the loss may be a blow for some traders. Now imagine that you bought a -0.70 delta put and the stock falls $1. You may still be at a loss in your trade, which can certainly be disheartening.

Granted, spreads are usually wide for a reason: either the stock is thinly traded or it may have a high relative volatility. I would prefer the latter if I were to trade an option with a large spread. Usually, trading stocks with poor volume isn't the soundest strategy (although some more advanced traders are successful at trading low volume stocks). In my opinion, try to find options with spreads less than $0.20, if possible. You can find these lower spreads in the bigger stock names that trade heavy volume (1mm plus), stocks like AAPL, QQQQ, IBM, and others. Sometimes higher spreads will be inevitable. Just be aware of them and be sure to look up and down the option chain to get an idea of the average spread size. Remember, the lower the spread, the less your immediate loss will be in a trade. I prefer to trade options with spreads less than $0.20; however, you can choose a number that you feel comfortable with.

I am waiting for the stock to rally a bit for the perfect entry, but for demonstration's sake, I placed a limit order "buy to open" 10 contracts at $13.50. Remember, placing a limit order will allow you to set the purchase or sale price, but not a fill. At the time I placed my bid, the asking price was $14.50, one dollar away from my bid. I was waiting for the stock to rally (the put then gets cheaper).

Open Interest   Open interest can tell us a great deal about a particular option. Open interest is the number of contracts held in an open position; it can be long or short. Some traders tend to forget that they can buy to open or sell to open a position. Traders should not always assume that because one contract has sizable open interest, every holder is long or short that option. For the retail options trader, open interest can give an indication of how interested people are in trading that option. Typically, higher open interest may lead to tighter bid-ask spreads, although this is not always the case. Open interest may increase as an option's life progresses, and it may decrease as the option gets closer to expiration. Again, none of these is a guarantee. As a general rule, it is good to see open interest of 100 or more, and to use caution when placing a trade that makes you more than 25% of the total open interest. Remember, when months are added the Monday after expiration day, you may see zero open interest in that strike, while there may be a great deal of open interest in that same strike in the prior (or next) expiration month. If that is the case, take the lower of the two months and cut it in half, which may be a good estimate of where the additional month's open interest may end up. This again is one of my quick formulas and it is *not* an assurance of open interest, just a best guess.

My option choice had 1,079 open interest, plenty for the 10 lot I traded. Try not to be more than 10% of the open interest. If you are trading less than 10 contracts, don't sweat open interest too much. Just be sure that your stock is trading adequate volume and the bid-ask spreads are reasonable.

Check Your Average Stock Volume   Volume is important. Remember that without volume, there would be no stock trading and potentially no change in prices. Think about it this way: You are trying to sell a vintage lamp with a real value of the lamp of $10. You can tell everyone that you are selling it for $100, $90, $80, $60, and so on. But until someone steps in and *pays* you something (most likely $10) a trade is not made, nor would that trade be recorded. Stocks work the same way. A stock finds its market value by people showing their best bids price and their best offers price. When these prices meet, that is a trade and that is the current price of the stock. The more players, investors, and traders participating, the more opinions there are on the stock and the more liquidity that the stock will have. This basically means that it will be easier to transact large amounts of shares (and options) at a single price. Volume is the cause and price is the effect, not vice versa.

Step 6. Monitoring and Exit   Once you've found the issue you want to trade, determined a suitable entry point, and located the put option you want to trade, you should determine a profit target as well as a stop-loss point for yourself. Remember, earlier in my call example we discussed several techniques such as using a stock's ATR as a means of finding a normal or average, movement for the stock over a given period of time. The goal here is to set realistic expectations in your stock and options trades; this should be done with puts as well.

Before executing the trade, note the ATR or historical volatility of the stock that you are trading so you can get an idea of its normal range. This range can be used to set goals and help manage an active trade. With the long put, you are buying to open to enter the trade and, when you are ready to exit, you must sell to close.

Although you are in the trade, remember that the long put has negative theta, which means that you are paying every day to be in that put or, in other words, time is working against you. Also remember that it is best if volatility rises because you are long vega; basically, you want that stock to move lower as fast as it can and—if it does not move in your desired direction—be sure that you control your risk and, in my opinion, have an acceptable stop-loss set. Don't forget, you do *not* have to lose all of your option's value if the trade does not move in your favor.

Once you are in a profitable situation, a professional trader would look at protecting that edge, or potentially taking the trade off. A great way for a retail trader to protect a profit and mechanize the trade is to use a trailing stop. Trailing stops allow a trade to move in a profitable direction, but will take the trader out if the position moves against him.

In this trade, I bought the put option at $13.50 and also put a good-to-cancel (GTC) order to sell the option at $14.80, as I would be happy with a 10% return on my trade. I was out of the trade in three days and moved on to the next trade that met my criteria.

TRADER TIP

Remember that every trade is a new one; in fact, every day that I am in a position I ask myself if I still would enter this trade as a completely brand new trade. If not, perhaps I want to evaluate being in the trade at all.

—Steve Claussen, Chief Options Strategist, OptionsHouse

TRADER TIP

When a stock or index is dropping, it is typical for volatility to be on the rise, thus benefiting the long put position. This can be considered an added benefit to the long put strategy. Remember, post earnings drops may happen with an actual decrease in volatility; always use caution when trading just ahead and through the earnings report.

BASIC STOCK AND OPTION SPREAD

The *collar* is a hybrid of stock and two options. I included it in the basic section, because it's a fairly simpler trade and can be used as temporary absolute protection for your long stock positions. It's basically a covered call with the additional purchase of a put, at or below the stock price.

The Collar

Covered Call + a Long Put = Relatively Cheap Protection for Long Stock

So, if we take what we learned from both the buy-write and covered call—that is, buy stock, sell call—all that you need to construct the collar is the addition of a long put, typically out of or at the money.

One collar is 100 shares of long stock, one at- or out-of-the-money short call, and one at- or out-of-the-money long put, with the call strike and put strike being different. The cost of the long put is partially, fully, and sometimes in excess offset by the credit from the sale of the short call. Of course, applying this strategy is easier said than done, and there is certainly a technique and reasoning that you need to apply the collar. As stated earlier, the call and put must have different strike prices and the call should be above the put in strike.

TRADER TIP

A short call and a long put with the same strike are equivalent to being short stock at that strike price; if you did that trade and bought stock at the same time, that would be called a conversion and is a directionless, generally riskless strategy.

So when would a trader use a collar? Suppose you had shares of stock in a company that you want to keep long term and would like the stock to stay within a certain range, perhaps because they are shares held in your IRA. For instance, let's assume that you have 1,000 shares of IBM, which, hypothetically is currently trading at $100 per share. This stock position is a large part of your retirement nest egg and the market is beginning to look a bit turbulent, possibly after rallying for some time. A collar can be a low-cost or costless way to protect your investment over time.

Collars can also be used ahead of an earnings report that you suspect may be volatile. The collar will help offer you relatively cheap or costless insurance on your stock position. Depending on how you structure the collar (which strikes you choose) you may even get a credit, which would actually reduce your cost basis in the stock.

The Collar = (Long stock + short call + long put [with different strikes])

The call strike is always greater than the put strike and usually both are out of the money, but not always.

Characteristics, sentiment, and risks for a collar are:

- *Market sentiment.* Neutral with a bias for protection to the downside and the potential for limited upside. This sentiment can vary with the choice of strikes and premium paid and/or received in the trade.
- *Risk.* Varies, but limited to cost basis in stock (pre-trade stock cost ± debit or credit for spread) minus put strike.
- *Potential reward.* Limited to upside call strike—cost basis.
- *Passage of time.* Varies.

- *Probability characteristics.* Protective strategy, sets absolute loss limits, while limiting upside, probability of profitability in trade depends on price at which the stock is owned and what strikes are chosen to sell call/buy put.
- *Time in trade.* Typically short term, generally used to protect over a known event; however, collars (credit collars preferably) can be used to protect a stock against a sharp downturn in a longer-term trade. Months of strikes can be staggered and adjusted with time.
- *When to apply this strategy.* You have a moderate to extremely aggressive bearish opinion of the stock.
- *How you will win.* If done for a credit, stock should stay between strikes above where you own the stock.

If done for a debit, and the stock drops, you can trade out of the collar to offset your loss in the stock. If the stock tanks way below your strike, you still retain the right to sell it back up at your put strike. Typically, the goal of the collar is to offer short-term absolute protection.

If you own the stock much lower, and just want to lock in a bottom price, collars can be done for even money (minus commission). This could be used in a retirement account where you need to maintain a minimum value of a large amount of stock, perhaps employing the strategy before an event or after the stock has had a strong rally.[4]

Breakeven at expiration = stock cost basis ± premium paid or received

How you will get hurt:

- *Stock stays flat·up to expiration.* You will gradually lose your time value and retain your intrinsic value if you had any to begin with. If the trade was done for a credit, this outcome will be desired. If the trade is done for a debit, this will cost you money if both option strikes are out of the money, because they will both expire worthless.
- *Stock rises.* You will typically make more from your stock than you will lose in the options. If the trade is done for a credit and the short call strike is at or above the stock price at the time of initiating the spread, *you will be profitable. Remember, if the stock is above the short call strike on expiration, you will be forced to sell your shares and limit your profit.*
- *Stock falls.* The put value will increase and the call value will decrease if the stock falls, creating a potentially profitable situation in those two options. However, you will be losing on your long stock position. If you still want to retain the stock position because you think the stock will recover, the collar can be removed for a profit. If your sentiment

has changed and you are no long bullish on the stock, the collar can be closed out (hopefully for a profit) and the stock sold.

Collar Greek attributes are:

- Delta

  Generally *net* positive as both the call and put are out of the money. Your stock delta will override the two smaller negative deltas of the short call and long put. The closer the options strikes are to the stock, the lower the net delta position will be.

  Delta can range from −.01 to −1.

- Gamma

  Gamma is really of minimal concern because the short call and long put will tend to neutralize each other. Generally, the goal is to have the collar expire with the stock just below the short call strike. Gamma will get more positive if the stock drops toward the long put strike and more negative as the stock moves to and above the short call strike.

- Theta

  Varies. If the collar is done for a credit and the stock is in between the long put strike and short call strike, you will collect theta. Once the stock falls below the long put strike, you begin to get short theta and the position is costing you money each day.

  With the stock above your short call, you will still be collecting theta, but you will also be limited in how much you can make because the short call obligates you to sell your stock at that strike. If you think the stock is going to continue to rise, close the collar out!

- Vega

  Varies. Typically with the stock near your short call strike you will have a minimal short vega bias; however, as the stock approaches the long put strike, your bias will actually change to become long vega because the put is gaining delta and is becoming the dominant option. Again, making a bet on volatility is not the objective in this strategy; focus on your cost basis in the stock and how much protection you want versus the amount of premium paid or collected in the trade.

- Rho

  Minimal risk.

The short call strike is always greater than the long put strike.

Figure 6.8 shows the risk characteristics of the collar. Note that unlike the covered call alone, this risk graph has flat horizontal lines above and below the breakeven point, which indicates limited risk and limited reward.

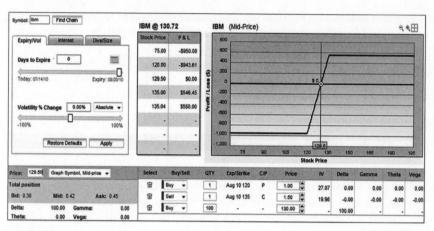

FIGURE 6.8 Collar Expiration Risk Graph

IBM Practical Application Use the collar strategy when you want to reduce your downside risk and you think that a stock is going to stay relatively flat or maybe move lower (certainly not explode to the upside). The collar allows you to lock in a sale price for the stock as long as the trade remains in effect.

Let's flash back for a moment to the year 2008: The market is performing well, everything seems great. When everything is looking rosy we generally forget about the need for a hedge (or downside protection) and tend to relax some of our trading rules because the irrational exuberance has taken hold not only of us, but of the masses, so any doubt you may have is diminished by the predominance of data that is flowing through the media and the net. Let's assume that back then IBM was trading at $100 per share and looked fairly strong from a technical and even fundamental perspective.

At that point, you are happy with the current price levels of your IBM stocks and you would be devastated if they were to fall a large amount. You have owned IBM for some time and your average cost basis is $70 per share.

Let's walk through an example of the collar strategy with IBM. In this example we are long 1,000 shares of stock, which means that we can sell 10 calls and buy 10 puts; don't forget that one contract controls 100 shares of stock.

In this case, we are going to just put the trade on as one collar, buying puts and selling calls at the same time. You can also "leg in" to the trade or, in other words, sell the calls first, then buy the puts or vice versa. Both the short call and long put are bearish, so there is generally no advantage to doing this unless you buy the put as protection first and then start to notice the stock strengthening and decide to wait on selling the call.

Strike Selection   Choosing the strikes for the call and the put really comes down to personal choice on costs and credit of the trade, as well as the amount of downside protection, and the opinion you have on the stock.

TRADER TIP

The higher the strike price of the call, the higher you think the stock can go; by selling a higher strike call you allow the stock more room to rally, but lessen the amount of premium received to offset the price of the put.

On the put side, the closer the put is to the stock price (the higher the delta) the more bearish you are on the stock and the more that put will cost.

So if you are more bullish, widen the space between the call and the put and move the call strike higher, allowing more room for the stock to run. If you are more bearish, tighten the space between strikes and sell the call strike closer to the stock price to get more premium.

My personal preference is to also include the implied volatility of the options and the historical volatility of the stock when calculating the possible moves that a stock could make in the time frame that you have the collar in place.

Be sure to also account for any earnings or corporate events that could be a catalyst for volatility. Earnings often bring abnormal movements along with them; the collar can be a way to minimize that increased volatility effect on your portfolio.

Here is how you can use volatility to find the expected range of a stock.

Historical Volatility in Your Calculations   If you are a bit more advanced (or if you have read this entire book) you may be familiar and comfortable with volatility. Historical volatility is an objective number expressed in annualized percentage terms. In other words, if IBM had an annual volatility of 30% and it was a $100 per share, this means that in the simplest terms, it's reasonable for IBM to vary 30% up or 30% down in a year about 70% of the time (one standard deviation). This does not mean that IBM cannot move more; it just means there is a much lower probability of that occurring. You can use the historical volatility of the stock to get an idea of how volatile it may be moving forward. This can help you with strike selection.

Remember, historical is just that—it is what has happened in the past.

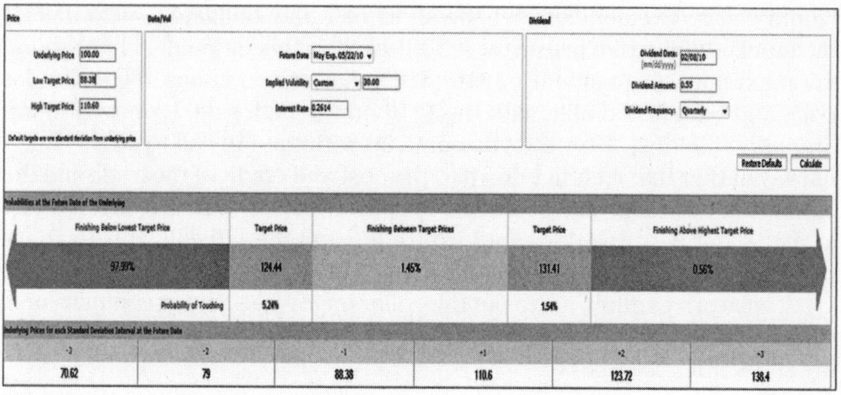

FIGURE 6.9 IBM Probability Calculator
Source: www.ivolatility.com and www.OptionsHouse.com.

Implied Volatility Implied volatility is a bit more subjective—it is a pricing component of the options that are trading and is *forward* looking. If the implied volatility of the options are, let's say, 40% hypothetically, then the market is pricing in some bigger potential moves for IBM. This could be due to perceived events in the stock itself, the sector, or even the market as a whole. Once you become more comfortable with the concept of volatility, you may be able to use this to your advantage; however, being knowledgeable about volatility, doesn't mean you'll be profitable. I generally will default to the higher volatility for a quick way of finding the probability of movement in a stock moving forward in the near term, so simply, if the implied volatility is greater, use it. If the historical volatility is great, then it might be my choice.

Figure 6.9 shows one of my favorite tools available at Options House.com (you can also find it at www.ivolatility.com) Basically, I plug in the stock price, IBM $100 and the volatility 30% (the calculator will populate the implied or historical as well), the month in which I intend to put the trade on, and the calculator tells me what the percentage chances are for the stock making certain moves in that time frame. In the following example, by May expiration (which is 60 days out) IBM has about a 70% chance of staying between 89 and 110. This just helps me get a gauge of its expected movement so I can better select strikes. Buying a May 70 put may be way too far out of the money if there is only a 1% chance that it could get down there.

Let's assume from here that I am fairly happy with my return on the stock, and as long as it stayed above $90 per share I would be okay with that. Let's also assume that for my account, if the stock went to $110 I would sell it. (Remember that the short call may obligate you to deliver the stock at the strike price you sell.) Based on this rationale, I have found my maximum loss amount of $10 ($100 share price minus $90 strike for put), and I am acceptable with the $110 on the high side. By now you are probably thinking, "How did you come up with the 110 call to sell?" Well, I did say earlier that it comes down to the cost and credit of the trade and the amount of downside protection that you want? So, hypothetically, looking at the 90 put with 160 days until expiration and the 110 call with 160 days till expiration, I can buy the put for $5.10 and sell the call for $5.10.

These prices allow me to put the collar on for free, minus commissions, which will hedge me if the stock drops below $90 and may force me to sell my stock if it goes to $110.

My maximum risk in this particular trade from this point until options expiration is $10 (the stock is currently at $100).

No matter how low the stock goes, I will lock in a gain of $20 on the stock ($90 strike on put minus the $70 cost basis)—as long as my position is in effect. (This is what Bernard Madoff stated that he was doing, but he did not actually place the trades.)

In trading, as well as in many parts of our lives, there is no such thing as a free lunch, and in this case, because we sold the 110 call, I have limited my upside, so my maximum profit in this trade is $40. My cost basis is $70. The short call obligates me to sell the stock at $110 if it is trading above that number on expiration $110 − $70 = $40.

Some traders prefer to buy the put for as long as they intend on being in the trade and either selling a call in the same time frame or selling a call with 30 to 40 days to expiration (DTE) so they can take advantage of accelerated time decay in the last month. When using this method, expect the trade to be a debit if the strikes are spaced evenly apart. Remember that you can continue to sell a call the next month and potentially increase or decrease your strike price according to where the stock is at that point.

If the stock rallies with strength to the upside, a more advanced technique would be to buy back the call (potentially at a loss), which would uncap the potential return. Some traders may choose to resell the call and perhaps repurchase a put, both of them with higher strikes.

If the stock drops sharply, remember, as a put owner, you have the right to sell that stock at the strike price. If you do decide to exercise that put, there are two things you must know:

1. By exercising the put option, you may be sacrificing some time value. If the stock seems like it may rebound, it may be more advantageous to sell the put in the open market.

2. If you do indeed exercise your put, you will no longer have a stock position, which means that there is potential that you will be left with a

naked out-of-the-money call. Be sure you completely understand your risk as of a short call before exercising the put because a short call can carry many potential dangers. A possible alternative to holding a short call would be to close the position.

While in the trade, because you are long stock, you will also collect and retain any dividends paid as you maintain your stock position. Be sure that you understand the potential tax implications if you are called away in your position or if you choose to exercise your long put. In addition, this strategy is complex and not suitable for all investors.

Another Collar Practical Application—PLL Back on March 10, 2010, Pall Corporation (PLL) was set to release earnings after the close of the next session. As PLL guided lower, Pall Corporation stated that it expected fiscal 2010 earnings of $1.95 to $2.05 per share. This guidance was on the low end of the scale and, in a statement, Pall Corporation said that for the previous six months, diluted earnings per share (EPS) were $0.98, compared to $0.68 a year earlier. Pro forma EPS, excluding restructuring and other charges as well as nonrecurring favorable items affecting interest expense and provision for income taxes (discrete Items), were $0.82 compared to $0.78 the previous year. The estimated impact of foreign currency translation increased both measures of six month 2010 EPS by $0.06. The current consensus earnings estimate is $2.07 per share for the year ending July 31, 2010.[5]

Before this news was released, I prepared a verbal reasoning and thesis of a collar trade on PLL Corporation.

My Note to Clients—March 10, 2010 Pall Corporation (NYSE: PLL), while maybe not the most exciting story on the Street, has its place in global fluid management, including filtration, separation, and so on. Their products are a part of many industrial markets including food and beverage, oil and gas, even municipal water filtration (to name just a few). As we become a "more green" society, PLL may stand to benefit.

Pall reports earnings tomorrow and I wanted to offer investors a look into PLL's history as well as a way to project into the number tomorrow.

The nine analysts that cover PLL are expecting earnings to come in between $0.46 and $0.49, with the consensus coming in at $0.47. PLL recently raised its quarterly dividend 10.3% to 16 cents per share. The stock falls right between the buy and hold ratings, with most issuing a neutral rating of sorts and one-third of the analysts rating the shares a strong buy.

In the past, the actual earnings date has been quiet; it has been the day after the fact when during which PLL tends to move. The past four earnings events have seen movements as follows: +8.6%, +1.9%, +7.8%, −17%. PLL

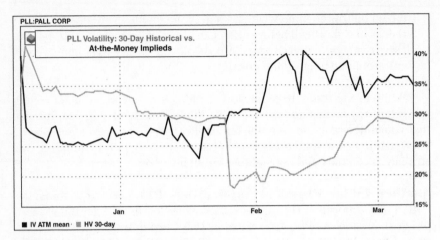

FIGURE 6.10   PLL Volatility Chart

has a tendency to move higher, but this is only about 65% of the time. Its bullish moves outweigh its bearish tendencies over earnings.

Since 2007, PLL has only missed analysts' projections in two quarters, occurring in the second quarters of 2008 and 2009. Second-quarter earnings are due tomorrow.

At 23 times trailing earnings, the stock may seem a bit rich here and it has had a tremendous run since its recent low of $33.50 back around February 11. The stock has stalled here in the past week and a half and even with the lack of movement, average implied volatility remains elevated at 35.5%, with the 30-day historical coming in around 28% (see Figure 6.10).

Note the strength in PLL's stock leading up to the earnings event in Figure 6.11, the 20-day SMA crossed above the 50-day, which is a bullish indicator.

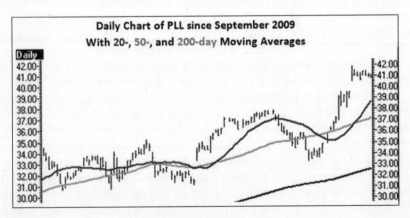

FIGURE 6.11   PLL Daily Chart 9/2009–3/2010

All of the moving averages are at $35 or below; that may be where support is, if PLL drops.

Based on what the stock has done in recent weeks and the history of its Q2 earnings report, I would approach with caution, although we are seeing strength in the macro recovery, which should feed PLL's earnings as well, as production/usage may be rising.

It really boils down to P/E, which I think is a bit rich; therefore, I am looking at an aggressive *covered call*, selling the April 40 call for $2.20 and buying the April 35 put for 20 cents. This will be a net credit of $2 and will reduce cost basis in the stock by that amount. Because the call has 90 cents of parity (intrinsic value), I am actually only capturing $1.10 in time value if PLL rallies from here.

In other words, if PLL rallies from this point, I may be required to sell my stock at $40, but since I received $2 to do this trade, it's the equivalent of selling PLL at $42, which is still $1.10 higher than where we are right now.

If the stock drops, I will buy back my call and sell my put, hopefully for a profit and retain my stock position.

Please be sure that you understand the risks associated with any trades that I discuss and ensure that the trade suits your thesis.

As it turns out that my thesis was correct and the collar served its purpose, I was able to realize a $1.30 profit from the short call and long put to offset the stock, which was trading down to $39 after the announcement: The collar could be closed for $0.70 (debit), which enabled me to capture the $1.30, after it was sold for $2.

Figure 6.12 shows the dramatic price drop in PLL on Friday, March 12, 2010.

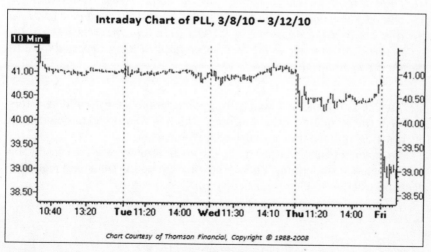

FIGURE 6.12 Intraday Chart of PLL's Earnings Move

From my analysis you will note that I took several things into consideration:

- Past earnings moves overall.
- Certain quarter's behavior (seasonal history).
- Moving averages, support, and resistance.
- Volatility (both historical and implied and their relativity to one another now compared to the past).
- Recent stock moves (stocks that tend to make large directional moves into the earnings report may lead me to look for more of a reversion to the mean and sway me into taking a directional bias against the recent move).
- What the masses were thinking (news, analysts, etc.).

Exiting the Collar   Pall Corporation (NYSE: PLL) opened on March 12 down more than 4% lower, dropping below the $39 mark after reporting quarterly earnings-per-share of 42 cents, missing estimates by a nickel. Revenue for the second quarter hit $560.4 million, which was a 3.1% year-over-year increase but also managed to fall shy of Street expectations. The bigger issue was this statement by Eric Krasnoff, chairman and CEO[†]:

> *Our prior EPS guidance for fiscal year 2010 forecast an earlier and stronger recovery for the Industrial markets and a benefit from foreign currency translation of $0.17. Applying an estimated benefit from foreign currency translation of $0.09 based on current exchange rates, we have retained the low end of our guidance at $1.95 and reduced the high end to $2.05 (excluding Discrete Items). Including the Discrete Items in the first half, EPS are expected to be in the $2.11 to $2.21 range.*

This updated guidance was a disappointment to analysts and investors and sent the stock lower this morning, which is what I had anticipated in my practical options trader analysis on Wednesday.

So, given the move this morning, the collar strategy was successful and now is where a trader must choose how to finesse the trade and make the decision whether to close it or keep it on.

[†]http://news.pall.com/article display.cfm?article id=4499

Quote Lookup:	**PLL** (NYSE): **PALL**			
[___] Go	Last: **38.93**	Chg: **$-1.91 -4.68%**		Open: **38.85**
Symbol Lookup	Bid: **38.92** [BTX]	Ask: **38.94** [BTX]	Size: **4 x 1**	High: **39.08**
	Shares: --	Net Delta: --	Pos Val: --	Low: **38.45**

OPTION CHAIN

CALL OPTIONS

Bid	Ask	Chg	Imp Vol	Vol	Opn Int	Delta	Gam	Theta	Vega	Pos	Series	Bid	Ask
											⊟ Apr 10 [35 days to expiration: Ap]		
13.50	14.40	-1.70	31.7	0	0	1	0	0	0	--	Apr 10 25.0	0.00	0.10
8.50	9.40	-1.75	31.7	0	0	0.999	0.001	0	0	--	Apr 10 30.0	0.00	0.10
3.90	4.50	-1.75	31.7	0	18	0.938	0.03	-0.008	0.017	--	Apr 10 35.0	0.20	0.45
0.85	1.15	-1.28	35.5	5	1020	0.575	0.087	-0.025	0.051	--	Apr 10 40.0	1.75	2.30
0.00	0.25	-0.40	36.3	0	3563	0.205	0.061	-0.02	0.041	--	Apr 10 45.0	5.50	6.60
0.00	0.10	-0.03	36.3	0	0	0.04	0.018	-0.006	0.014	--	Apr 10 50.0	10.60	11.50

FIGURE 6.13 PLL Options Chain—March 12

The option chains in Figure 6.13 show the calls much cheaper and the puts rising in value with the drop in PLL's stock. The good news is that the collar (options) can be closed this morning for about $0.70, which would result in a profit of $1.30 in the trade I referenced. (Originally selling the April 40 call for $2.20 and buying the April 35 put for 20 cents.)

That is with the stock down to $39, $2 from the $41 price level on Wednesday. So if you feel that the stock will recover from here, you could close the collar, which would reduce your loss to $0.70 (remember we made $1.30 on the collar) versus $2 if you owned only the stock. This leaves you with only long stock.

If you are concerned that the stock can drop further, you can choose to leave the trade on. These options don't expire until April and theoretically could continue to profit, but keep in mind that the put strike is fairly far away.

Implied volatility has been reduced this morning and if the stock were to drop again, volatility could jump back up. One caution here is the bid-ask spreads in the options, which are unusually wide. Use limit orders when executing options trades in this issue and don't be afraid to get aggressive with your limit amounts.

The bottom line is that the collar served its purpose and even though we didn't recoup all of the losses in the stock, we did reduce our losses by 70% in this case. Not to mention that if the stock had a catastrophic loss, we would have been protected.

FINAL THOUGHTS

Placing any trade, even a long call or put requires not only some work, but a method and checklist. You will be amazed at the speed at which you can execute your research, analysis, strategy selection, and money management once you have been trading for a while. Try not to break your rules; the guidelines that you set out for yourself are there to not only protect you, but to give you the rules of engagement and more importantly, disengagement. The goal of trading and/or investing is to provide consistent, low-volatility returns over a long period of time. If you follow your checklist and understand your risk, you will have longevity in the markets. If you choose a more haphazard, unstructured approach and engage without a plan, most likely you will find your investment career frustrating and perhaps short. Be sure to journal the results of your trades, especially the trades that went really well or extremely bad and try to mimic the good traits and avoid the bad ones. Options are an awesome tool that allows an infinite number of possible tactics to employ against whatever the market is throwing at you. In Chapter 7, I explain spreads, which are an excellent way to further decrease your risk, increase probability, and make time work *for* you instead of *against* you.

CHAPTER 7

Strategy: The Basic Spread Trades

Now let's focus on some of the traditional, basic option spread strategies.

When you combine multiple types and strikes of options and/or buy and sell them against one another as a combination (or spread), the characteristics of those single options change, giving the spread a personality that may be completely different from what you are used to if you only were to trade individual options.

Vertical spreads in particular are not only simple to apply and analyze, but they can either increase your probability of success in a trade and they can also greatly reduce your risk if you are making a "directional" trade, but reducing costs.

In every instance, a vertical spread has limited risk and limited reward. Even though the rewards are limited, they can sometimes be 100% or more return on the amount at risk, so "limited" doesn't necessarily mean mediocre.

VERTICAL SPREADS IN DEPTH

To help visualize the goal of the spread, sometimes it is best to think about the options at expiration and what they will be worth at that time to understand how your spread will eventually end up—this is called parity (no time value).

Obviously, to ignore or not understand the behaviors of that spread while you are in the trade is extremely foolish, as some spreads can completely change their behaviors depending on where their spread (strikes) lie in relation to the stock price. Vertical spreads are typically the first types of spreads that traders explore. Vertical spreads have fairly simple mathematical and behavioral rules that govern them and if you understand those basic sets of laws, you should have no problem interchanging long and short call or put vertical spreads, as they have similar but opposite behavioral characteristics.

When I refer to a *vertical spread*, this means that you would be buying and selling a call versus another call or put versus another put, one for one, in the *same* month. So if you bought one September 40 call and sold one September 45 call, that is a vertical spread; you could change the strike price, switch buy versus sell or make them both puts and it would still be considered a vertical spread.

- The term *vertical spread* means that the variable is the strike price; both options expire in the same month.
- A horizontal spread or calendar spread indicates that the variable is time or expiration month and the strike remains the same.
- A diagonal spread indicates that both strike and expiration month may be different in the spread.
- Think about the X and Y axis of a price graph where X typically represents time (horizontal) and Y typically represents price (vertical); this may also help you remember.

Table 7.1 gives you a quick snapshot at the behavior of the four basic vertical spreads we will discuss in this chapter. Use it as a ref guide to select your strategy when you are getting started or to jog your memory later on.

Verticals as an Added Cushion and Volatility Reducer

You really only have three choices when it comes to your investing: buy, sell, or hold.

When you take a position in a stock, it must move in your desired direction for you to be profitable.

Stock traders basically can only take a long or a short view on an underlying stock or ETF, but options traders are given much more flexibility in the way they invest and assume risk.

P&L volatility is a huge concern for many investors and the ability to reduce it is more and more the focus in the hedge fund community and among professional traders.

TABLE 7.1 Vertical Spread Characteristics

Description	Credit/ Debit	Market Stance	Max Gain	Max Risk	Time Decay	Vega
Bull call Purchase call with lower strike than one sold	Debit	Moderately bullish (need stock above short call on expiration)	Spread width−premium paid	Net premium paid	Bad (when out of the money Good (when in the money)	Long vega when out of the money; short when in the money
Bear call Sell call with lower strike than one purchased	Credit	Moderately bearish (need stock below short call on expiration)	Initial credit received	Spread width−premium received	Good (when out of the money) Bad (when in the money)	Short vega when out of the money; Long when in the money
Bull put Purchase put with lower strike than one sold	Credit	Moderately bullish (need stock above short put on expiration)	Initial credit received	Spread width−premium received	Good (when out of the money Bad (when in the money)	Short vega when out of the money; Long when in the money
Bear put Sell put with lower strike than one purchased	Debit	Moderately bearish (need stock below short put on expiration)	Spread width−premium paid	Net premium paid	Bad (when out of the money Good (when in the money)	Long vega when out of the money; Short when in the money

Depending on your opinion toward a particular company, you are really limited as a stock trader to more of a full "on or off" sort of sentiment and subsequently at the mercy of whatever volatility path that instrument (stock, ETF, index) follows.

Of course, you can choose to allocate only a certain percentage of your account to the trade (to manage your risk) or you can even diversify your portfolio to mitigate volatility and/or create a partial hedge in your account.

A Basic Diversification Example   If you bought ETFs in five different S&P 500 sectors on April 28, 2010, you would most likely have net losses in every one of your positions if you held the S&P 500 until July 1, 2010, when it was down at 1,010. Following you will see the price changes from April 28, 2010, through July 1, 2010, in these popular sector ETFs.

If you had allocated 20% of your account evenly into these five sectors, you would have a net loss of 13.2% over that time period. Individual stocks may have done better or worse, but ETFs may also in and of themselves offer another level of risk reduction through diversity.

By diversifying, in this case, you were able to moderate the major losing trades, but also worsened the better-performing investments in the same manner. This method of diversification through ETFs is one of several techniques that stock traders have at their disposal. The challenge with trading stocks and ETFs outright is that each share of stock has a delta of one, so for every share you own, you will make a dollar for every dollar the stock rises (and lose a dollar for every one that it falls). Although this is wonderful when you are long stock and it's going higher, it's not so much fun when you are long stock and it is dropping like a rock (or even down 13% as in the preceding situation).

It works the same when you decide to take a short position in a stock, only then you have unlimited risk to the upside and some additional margin requirements and costs. These can cut into your potential profitability, not to mention your stress levels.

If you have traded the markets at all or even read or watch financial news, you know that stocks don't go straight up or down. They tend to zigzag all over the place and generally form a bullish, bearish, or sideways trend when observed over certain periods of time.

Stock traders, whether long or short, will have one-to-one exposure to each dollar change in the stock itself. Because of this, stock traders may have to be more precise in their theses and or timing of their trades.

We options traders tend to take a more realistic, statistical, and, in my opinion, much less absolute view of the marketplace. I say *realistic* because many of us take on our risk based on volatility with minimal directional bias and *statistical* in that we look at typical patterns, news events, charts, and current and past options pricing to help choose an appropriate strategy (that doesn't have to be just buy, sell, or hold).

And taking a less *absolute* view means we don't have to be "all in" all of the time when it comes to an options strategy's sensitivity to stock movement. If you have gotten this far in my book, you probably have figured out that I just don't buy the fact that anyone can predict market prices and fluctuations with high precision.

How Can the Vertical Spread Mitigate Volatility Further? Vertical spreads, such as the bull put spread or bear call spread, can reduce your P&L's "connection" to a stock's movement. What these strategies allow us to do is act on the thesis that a stock, index, or ETF will stay above or below a certain price by a specific date, instead of the stock having to move, you can just make the "bet" that the stock will stay above or below a certain price. That price can be some distance away from the current price, allowing the instrument to actually move against you, but still potentially profit. This can be done by simply selecting the proper strikes to sell and buy.

Options traders certainly need to be correct to some extent as well, but with some strategies, like a vertical spread, options traders can be only "partially correct" and still achieve success. Let me explain.

Let's assume you were bullish on Goldman Sachs (NYSE: GS) back in May 2010 as a stock trader, but you were a bit nervous about the sector, the broad market, FINREG, and the company's legal situation. Of course, one option is to buy the stock at $139, which gives you unlimited upside and $139 of downside risk. For every dollar move in the stock, you will gain/lose $1 for every share you own. Therefore, if you decided to purchase 100 shares, you would gain/lose $100 for every dollar advance/decline in the stock.

If you were only moderately bullish and wanted to use options to reduce risk, you might explore selling a bull put spread strategy in July.

Because of the lower delta of a vertical spread, the spread's sensitivity to the underlying stock movement will typically be much less than the stock, meaning that your P&L will have less volatility. The delta of a vertical spread will typically be lower because you are selling one option against a long option, where the sale of a call option reduces the delta of the long option.

Table 7.2 shows the actual prices and deltas of three Goldman Sachs put options. Let's compare the risk of the individual options and what would happen if we create spreads with them.

If you were to buy one July 135 put, you would be short 34 deltas, or have about 34% exposure to the movement of GS, all while risking $6.70.

Your breakeven at expiration would be $128.30.

TABLE 7.2 Put Versus Put Spread Delta and Breakeven
Comparisons

Put Strike	Bid	Ask	Delta
July 125	3.85	4.00	−.21
July 130	5.05	5.15	−.27
July 135	6.55	6.70	−.34

If you were to buy one July 135 put for $6.70 and sell one July 130 put
for $5.05, your *net* delta position would be short 7 deltas, which means
you would have about a 7% exposure to the movements of GS with only
$1.65 at risk.

Your breakeven at expiration would be $133.35. Some traders use
short put spreads to limit risk and increase probability of success in a
trade. These attributes come at a price, however, and that price is limited profit (this limited profit can still be substantial when compared to the
reduced risk).

Out-of-the-money short vertical spreads typically have a higher probability of success because the stock doesn't have to necessarily move higher
for the trade to be profitable. This is not the case with a long stock position,
because the stock *must* move higher for you to realize a profit.

THE FOUR BASIC VERTICAL SPREADS—BASIC CHARACTERISTICS AND BEHAVIOR

This next section goes deeper into vertical spread behavior and more importantly, the relationships between them, so you better understand how
each of the four spreads are actually related to one another and are sometimes interchangeable.

Bullish Put Credit Spread

In a bull put vertical credit spread, you collect money at the onset of the
trade, but have to post some "just-in-case money" (margin), which will be
the width of the strike prices in the spread, minus the credit.

If you were to hypothetically sell the Goldman Sachs July 125/115 put
spread for $2.05 (which means selling the 125 put and buying the 115 put),
you are limiting your risk to the width of the strikes ($10), minus the credit

received ($2.05), which gives you a total downside risk in this example of $7.95.

The breakeven, or the point at which you will not make or lose money, on expiration, is $122.95. This means that GS could hypothetically fall to that level and on expiration you would still break even in the trade. Because of this characteristic, you have a statistical success advantage. This doesn't mean that if GS were to sell off you couldn't lose money in the weeks or days before the options expire.

Another advantage of this trade is the fact that GS could actually drop as far as $125 by July expiration and you would still retain the $2.05 credit, which is a 25% return on your risk. The disadvantage is that the $2.05 credit you receive is the maximum profit you can potentially make in the trade—not a penny more. For some stock traders, this factor may be hard to deal with. Greed, for many of us, is a tough emotion to control.

So if you are relatively bullish, content with a limited return potential, and want to increase your probability of success, you may want to examine the bull put spread strategy.

Change It to a Bullish Debit Call Spread   In a debit trade, you pay the full amount up front, and this is the most you can lose (it's exactly the same net cost of a credit spread because you have to put up margin with your broker).

Using the same scenario and strikes, there is a good chance that you would be able to *buy* the 115 call and sell the 125 call for $7.95, which would be an in-the-money bull call spread.

The spread, even though you are now using calls would behave almost *exactly* like the bull put spread. It would leave you with a profit potential of $2.05, which is the same potential profit as the short put spread. Cool, huh?

Bearish Call Credit Spread

In a bear call vertical credit spread, you collect money at the onset of the trade, but will have to post some "just-in-case money" (margin), which will be the width of the strike prices in the spread, minus the credit.

A bearish example would be selling the July 155/165 call spread for $2.10, (which means selling the 155 call and buying the 165 call). Here you are limiting your risk to the width of the strikes ($10) minus the credit received ($2.10), giving total *upside* risk in this example of $7.90.

The breakeven, or the point at which you will not make or lose money, at expiration, is $157.10. This means that GS could hypothetically rise to that level and when the options expire, you would break even in the trade (excluding commissions). Because of this characteristic, like the put spread example, you have a statistical success advantage because the stock can be trading anywhere from $157.10 down to zero and you can potentially profit. This doesn't mean that if GS were to rally you couldn't lose money ahead of expiration.

Another advantage of this trade is the fact that GS could actually rally to $155 by July expiration and you would still retain the $2.10 credit, which is a 27% return on your risk. The disadvantage is that the $2.10 credit you receive is the maximum you can potentially make in the trade.

By widening vertical spreads, you can increase your potential return (because the long strike will be cheaper), but you will increase your risk. By tightening your spreads, you will reduce your potential return, but lower your risk, generally speaking. If you are selling wider spreads, you are most likely more confident in your thesis on direction.

Change It to a Bearish Debit Put Spread   In a debit trade, you will pay the full amount up front, and this is the most you can lose (it's exactly the same net cost of a credit spread because you have to put up margin).

Using the same scenario and strikes as the bear call spread example, there is a good chance that you would be able to buy the 165 put and sell the 155 put for a net debit of $7.90, leaving you with a potential profit of $2.10, which is the same potential profit as the call spread.

The spread, even though you are now using puts would behave almost *exactly* like the bear call spread.

CREDIT SPREADS VERSUS DEBIT SPREADS

So which do you choose? Selecting which spread to employ depends on several factors:

- Bullish or bearish
- Probability preference
- Credit or debit (comfort level, risk tolerance)
- Price target in stock
- Cost or margin requirement
- Behavioral characteristics

Whether you buy or sell a call spread or put spread, you have to get yourself familiar with the behavior of that spread as well as the credit or debit characteristics discussed previously. The ultimate factor, when comparing a credit or debit spread should be which will you make the most money on and thus have the lowest risk.

The Behavior of Credit Spreads

If you are in the business of selling out-of-the-money verticals for credits and making time work in your favor, then in most cases you are probably betting on a support or resistance level in the stock. This is a fine technique, but when do you exit? It may be tougher to rationalize selling something first and then buying it back later, as many of us instinctually do like to let go of money once we believe we have it.

If you have a $5 wide spread that you sell for $1 credit, it may be hard to buy that spread back for $0.50 and think you're a big winner.

But if you look at it another way, maybe the rationale will help. Assume that you bought a stock for $4 and it went to $4.50 in a matter of a few weeks. Would you be happy with that 12.5% return on your money in less than a month? Most people would, although that depends on the person making the trades.

Upside-Down Risk/Reward versus Increased Probability The stock example assumes the same downside risk and return of a $5 credit spread sold for $1 and bought back for 50 cents. At any given time, your total risk was $4, no matter how far the stock dropped. This is also the margin requirement you will have in the trade. If you can buy the spread back for $3.50, you just made 50 cents on your $4 risk, minus commissions.

So aside from the risk and reward characteristics, which are upside down for a credit spread as opposed to a stock, stock has theoretically unlimited profit potential.

You have to think about the probability of that stock staying above or below your short strike (depending on call or put spreads). Statistical probability is in your favor if you are selling out-of-the-money credit verticals.

If you believe that there is a high probability that the stock will finish where you need it to, then it is acceptable to leave the trade on and let the options expire worthless. However, if there is a good chance that something could nudge your stock in the wrong direction or even pin the stock at your short strike, that may be a reason to act.

I have always thought that a bird in hand is better than two in the bush, but again, that is a personality trait unique to me.

I think at the end of the day, if you have a profit in the trade and don't feel particularly comfortable letting the trade expire, it is okay to remove risk and live to trade another day. In addition, if you know there is a pending event like an earnings report or drug approval before the trade expires, that may not be the time to take a gamble on an already profitable trade.

Bid-Ask Spreads—A Major Consideration

Every one of us would like to buy something at a low price and hopefully sell it at a higher price later to capture a profit. New traders might choose to buy an in-the-money bull call spread because they are comfortable with the concept and believe that the stock will stay above a certain level by the expiration date they choose. This is a perfectly good method, however, even though buying an in-the-money call spread is exactly the same as selling the out-of-the-money put spread with the same strikes; there is one major difference, *bid-ask spreads*!

Because the calls are in the money, they are going to be more expensive than the out-of-the-money puts on the same lines. They will also have a higher delta. Because of these two things, those calls will tend to have higher bid-ask spreads than the puts. If you choose to trade the call spread in place of the put spread, use caution and use limit orders.

TRADER TIP

If you are wanting to buy a call vertical as a substitute for a put vertical, but the calls have huge bid-ask spreads, a quick and dirty way to see what the call spread can be bought for is to take the amount you can sell the put spread for and subtract it from the difference in strikes.

Note the large bid-ask spreads in some of Google's options in Figure 7.1.

The 380/370 put spread can be sold for $1.10 at the market price, but because the options are cheaper, the max spread width is 0.30.

The call spread, however, would have to be bought for $11.10.

By the way, if you pay more than the spread width (10 in this case), you are guaranteed a loss!

CALL OPTIONS							PU)	
Bid	Ask	Chg	Vol	Opn Int	Pos	Series	Bid	Ask
79.90	82.50	-2.50	0	0	-	Aug 10 360.0	3.70	4.00
70.90	73.40	-2.75	0	0	-	Aug 10 370.0	4.70	5.00
62.30	64.80	-2.65	0	3	-	Aug 10 380.0	6.10	6.30
54.00	56.40	-2.55	27	1	-	Aug 10 390.0	7.70	8.00

FIGURE 7.1 GOOG Option Chain
Source: www.OptionsHouse.com.

If you use the technique I outlined and subtract $1.10 from 10 (the width of the spread), you should be able to buy that call spread for $8.90 or better.

CREDIT VERTICAL SPREADS

Selling a spread for your max potential profit with the goal of buying it back for less than you sold it for, the goal is to keep the difference (or the entire credit) as profit.

Selling a Put Spread (Bull Put Spread)

Following are the characteristics, sentiment, and risk of selling a put spread.

- *Market sentiment.* Moderately to very bullish—depends on where you place the spread.
- *Further out of the money.* Less bullish—spread is typically put on out of the money.
- *Further in the money.* More bullish.
- *Risk.* Return on risk varies, but overall dollar risk is limited to the difference in strikes minus premium collected (you will always collect premium when selling a put spread).
- *Potential reward.* Limited to the credit received.
- *Passage of time.* Good for out-of-the-money spreads, bad for in-the-money spreads.
- *Probability characteristics.* Stock *must* finish above short put strike price. I prefer to sell put spreads at or out of the money.
    The further the put spread is away from the stock price at the time of entry, the higher the probability of success. However, the higher the probability, the less credit you will receive for the spread.
- *Time in trade.* Typically 10 to 40 days until expiration, because put spreads are typically sold out of the money; the short put will have more time value than the long put, allowing you to collect theta.
- *When to apply this strategy.* You have a moderate bullish view on the stock and have found a support point and want to limit your risk.
- *How you will win.* Stock stays above your short strike by expiration. (*Breakeven at expiration = short strike price − premium collected.*)
- *How you will get hurt.*

- *Stock stays flat up to expiration.* If you sold your put spread at or out of the money (just below the stock price), a stock that stays flat can actually allow you to attain maximum profit in the trade.

    If you sold your put spread in the money, you will lose some or all of your investment depending on what strike you sold and the credit you received.
- *Stock rises.* You will gradually attain maximum profit as both put options become worthless, but stock must be above your short strike to attain max profit (you keep all of the premium you sold the spread for).

Following are the short vertical put spread Greek attributes:

- Delta

    Positive. Delta can range from 0.02 to 0.98.

    Because this spread is typically sold out of the money, it will generally have a lower positive delta > 0.60. When selling a put spread, focus more on the strike that you sold, the width of the spread, and the credit received as opposed to the delta. The lower delta tells us that these spreads are less sensitive to moves in the stock.

    The more in the money the put spread is, the higher the delta will be, as you will have a greater bullish bias and a possibly a lower probability of success.

- Gamma

    Negative when the spread is out of the money, and gradually will get positive as the spread moves in the money (which is not a good thing).

    The closer the short put is to the stock price, the more variance you will have in your P&L.

- Theta

    Varies. You are collecting theta when the stock is at or above the short put; you may begin to pay theta if the spread moves against you and into the money.

- Vega

    Varies. You are short vega when the spread is out of the money. If the spread moves against you, you will be long vega. Typically, at the onset of this trade you should have a moderate negative vega bias, being that I recommend this strategy be placed out of the money.

- Rho

    Minimal risk.

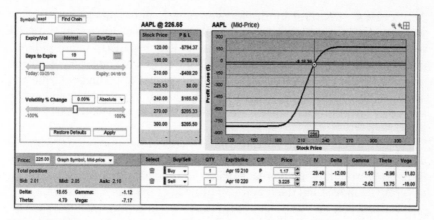

FIGURE 7.2   Out-of-the-Money Bull Put Spread Risk Graph with Greeks

In Figure 7.2, we see the Greeks when the spread is out of the money. This example shows the April 22, 2010, put spread (short the 220) with the stock at $225 and 19 days until expiration. Note the long delta, short gamma, positive theta, and short vega.

If the stock moves lower in the same day, note the shift in your Greeks. The position now becomes longer delta (you would need the stock to move further now) you begin to get long a bit of gamma and you are now paying theta (with no change in the stock price, the position is now costing you money every day). You are also long vega, which means that your P&L will increase if volatility rises. This is because your long put is closer to the money than your short put.

In Figure 7.3, we see the Greeks when the spread is *in* the money. Note the differences in the Greeks when the spread is positioned differently around the stock.

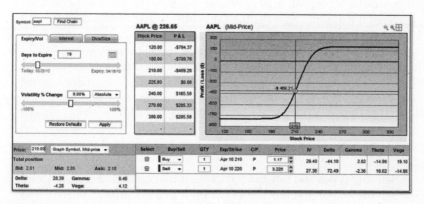

FIGURE 7.3   In-the-Money Bull Put Spread Risk Graph with Greeks

Academics   The first hurdle to overcome is understanding that when you sell a put spread it's actually a bullish trade (which can be confusing to some). When a put spread is sold, it is bullish because you are selling a put with a larger (negative) delta and buying a smaller (negative) delta put against it. Selling a larger delta put will inherently have a higher strike and a higher value than the put you are buying. Therefore you will be selling the spread or collecting a credit for the spread. You are also said to be "short" the spread.

When you sell a put spread, you are collecting money into your account; this is also called a *credit* trade. Short put spreads behave entirely differently from long put spreads. When you sell a vertical spread, you can never make more than the credit you bring in at the onset of the trade.

The first rule about the short put spread is when you are short a put vertical spread, you can*not* make more than what you initially sold the spread for, no matter what happens. So if you sell a put spread for $1 and the stock rallies way above your short put, that $1 you collected is all you will make. Unlike the long put spread, if you sell a put spread, typically you have a moderately bullish outlook on the stock, meaning that theoretically you want it to rise in value or at least stay above your short strike. If you choose to sell a put spread in the money, you are taking a much more bullish position and in that case would most likely need the stock to rise in value.

The second rule you must know when selling a vertical put spread is that you can sometimes lose more than the credit you brought in, meaning that if you sold the spread for a dollar and the stock goes down, you could potentially lose more than the dollar you brought in. The maximum amount you can lose is determined by the width of the spread (or difference between the put strike prices).

The third rule is that when you sell a vertical put spread, you cannot lose more than the difference in strikes, minus the credit you collected. In other words, if you sell a 100 put and buy a 95 put for a net credit of $1, you have a five-point spread that you collected $1 for, making your max loss $4. This is an example of an upside-down risk/reward ratio. You can make a dollar, but you have $4 of potential risk. This may sound like a bad deal if you look at just that part of the trade. Even though the risk can be potentially more than the reward, there is a reason why a trader may select this strategy. For example, the probability of success may be relatively high, depending on the strikes selected and the volatility in the underlying.

Examples of Gain/Loss   Consider the following:

> Sell the 55 put and buy the 50 put for a 1.00 credit = $4.00 max loss
> Sell the 55 put and buy the 45 put for a 2.00 credit = $8.00 max loss
> Sell the 55 put and buy the 40 put for a 3.00 credit = $12.00 max loss

Determining how wide you want to make your spread should be dictated by both the amount of the credit you take in and how far you think the stock could fall if things went wrong. The less likely you think it is that the stock will drop, widen your spread. The more likely you think it is that the stock will drop, narrow your spread.

Why Trade It? The goal of selling a vertical put spread is to have the stock finish *above* the put you sold at expiration. Basically, you want the stock to stay above the short strike all the way until expiration. Typically, this trade is executed with a spread that is already out of the money, meaning that both puts will have strike prices lower than the stock price.

So we have established that selling a vertical put spread is a bullish event. Now, the questions are: What strikes do we buy and sell and what month (or months) do we sell the spread in?

Remember the goal here: We want the stock to stay above the short strike up until expiration.

There are several different ways this trade can be executed. Keep in mind that I am sharing my personal views on this strategy. Typically, when I am selling a put spread, I sell them out of the money at the onset of the trade (below the stock price). This way the stock is already where I want it to be. Unlike buying a put spread, I will usually sell the put spread with 40 days or fewer days until expiration, because time passing by benefits my position. As long as my spread is out of the money, time decay will be working in my favor because both options will be getting cheaper and—because I collect a credit if the spread is worth zero at expiration—that is a good thing for me.

The mind-set of selling a spread can be quite different from buying one of the same type (call or put).

Remember, I discussed earlier how this trade may have an upside-down risk/reward ratio. This is because the trade should have a higher statistical probability of being successful. Let me explain.

Practical Example If you have a stock that you feel is going to rise in value and let's say that stock is trading at $50, if you were to sell the 40 put for $1.50 and simultaneously purchase the 35 put for $0.50, you now have a 40/35 bear put spread on for a credit of $1. Let's also assume that these options expire in 20 days, meaning that as long as the stock stays above $40 for the next 20 days you will retain your $1. Basically, the stock can do one of three things and you can still have a successful trade. The stock can rally from here, it can stay flat, or it can fall to $40 and you would still be profitable.

Now keep in mind that if the stock falls below $39, you will incur a loss. Your maximum loss potential in this trade is $4, because it is a $5 spread and you brought in $1. (Spread width minus credit equals risk.)

Let's take this concept a bit further. I am a statistical trader by nature, meaning that I look back at the historical volatility of a stock as well as the implied volatility to determine a realistic movement in a stock over a given period of time and then look at my potential reward and potential risk in a trade before I make my decision.

For example, let's say that historically over a month's time, a stock tends to fluctuate about 18% up or down, with the stock trading at $50. That's $9 higher or lower during a month's time. If we have sold our spread $10 away from the current stock price, this may give us a statistical edge. In our example, we sold the 40 put and bought the 35.

I can also tell you that even with a statistical edge, you can still potentially lose in this trade. Having probability on your side is a great thing, but anything can happen in the marketplace.

By practicing trading the strategy you will begin to find what works best for you. Practice trading can be done in a virtual account using fake money.

A Walk through a Basic Vertical Put Spread Sale   Here's what it looks like hypothetically. Let's say that you were bearish on ABC Corp. and thought it was going to stay above $100 for the next 20 days. It's currently trading at $110 (hypothetically on January 1, 2009).

You start looking at the options and are looking at the January 2009 puts, which expire in 21 to 15 days (expiration was on January 16). You can sell the 100 put for $1; it currently has a delta of 0.23 and the 95 put (which is further out of the money) can be bought for $0.25; it has a delta of 0.06. So if you were to sell the January 100 put for $1 and buy the January 95 put for $0.25 at the same time, you would actually be selling the January 100/95 put spread for a limit price of $0.75. Since the spread is $5 wide, your maximum profit potential in the trade would be $0.75, or 15%, on your risk. Your maximum risk in the trade is the spread width ($5) minus the credit received ($0.75), or $4.25. Maximum loss occurs when the stock is *below* the long strike at expiration. Your breakeven, at expiration, is your short strike minus the credit you received for the total spread.

Meaning that in our example, you would not make or lose money (excluding commissions) if the stock was at $99.25 at expiration. (100 [short strike] − $0.75 [credit received] = $99.25).

Some Notes on Behavior   When the put spread is out of the money, time is working for you, meaning that the spread gets cheaper as you move closer to expiration—which is a good thing because you are short the spread. When the spread is in the money, time is actually working against you, meaning that if both options are in the money or have strikes that are lower than the current stock price, the spread hurts you because it gets more expensive as you move closer to expiration.

The behavior of spreads can sometimes seem strange to a trader who is not familiar with them. This is why it is imperative to practice these trades in your virtual account before applying real money and remember that complex strategies are not suitable for all investors.

A Bull Put Spread Example Let's walk through an example of initiating a bull put spread on Google. Here is the strike selection and price; then I will explain the rationale.

GOOG Bull Put Spread

- Sell to open 10 April 500 puts.
- Buy to open 10 April 480 puts.
- The limit price (i.e., when you execute your order, you should collect at least this amount for the put spread) is $7.00. This limit price is currently way above the market price and will likely not get filled—read on for more details.
- Note: This is a credit spread. Both options should be traded simultaneously.

The Sentiment Back on February 25, 2010, GOOG was trading right around $521. I believed at the time, based on technicals and fundamental analysis that Google could hold the $500 mark for 50 calendar days. The stock did touch on some February lows, but I believed that this sell-off was a buying opportunity and that even if the stock had further downside (which means it was headed lower), GOOG will stay above the $500 level. Our strategy then is to have a limit offer in place for the April 500/480 put spread, which is currently trading for about $4.60. I decided to place the limit order at $7 limit, which was $2.40 higher than the current trading price, because I thought GOOG was going to sell off a bit more. But it was beginning to look tired to the downside; note the chart patterns in Figure 7.4.

The spread had a net delta of around 13. Of course, if GOOG trades another $15 to $20 lower and volatility creeps up, this spread could be trading for more than $7, but I still felt comfortable with the $500 support at that

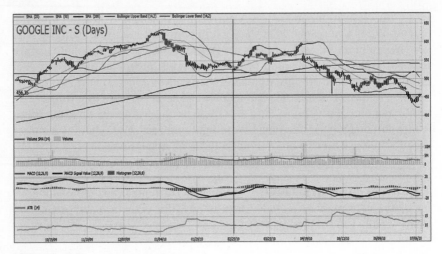

FIGURE 7.4 GOOG Daily Chart
Source: Courtesy of Lightwave Charts.

time. I wanted to offer it at $7 and be ready to capitalize on any sudden swoosh down. If I was not filled and the stock stabilizes around $520 in the next few trading days, I could have lowered my limit order to get into the position. But it was filled at $7.

Trade Analysis   GOOG was trading around $520.92, down about 2% on that day (see Figure 7.5).

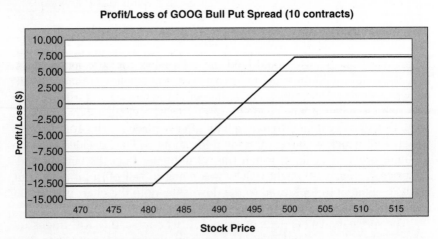

Chart Courtesy of OptionsHouse

FIGURE 7.5 GOOG Bull Put Risk Graph

Risk Attributes of the Bull Put Spread I Selected

The upside: Maximum profit for this credit spread is the $7 per spread collected on entry (minus commissions). The max profit will be achieved if GOOG shares are above $500 when the options expire on April 16. Return on risk is about 55 percent in 50 days.

The downside: Maximum risk is $13 per spread, or the difference between the strikes minus the credit received. For maximum loss to occur, GOOG would need to be trading below the long put strike (480) at April expiration. At this point, the 500 put is in the money by $20 and you would be assigned, forcing you to exercise the 480 put to cover. GOOG is currently about 8% above the lower strike.

Margin: The margin requirement for this spread could be as high as $13, or $1,300 per spread ($13,000 for a 10-lot).

Breakeven: Breakeven is the strike price of the sold put (500) minus the credit, or $493. Below this level, the spread begins to lose money. GOOG is currently trading about 5.4% above the breakeven point.

Probability of success: Here I used the OptionsHouse.com probable calculator to get a statistical measurement of the trade, just for rationalization purposes.

According to the calculator shown in Figure 7.6, this particular strategy has a 29.26% chance of losing money and a 70.74% chance of achieving some or all of the maximum potential profit. There is a 20.47% chance of suffering the maximum loss. This was assuming that day's implied volatility.

Trade Management Once I was in the GOOG trade, I closely monitored the price action in GOOG to see if it trades at a new lower valuation near $500. This is primarily an institutional stock, so I paid close attention to where large investors see value. My thesis was that with Google poised to earn near $25 this year, buyers will be eager to pay a 20 P/E forward multiple and keep the stock above $500.

Finishing Below Lowest Target Price	Target Price	Finishing Between Target Prices	Target Price	Finishing Above Highest Target Price
20.47%	480	8.79%	492.9	70.74%
Probability of Touching	38.53%		55.57%	

FIGURE 7.6 Probability of GOOG Trade Showing Prices and Percentages

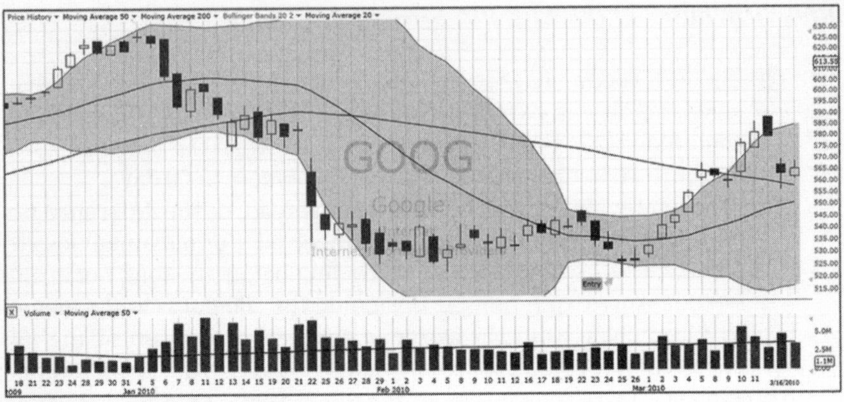

FIGURE 7.7 GOOG Rally

If that thesis and/or the stock's technicals break down, I would reevaluate my commitment to the trade and possibly exit to avoid catastrophe. This was more of an intermediate term trade, so I would obviously watch the charts for support, resistance, and any changes in the stock's relationship to moving averages.

Exiting the Trade before Expiration As you can see in Figure 7.7, the trade was working, as GOOG's price moved higher and higher. But remember that I had to contend with an earnings report, which our friends at Google love to announce right at options expiration. With the strong rally out of the gate on the Monday of expiration week and expiration Friday upon us, many out-of-the-money put options (and call options) were beginning to not only see some serious decay, but they will also realize the accelerated effects of gamma and thus delta as we approach Friday's close. The sharp changes in delta and the actual options premium will really start to become apparent this expiration week.

As Google approached $540, the 500- and 480-strike puts begin to have less and less of a delta, and remember that the gamma will increase the closer we are to expiration, causing even greater changes in delta and in options pricing.

Delta doesn't only tell us how much an option's price will change relative to the stock; it is also the percentage chance that the option will expire in the money.

So a delta of 0.10 (10%) also means that the option has roughly a 10% chance of expiring in the money (or, in other words, being worth anything!).

Don't forget that delta will either be 1 or 0—100 or zero—on expiry and *if* you are short the 500/480 bull put spread. This should lead to these puts being worthless at expiration, allowing you to retain the credit you collected when initiating the trade.

There was still a tremendous amount of doubt when it came to the strength of this market and of Google in particular; it has really been apparent when you survey the market action, especially late in the day. I saw the market starting to falter into the close on otherwise bullish days, which was *not* a sign of bullish strength and confidence.

GOOG has also had a tough time moving out of the $540 handle; it has been bumping its head on that level since January 29. With that said, it was time to examine exiting. Earnings are *not* typically a time for calm.

It does not hurt to sell into a little strength. And although I didn't book my max profit (that only occurs if both options are zero), I was able to sleep a bit better and move on to my next trade that may have a bit more edge.

I find that it is much easier to sell into strength than into a stock that is on the way down.

Result   The spread was bought back for $1.60, netting a profit of $4.40, or 34% of my total risk of $13.

Selling a Call Spread (Bear Call Spread)

The characteristics, sentiment, and risk of selling a call spread follows:

- *Market sentiment.* Moderately to very bearish—depends on where you place the spread.
- *Further out of the money.* Less bearish—spread is typically put on out of the money.
- *Further in the money.* More bearish.
- *Risk.* Varies, but limited to difference in strikes minus premium collected (you will always collect premium when selling a call spread in the same month).
- *Potential reward.* Limited to credit received.
- *Passage of time.* Good for out-of-the-money spreads, bad for in-the-money spreads.
- *Probability characteristics.* Stock *must* finish below short call strike price. I prefer to sell call spreads at or out of the money.

  The further the call spread is away from the stock price at the time of entry, the higher the probability of success. However, the higher the probability, the less credit you will receive for the spread.

- *Time in trade.* Typically 10 to 40 days to expiration, because call spreads are typically sold out of the money, the short call will have more time value than the long call allowing you to collect theta.
- *When to apply this strategy.* You have a moderately bearish view on the stock and have found a resistance point or top in a stock and want to limit your risk.
- *How you will win.* Stock stays below your short strike by expiration. (*Breakeven at expiration = short call strike price + premium collected.*)
- *How you will get hurt.*
  - *Stock stays flat up to expiration.* If you sold your call spread at or out of the money (just above the stock price), a stock that stays flat can actually allow you to attain maximum profit in the trade.

    If you sold your call spread in the money, you will lose some or all of your investment, depending upon what strike you sold and the credit you received.
  - *Stock rises.* You will gradually attain maximum profit as both put options become worthless.

The short vertical call spread Greek attributes are:

- Delta

  Negative—Delta can range from −.01 to −.97.

  Because this spread is typically sold out of the money, it will generally have a lower delta > 0.60. When selling a put spread, focus more on the strike that you sold, width of the spread, and the credit received as opposed to the delta. The lower delta tells us that these spreads are less sensitive to moves in the stock. The closer the short put is to the stock price, the more variance you will have in your P&L.

- Gamma

  Negative when the spread is out of the money, and gradually will get positive as the spread moves in the money (which is not a good thing).

- Theta

  Varies. You are collecting theta when the stock is at or above the short put; you may begin to pay theta if the spread moves against you and into the money.

- Vega

  Varies. You are short vega when the spread is out of the money. If the spread moves against you, you will be long vega. Typically, at the onset of this trade you should have a moderate negative

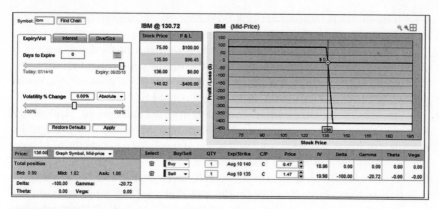

FIGURE 7.8 Bear Call Spread Expiration Risk Graph

vega bias, being that I recommend this strategy be placed out of the money.

Figure 7.8 shows us the risk graph of a bear call spread at expiration; it looks identical to the bear put spread risk graph with limited risk and limited reward.

Bear Call Spread Academics When you sell a call spread, it's actually a bearish trade, which also can be confusing to some because of the use of call options to take a bearish stance on the stock. When a call spread is sold, typically it is bearish because you are selling a call with a larger delta and buying a smaller delta call against it.

Selling a larger delta call means that it will inherently have a lower strike, higher delta, and a higher value than the one you are buying; therefore, you will be "selling" the spread—or collecting a credit for the spread. You are also said to be *short* the spread.

When you sell a call spread, you are collecting money into your account; this is also called a *credit* trade. Short call spreads behave entirely different from long call spreads.

A short call spread is similar in behavior to an in-the-money bear put spread, but it is a credit trade.

The first rule about short call spread is that when you are short a call vertical spread, you can*not* make more than what you initially sold the spread for, no matter how far the stock drops. I will illustrate this in a moment.

If you sell a call spread for $1 and the stock plummets, that $1 is all you will make. Unlike the long call spread, if you sell a call spread, typically you have a moderately bearish outlook on the stock—meaning that you want it to drop in value.

The second rule you must know when selling a vertical call spread is that you can sometimes lose more than the credit you brought in, meaning that if you sold the call spread for a dollar and the stock goes up, you could potentially lose more than the dollar you brought in.

The third rule is that when you sell a vertical call spread, you cannot lose more than the difference in strikes, minus the credit you brought in. Meaning that if you sell a 95 call and buy a 100 call for a net credit of $1, you have a five-point spread that you collected $1 for, making your max loss $4. This is an example of an upside down risk and reward ratio. You can make a dollar, but you have $4 of potential risk. Like selling a put spread, this may sound like a bad deal if you just look at that part of the trade, but there is a reason why a trader may select this strategy, which is typically because there is a higher probability of success in the trade and limited loss potential when compared to short stock.

Risk Examples Before you widen your spread width and chase the higher returns, consider the following three examples of risk in a vertical credit spread:

1. Sell the 50 call and buy the 55 call for a 1.00 credit = $4.00 max loss.
2. Sell the 50 call and buy the 60 call for a 2.00 credit = $8.00 max loss.
3. Sell the 50 call and buy the 65 call for a 3.00 credit = $12.00 max loss.

Determining how wide you want to make your spread should be determined by both the amount of the credit you are taking in and how far you think the stock could rally if things went wrong. The less likely you think it is that the stock will rally, widen your spread. The more likely you think it is that the stock will rally, narrow your spread.

The goal of selling a vertical call spread is to have the stock finish *below* the call you sold at expiration. Basically, you want the stock to stay below the short strike all the way until expiration. Typically, this trade is executed with a spread that is already out of the money, meaning that both calls will have a strike price higher than the stock price.

We have established that selling a vertical call spread is a bearish event. Now, the question is what strikes do we buy and sell and what months do we sell the spread in?

Remember the goal: We want the stock to stay below the short strike up until expiration.

There are several different ways this trade can be executed; keep in mind that I am sharing my personal views on this strategy.

Typically, if I am selling a call spread, I like to sell them out of the money to begin with. This way, the stock is already where I want it to be. Unlike buying an out-of-the-money call (OTM) spread, I will usually sell (OTM) spreads with 30 or fewer days to expiration, as passing time benefits my position. As long as my spread is out of the money, time decay will be working in my favor because both options will be getting cheaper. Because I had traded for a credit, if the spread is worth zero at expiration, it is a good thing for me.

The mind-set of selling a spread can be quite different from buying one.

Remember earlier that I discussed how this trade may have an upside down risk/reward ratio, partially because the trade may have a higher statistical probability of being successful. Let me explain.

If you have a stock that you feel is going to drop in value (let's say that stock is trading at $50), if you were to sell the 60 call for $1.50 and simultaneously purchase the 65 call for $0.50, you now have a 60/65 bear call spread on for a credit of $1. Let's also assume that these options expire in 20 days, this means that as long as the stock stays below 60 for the next 20 days you will retain your $1. Basically, the stock can do one of three things and you can still have a successful trade. The stock can fall from here, it can stay flat, or it can rise to 60 and you would still be profitable. Keep in mind that if the stock rises above $60 you will begin to lose money and above $61, incur a loss, your max loss potential in this trade is $4, because it is a $5 spread and you brought in $1 (spread width minus credit equals risk).

Let's take this concept a bit further. I am a statistical trader by nature, meaning that I look back at the historical volatility of a stock as well as the implied volatility to determine a realistic movement in a stock during a given period of time. I then look at my potential reward and potential risk in a trade before making my decision.

For example, let's say that historically (over a month's time), a stock tends to fluctuate about 18% higher or lower, with the stock trading at $50, that's $9 in either direction over a month's time. If we have sold our spread $10 away from the current stock price, this may give us a statistical edge. I can also tell you that even with a statistical edge, you can lose in this trade; having probability on your side is a great thing—but anything can happen in the marketplace.

Combining your statistical analysis with a bearish fundamental or technical thesis will increase probability of success.

By practice trading the strategy, you will begin to find what works best for you. Practice trading can be done in a virtual account using fake money, which will help ensure that you understand the sometimes unpredictable behavior of a spread and will help you to refine your exit criteria.

Practical Example   Let's walk through a basic vertical call spread sale. Here's what it looks like hypothetically:

Let's say that you were bearish on ABC Corporation and thought it was going to stay below $120 for the next 20 days; it's currently trading at $110 (on January 1, 2009). The stock has been rallying with the broad market, but its fundamentals are not the best. The P/E ratio of the stock is high, compared to its peers and the stock is beginning to look shaky. You're thinking that the stock most likely will not move much higher from here and will experience a short-term retracement and then struggle to break up through its recent high of $113 because you have notice that when it rallied to this range before, it failed.

You start looking at the January 2009 calls, which expire in 15 days. You can sell the 120 call for $1. It currently has a delta of 0.23 and the 125 call (which is further out of the money) can be bought for $0.25; it has a delta of 0.06. If you were to sell the January 120 call for $1 and buy the January 125 call for $0.25 at the same time, you would actually be selling the January 120/125 call spread for a limit price of $0.75. Because the spread is $5 wide, your maximum profit potential in the trade would be $0.75, or 18%, on your risk of $4.25. Your maximum risk in the trade is the spread width ($5) minus the credit received ($0.75), or $4.25. Maximum loss occurs when the stock is above the long strike at expiration. Your breakeven at expiration is your short strike plus the credit you received for the total spread.

In our example, you would not make or lose money (excluding commissions) if the stock was at $120.75 at expiration (120 [strike] + $0.75 [credit received] = $120.75).

Entry   The best time to enter a short call spread is right before you feel the stock is going to drop, usually on a day when the stock is rallying, but on low volume and beginning to look weak into the close. You can enter once the stock has begun to drop, but you will most likely receive less premium for your spread because the calls lose value when stocks decline.

Before even entering the trade, find an acceptable loss that you are willing to take in the spread. In some cases, it may be okay to accept the maximum loss in this trade, which would be $4.25. But if the stock begins to rally or if something fundamentally changes with the stock or broad market causing a surge of buyers, which seem like they are in it for the long haul, it may be best to cut the cord and limit your losses.

Many times, when I sell a call spread, I am willing to lose more than twice the credit I received. So if I sold a $5 call spread for 0.80, I may be willing to lose $1.60 on the trade, which would mean I would buy it back for $2.40 (0.80 credit initially + 1.60 loss potential = $2.40 stop). You can also base your stop loss on a point in the underlying stock; however, realize that if the stock rallied quickly, in this case to $119, you might immediately see your P&L go negative, but if the stock stalls and just sits there, you would gradually become profitable and may even make your max profit.

Typically, if the stock begins to rally through my short strike and looks strong, I will look to exit the trade. You don't want one loss wiping out five good ones.

Here are some notes on behavior. When the call spread is out of the money, time is working for you, meaning that the spread gets cheaper as you move closer to expiration, which is a good thing because you are short the spread. When the spread is in the money, time is actually working against you, meaning that if both options are in the money or have strikes that are lower than the current stock price, the spread hurts you because it gets more expensive as you move closer to expiration.

Preferred Technical Example   In Figure 7.9 you can see a double top formation in ACI at the $28 level; this would be a level to examine selling a call spread. When/if the stock approached that level again, if it began to exhibit weakness, that is, lower volume and decreasing momentum, it might be a good candidate for the bear call spread.

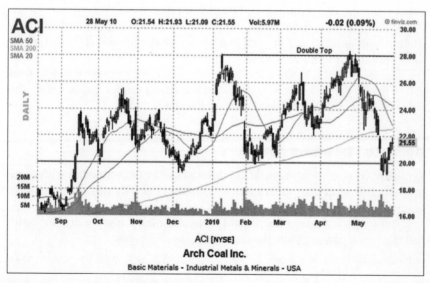

FIGURE 7.9   ACI Daily Chart
Source: Courtesy of www.Finviz.com.

TRADER TIP

Remember that a bear call spread is basically the same as a bear put spread with the same strikes, only a bear call spread is a credit trade and the bear put is a debit trade. Timing, monitoring, and exiting are the same.

DEBIT VERTICAL SPREADS

You must pay your maximum loss up front; the goal is to sell them for more than you originally paid, netting a profit.

The concept of buying a vertical spread may be easier for new traders to grasp because it falls back in line with what most of stock and beginner options traders are used to—paying for something up front. The idea of paying for something then and hopefully selling it for more than what you paid is a method that most traders already employ, so the mechanics of the trade are familiar and therefore the behavior and money/risk management of the trader is generally easier. If you are not yet comfortable with the concepts of credit spreads, remember that you can substitute an in-the-money debit spread for an out-of-the-money credit spread and vice versa.

Rules of the vertical still apply, only when you are buying a vertical you always *buy* the deeper in-the-money call or put.

A long vertical spread still means that you are buying and selling a similar type option (call or put) one to one (buy one and sell one) in the same month with different strikes.

The goal of the long vertical spread is to have the stock finish at or above the strike you sold in the case of the call spread, or at or below the put strike you sold in the case of the put spread.

Where to Place Your Spread

Typically, long vertical spreads are done at or out of the money with more time to expiration than short vertical spreads, generally with three or more months until expiry.

The long vertical spread should be positioned at a point at which you feel the stock can get to by the time the spread expires.

Swapping a Long Spread for a Short Spread

However, in-the-money *long* verticals will behave the same as the opposite type short vertical spread in the same month. Simply translated, the long 45/50 call spread will behave exactly the same as selling the 45/50 put spread when buying and selling the same strikes.

So if you bought the 45 call and sold the 50 call, it would be the same as buying the 45 put and selling the 50 put. The behavior of the spreads in terms of the Greeks would be identical. Even the profit and loss potential would be exactly the same.

Here is the conversion chart:

In-the-money *debit call* spread = Out-of-the-money *credit put* spread with same strikes and action (buy/sell)

In-the-money *debit put* spread = Out-of-the-money *credit call* spread with same strikes and action (buy/sell)

BUYING A PUT SPREAD (BEAR PUT SPREAD)

Some characteristics, sentiment, and risks of buying a put spread are:

- *Market sentiment.* Moderately to very bearish—depends on where you place the spread.
- *Further out of the money.* More bearish—spread can be placed anywhere.
- *Further in the money.* Less bearish; you would just need the stock to stay below the short put strike.
- *Risk.* Varies, but limited to premium paid.
- *Potential reward.* Limited to spread width minus premium paid
- *Passage of time.* Good for out-of-the-money spreads, bad for in-the-money spreads.
- *Probability characteristics.* Stock *must* finish below short put strike price. If I think the stock is going to just creep lower over a period of time, I would buy a put spread out of the money, which has a lower probability, but higher potential payoff. You can also buy a put spread in the money, which is the synthetic for selling an out-of-the-money call spread with the same strikes.

  The further the put spread is below (out of the money) from the stock price at the time of entry, the lower the probability of success. However, the lower the probability, the greater the potential profit and vice versa.
- *Time in trade.* Typically 20 to 180 days to expiration, can vary greatly.

- *When to apply this strategy.* You have a moderately bearish view on the stock and have found a resistance point or top in a stock and want to limit your risk.
- *How you will win.* Stock stays below your short strike by expiration. (*Breakeven at expiration = short put strike price minus premium collected.*)
- *How you will get hurt.*
  - *Stock stays flat up to expiration.* If you bought your put spread at or out of the money (short strike just below the stock price) a stock that stays flat can actually allow you to attain maximum profit in the trade.

    If you bought your put spread in the money, you will make all potential profit if the stock is below the short put strike
  - *Stock rises.* You will gradually lose money as both put options become worthless. You will lose everything if the stock is *above* the *long* put strike on expiration.

The long vertical put spread Greek attributes are:

- Delta

  Negative. Delta can range from -0.01 to -0.97.

  Because this spread is typically bought at or out of the money, it will generally have a lower delta > 0.60. When buying a put spread, focus more on the strike that you sold, width of the spread, and the price paid as opposed to the delta. The lower delta tells us that these spreads are less sensitive to moves in the stock. The closer the short put is to the stock price, the more variance you will have in your P&L.

- Gamma

  Negative when the spread is in the money, and gradually will get positive as the spread moves out of the money (which is not a good thing).

- Theta

  Varies. You are collecting theta when the stock is at or below the short put. You may begin to pay theta if the spread moves against you and out of the money (stock moves higher).

- Vega

  Varies. You are short vega when the spread is in the money. If the spread moves against you, you will begin to get long vega.

- Rho

  Minimal risk.

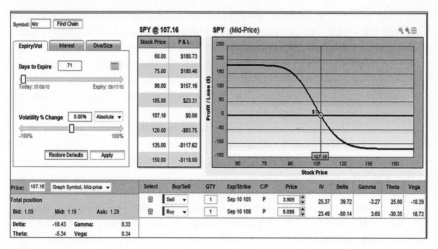

FIGURE 7.10 Bear Put Spread Risk Graph with Greeks

Figure 7.10 displays the limited risk/reward characteristics of the bear put spread.

Why Trade a Bear Put Spread?

Put spreads can be used because they may be cheaper than just buying a put outright and potentially less risky than selling a put outright, you will also tend to have less sensitivity to changes in volatility as well as changes in the stock price because of the lower delta of the spread.

Put spreads, like call spreads, are limited in both risk and reward; we discuss that in a moment. Put spreads involve the purchase and sale of two or more puts, one for one.

There are also different types of put spreads, including vertical, horizontal, and diagonal. For this discussion, we focus on vertical, nonratio put spreads. Vertical means that both put options are expiring in the same month. Nonratio means that for every one put we buy, we will only be selling one put against it. If you have already traded call spreads or at least researched them you will find many similarities between call spreads and put spreads, just a slight difference in directional behavior.

The main difference is when you buy a put spread, you are bearish; when you sell a put spread you are bullish, opposite of the call spreads.

The Components Put options can be used in many different ways. Some options traders buy put options to speculate on a stock's potential downward movement. Buying a put can reduce your risk, or upside exposure to a stock, because you may pay less for your put options versus shorting the stock—not to mention that being short a stock is theoretically unlimited in risk. Buying a put certainly has its share of risk, but that risk is limited to the premium paid. So if you bought the January 100 put for $2, and the stock rose to $200, you would lose only the $2 premium.

Selling puts naked, on the other hand, can be more risky. Short puts by themselves have a maximum risk of the strike price minus the premium. So if you sold that same January 100 put for $2 and the stock went to zero, you would lose $98 (strike-premium).

Short puts are commonly used as a stock acquisition tool as discussed in the short put strategy section.

To reduce risk, a short put can be done with a hedge of some sort, something to offset risk, something like stock or another option.

When you combine the long and short put together in the same month, you create a vertical put spread, which can be either bought or sold.

Bear Put Practical Application   When a put spread is bought, it is bearish because you are buying a put with a larger delta and selling a smaller delta put against it. Buying a larger delta (which inherently will cost more) will have a higher strike than the one you are selling; therefore, you will be "buying" the spread. You are also said to be long the spread. Remember, delta is the rate of change in the options price for every one dollar move in the stock. Because you are buying the put with the larger delta, that put is in control, so to speak, which means the spread is bearish.

When you buy a spread, you are paying money out of your account; this is also called a *debit* trade. In the world of options, there are certain rules that are governed by the laws of mathematics. Don't worry if you're not a math whiz. One of the rules I am going to let you in on is that, in a debit vertical spread, based on the upcoming discussion, you can*not* lose more than what you pay; this applies to both call and put spreads. This doesn't mean that you can't lose money, but it does let you know right at the onset of the trade what your risk is. If you buy a put spread, typically you have a moderately bearish outlook on the stock, meaning that you want it to fall in value. Another rule you must know when buying a vertical put spread is that the spread will never not be worth more than the difference in strikes, meaning that if you buy a 100 put and sell a 90 put you have a 10-point spread. That spread can't be worth more than $10. If you pay $5 for that spread, your maximum profit potential is $5, or 100%, in that case.

At expiration, the bear put spread will be at its maximum value if the stock is below the put you sold. In basic terms, you want the stock to fall below the short strike before the time the spread is set to expire. This does not mean that you cannot be profitable if the stock does not reach the short strike by expiry, but as a general rule, if you are just getting started, the basic goal is to have the stock get below the short strike. So we have established that buying a vertical put spread is a bearish event. Now, the question is: What strikes do we buy and sell and what months do we purchase the spread in?

There are several different ways this trade can be executed; keep in mind that I am sharing my personal views on this strategy. Typically, if we are buying a put spread, we will usually buy enough time for our spread to potentially become profitable. If I feel a stock is going to go down in value over the next three to four months, I want to be sure that I buy a spread that doesn't expire in two months; maybe the best choice would be to buy one with expiration of five or six months, just slightly longer than I anticipate being in the trade. By practice trading the strategy, you will begin to find what works best for you. Practice trading can be done in the virtual account using fake money.

A Walk through a Basic Vertical Put Spread Purchase   We will assume it's January 1, 2009. Let's say that you thought ABC Corporation was going to go from $105, which is its current trading price, to $90 or lower over the next three months.

You start looking at the options and find the June 2009 puts. The 115 put will cost you $17 to buy; it currently has a delta of –0.68. The 90 put can be sold for $6.50. It has a delta of −0.37. If you were to buy the June 115 put for $17 and sell the June 90 put for $6.50 at the same time, you would actually be buying the June 115/90 put spread for a limit price of $10.50. The spread is $25 wide, so your maximum profit potential in the trade would be $12.50, or 119%. Your maximum risk in the trade is your original investment of $10.50, or $1,050 per spread, meaning loss occurs when the stock is *above* the long strike at expiration. Your breakeven at expiration is your long strike minus what you paid for the total spread. Meaning that in our example, you would not make or lose money (excluding commissions) if the stock was at 104.50 at expiration. (115 [strike] − 10.50 [cost of spread] = $104.50).

Notes on Behavior   When the put spread is out of the money, time is working against you, meaning that the spread gets cheaper as you move closer to expiration—which is obviously not beneficial because you are long. When the spread is in the money, time is actually working for you, meaning that if both put options are in the money or have strikes that are higher than the current stock price, the spread benefits, or gets more expensive, as you move closer to expiration.

BUYING A CALL SPREAD (BULL CALL SPREAD)

Some characteristics, sentiments, and risks of buying a call spread are:

- *Market sentiment.* Moderately to very bullish—depends on where you place the spread.
- *Further out of the money.* More bullish.
- *Further in the money.* Less bullish—goal of trade is to have the stock finish above short call strike.
- *Risk.* Varies, but limited to premium paid (you will always pay premium when buying a call spread).
- *Potential reward.* Limited to width of strikes minus premium paid.
- *Passage of time.* Good for in-the-money spreads, bad for out-of-the-money spreads.
- *Probability characteristics.* Stock *must* finish above short call strike price. Shorter-term call spreads should be bought in the money, longer-term call spreads can be bought further out of the money. The longer time you have in the trade, the more time the stock has to get above the short call strike.

  The further the call spread is away from the stock price at the time of entry, the lower the probability of success, but higher potential profit, that is, the spread will be cheaper.
- *Time in trade.* Anywhere from 3 to 180 days to expiration, the further out in time and the closer the strikes are to one another, the less sensitivity the spread will have to changes in the stock price.
- *When to apply this strategy.* You have a moderate bullish view on the stock and have found a support point and want to limit your risk.
- *How you will win.* Stock stays above your short strike by expiration. (*Breakeven at expiration = long call strike + premium paid for the spread.*)
- *How you will get hurt.*
  - *Stock stays flat up to expiration.* If you bought your call spread at or in the money (just below the stock price), a stock that stays flat can actually allow you to attain maximum profit in the trade as long as it's above strike upon expiry.
  - *Stock rises.* You will gradually attain maximum profit as both call options move to parity (their actually intrinsic value), but stock must be above your short strike to attain max profit.

The long vertical call spread Greek attributes are:

- Delta

   Positive. Delta can range from 0.02 to 0.98.

   The more in the money the call spread is, the higher the delta will be and you will have a greater bullish bias, although if the call spread continues to move very deep in the money, the P&L variation will reduce as both call deltas move to 1 and offset one another.

   If the call spread is out of the money, the delta will be less, but you will *need* the stock to move higher if you want to get profitable.

- Gamma

   Negative when the spread is out of the money, and gradually will get positive as the spread moves in the money (which is not a good thing).

   The closer the short call is to the stock price, the more variance you will have in your P&L.

- Theta

   Varies. You are collecting theta when the stock is at or above the short call (spread is in the money); you may begin to pay theta if the spread moves against you and out of the money. Out-of-the-money call spreads will cost you money each day in theta.

- Vega

   Varies. You are short vega when the spread is in the money. If the spread moves against you and out of the money, you will be long vega.

- Rho

   Minimal risk.

Academics   After you have become comfortable with how call options behave in the marketplace and you are confident with trading both long and short calls, you may choose to start exploring call spreads.

Call spreads can be used because they may be cheaper than just buying a call outright and potentially less risky than selling a call outright. They can also be positioned to increase the probability of success. This occurs when you buy an in-the-money call spread or sell an out-of-the-money call spread.

Call spreads, typically, are limited in both risk and reward; we discuss that in a moment. They involve the purchase and sale of two or more calls. There are also different types of call spreads—vertical, horizontal, and diagonal. For this discussion, we discuss vertical, non ratio call spreads. Vertical means that both call options expire in the same month. Non ratio means that for every one call we buy, we only sell one call against it.

Now, before you get all nervous with the foreign words, let's break d⌐wn the concepts involved.

Call options can be used in many different ways; some options traders buy call options to speculate on a stock's potential upward movement. Buying a call can reduce your risk (or downside exposure to a stock) because you may pay less for your call options versus simply buying the stock. Buying a call certainly has its share of risk, as we have discussed in our long call practical discussion.

Selling calls naked, on the other hand, can be extremely risky when done without a hedge. A hedge might be something like the simultaneous purchase of stock or another long call. Some traders are comfortable with the concept of buying a stock and selling a call against it, which is called a buy-write or covered call. In a buy-write (or covered call) we still may have significant downside risk. If we want to take risk reduction a bit further, we first have to define risk. As a professional trader, I view risk as the maximum I can lose in a trade—others may have a different view. For instance, if I buy 100 shares of a stock at $100 per share, my total risk in that investment is $10,000 dollars, period. If I sell a 110 call for $2 against the stock that I bought at $100, my risk is now $98 per share, because the credit from the call reduced my cost basis in the trade. I had to give up something for that risk reduction; in that example I gave up some of my potential profit. The max I can make in this trade is $12; here my cost basis was $98 and I sold the $110, which would obligate me to sell the stock at $110 on or potentially before expiration. I am using this example as we begin discussing call spreads because we have to understand risk, cost basis, max profit potential, and return on risk.

I said earlier that call spreads are limited in risk as well as reward. That is certainly an open statement; another thing you must know is that call spreads can either be bought or sold.

When a call spread is bought, it is bullish because you are buying a call with a larger delta and selling a smaller delta call against it. Buying a larger delta will inherently cost more and will have a lower strike than the one you are selling; therefore you will be "buying" (or *long*) the spread. Delta is the rate of change in an options price for every one dollar move in the stock. The higher the delta, the more expensive the option costs in the same expiration month.

Bull Call Spread Practical Application #1   When you buy a spread, you are paying money out of your account; this is also called a *debit* trade. In the world of options, there are certain rules that are governed by the laws of mathematics. Don't sweat it if you're not a math whiz; it's okay. One of the rules I am going to let you in on is that, based on the following discussion, in a debit vertical spread, you can*not* lose more than what you pay. This doesn't mean that you can't lose money, but it does let you know right at the onset of the trade your amount of risk. If you buy a call spread, you typically have a moderately bullish outlook on the stock, meaning that you want it to rise in value. There is another rule you must know when buying a vertical call spread—the spread will not be worth more than the difference in strikes. This means that if you buy a 90 call and sell a 100 call you have a 10-point spread and that spread isn't worth more than $10. If you pay $5 for that spread, your maximum profit potential is $5, or 100%, in that case.

At expiration, the bull call spread will be at its maximum value if the stock is above the call you sold. In basic terms, you want the stock to rise above the short strike before the spread's expiration date. This does not mean that you cannot be profitable if the stock does not reach above the short strike by expiry, but as a general rule (if you are just getting started) the basic goal is to have the stock get above the short strike. So we have established that buying a vertical call spread is a bullish event. Now, the question is: What strikes do we buy and sell and what month do we purchase the spread in?

There are several different ways this trade can be executed. Keep in mind that I am sharing my personal views on this strategy. Typically, if we are buying a call spread, we will usually buy enough time for our spread to potentially become profitable. If I feel that a stock is going to go up in value over the next three to four months, I want to be sure that I buy a spread that doesn't expire in two months, unless I think the stock will get up above my short call strike before that time or if the spread is already in the money.

If I am more of an intermediate-term trader who believes the stock will see a moderate rise over the next four to five months, perhaps the best choice would be to buy one with expiration in five or six months, which is slightly longer than I anticipate being in the trade. By practicing the strategy, you will begin to find what works best for you. Practice trading can be done in a virtual account using fake money.

A Walk through a Basic Vertical Call Spread Purchase Going back to the previous example of ABC Corporation, let's now assume the opposite. If you thought ABC was actually going to go from 105, its current trading price, higher to $120 or more over the next three months.

Using similar analysis, but now with calls, you examine the options and find the June 2009 calls. The 95 strike will cost you $17 to buy and currently has a delta of 0.68. The 120 strike can be sold for $6.50 and has a delta of 0.37. If you were to buy the June 95 call for $17 and sell the June 120 call for $6.50 at the same time, you would actually be buying the June 95/120 call spread for a limit price of $10.50. The spread is $25 wide, so your maximum profit potential in the trade would be $12.50, or 119%. Your maximum risk in the trade is your original investment of $10.50, or $1,050 per spread. Maximum loss occurs when the stock is *below* the long strike at expiration. Your breakeven at expiration is your long strike plus what you paid for the total spread. Meaning that in our example, you would not make or lose money (excluding commissions) if the stock was at $105.50 at expiration (95 [strike] + $10.50 [cost of spread] = $105.50).

Expiration breakeven: Long call strike + premium paid.

Notes on Behavior   When the call spread is out of the money, time is working against you, which means the spread gets cheaper as you move closer to expiration—which is not what you want because you are long. When the spread is in the money, time works for you, meaning that if both options are in the money or have strikes that are lower than the current stock price, the spread benefits (or gets more expensive) as you move closer to expiration.

Real Bull Call Example   It's June 1, 2010, and the market has been recently corrected, but is having an extremely tough time building momentum. The S&P and Dow Jones have given back all their gains for the year. Price-to-earnings multiples on the S&P 500 are at low historically levels and for the most part, companies seem to be growing. Unemployment is high, but looks to be improving. Europe is still shaky and the euro has been weakening against the dollar, causing dollar-denominated commodities and oil to slide lower. U.S. multinational companies may experience weakness due to the strong dollar. Many short-term technicals have broken down on the major indexes and on many of the stocks that are contained within. Some select stocks and longer-term technical indicators seem to be intact, suggesting a continuation of the bull market, with this being a momentary pullback. Although the bulk of the news is moderately positive, there are still risks and consequently, volatility, and the S&P 500 Volatility Index (VIX) remains elevated.

How do we trade this moderately bullish, but skeptical sentiment?

From an options trader's perspective, there are some specific parts of that thesis that need to be taken into consideration specifically to determine the best strategy:

- Moderately bullish sentiment.
- High volatility.
- Long-term support levels.
- Underlying concern for systematic sovereign risk.
- Limited growth potential.

Rationale   A bull call spread may provide a solution in this instance, as it offers limited risk, lower vega exposure, and the ability to set the maximum risk by adjusting spread width—a lower upfront cost than just purchasing a call outright, but still an excellent return on risk given the limited upside anticipation.

This is where you need to find and decide on a candidate. The S&P 500 Spyders ETF (SPY) would be the broadest way to express this view; however, there are other specialized ETFs and even individual stocks that you may think will fit your thesis best and satisfy your desired outcome. For me, there are three ways I would approach this situation.

First, I could find a quality, low beta stock that is more defensive in nature and has been beat up pretty bad with a low earnings multiple, looking for a pop in that individual stock.

Second, I could target a sector with an ETF that has underperformed in the rallies, but bore all the brunt of the sell-offs, looking for value there.

Third, I could just buy the SPY or the SPDR Dow Jones Industrial Average ETF (DIA) looking for a broad market recovery. This method has pros and cons; a pro would be the fact that I am hedged in the SPY with 500 different stocks and 30 in the DIA, but at the same time, the con is that those indexes could flounder over the next couple months as sectors within them rotate and the losers cancel out the winners, making for a flat trade.

The benefit here is that if I choose the SPY, I could structure the strikes in a way that doesn't require much upside in the index for me to attain a decent return.

For this trade, looking at the forward P/E of the S&P 500, which was about 13.11 times earnings on June 1, 2010, and the chart, I felt that there was a large amount of value and a viable trade for the intermediate term (one to three months) in the SPY.

I chose a spread that expired in September 2010, which was 112 days away; it was six points wide and was partially in the money, for several reasons.

A $6 wide spread that cost me $3.55 to buy allows me to potentially make another $2.45 on the trade in about four months if SPY is above $112 on September expiration. This is almost a 70% return on my risk capital, or about 230% annualized return.

The reason why I partially put this spread in the money was the breakeven. Remember earlier when I noted that I thought the recovery may be shaky? Well, with the uncertain prospects, I didn't want to have to require SPY to have to do much. The breakeven on this trade is $109.55 (long strike + premium paid), and SPY is currently trading at 109.37, which means that if the index just moves up 0.18, I will be at a point where I won't make or lose any money, all while having only $3.55 at risk at all times, no matter how bad things get.

Is This a Good Return? How do you rationalize return on the bull call spread? Statistically, in the SPY example, the trade is much like buying the stock in terms of its success, in that the breakeven is close to the stock price (109.55 for spread versus 109.37 for the stock). Because of this, I want to be sure that my return potential on the spread is commensurate with the statistical returns of the index.

TRADER TIP

If the breakeven was much higher, the statistical probability of success is lower, but the potential return should be greater.

   If the breakeven was below the current stock price, the stock is already where it needs to be for me to make max profit in the trade, so the odds are in my favor and, therefore, I should expect to make less return.

And, how do you find a realistic return? Remember average true range (ATR)?

An easy way to figure out a realistic return in a given period of time is to look at either the stock's ATR or standard deviation for that time period. There are calculators and tools that allow you to do this.

If you are going to be in a trade for:

- One to six days, use the daily ATR.
- One to four weeks, use the weekly ATR.
- One to four months, use the monthly ATR.[1]

You can also use one standard deviation in your selected time frame. Standard deviation is the dollar representation of volatility over a given period of time. I talked about this in an earlier chapter.

For example, based on the implied volatility of the at-the-money options in September in SPY (27% IV), one standard deviation in the SPY four months out would be about $16.50, up to $125 and down to about $93.

There is about a 28% statistical chance that SPY would touch $93 to the downside. This is just an example; you can obviously adjust your risk to your comfort level, but placing your stop loss too close may prematurely exit you from the trade—too far and you may be risking too much.

This method, along with technical analysis, can be used to figure not only stop losses and targets, but also to compare the potential return of your options strategy with that of a stock position. The upside shows a 36% statistical probability that SPY could touch $125, which would be one standard deviation up.

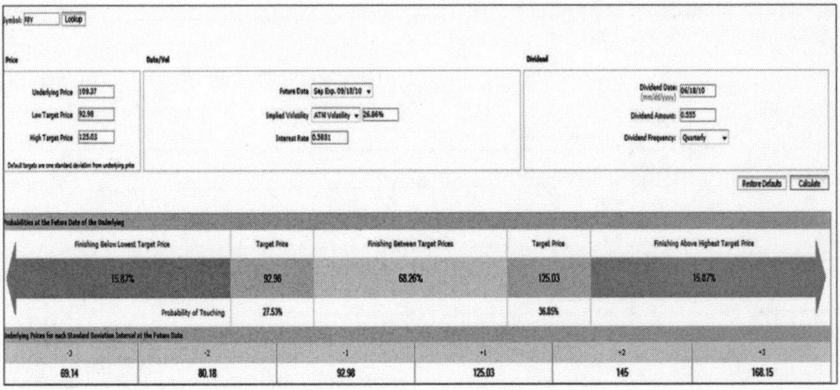

FIGURE 7.11 SPY Probability Chart
Source: Courtesy of www.OptionsHouse.com.

If we assume that SPY moves in the direction we want it to, one standard deviation (SD) of 16.50, that would be a return on risk of 15% ($16.50 1SD/$109.37 SPY stock). This still pales in comparison to the return of 70% on our risk in the bull call spread.

We also have to consider real market conditions; can the S&P really get up to 1,250 within that time frame, which would be one SD? Statistics are one thing, market sentiment, news, earnings, technicals, and the myriad of real market forces are another.

Furthermore, to achieve a 70% return on our stock trade, SPY would have to go to almost 186, which would mean the S&P 500 would have to rally to roughly 1,860 or more, a level never seen in the index.

Figure 7.11 shows the expected statistical probability and standard deviations of the SPY over the next four months (from 6/1/2010 to 9/17/2010) one SD in that time frame was projected at about $15 or 14%.

Setting Stops Before any trade takes place, you must establish an exit strategy or set stop loss levels. Because bull call spreads are limited in risk and sometimes can have a high probability of statistical success, your stop loss may be your total risk in the trade. I mean, think about it; if you were a longer-term trader who intended on holding SPY for several months, your stop loss may be upward of $12, which is the monthly ATR (average true range) of SPY. In this trade, no matter what happened to SPY, your max risk would be $3.55, so for your risk management in this trade, you may allow the trade to go to max loss.

If the $6 wide call spread was in the money, it would cost more, but have a higher probability of success because the stock is already where it

FIGURE 7.12 Daily SPX Chart
Source: Courtesy of Lightwave Charts.

needs to be on expiration for you to make money. The increased cost will increase risk because it costs more.

With many debit vertical spreads, because of their nature (risk/cost is commensurate with probability) stop losses and money management may be done on the front end, in that you limit the amount of spreads you buy to an acceptable level, assuming the worst-case scenario.

In other words, make sure that you understand the probability characteristic of your trade; you don't have to lose your entire investment, but if that is the way you want to trade (risking the entire spread), just use the number of spreads to meter your risk.

You can use technicals to assist you in setting stops and targets; moving averages and support/resistance levels like those in Figure 7.12 can be trigger points for entry and exit.

Bull Call Spread Practical Application #2   Back in early June 2010, Boeing had announced plans to ramp up production of its ever-popular narrow-body 737 jet. Boeing (BA) was producing 31.5 jets per month and was aiming to increase that number to 35 by the end of 2012. There seemed to be a sense of urgency within Boeing because it was the company's second increase in production in a month's time. At that time there was a backlog of more than 2,000 orders for their best-selling plane, according to the *Wall Street Journal*. Executives at Boeing noted increased demand for new planes as well as the exercise of existing options already held by carriers. The bottom line is that this increased demand and subsequent increase in production seemed at the time to be a sign of global economic improvement (or at least stabilization within the air travel space).

Airbus also found itself in a similar situation with its Airbus A320, which competes with the 737. Airbus will also be increasing its production from 34 planes to 36 per month to meet its backlog of more than 2,300 planes. The dance between the two will be somewhat in sync as neither wants to find itself standing alone in a tightly woven, highly competitive sector that has some new players entering the space with jets that compete directly with the 737 and A320. Canadian equipment manufacturer Bombardier, for example, was nipping at the heels of the world's largest commercial jet makers.

According to its website, Bombardier's CSeries jet will seat 100 to 149 passengers and use the Pratt & Whitney PurePower PW1000G high-efficiency engine. Bombardier calls the engine *game-changing*. The plane's unique design will supposedly operate with 15% less cost and use 20% less fuel than a comparably sized jet. The vehicles also boast wider seats and windows than comparable models in production.

Of course, BA and EADS (the parent company of Airbus) were looking to revamp their most popular lines as well, with industry experts not expecting a total revamp until after 2020. Much of the decision was whether there would be a real game-changing engine design. It would cost billions for both manufacturers to design, test, and successfully release a completely new aircraft. In the meantime, the two major players can incorporate a more efficient engine into the current design to increase efficiency and noise reduction, though there could be negative ramifications regarding the backlogs on their current models. The week prior, Airbus COO John Leahy hinted that an A320 replacement may not come until 2027.

Regardless, if demand looked and remained strong and carriers such as American Airlines looks to replace its fleets of aging MD-8Xs (American has 272 of them) and other aircraft, this could bode well for BA. American operates an all-Boeing et leet at present.

United, on the other hand, replaced its older 737s with A320s and it may be replacing its last 737s with the CSeries jets, which is a bonus for Bombardier.

There are obviously dozens and dozens of airlines globally, all with different needs, route maps, and budgets. Ultimately, it is extremely difficult to know who will come out on top. Boeing is one of two major manufacturers of large jets, and if global demand increases (causing production to continue to rise), BA could experience an earnings boost. Boeing believes that its customers will remain loyal and will be looking to Boeing to lead with new products.

Why choose an at-the-money bull call spread (see Figure 7.13)?

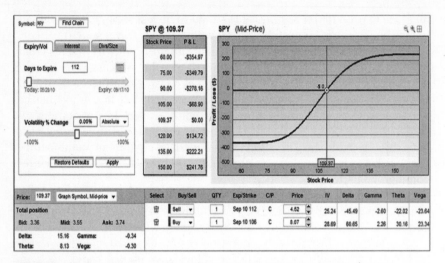

FIGURE 7.13　SPY At-the-Money Bull Call Spread Risk Graph with Greeks

Figure 7.14 shows support and resistance levels in Boeing. Because levels are rather tight and the bullish news is more moderate and long term, a bull call spread may be appropriate

Based on the news analysis, there seemed to be some moderately bullish news coming down the pike. There were also some technical issues to deal with, namely a 52-week high at that time of around $76. A bull

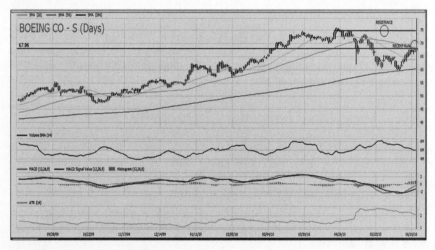

FIGURE 7.14　BA Daily Chart Showing Short-Term Support and Resistance
Source: Lightwave.

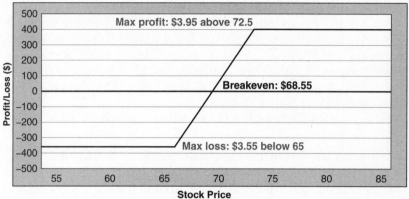

FIGURE 7.15 BA Risk Graph with P&L

call spread comes to mind here, because the bullish catalysts are a bit more moderate and longer term, not to mention the market in general was a bit squirrely back then, and BA had just rallied for almost eight days straight, which left me reluctant to take a ton of bullish risk at that moment.

I didn't know if BA was getting back to its April high of $76, but thought that it could get above $72.50 in a month or so. It was trading at $68 at the time (see Figure 7.15). Typically, bull call spreads are used if you have a moderately bullish opinion on the underlying stock, with the maximum profit being attained if the stock is above the short call strike by expiration. For example, the November 65/72.50 call spread could be bought for $3.55 (buying the 65 call and selling the 72.50 call). This means that the maximum risk in the trade would be $3.55 and the max potential profit is $3.95, or the difference in the strike prices minus the premium collected. If BA is trading above $72.50 at November expiration, you could potentially return 111% on your risk. Breakeven for this strategy is $68.55, which essentially means that the stock only needs to be 55 *cents* higher than where it is today for me to be breakeven at expiration.

Verticals Can Mitigate Volatility and Other Risk   It is important to note that this trade would have minimal vega exposure (the spread would be minimally impacted by changes in volatility). This is different from buying a call outright or selling a put outright, which are both bullish acts, but have more sensitivity to changes in implied volatility. The bottom line is that if you are unsure of where volatility is going or if it has just spiked or dropped sharply and you are concerned about a reversion to the mean, using a vertical spread can reduce your vega exposure.

Vertical spreads can also lessen overall volatility in your portfolio, because they can be structured to have a lower delta than just buying or selling an option outright. The width of the difference in strike prices in a vertical spread can have dramatic effects on several behavioral characteristics of the spread including P&L variation, delta, vega, theta, and so on. Be cognizant of how your spread changes.

Here are some characterizations of vertical spreads you must know:

- The wider the spread, the more sensitive the spread will tend to be to stock movement, because the difference in delta becomes more drastic the further away the options are from one another (depending on placement).
- The wider the spread, the more potential reward, but greater risk.
- Narrower spreads offer lower risk/cost, but lower profit potential.

Picking the Right Strike Prices and Width of Spread   Determining the width of your spread and which strikes to buy and sell is really a matter of personal preference and sentiment on the stock. As I mentioned earlier, the further your spread is above the stock price, the cheaper it will be, in turn offering you the potential for an increased return. The reality is that you should choose the short call strike at an area where you feel very *confident* that the stock will be above on expiration day. If you are less bullish, move your short strike lower. You can even buy a call spread in the money if you wish; just be prepared to pay more and get less return.

Long call spread behavior will vary greatly depending on the positioning and width of strikes. Remember that out-of-the-money call spreads will be costing you theta each day, where in-the-money call spreads will allow you to collect theta.

If you are feeling a little less bullish or are nervous about the current market conditions, you can narrow your strikes closer together.

Typically, I trade spreads that are $5 wide. For stocks over $100, I may increase that to $10. For lower-priced stocks and some ETFs, I may reduce my spread width to $2, or even a dollar. Because I like odds in favor of and not against me, I tend to position bull call spreads at or in the money. But if I do find a stock that I think could really explode to the upside, but I don't want to risk as much with buying a long call, an out-of-the-money bull call spread can be suitable. I still rationalize my positioning of the short call strike with past stock movements or levels. You can use forward earnings projections combined with your short call strike price to see if the P/E ratio at that price at some finite point in the future seems cheap or expensive.

At Expiration

ABC Stock	59.50	60.00	60.50	62.00	65.00	70.00
60 Call Short	00	00	.50	2.00	5.00	10.00

——————— subtract short call value from long value ———————

| 55 Call Long | 4.50 | 5.00 | 5.50 | 7.00 | 10.00 | 15.00 |

——————— sum of both calls gives your spread value ———————

| Spread Value | 4.50 | 5.00 | 5.00 | 5.00 | 5.00 | 5.00 |

FIGURE 7.16 Expiration Profit and Loss Scenarios for Bull Call Spread

Behavior of the Bull Call Spread One of the most common complaints of bull call spread buyers, both new and seasoned, is that you could buy the 55 to 60 bull call spread with the stock at 55, and in a short amount of time the stock rallies to $60.50 and your call spread is worth only $3.50. What gives? New traders often deal with this and become extremely frustrated, so let's address it. First off, if that did indeed happen in a short amount of time, chances are that you are profitable in the trade and if the stock seems to be weakening, or you are afraid of a pullback, it's okay to exit the trade as a spread. But why isn't the spread worth $5? The answer is time value. Now that the short call (60 strike) is closest to the stock price, it is at the money, and if you remember, at-the-money options have the most amount of time value compared to other options in their month.

If the stock stays above $60 (in this case), that 60 call's time value will continue to erode away, and on expiration, you will be left with pure parity or intrinsic value and the net value of the spread will be $5 anywhere above $60, as illustrated in Figure 7.16.[2]

If the stock continues higher and that short call goes deeper in the money, it will also lose time value and the spread will move closer to its maximum value. How deep the spread has to be in the money to be trading for close to parity depends on the price of the stock and the implied volatility of the options themselves.

How will changes in implied volatility affect your spread?

- If your spread is totally in the money and volatility decreases, this will be beneficial to your P&L.

• If your spread is out of the money and volatility decreases, this will
hurt your P&L.

Make yourself aware of the net delta of your spread, so you will have an idea of
the sensitivity your spread will have to changes in the stock price.

Exiting and Expiration   As one of my favorite bullish strategies and
one of the easier spreads for beginners to employ because of its similarity
to a long call, the bull call spread does need to be monitored. Because
you have sold a call against another call, the variation of your P&L will be
reduced when compared to just buying a call outright.

At-the-money bull call spreads will generally have the most variation
in P&L.

What you must remember is that when you purchase a call spread (and
a put spread for that matter) you have limited risk, but also limited reward.
Because of this, you must be more conservative in your profit targets. For
example, if you buy a call spread for $3 and it goes to $4, that would be a
33% return on your risk. Not too shabby. Depending on how much of your
account you allocate to each trade, you may be willing to risk the entire
premium spent on the spread or if you risked a substantial portion of your
account and the trade goes against you, you may want to salvage what you
can, perhaps a 50% stop loss, which if you buy the spread for $3 and if it
goes to $1.50, you will exit.

Risk and monitoring the trade also has much to do with what strikes
you use. If you bought an in-the-money bull call spread, the stock only has
to stay above the short call strike for you to make your max profit. So
in that case, because you have a higher probability of success, you may
choose to allow a bit more wiggle room in any loss you are willing to
tolerate.

If you bought the spread out of the money, it will be cheaper, but in that
case, the stock must move for you to make money. In this case, if the stock
really looks like it's not going to move higher, it may be best to salvage
what you have left and move on.

There are some traders who buy very cheap out-of-the-money call
spreads and take a long shot on the stock rallying. In this case, be sure
to *take* your profit when you have one, because it may be gone in the blink
of an eye.

MARKET DIRECTION NEUTRAL SPREAD STRATEGIES

Sometimes we may lack an opinion on the direction of a stock. Perhaps we believe that it's going to move big, but we are not sure about direction. Maybe we believe that the market as a whole is going to get more volatile and we want to make that bet with limited risk. This can be done with the purchase of a straddle or strangle. On the other hand, sometimes we may believe the opposite, that the market will remain within a range and volatility will recede. That sort of thesis may warrant a sale of a straddle or strangle. All of these sentiments could merit what we call a *neutral* strategy. Let's explore them.

Long Straddle

The characteristics, sentiments, and risks of a long straddle are:

- *Market sentiment.* Neutral/directionless, but with big movements expected after trade is executed. Depending on what strike price you choose in relation to the stock, the trade can have a bullish or bearish bias.
- *Call further in of the money.* The straddle will have a higher delta and become profitable faster if the stock rises.
- *Put further in the money.* The straddle will have a lower delta (negative) and will become profitable faster if the stock drops.
- *Risk.* Limited to premiums paid for both the put and the call.
- *Potential reward.* Unlimited to the upside, limited to strike minus premium paid to the downside.
- *Passage of time.* Very bad for long straddles, especially when they are bought using at-the-money strikes, being that those options have the most amount of theta.
- *Probability characteristics.* Varies, but odds are against you. The stock must move or volatility must increase faster and greater than the amount of theta you are paying per day.
- *Time in trade.* Typically, straddles are bought with at least 45 days to expiration, but can be bought with much longer time durations if you are making a bullish bet on volatility rising. They can also be bought with shorter durations if you believe that the stock will make a drastic move in the near term that will be more than the premium you paid for the entire straddle.
- *When to apply this strategy.* You have a belief that the stock will experience a drastic change in price over the duration of the spread.

Optimally, that movement will be more than the cost of the spread itself.

You have a bullish bet that implied volatility will rise faster and greater than the amount of theta you are paying in that time frame.

- *How you will win.* Stock moves up or down past your breakeven points (strike ± premium paid).
- *How you will get hurt.*
  - *Stock stays flat up to expiration.* If the stock does nothing and/or volatility drops, this can hurt your P&L. Remember that the passage of time is bad for a long straddle.

Some long straddle Greek attributes are:

- Delta

  Positive to negative, depending on which option is further in the money. Delta can range from −1.00 to +1.00 (for a truly neutral trade, delta should be around 0.50).

  The more in the money the call is, the higher the delta will be, as you will have a greater bullish bias.

  The more in the money the put is, the lower the delta will be, as you will have a greater bearish bias.

- Gamma

  Long straddles are always long gamma, because you have bought both a call and a put. Gamma will be greatest in the spread when the strike price chosen for the call and put is closest to the stock price.

  Long gamma means that you want the stock to move and can potentially become profitable no matter which direction the stock moves in.[3]

- Theta

  You are always short, or paying theta, as you are long both the call and the put.

- Vega

  Because you are long both options, you will always want vega to move higher, no matter where the stock is in relation to the strike(s) you have bought.

Note that the unlimited profit potential to the upside and high profit potential to the downside indicated by the V shape of the risk graph in Figure 7.17. Even with all that upside potential, you must consider the area at the base of the V, where you are going to lose money if the stock doesn't move.

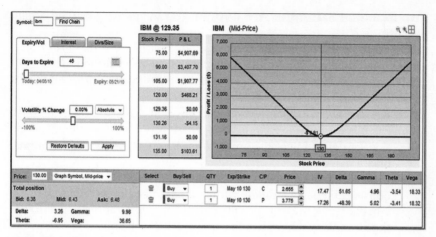

FIGURE 7.17 Long Straddle Risk Graph with Greeks

Academics The long straddle is used to express a neutral directional sentiment, but with the intent that the stock will move away from your strike price far and fast. Out of all the market-neutral strategies, the straddle can be the most aggressive in terms of *needing* the stock to move, particularly when the straddle is purchased at the money. The strategy involves the purchase of a call and a put with the same strike in the same month.

Because the strategy involves the purchase of two options as the entire spread, this strategy tends to have a higher relative theta than other spreads, and also, when bought near the money, may have great sensitivity to changes in implied volatility. The straddle strikes can be anywhere in relation to the stock price, though many traders tend to associate the straddle with the at-the-money strikes. Because you are purchasing both options, the risk of the straddle is the premium paid. The breakeven points, on expiration, in the long straddle is the straddle strike plus and minus the premium.

Let's examine what the breakeven and profitability profiles look like for long straddles. In the long straddle, you are *losing* money in between the breakevens on expiration.

Breakeven Example

- Long 1 January 30 call for 3.00 and Long 1 January 30 put for 2.80.
- Straddle Cost $5.80.
- Breakevens 35.80 to the upside, 24.20 to the downside.
- If the stock moves past these points before expiration, you are ensured a profit as well.

Two Reasons Straddles Are Bought   Straddles are generally bought because:

1. The trader believes that the stock will be outside of either the upper or lower breakevens by the straddle's expiration date, without having a directional bias and taking limited risk.
2. The trader believes that implied volatility will rise faster than theta will decay the straddle.
   - You can also adjust the straddle's placement to take a directional bias.
   - If you believe that there is a better chance of the stock dropping, consider buying a straddle with a strike price that is higher than the current stock price. This will give the put a greater delta and in turn the straddle will have a net negative delta at the onset.
   - If you believe that there is a better chance the stock will rally, purchase the straddle with a strike price below the stock price, which will give the call a greater delta and in turn the straddle will have a net positive delta at the onset.

Long Straddle Strike Positioning

1 Long Call	+	1 Long Put
CALL	+	PUT
Strike		*Strike*
40		40
45	Max ⇕ Reward	45
Long 1 50		50 Long 1
55	Unlimited	55
60		60

Paying Theta   The long straddle can be an expensive strategy to keep on if unhedged, especially when the straddle is bought close to expiration. Before you buy a straddle, be sure that you are okay with the amount of theta that you are paying per day and remember that theta increases as you move closer to expiration.

If the straddle is bought with 60 days or greater, volatility increase typically becomes the bigger bet. In other words, options that expire further out in time have a greater vega, or sensitivity, to changes in implied volatility. If you have an opinion that volatility will rise, buy a longer-dated straddle.

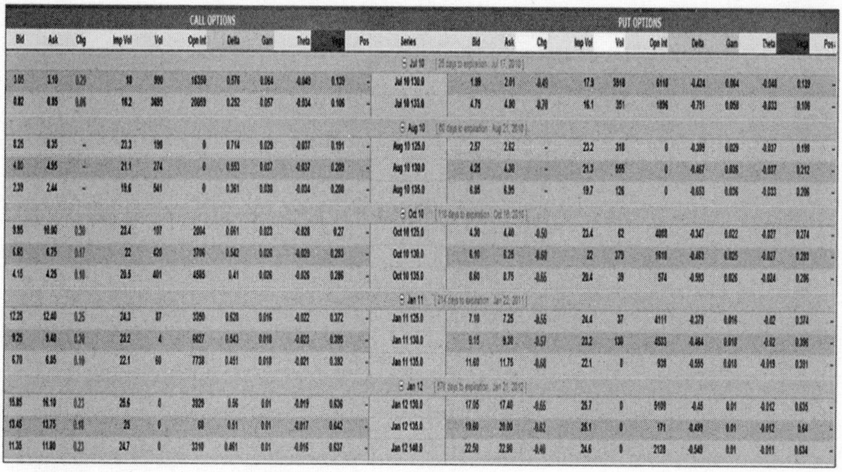

CALL OPTIONS												PUT OPTIONS										
Bid	Ask	Chg	Imp Vol	Vol	Open Int	Delta	Gam	Theta	Vega	Pos	Series	Bid	Ask	Chg	Imp Vol	Vol	Open Int	Delta	Gam	Theta	Vega	Pos
											Jul 10 [25 days to expiration, Jul 17, 2010]											
3.05	3.10	0.25	18	990	16350	0.576	0.064	-0.049	0.139	-	Jul 10 130.0	1.99	2.01	-0.45	17.8	3918	6118	-0.424	0.064	-0.048	0.139	-
0.82	0.85	0.06	16.2	3495	20859	0.252	0.057	-0.034	0.106	-	Jul 10 135.0	4.75	4.90	-0.70	16.1	351	1896	-0.751	0.059	-0.033	0.106	-
											Aug 10 [60 days to expiration, Aug 21, 2010]											
8.25	8.35	-	23.3	198	0	0.714	0.029	-0.037	0.191	-	Aug 10 125.0	2.57	2.62	-	23.2	318	0	-0.309	0.029	-0.037	0.198	-
4.80	4.95	-	21.1	274	0	0.553	0.037	-0.037	0.209	-	Aug 10 130.0	4.25	4.30	-	21.3	555	0	-0.467	0.036	-0.037	0.212	-
2.39	2.44	-	19.6	541	0	0.361	0.038	-0.034	0.208	-	Aug 10 135.0	6.85	6.95	-	19.7	126	0	-0.653	0.036	-0.033	0.206	-
											Oct 10 [116 days to expiration, Oct 16, 2010]											
9.85	10.00	0.30	23.4	107	2004	0.661	0.023	-0.028	0.27	-	Oct 10 125.0	4.30	4.40	-0.50	23.4	62	4083	-0.347	0.022	-0.027	0.274	-
6.65	6.75	0.17	22	420	3706	0.542	0.026	-0.029	0.293	-	Oct 10 130.0	6.10	6.25	-0.60	22	375	1618	-0.463	0.025	-0.027	0.293	-
4.15	4.25	0.10	20.5	401	4585	0.41	0.026	-0.026	0.286	-	Oct 10 135.0	8.60	8.75	-0.65	20.4	39	574	-0.593	0.026	-0.024	0.296	-
											Jan 11 [214 days to expiration, Jan 22, 2011]											
12.25	12.40	0.25	24.3	87	3359	0.628	0.016	-0.022	0.372	-	Jan 11 125.0	7.10	7.25	-0.55	24.4	37	4111	-0.379	0.016	-0.02	0.374	-
9.25	9.40	0.36	23.2	4	6627	0.543	0.018	-0.023	0.395	-	Jan 11 130.0	9.15	9.30	-0.57	23.2	130	4533	-0.464	0.018	-0.02	0.396	-
6.70	6.85	0.10	22.1	60	7738	0.451	0.018	-0.021	0.392	-	Jan 11 135.0	11.60	11.75	-0.60	22.1	0	938	-0.555	0.018	-0.019	0.391	-
											Jan 12 [578 days to expiration, Jan 21, 2012]											
15.85	16.10	0.23	25.6	0	3329	0.56	0.01	-0.019	0.636	-	Jan 12 130.0	17.05	17.40	-0.65	25.7	0	9109	-0.45	0.01	-0.012	0.635	-
13.45	13.75	0.10	25	0	68	0.51	0.01	-0.017	0.642	-	Jan 12 135.0	19.80	20.00	-0.62	25.1	0	171	-0.499	0.01	-0.012	0.64	-
11.35	11.80	0.23	24.7	0	3310	0.461	0.01	-0.016	0.637	-	Jan 12 140.0	22.50	22.90	-0.40	24.6	0	2128	-0.549	0.01	-0.011	0.634	-

FIGURE 7.18 IBM Option Chain—Note Vega
Source: Courtesy of OptionsHouse.com.

Betting on Vega If you look at Figure 7.18, you can see how vega increases the further out in time you buy the straddle. These are the at-the-money options on IBM, with the stock at about $131. The straddle in July has a net vega of about 0.28, which means that it will change about 28 cents (28 real dollars) for each 1% *absolute* change in implied volatility, where the January 2012 straddle has a net vega of 1.28, which means that a 130 straddle in 2012 will change by 128 real dollars for every one dollar absolute change in implied volatility.

TRADER TIP

Watch out for the volatility crush—the straddle before earnings mistake. Some traders use straddles ahead of a big event to potentially profit from a large move in the stock. If the stock moves away from your strike by an amount greater than the premium you paid for the entire spread, then you are in the clear, as either the put or call's parity value will enable you to be profitable in the trade. However, even though straddles can profit from a large move in the stock, there are also other forces at work that you must be aware of. If you buy an at-the-money straddle, you are basically buying the most amount of volatility for that month, because the at-the-money strikes have the highest vega.

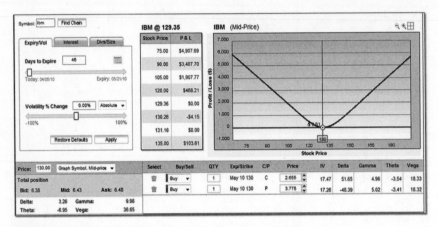

FIGURE 7.19 IBM Straddle Risk (P&L) Graph and Greeks

Variations To reduce risk but widen breakevens, a strangle can be used. A long strangle is almost identical in market sentiment and Greek sensitivity; however, instead of buying a call and a put with the same strike, an out-of-the-money call and an out-of-the-money put are bought in the same month, with different strikes. The strangle will cost less than a straddle, but will have different breakevens on expiration and will also have less gamma.

In the P/E in Figure 7.19 for the IBM straddle, the vega is almost 37, which means that for every 1% absolute change in implied volatility, the position will lose or gain roughly $37 per spread. Compare that to the delta of less than four. Volatility can and will hurt you if it drops sharply.

In fact, it is extremely common for volatility to decrease sharply after an event such as earnings or an FDA ruling becomes known. In fact, IBM implied volatility, in 2009 to 2010, dropped an average of 15 percentage points after earnings. (You can find this data by using a historical volatility chart and comparing implied to observed volatility over earnings periods.)

If you were long the straddle in Figure 7.20, that could have equaled a $555 in vega alone, which means the stock would have to move further for you to be profitable. This is why traders can have a stock make a fairly large move in the stock and still lose money buying a straddle ahead of an event. There are other ways that a trader can make a bet on a large move in the stock while having less long vega exposure. The good thing is that as long as your stock, ETF, or index moves outside of your breakeven points up or down, you can profit, but the post-earnings volatility crush can be a serious obstacle on your road to profitability in the straddle.

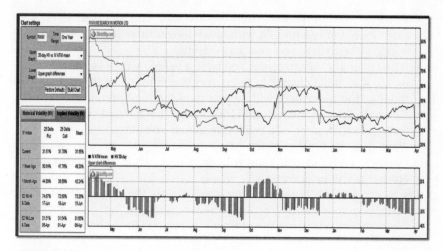

FIGURE 7.20 Volatility Chart Example (Historical and Implied)—Look at Historical Changes in Both

Short Straddle

The characteristics, sentiment, and risks of a short straddle are:

- *Market sentiment.* Neutral/directionless, with few or no market fluctuations after trade is executed. Depending on what strike price you choose in relation to the stock, the trade can have a bullish or bearish bias.
- *Call further in of the money.* The straddle will have a greater *negative* delta and will give the spread a bearish bias at the onset.
- *Put further in the money.* The straddle will have a greater *positive* delta and will give the spread a bullish bias at the onset.
- *Risk.* Unlimited to the upside, limited to the downside (strike sold minus premium collected).
- *Potential reward.* Limited *only* to premium received, max gain will be if straddle expires with strike price equal to stock price.
- *Passage of time.* Very good for short straddles, especially when they are sold using at-the-money strikes, being that those options have the most amount of theta. Theta accelerates in the last weeks of the straddle's life.
- *Probability characteristics.* Varies. If you sell a straddle, the probability of the stock expiring right at your strike price is very low; however, the more premium you collect, the wider your profitable zone will be. Unfortunately, big premiums often mean big volatility, which will hurt you.

- *Time in trade.* Typically, straddles are sold with less than 45 days to expiration, but can be sold with much longer time durations if you are making a bearish bet on volatility (falling).
- *When to apply this strategy.* You have a belief that the stock will experience a minimal change in price over the duration of the spread. Optimally, that movement will be less than the total premium collected. Generally, the straddle should be sold in a heightened volatility state, with the anticipation of a reduction in that volatility.
- *How you will win.* Stock stays between your breakeven points (strike ± premium paid) and volatility drops, while time passes by.
- *How you will get hurt.*
  - *Stock makes a big move after you initiate the spread.* If the stock starts to move and volatility increases, this can hurt your P&L. Remember that the passage of time is very good for a short straddle.

The short straddle Greek attributes are:

- Delta

  Positive to negative depending on which option is further in the money. Delta can range from –1.00 to +1.00. To be truly direction neutral, delta should be close to zero.

  The more in the money the short call is, the more negative the delta will be, as you will have a greater bearish bias.

  The more in the money the short put is, the more positive the delta will be, as you will have a greater bullish bias.

  Positioning a short straddle's bias will be the opposite of a long straddle.

- Gamma

  Short straddles are always short gamma, because you have sold both a call and a put. Gamma will be greatest (negative) in the spread when the strike price chosen for the call and put is closest to the stock price.

  Short gamma means that you want the stock to remain right at the strike price sold and any deviation from that point will have an opposite effect on delta and may also affect profitability.[4]

- Theta

  You are always long or collecting theta in a short straddle.

- Vega

  You are always short vega when you sell a straddle, meaning that you want volatility to drop after making the trade.

Short Straddle Academics   You must really have a grip on risk, not to mention a rather strong stomach if you get into the business of selling naked straddles. There are certainly rationales and situations for just about every option strategy, but this one can really hurt you if the stock really starts to move in either direction.

When to Trade   The short straddle is used to express a neutral directional sentiment, but with the intent that the stock will remain low in volatility and preferably expire with the straddle strike price right at the stock price with little or no movement until that time. Out of all the market-neutral-type strategies, the short straddle does carry the highest risk, which is theoretically unlimited because of the short call. The strategy involves the sale of a call and a put with the same strike in the same month. Because the strategy involves the sale of two options as the entire spread, this strategy tends to have a higher relative theta (you will be collecting time decay) and when sold near the money may have great sensitivity to changes in implied volatility (you will want volatility to decrease. The short straddle strike can be anywhere in relation to the stock price, though many traders tend to associate the straddle with the at-the-money strikes. Preferably, you would want to choose a strike where you believe the stock will be when the straddle expires. The risk of the straddle to the downside is limited to the strike price minus the premium you collect; the risk to the upside is unlimited. The breakeven points, on expiration in the short straddle is the straddle strike plus and minus the premium collected (your profitable zone will be in between those breakevens).

Let's examine what the breakeven and profitability profiles look like for short straddles. In the short straddle, you are *making* money in between the breakevens on expiration.

Breakeven Example
- Short 1 January 30 call for 3.00 and Short 1 January 30 put for 2.80.
- Straddle Premium collected $5.80.
- Breakevens are $35.80 to the upside, $24.20 to the downside (inside these levels is your profitable zone).[5]

Two Reasons Straddles Are Sold   Straddles are generally sold for two reasons:

1. The trader believes that the stock will be inside of the upper and lower breakevens by the straddle's expiration date, without having a directional bias.

2. The trader believes that implied volatility will fall and wants to collect theta in a sideways market.
   - You can also adjust the straddle's placement to take a directional bias.
     - If you believe that there is a better chance of the stock dropping, then sell a straddle with a strike price that is lower than the current stock price; this will give the straddle a negative delta at the onset of the trade, because the short call is already in the money and the straddle will have a net negative delta.
     - If you believe that there is a better chance the stock will rally, sell the straddle with a strike price higher than the stock price, which will give the put a greater (positive) delta and in turn the straddle will have a net positive delta at the onset.

Selecting Strikes in the Short Straddle   Find the best strike that you believe the stock will stick to for the duration of the trade. Here is a visual representation of what the short straddle will look like and what you want the stock to do based on the individual parts. You will want to sell a straddle at a strike you believe the stock will stick to.

Short Straddle Strike Positioning

1 Short call	+	1 Short put
CALL	+	PUT
Strike		*Strike*
40		40
45	Max Profit	45
Short 1 50	⟵⟶	50 Short 1
55	@50	55
60		60

Expiration Concerns   Because the short straddle is composed of both a short call and a short put with the same strike, there is a guarantee that one of them will be in the money (unless the stock expires right at the strike price) on expiration. Furthermore, because the short straddle is frequently employed close to expiration to take advantage of time decay, there is a good chance that you may find yourself maintaining the position at or near expiration. For both of these reasons you must make yourself aware of your strategy headed into expiration along with its risks. I highly suggest that you have a plan in place ahead of time, which includes contingencies for what to do if the stock begins to move away from your short strike, in which the best solution would be to buy back the entire straddle. If you

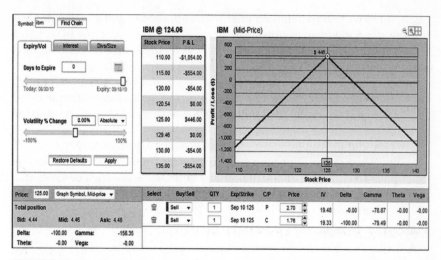

FIGURE 7.21 Short Straddle Risk Graph—Note the Small Profit Zone (Triangle) at the Top

hold the short straddle into expiration and your short call is in the money, it will most likely be assigned, leaving you with a short position in the stock come Monday morning as long as you have the cash in your account to cover the margin requirement.

If you do *not* have the cash in your account to cover the margin, your broker may *buy* the straddle back for you, which may be an undesirable outcome. These same risks apply if the stock finishes below the strike, which would put the short put in the money and thus cause an assignment, leaving you with a long stock position come Monday. If you are comfortable with having short or long stock on Monday, that is certainly an option that you have; just realize that anything can happen over the weekend and if on Monday, your long stock and it's down $10, your P&L may be much worse off than if you had just bought back the straddle on expiration day. This can obviously work in the other direction as well.

Long Straddle versus Short Straddle

Sometimes you can find a volatile stock that you think would be best suited to a long straddle, may actually be better suited to a short straddle. Here I will compare the two trades on one stock, Research in Motion.

An Experiment in Profitability I wanted to show you the advantages and disadvantages of both strategies and what might happen in both trades using one stock. There are arguments for both sides of the trade. At this point, there was news that their new Torch phone was going to be released, but the exact date had not been set. I only knew it was coming in the third quarter of the year and that expectations were high. On this date, the July options had 24 days to expiration and the August options had 59 days to expiration. Remember, when you are buying a straddle, you want enough time for the trade to work out; you want that stock to move outside those breakeven points. Typically, I buy straddles with more than 45 days to expiration.

When you are selling a straddle, you obviously want to get as much premium as you can, but limit your exposure time in the stock, so you don't have to endure as many potentially volatile events such as economic and corporate data releases.

Practical Comparison—RIMM   RIMM, June 22, 2010, stock is trading at $58.48 (see Figures 7.22 and 7.23).

Selecting Strike and Expiration Date   Looking at the option chains, the two months that are closest to expiration would both fit my basic criteria for going long or short with their expiration dates: August expiration is appropriate for the long straddle and July for the short straddle.

Selecting a strike price is key. The factors to think about are any directional bias you may have, along with the amount of premium you

FIGURE 7.22   Daily Chart of RIMM
Source: Courtesy of Lightwave.

			Jul 10 [24 days to expiration : Jul 17, 2010]		
28.15	28.95	—	Jul 10 30.0	0.00	0.02
23.20	24.00	—	Jul 10 35.0	0.03	0.04
20.75	21.40	—	Jul 10 37.5	0.05	0.07
18.30	18.60	—	Jul 10 40.0	0.11	0.12
15.95	16.10	—	Jul 10 42.5	0.19	0.21
13.55	13.70	—	Jul 10 45.0	0.32	0.34
11.25	11.40	—	Jul 10 47.5	0.52	0.54
9.05	9.20	—	Jul 10 50.0	0.82	0.85
7.05	7.15	—	Jul 10 52.5	1.27	1.30
5.20	5.30	—	Jul 10 55.0	1.94	1.96
3.65	3.75	—	Jul 10 57.5	2.86	2.91
2.44	2.46	—	Jul 10 60.0	4.10	4.20
1.51	1.54	—	Jul 10 62.5	5.65	5.80
0.89	0.92	—	Jul 10 65.0	7.55	7.65
0.50	0.52	—	Jul 10 67.5	9.65	9.80
0.28	0.29	—	Jul 10 70.0	11.90	12.05
0.10	0.11	—	Jul 10 75.0	16.70	16.90
0.03	0.06	—	Jul 10 80.0	21.65	21.85
0.00	0.03	—	Jul 10 85.0	26.15	26.90
0.00	0.03	—	Jul 10 90.0	31.05	31.85
			Aug 10 [59 days to expiration : Aug 21, 2010]		
9.70	9.85	—	Aug 10 50.0	1.42	1.46
6.05	6.20	—	Aug 10 55.0	2.78	2.82
4.60	4.70	—	Aug 10 57.5	3.75	3.85
3.35	3.40	—	Aug 10 60.0	5.00	5.10
2.36	2.39	—	Aug 10 62.5	6.50	6.60
1.60	1.63	—	Aug 10 65.0	8.20	8.35
1.05	1.07	—	Aug 10 67.5	10.15	10.30
0.66	0.70	—	Aug 10 70.0	12.25	12.40

FIGURE 7.23 RIMM Option Chains on June 22, 2010

are selling or buying it for. Refer back to the individual strategies for that data.

For comparing these trades, I have decided to take a more neutral stance on the direction of RIMM by purchasing the 57.50 straddle, which is just a dollar away from the current stock price of $58.48.

The Long Straddle Trade

Buy the August 57.50 straddle for $8.35.

- The expiration breakevens are $65.85 (upside) and $49.15 (downside).
- The profitable zone on expiration is outside breakeven prices.
- Max risk is $8.35.
- Max profit is unlimited.

The Short Straddle Trade

Sell the July 57.50 straddle for $6.60.

- The expiration breakevens are $64.10 (upside) and $50.90 (downside).
- The profitable zone on expiration is in between breakeven prices.
- Max profit is the $6.60 I collected.
- Max risk is unlimited.

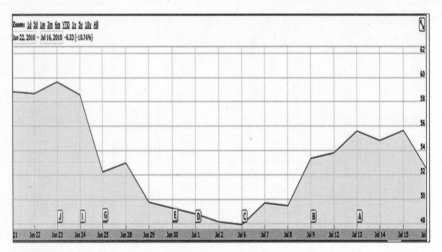

FIGURE 7.24   RIMM's Price from June 22, 2010—July Expiration
Source: Courtesy of Google Charts.

Monitoring and Exiting the Trades

Short Straddle

What happened over the next 24 days is:

- High over $59, low around $48—Were you sweating?
- Volatility jumped around June 25 (detrimental to position).
- Straddle expired with RIMM at $52.15 (profitable by $1.25).

    The short straddle trade would have eventually worked out, but it was a bit unnerving when the stock was below $50 for six days, until it leaped back up above $53. The point is that with the short straddle you are praying not only for the stock to stay within your breakevens (profitable zone) but any jumps in volatility or sudden moves in the stock can really hurt your P&L and potentially cause you to exit the trade for a loss, because of the possibility of continued risk. Figure 7.24 shows the price from June 22 through expiration.

Long Straddle

What happened over the next 59 days is:

- High over $59, low of $47.90 (on July 6)—Did you exit when you had the chance?
- Volatility jumped around June 25 (helped position).
- Straddle expired with RIMM at $48.72 (profitable by $0.43).

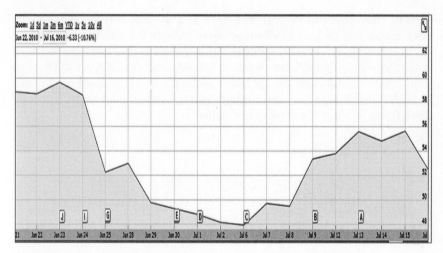

FIGURE 7.25 RIMM's Price from June 22, 2010—August Expiration
Source: Courtesy of Google Charts.

The long straddle also worked out, but the lack of unlimited risk kept me a bit more willing to stay in the trade, because I had less to lose. Check out RIMM's movements up until August expiration in Figure 7.25.

Results The long straddle in the case, after becoming profitable early on in July and then unprofitable when the stock rose back above $55, did manage to finish with a modest profit, as the stock took a nose dive in the last couple days leading into expiration. The question you have to ask yourself is when would you have exited the trade and do you think you would have made money. Looking back at Figure 7.25, on July 6, chances are you were happy, but did you get greedy and stay in? This is why it's paramount to have a profit target, not to mention test and perfect your methods and take profits when you have them. That pleasure you were experiencing in early July would have turned to stress when the stock started climbing back into your loss zone (between your breakeven points).

The point of this comparison is to show that several strategies can work, even on the same stock, at the same time. Managing them and understanding your risks will be your keys to success.

FINAL THOUGHTS

Combining individual options into basic spreads can really increase your probability of success and offer more precision in alighting your sentiment to your risk. This can be a great help if you are not very good at timing your trades and picking stocks that move exactly the way you want them to. In other words, certain spreads allow you to be partially correct and still make money in the trade. Vertical spreads and straddles are fairly easy to understand and once you get those concepts down, you are now ready to begin combining verticals into butterflies, condors, and more. You will learn those strategies and more in Chapter 8.

CHAPTER 8

Strategy: The Advanced Option Spreads

E mploying the strategies contained in this chapter requires a higher level of options understanding. You should have a firm grasp on the Greeks and have a thorough knowledge of buying and selling both calls and puts. Don't be afraid to paper trade these strategies and monitor their behavior in the open market. Because many of these strategies contain three or more different options, the behavioral characteristics can be foreign to a new trader.

MARKET NEUTRAL, VOLATILITY, AND EARNINGS SPREAD STRATEGIES

The basic options strategies and basic vertical spreads you have learned can now be combined to form new strategies that give you more opportunity to further reduce risk and add precision to your trades. While these strategies may seem complex, many of them are simply combinations of two vertical or other spreads. Dissect the components, learn the rules that govern their risk and reward, and test their behavior in a practice trading account before going live. They are not as difficult as you may think.

Butterflies, Iron Butterflies, Condors, and Iron Condors

I lumped these four strategies together because of their similarities in structure, risk, and preferred outcome, but for the sake of brevity and keeping you focused, I go into great depth on the Iron Condor strategy specifically, which I believe for the beginner may be the easiest to grasp and to employ, although based on what you have learned about vertical spreads, you should be able to trade any and all of these, because all four are simple combinations of two vertical spreads that can be composed of both call spreads, put spreads, or one of each. Butterflies are also called *flies* or *flys*.[1]

TRADER TIP

Regular (not iron) butterflies and condors can be confusing when it comes to being long or short. If you are short a *fly* or condor you are usually paying for the spread and when you are long a fly or condor, you are usually collecting a credit!

Butterflies

A butterfly is simply the combination of two vertical call spreads that are of equal width (long and short strike) that share a strike price in the middle. Both spreads expire in the same month. You can think of the butterfly as a one-to-one combination of strikes equidistantly apart. Buy one, sell two, buy one or sell one, buy two, sell one.

Butterflies can either be bought or sold. In the options world, it matters what you do to the "wings," which are the outer strikes. If you bought the wings, you are long the butterfly.

Some examples are:

- Buy 1 call (30 strike), sell 2 calls (35 strike); buy 1 call (40 strike) would be a long call butterfly.
- Buy 1 put (30 strike), sell 2 puts (35 strike); buy 1 put (40 strike) would be a long put butterfly.

The options can both be call spreads or put spreads, but not mixed and believe it or not, it doesn't matter which you use in terms of the ultimate goal and Greek sensitivities of the spread itself. It purely is where you can buy it cheaper or sell it for more.

Remember, it is always either calls or puts in a regular butterfly.

Long Butterfly (Long Fly) Calls or Puts

If a butterfly is bought, which can be a call or put fly, you want the stock to expire right at the center strike. This is where you would realize the most profit, so this is really a range-bound sort of strategy. It could be also used if you think the stock is going to end up as a certain price on or near expiration. Even though a butterfly may be cheaper than buying a call or put to speculate on the move, be sure that you consider commissions in the trade, as some brokers will charge per leg and even if they don't, each butterfly is a four-contract transaction.

You will always pay to be long a butterfly; however, you could leg into a long butterfly for a credit, which means that you are guaranteed a profit of whatever credit you received. You would also have the potential to make more if the position expired with the stock right at the center strike price.[2]

The butterfly can be placed out of the money using calls above the stock price or puts below the stock price to make the bet that the stock will end up at a certain area. This can be done for a very low cost and can have a large percentage return when compared to simply buying an out-of-the-money option with the same center strike.

Below you see the graphical representation of long butterfly strike selections. A long butterfly can either use calls or puts, but does not use both. The strike positions and 1–2–1 (long-short-long) formation remains the same for both. Whether you use calls or puts, the max profit would occur if the stock was at the center strike when the butterfly was expiring.

Long Butterfly Strike Positioning					
2 Call Spreads	or		2 Put Spreads		
LONG CALL FLY			LONG PUT FLY		
CALLS	or		PUTS		
Strike	⇧		Strike		
40			40		
Long 1	45	Max Profit	45	Long 1	
Short 2	50		50	Short 2	
Long 1	55	@50	55	Long 1	
	60		60		

Breakevens (Profitable Zone) Before you enter into a long call or put butterfly, you need to find where your profit zone will be. In other words, where can the stock be for you to make money. If the max profit is made when the stock is right in the middle of the fly, it would also make sense that you make less money the further away the stock is from the center strike. Here is the formula:

> Profitable zone is between lower strike + net debit and higher
> strike − net debit

For example, if you paid $1 for the above fly, you will be profitable on expiration anywhere between 46 and 54.

The characteristics and sentiments of the long butterfly are:

- *Market sentiment.* Neutral/directionless, range bound. You want spread to expire right at center strike.
- *Risk.* Limited to premiums paid for total fly.
- *Potential reward.* Limited to width of strikes (which should be equidistantly apart) minus net debit.
- *Passage of time.* Bad if you are not in your profitable zone; good if you are within the profitable zone.
- *Probability characteristics.* Varies, but if the spread is placed with the short strike at the current stock price, probability of success rises because the stock can potentially move up or down with you still resulting in a profit.
- *Time in trade.* Typically, butterflies are bought with less than 45 DTE and sometimes much less, although exceptions can be made.
- *When to apply this strategy.* You have a belief that the stock will *not* experience a drastic change in price over the duration of the spread. Optimally, it is a stock that tends to be range bound with minimal corporate events scheduled up until expiry.

Some long butterfly Greek attributes are:

- Delta

  Delta is zero when the stock is at the center strike because the delta of the opposing spreads cancels each other out. As the stock rises, the delta gets shorter (because you want the stock to be right at the center strike at expiration) and reaches its apex around the upper long strike at which point it begins to move back to zero the higher the stock goes.

  As the stock drops, the delta gets longer (because you want the stock to be right at the center strike at expiration) and reaches its apex around the lower long strike at which point it begins to move back to zero the lower the stock goes.

- Gamma

  Gamma is generally negative with the long fly, and is greatest when the stock is right at the center strike. You may notice that if the trade is outside of its breakevens, gamma will turn positive.

- Theta

    If the stock is within its breakeven levels, time decay is generally beneficial to the position. If the stock is outside of the spread's breakeven levels, time decay is generally a detriment to the position.

- Vega

    When the stock is between the long strike prices, the position is short vega (you want volatility to drop). If the stock is outside of the long strikes, the position becomes long vega.

A long butterfly can be constructed of two call spreads *or* two puts spreads, *not* a combination of both. It does not matter whether calls or spreads are used; the strike prices determine risk, cost, and Greeks. Max profit will be if spread expires with stock at center strike. Maximum loss will be if spread expires with stock above or below the wing strikes. The most you can make is the width of the spreads ($5 in the case above) minus what you paid for the spread.

Some traders describe the long butterfly risk graph at expiration as the *witch's hat*. Can you see that formation in Figure 8.1?

Short Butterfly (Short Fly) Calls or Puts If a butterfly is sold, which can be a call or put fly, you want the stock to expire anywhere above or below the short or outer strikes. This is where you would realize the most profit, so it tends to be more of a volatility strategy or one that is used when you think the stock is about to make a large move and *not* revert back to

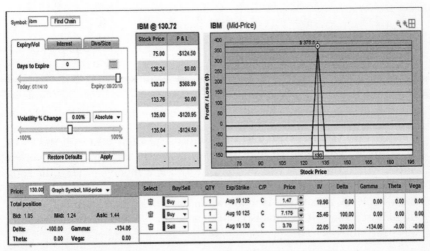

FIGURE 8.1 Long Call Butterfly Risk Graph 125/130/135

where it was trading. It could be also used if you think that the stock is going to end either above or below a certain level by expiration. Even though a butterfly may be cheaper than buying a straddle or strangle to speculate on the move, be sure that you consider commissions in the trade, as some brokers will charge per leg and even if they don't, each butterfly is a four-contract transaction. Also be sure check and compare your breakevens. Short butterflies are also limited in reward and in risk, but you can lose more than the credit you receive for the trade.

You will always collect a credit to be short a butterfly, and remember that the credit you receive is the most you can make in the trade. You can leg into the spread to try to maximize the credit you receive.[3]

Below you see the graphical representation of short butterfly strike selections. A short butterfly, like the long, can either use calls or puts, but does not use both. The strike positions and 1–2–1 (short-long-short) formation remains the same for both. In the short fly, whether you use calls or puts, the max profit would occur if the stock was above or below your outer or short strikes when the butterfly was expiring.

The only reason to select a call fly over a put fly or vice versa is the premium you collect. Whichever fly (call or put) yields more premium, that is the one you will select.

**Short Butterfly[4]
Strike Positioning**

2 Call Spreads				or		2 Put Spreads		
SHORT CALL FLY				or		**SHORT PUT FLY**		
	CALLS			or			**PUTS**	
	Strike			⇧			*Strike*	
	40			Max Profit			40	
Short 1	45			Below Short Strike		45		Short 1
Long 2	50			or		50		Long 2
Short 1	55			Above Long Strike		55		Short 1
	60			Max Profit			60	

⇩

Breakevens (Profitable Zone) Before you enter into a short call or put butterfly, you need to find where your profit zone will be. In other words, where the stock can be for you to make money. Unlike the long fly, when you sell a fly, you want the stock as far as possible from the center strike. If the max profit is made when the stock is above or below your outer short strikes, it would also make sense that you make less money the closer the stock is to the center strike. Here is the formula:

- Your upper breakeven will be above your higher short strike minus your credit received.

- The lower breakeven level will be the low short strike plus the credit you receive.
- With the stock in between those levels you will lose *more* money than the credit you received. Above or below those levels you will retain a portion of your credit until the stock is outside of the highest and lowest strikes, at which time you will retain your entire credit.

For example, if you collected $1 for the above fly, you will be profitable on expiration with the stock above 54 or below 46, which would also be your profitable zone. The more you collect, the lower the chance you have of losing money, because your breakevens are closer to one another. You would lose the most money with the stock at 50.

Some characteristics and sentiments of the short butterfly are:

- *Market sentiment.* Neutral/large move to a level outside the short strikes you choose. You are anticipating a significant event or catalyst that will move the stock.
- *Risk.* Limited to width of strikes minus credit received. You can lose *more* than the credit you brought in.
- *Potential reward.* Limited to credit received.
- *Passage of time.* Bad if the stock is stuck between your breakeven points, good if you are in the profitable zone (which is outside your breakevens) or preferably the outside of outer strikes.
- *Probability characteristics.* Varies, but if the spread is placed with the short strike at the current stock price, probability of success rises because the stock can potentially move up or down with you still resulting in a profit.
- *Time in trade.* Typically, butterflies are bought with less than 45 DTE (days to expiration) and sometimes much less, although exceptions can be made.
- *When to apply this strategy.* You have a belief that the stock will *not* experience a drastic change in price over the duration of the spread. Optimally, it is a stock that tends to be range bound with minimal corporate events scheduled up until expiry.

Some short (call or put) butterfly Greek attributes are:

- Delta

  With time to go to expiration, delta is lowest when the stock is at the center strike; however, it will begin to increase if the stock stays there as you approach expiration. The delta will become 1 if the stock expires anywhere between your breakevens (when you are losing money). As the stock moves above the center strike, delta will increase, as you want the stock to move higher. It will peak around the upper short strike and then begin to decrease, as profit potential is limited. Delta will be zero with the stock above the upper short strike.

As the stock moves below the center strike, delta will get shorter, as you want the stock to move lower. It will peak around the lower short strike and then begin to decrease as profit potential is limited to the downside as well. Delta will be zero, with the stock below the lower short strike.

- Gamma

    Gamma is generally positive with the short fly, and is greatest when the stock is right at the center strike. You may notice that if the stock is outside of the outer strikes of the butterfly, gamma will turn negative.

- Theta

    If the stock is outside its breakeven levels, time decay is generally beneficial to the position. If the stock is inside the spread's breakeven levels (ultimately outside the outer strikes), time decay is generally a detriment to the position. The bottom line is that you want the butterfly to be in a profitable position if you want to collect time decay.[5]

- Vega

    When the stock is between the short strike prices, the position is long vega (you want volatility to rise). If the stock is outside of the short strikes, the position becomes short vega.

In Figure 8.2, we see the "V" formation that dips below the breakeven in the center, but rises above breakeven to limited profit in either direction.

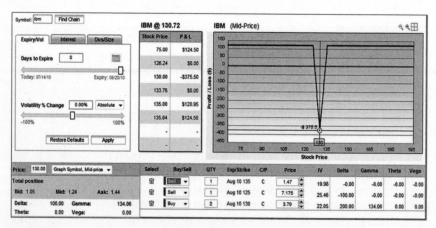

FIGURE 8.2 Short Call Butterfly Expiration Risk Graph 125/130/135

This is the visual representation of risk and reward for the short fly (call or put).

BUTTERFLIES VERSUS CONDORS

Butterflies and condors are similar in that they are constructed by either the sale or purchase of two call spreads *or* two put spreads. The Greek attributes are also similar, however; condors differ in that they *do not* share a center strike like a butterfly. A condor has space in between the two spreads:

1. Butterflies are spread among three strike prices.
2. Condors are spread among four strike prices.

Because of this, there are wider berths and thus wider breakevens (both positive and negative) when it comes to selling a condor, and in turn, the allowance for a long condor to have a higher percentage chance of success. Obviously, these characteristics come with a price. Let's look at a long condor first: its Greeks are exactly like the long butterfly, only the stock has a wider range to stay within for maximum profitability.

Long Condor

If you were to compare a butterfly to a condor in the animal kingdom, I know you could find many differences. In the options world, we focus on one, *wingspan*! The wingspan, or distance between the center strikes, is wider in a condor than it is in a butterfly. In the long condor, the characteristics are very similar to a long butterfly, but there are some subtle differences. Let me explain.

Profitability   In a long butterfly (call or put), the max profit would only be with the strategy expiring with the stock right at the center strike. Any deviation from that point would take away from profitability.

In the long condor, the strikes are spread out, which means that as long as the stock stays *anywhere* between the two short center strikes (which are also called the body), the spread will be worth its max value. This higher probability comes at a cost, less potential profit. In a long condor, the debit that you pay for the spread will be more than if you traded a similarly spaced and positioned long butterfly. Call and put condors both have similar behaviors. The max you can make is the width of the outer strikes minus the debit paid.

Losses Just like the long butterflies, long condors will begin to lose money if the stock moves above or below your breakeven points, but because the condor is spread out, the stock has to move farther for the maximum loss to occur when compared to a similar width butterfly.[6]

Below you see the graphical representation of the long condor strike selections. A long condor can use either calls or puts, but does not use both. The strike positions and 1–1–1–1 (long-short-short-long) formation remains the same for both. Whether you use calls or puts, the max profit would occur if the stock was between the two short center strikes when the condor was expiring.

Long Condor Strike Positioning

	2 Call Spreads	or	2 Put Spreads	
	Long Call Condor		**Long Put Condor**	
	CALLS	or	**PUTS**	
	Strike	⇧	*Strike*	
Long 1	40	Max Profit	40	Long 1
Short 1	45		45	Short 1
Short 1	50		50	Short 1
Long 1	55	Between	55	Long 1
	60	45 and 50	60	
		⇩		

Figures 8.3 and 8.4 display the risk graphs for long call and put condors respectively (both have the same risk and Greek sensitivity). A long condor

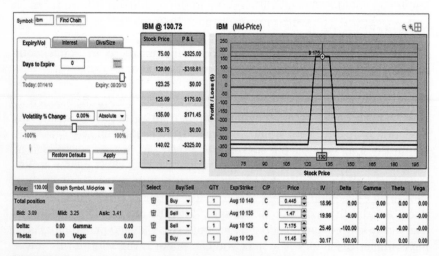

FIGURE 8.3 Long Call Condor Expiration Risk Graph

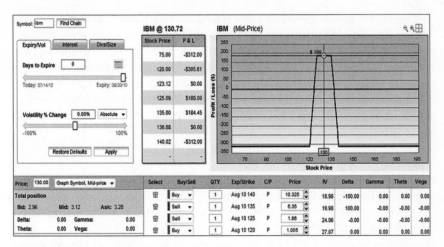

FIGURE 8.4 Long Put Condor Expiration Risk Graph—Same Risk/Reward Profile as the Long Call Condor

risk graph will always have that flat portion at the center peak. It is there where you will make the most money.

Long (Call or Put) Condor Greek Attributes/Sentiment Greeks are similar to long (call or put) butterfly, just with wider space between spreads that lessen the speed at which the Greeks change when the stock is in between the inner strikes.

Short Condor

Like the long condor, the short condor is the short butterfly's wider cousin. The wingspan may be wider, but the characteristics and sentiment are similar, with just a few nuances. Let's discuss them.

Profitability In a short butterfly (call or put) the max profit would only be with the strategy expiring with the stock outside of the breakeven levels, which is the center strike plus or minus whatever was paid for the short fly. If the stock expires anywhere in between those levels, you would experience a loss. Max loss would be with the butterfly expiring with the stock right at the center strike.

The condor's behaviors are similar, but in the condor, the strikes are spread out, which means as long as the stock stays *anywhere* above or below the two outer short strikes, the spread will be worth its max value. Since the condor is spread out, it will be harder statistically to achieve this,

because you are requiring the stock to market a larger move (depending
on where you place the spread). This lower probability is the reason why
short condors will generate a greater credit than short butterflies. (Your
rate of potential return on your risk will be higher.) In a short condor, the
amount that you collect for the spread will be more than if you traded a
similarly spaced and positioned short butterfly, thus allowing the potential
profit to be greater (but with lower probability). Call and put condors both
have similar behaviors.

Losses   Just like the short butterfly, short condors will begin to lose
money if the stock stays between your breakeven points (between inner
strikes is the max loss), but because the condor is spread out, the stock
has to move farther for the trader to avoid maximum loss when compared
to a similar width butterfly.[7]

Below you see the graphical representation of the short condor strike
selections. A short condor, like the long, can either use calls or puts, but
does not use both. The evenly spaced strike positions and 1–1–1–1 (short-
long-long-short) formation remains the same. In the short condor, whether
you use calls or puts, the max profit would occur if the stock was above or
below your outer or short strikes when the condor was expiring. The most
you can make is the credit, the most you can lose is the width of the outer
strikes minus the credit.

Short Condor Strike Positioning

2 Call Spreads	or	2 Put Spreads
Short Call Condor		**Short Put Condor**
CALLS	or	PUTS
Strike	⇧	*Strike*
Short 1 40	Max Profit	40 Short 1
Long 1 45		45 Long 1
Long 1 50		50 Long 1
Short 1 55	Outside	55 Short 1
60	45 and 55	60

⇩

Figure 8.5 shows us the risk graph of the short condor. Remember that
your max profit will be above or below your outer strikes.

Short (Call or Put) Condor Greek Attributes/Sentiment   Greeks
are similar to the short (call or put) butterfly, just with wider space between

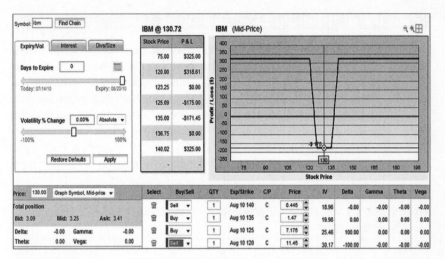

FIGURE 8.5 Short Condor Expiration Risk Graph—Same for Both Call and Put Short Condors

spreads that lessen the speed at which the Greeks change when the stock is in between the inner strikes.

IRON SPREADS

Whenever the term *iron* is used, this means that the spread is a combination of a call spread and a put spread, both of which are either sold or bought. The strikes of the call and put spreads are generally the same width apart, but don't have to be. In other words, if I sold the 50/55 call spread, I may sell something like the 40/35 put spread as well, keeping the risk balanced on each side. (In that case, I would have sold an iron condor, because there were four different strikes used.) This is not a steadfast rule, but it generally makes things easier. The width of the actual spreads from one another can be as wide or as close as you wish; there is no standard. Just remember that if you are calling it an iron spread, you are using a call spread and a put spread and you are buying and selling both. Typically, but not all the time, both spreads are placed out of the money and you are either making the bet that the stock will either stay between your closest strikes (selling an iron) or that the stock will explode beyond the long strikes (buying an iron). Iron condors have the same Greek behavior as their regular condor cousins. The only difference here is that you are combining a call spread *and* a put spread.

TRADER TIP

When trading an iron spread (butterfly or condor) you are short the spread when you collect money to do the trade and long the spread when you pay money to do the trade. This differs from regular butterflies and condors where you are long if you "buy the wings" of those spreads, which would mean that you actually collect a credit, and short if you are "short the wings," which means you actually pay for the spread. I didn't make this up; you can thank our options founding fathers for the confusion.

IRON BUTTERFLY VERSUS IRON CONDOR

Figuring out if the spread is an iron butterfly or iron condor is very simple. Here is the simple rule. In an iron condor the total spread encompasses four different strike prices and in an iron butterfly, just like in a regular butterfly, a strike price is shared between the two spreads, and the spread encompasses only three strike prices. Let's examine iron butterflies first.

Short Iron Butterfly

The strike positioning of the short iron butterfly is a bit different from a regular fly. In this strategy, you will use *both* calls and puts, essentially combining a bear call vertical and a put vertical that share a center strike price (the short strike). The maximum profit would occur if the short iron butterfly expired right at the short strike, $50 in the example below.[8]

Short Iron Butterfly Strike Positioning

Call Spread	+	Put Spread
CALLS	and	PUTS
Strike		*Strike*
40		40
45	Max Profit	45　Long 1
Short 1　50	<———————>	50　Short 1
Long 1　55	<-------->	55
60		60

In the above example, you are short the 50/45 put spread, which is bullish (you want the stock at 50 or *higher* on expiration) and you're also short the 50/55 call spread (you want the stock at 50 or *lower* on expiration). Initially, you're probably thinking why the heck would I place one strategy that is profitable at 50 and above and another that is profitable only at 50 or below? That would mean the stock would have to be right at $50 on expiration for me to make the most money! Well, you are correct. The max profit in this iron butterfly would actually be attained if the stock expired right at $50. But let's assume for this example that you collected 3 between both spreads. (Remember that they are both credit spreads.) Since you collected money, this means you have two breakeven points, one to the upside and one to the downside of the center strike. The more money you collect, the wider the profit zone on expiration.

Breakevens (Profit Zone) If you collected $3 for the preceding trade, the stock can actually end up anywhere between 47 and 53 on expiration and you would potentially make money (breakeven = shared center strike ± the credit that you received).

Options are truly amazing. If you look at Figure 8.6, you will notice that the short iron condor risk graph is identical to the long standard butterfly risk graph.

Practical Application This trade is similar in practical reasoning to the long standard butterfly. The reason you might choose one over the other would be the ability to attain more premium or if you better grasp using two short verticals, rather than a long and short combined.

Risk in this Trade Because the stock can only be at one price on expiration, the maximum risk in this trade is only $2, meaning that when

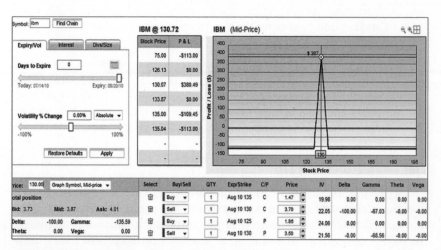

FIGURE 8.6 Short Iron Butterfly Expiration Risk Graph

you sell an iron butterfly, the most you can lose is the width of the spread strikes (if one is wider, then use that) minus the credit received. You can't lose on both spreads!

In this example, both spreads are $5 wide and the maximum loss would be taken if the stock finished above or below your long strikes (45 or 55). But risking two to make three might seem advantageous if you think the stock will finish right at or near $50.

Greek/Sentiment Considerations   There are several reasons that a trader may employ a short iron butterfly, but they all basically indicate you have a stock that is going to stay within a very tight range by expiration. Iron butterflies can potentially become profitable before expiration and can be exited at anytime if you are profitable or to avoid losses. The Greeks are similar to a regular **long** call or put butterfly. Some of these are:

- Theta

  Like some of the other strategies we have discussed, this one allows you to potentially collect theta, so if the stock is staying in your expected range and volatility is not on the rise, the position will progressively earn a little bit of money each day, because the options you sold have more time value than the ones you bought.

- Vega

  This position is short vega when you are within your profitable zone (stock is between breakeven points or near center strike) meaning that you want implied volatility to fall once you are in the trade. Even if the stock is not moving, a jump in implied volatility could hurt your position. If the stock moves outside of your profit zone, and beyond your outer strikes, the position may become long vega.

- Delta

  Simply put, you want the stock to stay right at or as close to the strike price that you are short. If the stock rises, you will actually get short delta, because you want the stock to come back to the strike price, and the opposite goes for when the stock drops. You will get long delta because you want the stock to rise.

The Long Iron Butterfly

The strike positioning of the long iron butterfly is a bit different from a regular fly. In this strategy, you will use *both* calls and puts, essentially combining a bull call vertical and a bear put vertical that share a center strike price (the long strike). The max profit would occur if the stock was above or below the outer short strikes, $45 and $55 in the following example.

Long Iron Butterfly Strike Positioning

2 Call Spreads	or	2 Put Spreads
Long Call Fly		Long Put Fly
CALLS	or	PUTS

		Strike		Strike	
		40	Max Profit	40	
		45	Below Short Strike	45	Short 1
Long 2	50	⟵⟶	50	Long 2
Short 1	55	or			
			Above Long Strike	55	
		60	Max Profit	60	

In the above example, you are long the 50/45 put spread, which is bear-ish (you want the stock below 45 by expiration) and you are also long the 50/55 call spread (you want the stock above 55 on expiration). You pay something for both spreads and you just want that stock to get as far away from those outer strikes as possible. Again, you're probably thinking why the heck would I for two spreads, when only one can be profitable at expi-ration? The reason here is obviously because you have a feeling the stock will move in a big way; you just don't know where.

Profitability   The max profit in long iron butterfly would be attained if the stock expired either below the short put or above the short call strikes on expiration. But the profit is limited. Profit is limited to the distance be-tween strikes minus what you paid. Let's assume for this example that you paid $2 for the iron butterfly. The strikes are spaced $5 apart, and since you paid $2 for the entire spread, the most you could ever make would be $3.

TRADER TIP

Even if you buy an iron butterfly and the stock makes a dramatic move outside of either of your short strikes, the spread may not trade at its maximum value before expiration because of time value, which may be left in the options that you are short. Don't get frustrated; remember your return on risk. If you bought the spread for $2 and you can sell it for $3—that is a 50% return!!

Breakevens   (Similar to short call or put butterfly.) To find your breakeven levels in the long iron butterfly, you simply add and subtract what you paid for the spread from the center strike. Those two numbers

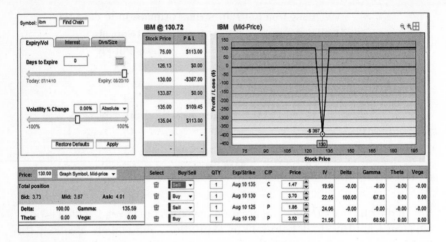

FIGURE 8.7 Long Iron Butterfly Expiration Risk Graph

are the levels the stock must be at for you to make or lose nothing on the trade.

Losses   Like the short butterfly, maximum loss will occur if the stock pins at the center strike on expiration. Although this may be highly unlikely, if you trade a stock that has a history of gravitating toward strikes, like GOOG tended to do in the late 2000s, you may want to evaluate an exit. You will be losing money in the trade if the stock expires within the breakeven levels discussed earlier (see Figure 8.7).

Greek Considerations/Sentiment   The Greeks are similar to a regular *short* call or put butterfly.

There are several reasons that a trader may employ a long iron butterfly, but they all basically indicate you have a stock that is going to experience a huge move outside of your outer short strikes. Iron butterflies can potentially become profitable before expiration and can be exited at any time if you are profitable or to avoid losses.

Practical Application   The practical application of the long iron butterfly is going to be similar to the short regular butterfly. In the long iron butterfly, you want the stock to move outside of the strikes that you are short (the outer strikes or wings). You will always pay for a long iron butterfly and the profit will be limited to the width between the strikes minus the premium you paid for the entire spread. Because of this, you are generally going to employ a long iron butterfly just ahead of an expected catalyst for a stock suck as earnings or a major news or economic data release. It can also be used if you just don't think a stock will stay at its current level by a certain expiration date.

Iron Condors

There are two types of iron condors, just like the butterfly, only condors encompass four strikes. They are therefore spread wider, hence the name *condor*.

Many of the same Greek sensitivities apply to iron condors as they do with iron butterflies, only with condors they tend to be even less dramatic because they are generally spaced out of the money and by definition farther apart than butterflies are.[9]

The iron condor both long and short involves a long or short call spread combined with a long or short put spread. Both spreads are typically out of the money, and if you bought the call spread, you would also be a buyer of the put spread (long iron condor). If you sell the call spread, you would also sell the put spread (short iron condor). As you will note, the long or short in the case of the iron condor refers to whether you pay (long) or collect (short) premium. Both the call spread and put spread do not have to be equidistant from where the stock is trading. For a traditional iron condor, however, the strikes of the individual spreads should be the same. So if the call spread was $5 wide (sold the 45 and bought the 50 call, for example), the put spread should also be $5 wide (sell the 30 put and buy the 25).

The spreads *cannot* share a strike price for the trade to be considered an iron condor.

TRADER TIP

If the call and put spreads are of different widths (e.g., the call spread is $5 wide and the put spread is $10 wide), the strategy is called a broken wing iron condor and has different risk characteristics from what I am describing here.

What Is the Desired Outcome?   The desired outcomes are:

Long—When you buy an iron condor, you are making the bet that the stock will make a large move, up or down, preferably past one of the outer (short) strikes in the spread by expiration, or at least move past your breakeven point, which I will discuss in more detail.

Short—When you sell an iron condor, you are making the bet that the stock will remain within the inner (short) strikes of the spread by expiration.

Structure and Composition   The width in between the call spread and the put spread can be as wide or as narrow as you wish. The narrower the distance between the spreads, the more expensive the iron condor will be.

Buyers (Long Iron Condor)   For the buyer of the spread, this higher cost may mean higher risk (because of the greater cash outlay) but also could mean a higher statistical probability of success because a narrower spread means that the stock doesn't have to travel as far for the spread to move to its maximum value. If the buyer of an iron condor chooses to buy a call spread and a put spread that are far apart from one another, of course they will be cheaper, but the statistical probability of that stock moving further by expiration becomes less and less. Remember the buyer of a condor wants the stock to move outside the outer short strikes.

Sellers (Short Iron Condor)   For sellers of iron condors, the same rules apply—the closer the call and put spreads are to one another, the greater the premium collected will be—however, the greater the statistical risk for the trader because the breakeven levels will be closer. Most sellers will space the call and put spreads as far away from one another where they can still get an acceptable premium, usually at levels outside of support and resistance for the stock. Remember, the seller of the iron condor wants the stock to stay in a range between the inner short strikes.

Max Risk/Max Reward   Figuring out the maximum risk and reward for an iron condor is easy.

Buyers   For the buyer of an iron condor, the risk is always limited to whatever is paid for the entire spread. Even though you are theoretically buying a call and put vertical spread, you would enter only one price to buy them both. Finding the potential reward is also simple. On expiration, you can fully profit on only one of the spreads, not both, so to find the max profit potential, take the total premium paid for the iron condor and subtract it from the width of one of the spreads (they should both be equal). If the call and put spreads are $5 wide and you paid $2 for the condor, the most you can make is $3.

Sellers   For the seller of an iron condor, the risk is always limited to the width of one of the spreads (the wider of the spreads if the spreads aren't equally spaced) minus the net credit received on entry. Even though you are theoretically selling a call and put vertical spread, you would enter only one price to sell them both. This is your net credit. You can also lose on only one spread or the other, not both, because the stock can only be at one price on expiration. This is why risk is limited to only one side. If the call and put spreads are $5 wide and you collect $2 for the condor, the most you can lose is $3, so you would be risking $3 to make $2.

Finding the potential reward is also simple. On expiration, with a short iron condor you can actually profit fully on both of the spreads. This only occurs when the entire spread expires with the stock between the short *inner* strikes (at which point all options expire worthless). At this point you would retain the net credit you received. Max profit in a short iron condor is *always* the net credit you bring in.

Commissions Although both the long and short iron condor can be a great strategy to employ with limited risk (and limited reward) there are four options (also called legs) involved in each condor that is traded. Be sure to check with your broker to determine commission costs, as they may eat up a portion of your profits. Some brokers charge a single commission for a spread (up to four legs); others treat the legs of the spread as individual options.

Visualization of the Iron Condors Hopefully by now the relationships between regular and iron butterflies and regular condors and iron condors are becoming more clear. They are all basically interchangeable. The only reason to choose one over the other would be to find the one with the least risk and greatest return. Below you will see the strike price positioning for the short and long iron condors. Just like we took a long regular butterfly and turned it into a short iron butterfly by using a combination of calls and puts versus one or the other, condors become iron condors when you do the same.

Check out the following lists and Figures 8.8 and 8.9.

Short Iron Condor Strike Position

1 Short Call Spread Bearish	+	1 Short Put Spread Bearish
CALLS	and	PUTS
Strike		*Strike*
40	Max Profit	40 Long 1
45		45 Short 1
50	<———————>	50
Short 1 55	Between	55
Long 1 60	45 and 55	60

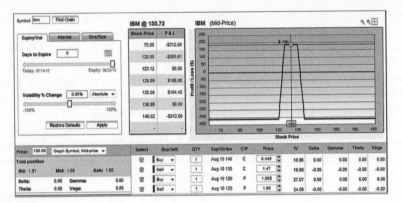

FIGURE 8.8 Short Iron Condor Expiration Risk Graph

Note the larger area of potential profit above the breakeven line when compared to a short iron butterfly.

Long Iron Condor Strike Positioning

1 Short Call Spread	+	1 Short Put Spread	
Bearish		Bullish	
CALLS	and	PUTS	
Strike		*Strike*	
40	Max Profit	40	Short 1
45	Below Short Strike	45	Long 1
50	⟵ or ⟶	50	
Long 1 55	Above Long Strike	55	
Short 1 60	Max Profit	60	

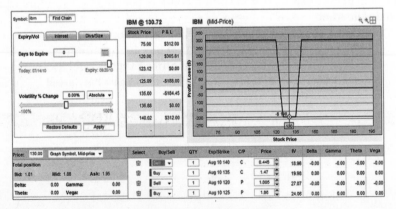

FIGURE 8.9 Long Iron Condor Expiration Risk Graph

Note the larger area of potential loss below the breakeven line when compared to a long iron butterfly.

Breakevens (Profitable Zones)   Finding the breakevens for an iron condor, short or long, is fairly simple. It must be done before you place the trade so you can be sure the breakevens jive with your thesis on where you think the stock will be over the life of the trade. Let's now explore how to find the breakevens and profitable zones for long and short iron condors.

Buyers   Just like buying an iron butterfly, you are expecting a big move in the stock either up or down. Because the strikes are spread further out, it will take a larger move in the stock for you to reach your profitable zones, which lie at some point above and below your inner long strikes.

To find your upside breakeven at expiration, take the net amount you paid for the iron condor and add it to the long call strike. The sum of those numbers will be your upside breakeven point at which you *begin* to *make* money. You will continue to profit until the stock rises to the short call strike, at which time your profit will be capped out.

For example, if you bought a condor for $1 and your call spread strikes are long the 50, short the 55, your profitable zone is from $51 to $55 (above 55 you would still profit, only that profit is capped at $4, which is the distance between the call spread strikes minus the net premium paid).

To the downside, you will subtract the amount you paid for the condor from the long put strike; that remainder is your downside breakeven at which point you would begin to make money on expiration. You will continue to profit until the stock falls to the short put strike, at which time your profit will be capped out.

For example, if you bought that same condor for $1 and your put spread strikes are long the 40, short the 35, your profitable zone is from $39 to $35 (below $35 you would still profit, only that profit is capped at $4, which is the distance between the put spread strikes minus the net premium paid).

TRADER TIP

If you buy an iron condor, you will lose your entire premium paid if the spread expires with the stock between the inner long strikes. However, if the stock moves quickly, you can see profitability in the spread even if the stock doesn't reach your expiration profit zone. Don't be afraid to take profits if you think the stock is going to stop moving or revert back to where it was before, at which time you may find yourself in a losing situation.

Sellers Just like selling an iron butterfly, you are expecting minimal movement in the stock, but unlike the butterfly, the condor, because of the strike spacing, will allow the stock a wider berth and in turn allow you a greater chance of making the maximum profit in the trade. This increased width also means your profitable zone will be wider than in a short iron butterfly.

To find your profitable zone at expiration, take the net amount you received for the iron condor and add it to the long call strike; the sum of those numbers will be your upside breakeven point at which you *begin* to *lose* money. You will continue to *lose* until the stock rises to the short call strike, at which time your *loss* will be capped out.

As an example of upside breakeven, consider that if you sold a condor for $1 and your call spread strikes are long the 50, short the 55, your profitable zone is from the current stock price up to $51 on expiration. Above 51 you would begin to lose money. That loss is capped at $4, which is the distance between the call spread strikes minus the net premium collected on the entire spread.

To the downside, you will subtract the net amount you collect for the condor from the short put strike. The remainder is your downside breakeven, at which point you would begin to *lose* money on expiration. You will continue to lose money until the stock falls to the long put strike, at which time your losses will be capped out.

A downside breakeven example would be if you sold that same condor for $1 and your put spread strikes are short the 40, long the 35, and your profitable zone is from the current stock price down to $39. Below 35, you would begin to lose money. That loss is capped at $4, which is the distance between the put spread strikes minus the net premium collected on the entire spread.

TRADER TIP

You can often lose more than the credit you receive when you sell an iron condor; don't be afraid to take risk off the table if you think that the stock is going to keep moving in one direction.

Also remember that you can become profitable before expiration and also lose money even if the stock doesn't get outside your expiration profitable zone. If you feel that the stock will remain within that zone, you can leave the spread on and it will eventually become profitable if the stock remains within that range.

Long iron condor characteristics and sentiments are:
- *Market sentiment.* Neutral/large move to a level outside the short strikes you choose. You are anticipating a significant event or catalyst

that will move the stock. Generally cheaper than a long iron butterfly, but will require a larger move in the stock.

* *Risk.* Limited to the premium paid.
* *Potential reward.* Limited to the width of either the put spread or call spread minus the premium paid, you can profit from only one of the spreads contained within the condor, not both.
* *Passage of time.* Bad if the stock is stuck between your breakeven points. If stock is between long strikes, you will be paying to be in the position.
* Good if you are in the profitable zone (which is outside your breakevens) or preferably the outside of outer strikes, at which point you have reached max profit and will collect time decay.
* *Probability characteristics.* Varies on how far the spreads are spaced apart and how much is paid for the entire condor. The closer the long strikes are to the current stock price, the higher the probability of the stock moving through the strikes; however, the closer the long strikes are to the stock, the more the condor will cost, thus increasing risk.
* *Time in trade.* Typically, iron condors are bought with a suitable amount of time for the stock to move outside of the short strikes. The time in the trade may encompass a corporate or economic event that is a potential catalyst for movement. Generally, they are bought with 30–90 DTE, but can sometimes be placed with less time, if you think the stock will make a quick move to a certain level. If this is your choice, realize that you may experience accelerated time decay if the stock doesn't move in the last two weeks of the spread's life.
* *When to apply this strategy.* You have a belief that the stock will experience a drastic change in price over the duration of the spread.

Some long iron condor Greek attributes are:

* Delta

   With time to go to expiration, delta is lowest when the stock is equidistant from the inner long strikes of spread; it will begin to increase if the stock moves higher and will peak at the short strike and then begin to decrease if the stock continues to move higher because your profitability is capped. The same works to the downside, only the delta will increase negatively, peaking at the short put strike and then begin to move back to zero if the stock continues to drop.

* Gamma

   Gamma is generally positive with stock in between the inner strikes, because you want the stock to move. Gamma will peak right around the long call or put and then will turn negative as the stock approaches the outer short strikes, as that's the most this position can make and the point at which you don't really need the stock to move any further.

- Theta

    If the stock is inside its breakeven levels, time decay is generally hurtful to the position. If the stock is outside of the spread's breakeven levels (preferably outside the outer strikes), time decay is generally helpful to the position. The bottom line is that you want the condor to be in a profitable position if you want to collect time decay, meaning that you want the stock to get to where it needs to be on expiration and you will then collect money to be in the trade.

- Vega

    When the stock is between the long strike prices (not in profitable zone), the position is long vega (you want volatility to rise). If the stock is outside of the short strikes, the position becomes short vega.

Short iron condor characteristics and sentiments are:

- *Market sentiment.* Neutral/range bound move within certain levels that you select. You are anticipating no catalyst or believe that any upcoming news or events will not send the stock above or below your breakeven points or preferably beyond your inner short strikes. The credit received will generally be less than an iron butterfly, positioned around the stock, but will allow more movement in the stock and perhaps a higher probability of success.
- *Risk.* Limited to the difference in the strikes of *either* the call spread or put spread, minus the premium received.
- *Potential reward.* Limited to the net premium received for the entire short iron condor.
- *Passage of time.* Good if the stock is stuck between your breakeven points. If stock moves beyond your profitable zone, time will hurt the position.[10]
- *Probability characteristics.* Varies on how far the spreads are spaced apart and how much premium is collected for the entire condor. The short iron condor has a higher probability of success statistically than a long iron condor. The closer the short strikes are to the current stock price, the higher the probability of the stock moving through the strikes, which would mean reduced probability, but a greater premium collected. The spacing of strikes is the key to success in this trade.

TRADER TIP

Don't forget that the spacing of the outer spreads themselves (the wings) will increase or decrease your risk/reward. The wider the call and put spread strikes are, the more premium you will collect, but this also increases your potential loss amount.

- *Expiration date.* Typically, iron condors are sold with shorter durations, to take advantage of the accelerated time decay that occurs in the last month of an option's life. Also, remember that the longer you are in a strategy like this, the more you leave yourself and the position susceptible to events that may create volatility in the stock, both corporate and economic. So you will want to account for those events when selecting your strikes before you enter.

  Generally, I sell irons with 15 to 50 days to expiration, but they can sometimes be placed with even less time. It's all about support and resistance for the stock and the strength of your belief that the stock will stay between your short strikes. There is also a preference that implied volatility is relatively high when you put the trade on!

  When to apply this strategy. You have a belief that the stock will be completely range bound over the duration of the spread.

Some short iron condor Greek attributes are:
- Delta

  With time to go to expiration, delta is lowest when the stock is equidistant from the inner long strikes of the spread; it will begin to decrease if the stock moves higher and will peak at the short strike, and then begin to decrease if the stock continues to move higher. Because the same works to the downside, only the delta will increase negatively, peaking at the short put strike and then begin to move back to zero if the stock continues to drop.[11]
- Gamma

  Gamma is generally negative with stock in between the inner strikes, because you want the stock to stay equidistant between your short strikes. Gamma will peak right around the mid-point between the short strikes and will get more positive as you approach your breakeven points. It will peak right around your long strikes and will begin to decrease again as the stock moves outside those levels.

- Theta

  If the stock is inside its breakeven levels, time decay is generally beneficial to the position. If the stock is outside of the spread's breakeven
  levels (or worse, outside the outer long strikes), time decay is generally hurting the position. The bottom line is that you want the
  condor to be in a profitable position if you want to collect time decay, meaning you want the stock to get to where it needs to be (between short strikes on expiration, and you will then collect money
  to be in the trade).

  When the stock is between the long strike prices, the position is short
  vega (you want volatility to fall). If the stock is outside of the short
  strikes, the position becomes long vega.

TRADER TIP

In both long and short iron condors, you can use a probability calculator, such
as the one found on www.iVolatility.com to look at the statistical probability of a
stock staying either within a certain range or traveling outside it. Statistically, the
probability is always greater that a stock will stay within a certain range within
its current price rather than make a move to a level above or below its current
price; this is why the risk/reward is always lower when you buy an iron condor
versus selling them. Of course, statistics can never measure what is happening
in the real world, just make sure that your thesis is realistic, and be careful
when betting a long shot. Be sure to combine your statistical measurements
with charts and real-world price observations.

Practical Example of the Short Iron Condor   I thought that it
would be best to take you through an actual trade I did in the S&P 500 Cash
Index (SPX) back in 2010 and walk you through my thought process, risk
analysis, and results for you to better get a handle on this popular trade.

A Range-Bound SPX   On August 20, 2010, after disappointing jobs data
and weak data from the Philly FED, the market (S&P 500) continued to
slide to about 1,071; this was after a 1.5% tumble the previous day. It was
also options expiration Friday, which historically has been a bearish day
for the markets. The S&P 500 was also nearing a support level and bounced
right near its lower Bollinger band, which indicated an oversold condition
in the index. Earnings season was winding down and I thought that it might
be a good time to employ an iron condor. Of course, even with earnings out
of the way, I still had predominantly weak economic data, but it seemed
like most market participants were expecting the worst. I also noticed that

FIGURE 8.10   Daily SPX Chart—Searching for Support and Resistance
Source: Lightwave Charts.

technicals, namely 50- and 200-day moving averages were getting a lot of attention in the media and by the markets themselves.

I thought that the trade would be best placed for September expiration, as I don't want to get into next earnings season, which begins in early October. I also know that fall and winter tend to be more volatile seasons than summer for the equity markets.

Looking at the price chart shown in Figure 8.10, I thought that the SPX was closer to the support levels of its recent channel; therefore, I would position the put spread portion of the iron condor closer to the current SPX price, thus allowing some more room for the SPX to rally. Mean reversion is common, meaning that when a stock or index has been falling for an extended period in an abnormal manner, without catastrophic news, a bounce will typically occur, and the underlying asset will rise in value, perhaps to a previous resistance point or to a Fibonacci level.

TRADER TIP

In high-dollar stocks and indexes like the SPX, bid-ask spreads in the options tend to be wide. Because of this, I highly suggest using limit orders and working your bids and offers just around the mid-value point of the spread. In my trade in the SPX, if I were to go in with a "market sell" order, I would be giving up $3.80 compared to $9, which was where I was filled at. Always start in the middle and adjust if you need to; pay a little more than the mid-price if you are a buyer, and sell for a little less than the mid-price if you are selling the spread. Spreads have a higher chance of mid-point execution because of the reduced need for the market maker to hedge when compared to just buying or selling an in-the-money option.

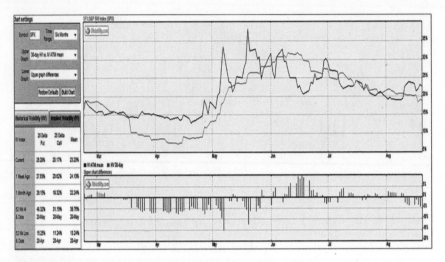

FIGURE 8.11   SPX Six-Month Volatility Chart (HV and IV)
Source: Courtesy of iVol.

Implied Volatility Considerations   In a perfect world, when selling an iron condor you would want to do so in a period of relatively high volatility, with the anticipation that it will drop. Looking at a comparison below, you will notice the black line (implied vol) is not only above the green (observed vol) but the level of implied volatility is on the neutral to slightly elevated side when compared to the past six months of data. In Figure 8.11, you can see the spikes in May and June when the market was dropping and during the flash crash. There is no perfect guideline for where implied volatility should be in relation to historical; rather, it is preferred to see it in an elevated state and preferably on the way down, as this will help your net short vega in the short iron condor.

What you will find interesting in the SPX chart in Figure 8.12 is that I drew a Fibonacci line from the highest point to the lowest point of the largest move in the past 50 days on August 20, 2010, and you can see the different Fibonacci levels drawn and how the stock responded to those levels. What I found even more interesting was that on expiration Friday, the index settled exactly at the 50% retracement level of that move, within one penny (this is an $1,100 index).[12]

FIGURE 8.12 Daily SPX Chart Showing Fibonacci Levels—Note the Effect of the Levels on Price

TRADER TIP

The Fibonacci levels sequence starts with the number 1. Each additional number is the sum of the two numbers preceding it. For example, $1 + 0 = 1$, $1 + 1 = 2$, $2 + 1 = 3$, $3 + 2 = 5$, $5 + 3 = 8$, and so on. If you take each number of the Fibonacci sequence and divide it by the previous number in the sequence (i.e., 2/1, 3/2, 5/3, 8/5), a pattern appears. As the numbers increase, the quotient approaches what's called the *golden ratio*, which is approximately 1.6180339887. Much of the history and knowledge about this ratio is beyond both the scope of this book and my present knowledge on the subject. Just know that most charting packages include the ability for you to draw Fibonacci lines on a chart and it does the math for you by showing you the different Fibonacci levels. You can also research this further.

Fibonacci levels are used by technical analysts typically in conjunction with other indicators. I use them to find support and resistance levels within a stock using daily, weekly, or monthly charts. If a certain Fibonacci level coincides with a moving average or other indicator, it only strengthens my support or resistance level hypothesis.

Strike Selection Strike selection is probably the most crucial part of the iron condor, along with the amount of premiums you are paying and/or collecting. Don't forget, you have a total of four strikes to decide on, the results of which can be either rewarding or devastating. Let me walk you through my rationale.

Inner Strike Selection   Choosing what inner strikes to use is a balance between the range you think the stock or index can stay within combined with the amount of premium you can receive in the spread once you determine what your outer strikes will be. In addition to choosing how wide your inner strikes are going to be, you may need to skew the strikes higher or lower if you think that the stock is at the upper or lower end of its expected range, or if you think it's right in the middle of the expected range, you can choose to place the strikes equidistantly from the current price of the stock. In my SPX example, I skewed the inner spread strikes higher and placed my put spread closer to the current price of the SPX because I thought it was closer to the lower end of its range.

Outer Strike Selection   Selecting the outer strikes also takes some practice. The distance from the inner strikes that you sell to the outer strikes that you will be buying determines two things:

1. The amount of total premium received, which influences your breakevens.

   The farther the outer strikes are from the inner strikes, the cheaper they will be because they will be further out of the money. The less you pay for those strikes will mean you will retain more of the credit you brought in for the short strikes. The farther the outer strikes are from the inner strikes the wider the breakevens, but there is no such thing as a free lunch, which leads me to my next point about outer strike selection.

2. The amount to total risk you are willing to take.

   The farther the outer strikes are from the inner strikes the more you can potentially lose in the trade. Remember that those outer strikes are like your stop loss; the most you can lose in a short iron condor is the difference between one inner strike and one outer strike minus the premium you received for the spread.

Figure 8.13 shows you what a typical spread order ticket might look like. When trading a spread, especially one with four legs, don't be afraid to use limit orders and negotiate your bids and offers. You don't have to just pay what is being asked and vice versa.

In this trade, the inner and outer strikes are spaced $20 apart, which means that since I sold the entire spread for $9, the maximum I could lose in this trade would be $11 (inner and outer strike width, minus premium received).

Symbol:	SPX							▾ ☒ Shrink Ticket
	Action	Expiry	Strike	Call/Put	Quantity	Pos	Bid	Ask
Leg 1	Sell ▾	Sep 10 ▾	1,055.00 ▾	Put ▾	1	🗑 ↻	0	19.40	22.50
Leg 2	Buy ▾	Sep 10 ▾	1,035.00 ▾	Put ▾	1	🗑 ↻	0	13.70	16.60
Leg 3	Sell ▾	Sep 10 ▾	1,120.00 ▾	Call ▾	1	🗑 ↻	0	5.20	7.20
Leg 4	Buy ▾	Sep 10 ▾	1,140.00 ▾	Call ▾	1	🗑 ↻	0	2.20	2.80
Price:	Limit Sell ▾ $	9.00 ⬍			Market: $5.20 Sell			
Duration:	Day ▾				☐ All or None			
Estimated cost of trade before calculating commission charges:								
You receive $900.00 - Commission - Fees								

FIGURE 8.13　SPX Option Trade Ticket on August 20, 2010

Breakevens　To find the breakevens in the trade, the math is easy. For the upside, simply add the total premium in the spread to the short inner call strike (1,120), which would give us 1,129 upside breakeven on expiration. To find the downside breakeven at expiration, simply subtract the total premium from the short inner put strike (1,055), which gives us 1,046 as our downside breakeven. So in this trade SPX just has to stay between 1,129 and 1,046 for me not to lose money.

Use a Probability Calculator　Use a probability calculator to find a realistic range. There are many resources that offer a future price probability calculator based on implied or historical volatility; www.ivolatility.com is one of the websites that offers this type of tool, which will allow you to view the statistical probability of your trade winning and losing. Be careful when using statistics. Remember that anything can happen in the real world, but at least using a calculator gives you more of an objective view that you can use in conjunction with your fundamental and technical thesis. You will be asked to input an expiration date and a volatility factor. For the volatility factor, I look at the money-implied volatility and the 30-day historical volatility; I use whichever is greater in my forward calculation to be more conservative.

Use your breakeven points to calculate statistical probability on expiration.

In Figure 8.14, I entered my breakeven levels into a probability calculator to view my statistical chances in the trade. Although this can help with rationale, don't fall into the trap of putting all your faith in statistics.

Probabilities at the Future Date of the Underlying					
Finishing Below Lowest Target Price	Target Price	Finishing Between Target Prices	Target Price	Finishing Above Highest Target Price	
36.01%	1046	44.49%	1129	18.7%	
Probability of Touching	69.73%		40.39%		

Underlying Prices for each Standard Deviation Interval at the Future Date					
-3	-2	-1	+1	+2	+3
886.11	943.07	1003.68	1136.84	1209.91	1287.67

FIGURE 8.14 SPX Trade Probability
Source: Courtesy of www.OptionsHouse.com.

Legging In versus All In   Since the short iron condor is basically the combination of bull put spread and a bear call spread, you can "leg in," or execute, each spread separately. For example, if a stock has been selling off and you think it's ready for a mean reversion (bounce), you could sell the put spread first (which is the bullish portion) and then once the stock rallies, you could execute the call spread side (the bearish portion). Some advantages and disadvantages are:

> The **advantages** of this method may allow you to not only maximize the amount you get for each spread and in turn the entire condor, but you can also potentially widen the distance between the inner strikes because the stock's movement will allow you to gain value in both the call and put spreads. Use this method if you are really good at timing the market or a particular stock and you are comfortable with the way an iron condor is constructed.

> The **disadvantage** of legging in could be that the stock never bounces and you have to sell the put spread for less or vice versa if you were selling the put spread first. Also, depending on your broker, commissions may be higher if you complete the spread in two parts. Also, depending on your broker, you may be required to put up margin in *both* the call and put spread, when in most cases, when they are executed at the same time, you will only need to put up margin in one, because you can lose on only one side.

Trade Update September 8, 2010—SPX at 1,098   You can see in Figure 8.15 that the options have gotten much cheaper. What you will also notice is how the SPX market makers can easily take advantage of novice traders with the wide spread. When we first went to enter this trade, the market price was $5.20, but I was able to sell it at $9. Now that the options have gotten cheaper, the bid-ask spreads aren't as wide, but they still are too wide to just enter a limit order. Always use limit orders when

Symbol:	SPX							▼ Shrink Ticket
	Action	Expiry	Strike	Call/Put	Quantity		Pos	Bid	Ask
Leg 1	Buy ▼	Sep 10 ▼	1,055.00 ▼	Put ▼	1	🗑 ♻	0	2.35	3.10
Leg 2	Sell ▼	Sep 10 ▼	1,035.00 ▼	Put ▼	1	🗑 ♻	0	1.05	1.65
Leg 3	Buy ▼	Sep 10 ▼	1,120.00 ▼	Call ▼	1	🗑 ♻	0	3.60	4.30
Leg 4	Sell ▼	Sep 10 ▼	1,140.00 ▼	Call ▼	1	🗑 ♻	0	0.70	1.00

Price:	Limit Buy ▼ $ 4.00 ⬍	Market: $5.65 Buy
Duration:	Day ▼	☐ All or None

Estimated cost of trade before calculating commission charges:
You spend $400.00 + Commission + Fees

FIGURE 8.15 Option Trade Ticket on September 8, 2010, in SPX Iron Condor

trading stocks with wide spreads (more than 10 cents). This trade could have actually been a loser if I just used market orders.

At this point I have a decision to make, I could buy back the entire spread for $4 and make a $500 profit, which is a 45% return on my total risk of $1,100 or I could choose to just leave it on for a little while longer. September expiration occurs in nine days; there is plenty that can happen in that time.

I have been in this trade for 18 days and I have to be honest with you, even though the charts don't look that bad, there were some sweaty moments. I feel really good about a 45% return in 18 days and the market just seems skittish to me, so I am going to remove my risk and take the trade off (see Figure 8.16).

Outcome Had I Held to Expiration Before I get into what happened on September expiration, I want to remind you about SPX, VIX, DJX-RUT, OEX, and select cash settled indexes. If you recall the section on cash settlement, I discussed how positions in these types of securities will offer you an absolute profit-or-loss figure upon expiration. You will *not* be left with long or short stock after expiration. More important is *when* some cash-settled indexes actually expire. Most options we trade expire on the third Friday of the month and the closing price of the underlying security (stock) is what is used to determine whether the option is in, at, or out of the money and helps determine if that option should be exercised or not.

Last Day to Trade Is Thursday In some cash-settled indexes, such as the SPX, the options will cease trading at 4:15 Eastern Standard Time on

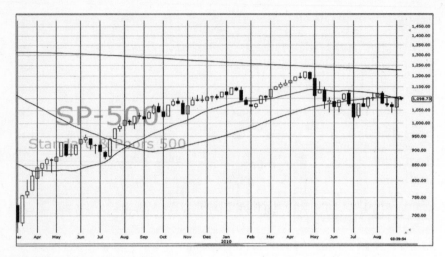

FIGURE 8.16   SPX Weekly Chart from August 2010 Back—Freestockcharts.com

the *third Thursday* and will be marked to a value determined on *Friday morning*. This settlement value is *not* the opening print of the index itself, but is actually the opening print of *all* of the individual stocks contained within the index.

Regarding the SPX settlement value:

> Settlement values for various indexes can be found at
> www.cboe.com/data/Settlement.aspx.
>   • The September 2010 SPX "settlement value" was 1,131.15.
>   • The opening print of the SPX on September 2010 expiration Friday was 1,126.39.
>   • The closing price of the SPX on September 2010 expiration was 1,125.59.

The SPX settlement value is obviously the one that counts, but you can see how traders with minimal knowledge of the expiration and settlement process potentially could find themselves in a serious pickle.

The settlement value (which is usually posted around 10:30 Central Standard Time on Friday) was higher than both the opening price of the SPX and the closing price of the SPX. In this case, that would have hurt me, not helped.

Remember that one week ago, I closed the position out for a profit. Had I held this until expiration and let it settle into cash, the trade would have resulted in a $2.15 *loss*.

Here is the math:

I sold the entire iron condor spread for $9 (credit).
If I would have held, I would have lost money, because the SPX finished
    at 1,131.13; my 120 call realized a $11.15 *loss* (all other options ex-
    pired worthless).
$9 − $11.15 = −$2.15 (net loss in trade).

Do you see why I encourage taking or protecting profits when you have
them?

TRADER TIP

If you are trading individual stocks around earnings, the more analysts that
cover a stock, typically, the less chance you have for surprises, but this certainly doesn't mean that the stock cannot do something dramatic. Look at how
it has traded over earnings in the past to gain insight to its typical behavior.
Trading in indexes may also help mitigate earnings surprises, but they will *not*
eliminate them.

FINAL THOUGHTS

Even the most complex of options strategies can be understood by looking
at each individual component. I have seen so many new options traders
struggle with the more complex tactics, because they just can't seem to
wrap their hands around the combined behaviors of multiple options. Take
your time and disassemble a spread that you are having trouble with. For
example, instead of thinking about the short iron condor as a whole, start
breaking it into pieces. Picture it as a bear call vertical spread and a bull put
vertical spread placed at the same time. Use the characteristics of each to
find the total characteristics of the whole. Repetition is a propellant to per-
fection. When you are ready to fine-tune your advanced knowledge, move
on to Chapter 9.

Advanced Concepts

We habitually underestimate the effects of random-ness. Our stockbroker recommends that we invest in the Latin American mutual fund that "beat the pants off the domestic funds" five years running. Our doctor attributes that increase in our triglycerides to our new habit of enjoying a Hostess Ding Dong with milk every morning after dutifully feeding the kids with a breakfast of mangoes and nonfat yogurt. We may or may not take our stockbroker's or doctor's advice, but few of us question whether he or she has enough data to give it. In the political world, the economic world, the business world—even when careers and millions of dollars are at stake—chance events are often conspicuously misinterpreted as accomplishments or failures.

—Leonard Mlodinow
The Drunkard's Walk

This chapter explores concepts and strategies that go beyond the basics and some of which carry more risk and a more comprehensive knowledge of options if you plan on "testing" them. Please be sure that you understand any strategy and concept fully before applying in a live market environment. Aside from the strategies contained, this chapter also offers you a deep look into the relationships that options have not only with their underlying asset, but with each other.

PUT-CALL PARITY, INTEREST RATES, DIVIDENDS, AND FORWARDS

There is a balance that exists between calls and puts; in other words, if a call is trading for X, the put, in most cases should be trading for Y and vice versa. I am now going to take you through some of that rationale and theory. Realize that in today's highly technological and computer-driven marketplace, you will be hard-pressed to find a market that is out of balance without reason. Basically, it is extremely difficult to find risk-free arbitrage as a retail trader. So if you use some of the techniques that I'm about to teach you and find that the put or call seem mispriced, there is probably a reason for it; don't go firing off trades thinking that you're capturing risk-free arbitrage, because it's probably not true. Several factors like a changing interest rate environment, a stock that is hard to borrow (or is getting even harder to borrow), changing dividend rates, or other reasons can throw put and call parity out of balance.

Interest Rates

The balance in price between calls and puts is a tug of war between interest and dividends; both can have a profound effect on options prices. Remember that call owners do not receive dividends and put owners don't have to pay them. Options prices are adjusted for upcoming dividends until their expiration date. (I covered exercise and assignment in Chapter 4.)

Generally speaking, call options will more expensive in stocks (relative to puts) without dividends and are not hard to borrow, because of interest.

One technique to find the put-call parity, or price difference, between a same strike call or put would be to use the forward value of a stock or exchange-traded fund (ETF) at a certain point in the future. The first step to finding the forward value of a stock is to use the appropriate risk-free interest rate for the time to expiry (forward date), take that dollar amount, and then simply subtract from that the dividends that would be paid up until that date as the final step. What you're left with is a forward price. Typically Treasuries with the corresponding expiration date are used to find this risk-free rate.

TRADER TIP

The reason that a stock has a forward value is the cost of money (opportunity cost). You are able at any time to take the same amount of money you would invest in a stock and put it into a risk-free Treasury instrument, earning you interest and thus increasing the theoretical value of your money out in time.

Let's suppose that IBM stock is trading for $100 and we are examining the January 2011 100-strike call and 100-strike put. I am going to give you two ways to look at the relationship between the stock and both the call and put. First, we have to be sure that we are using the correct rate (this can vary from person to person).

Assume for this example that January LEAPS options expire exactly 469 days from today.

When January 2011 expiration was 469 days in the future, the current yield on the 12-month Treasury was 0.35%. Now divide 469 (days until expiration) by 365 (days in a year) = 1.28 (our interest multiplier). When finding our forward price, we are going to multiply the stock price of IBM by the interest we *would* have received if we had invested that money in a risk-free asset. So that is (100 [stock price] * .0035 [annual rate * 1.28 [interest multiplier]) = $0.45.

This interest will *raise* the forward price of IBM to $100.45. We are not finished; now we have to subtract any dividends, as that would lower the forward price of the stock.

Let's say that IBM had several dividends scheduled between September 2009 and January 2011 expiration: 11/09: $0.55, 2/10: $0.55, 5/10: $0.59, 8/10: $0.59, 11/10: $0.59. That is a grand total of $2.87.

If I subtract the total dividends ($2.87) from $100.45, I get $97.58, which would be the expected forward price for IBM on January 2011 expiration.

Figure 9.1 gives you a graphical depiction of forward price, with interest raising the forward and any dividends lowering it.

Forward Price

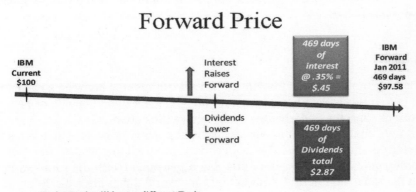

- Each Month will have a different Basis
- Basis = Interest-Dividends
- Forward price will be unique for each month
- If forward is higher, calls should be more expensive than puts
- if forward is lower, puts should be more expensive than calls

FIGURE 9.1 Forward Price Visual

$$F = S_0 e^{(r+q)T} - \sum_{i=1}^{N} D_i e^{r(T-t_i)}$$

FIGURE 9.2 Forward Arithmetic

Finding the forward price will also tell me that the IBM 100 puts (currently at the money) should be trading about $2.42 over my 100 calls, because now the 100 puts have $2.42 more value based on the forward pricing calculations. This is a basic example of put-call parity. This method is a bit more quick and dirty as opposed to using the following compounding interest formula to find the forward; if you're into algebraic expressions, Figure 9.2 shows the arithmetic for finding forward price:

Where F is the forward price to be paid at time T

e^x is the exponential function (used for calculating compounding interests)

r is the risk-free interest rate

q is the cost of carry

S_0 is the spot price of the asset (i.e., what it would sell for at time 0)

D_i is a dividend that is guaranteed to be paid at time t_i where $0 < t_i < T$.

You could also find a forward price calculator on the Internet to make your life a bit easier.

Basis

Basis is another way of looking at the value differential between a call and a put. You calculate basis by determining the costs and benefits of being long or short the underlying security versus the option.

We could also look at our specific cost of carry or basis, which is also referred to as the *reversal* or *conversion rate* used to calculate the value differential between a call option and a put option with the same strike in the same month. In the market makers' world things are a bit different. When professional market makers hold short stock in their accounts, they are collecting what is called a *short stock rebate*; in other words, they are getting paid to be short stock. In a retail trader's account, short stock positions usually cost money. On the flip side, maintaining a long stock position will cost the trader money (they are still entitled to dividends).

- Every trader is different and can borrow money at slightly different rates.
- You can find basis (or the conversion/reversal rate) for any strike in any month.

Multiply the strike price times the interest until expiration (using appropriate risk-free rate) and then subtract the dividends; this resulting amount is your basis. You can use the basis to find where the put should be trading at in relation to the call, and vice versa.

If the call price is known, you subtract basis from the amount the call is trading over parity to find the put's value. If the put price is known, you will add basis. (If the call has parity value or intrinsic, the same-strike put will not, and vice versa.)

This put and call parity relationship will hold as long as there is not an unusual situation in the stock, such as the stock being hard to borrow, where the puts may be elevated to account for the lack of interest collected on short stock (it may even be negative).

That basis figure can be considered the theoretical value for the conversion or reversal, which I will discuss shortly.

Changing Interest Rates

If you're a beginner, this will probably not have much effect on your trading life but it never hurts to explore some of the more esoteric forces that are pushing and pulling on the options markets.

In late 2009 and early 2010, contemplating a rise in interest rates was certainly a bit premature. The looming specter of a rising interest rate was really a nonissue at that time with inflation low, economic growth anemic, consumer spending down, and unemployment high. But we may not be able to avoid the inevitable for long. In reality, rates rise and fall and inflation can sneak up pretty fast.

This is not about my opinion on the issue, but rather a simple explanation of how rising rates may affect options prices—both calls and puts—and what you need to know as a retail trader. If you're not a math whiz, no need to worry, I'll keep this simple. Those of you who are familiar with put-call parity may also be familiar with basis or carrying cost.

So what if interest rates are in increasing mode? Or decreasing? How do you know which rate to use? I find it fascinating to play around with put-call parity and try to back out the interest calculations that the market makers are using.

More importantly, this is where Rho comes in.

The Rho for a call and put with the same strike price and the same expiration month are not equal.

For the call owners out there, an interest rate hike will make your calls more expensive, which obviously is a good thing for you as an owner. Put owners will experience the opposite effect; they may see values drop as interest rates rise. The bottom line is that an option does have sensitivity to interest rates, and here are some bullets to help you along:

• All futures options have a negative Rho, by the way.
• Deep out-of-the-money options have lower Rho, while at-the-money and in-the-money options have a relatively higher Rho.
• More expensive stocks will have higher relative Rho than cheaper stocks because higher dollar amounts invested would have greater interest rate returns.

There are actually options strategies that have only Rho or interest rate risk. Strategies such as the "jelly roll" are examples of this. For most of you, mastering interest rate risk will not be your focus, although you can certainly choose to assume that risk if it is indeed your focus. There are many more intricacies to finding Rho and forwards, which you can choose to explore in further reading.

SYNTHETICS AND MORE ON PUT-CALL PARITY

You've learned about delta, gamma, theta, and other measurements, called the *Greeks*. Greeks are how we professional traders analyze an option trade's sensitivity to certain changes in the market environment. They are used to help predict the behavior of our position as it moves through changes in time, stock price, volatility, interest rates, and even dividends (dividends affect the prices of options directly).

Put-call parity on the other hand is the actual price relationship between a call options price compared to a put option with the same strike and expiration.

In other words, if we know what the call is trading for and what interest rates and dividends are in a particular stock (some stocks are harder to borrow than others) we can surmise what the put should be worth (and vice versa) without even looking at the Greeks.

You can actually know for certain what the value of the call is if we know what the put is trading for and the other way around. Many professionals in the early days used this to their advantage to find markets that were out of line. These days, finding mispriced options is much more difficult, with the advent of computerized trading and black box systems that scan the market looking for possible arbitrage opportunities between calls and puts or even spreads.

You will often hear traders say calls are puts and puts are calls, meaning that they are somewhat interchangeable. You can combine calls, puts, and stock to create entirely new risk characteristics and augment your call position to imitate a put position and vice versa; this procedure of combining an option with stock is known as creating a *synthetic*. You can even combine options to create a synthetic long or short stock position.

Before I get deeper into put-call parity, it is imperative that you understand the basic synthetic relationships among calls, puts, and stock.

Synthetics

Following are the six basic synthetic positions; in other words, how a combination of calls, puts, and stock can be assembled with one or more of each to create a completely different strategy and risk profile. The synthetic should behave almost identical to the actual position it synthesizes. It's just a way to substitute risk. Sometimes certain transactions can be cheaper or more expensive than others, which is why a professional looks at the most efficient way to take risk.

This is the list of the different combinations of stock and options that can be used to create a synthetic position.

The six synthetics are:

1. Long call = 1 long put and 100 shares long stock.
2. Long put = 1 long call and 100 shares short stock.
3. Short call = 1 short put and 100 shares short stock.
4. Short put = 1 short call and 100 shares long stock.
5. Long stock = 1 long call and 1 short put (same strike).
6. Short Stock = 1 Long put and 1 short call (same strike).

TRADER TIP

If you are *buying* an option, the synthetic will always come out to *buying* the other option. If you are *selling* an option, the synthetic will always come out to *selling* the other option.

In addition, the synthetic (options) will always have the same month and strike price. Remember that when you complete a synthetic, you have made the trade, without having to actually place another order. So if I were to buy a call and sell stock, I have synthetically bought a put, which doesn't mean I will have a long put in my account.

Example of a Synthetic Position   If I wanted to have the same risk as being short stock, I could buy a put and sell a call with the same month and strike. By doing this, I create an identical risk position to short stock.

Now why would anyone want to have the same risk as short stock? Well, as options traders, we want to buy what is cheap and sell what is expensive.

If you were to create a September 145 short stock synthetic position by purchasing a 145 put and selling a 145 call for a 0.55 net credit, it would be essentially the same taking a short position in the stock at $145.55, which would also be your profit and loss (P&L) breakeven in the underlying stock.

There are interest and dividend considerations to think about when creating synthetics. Remember that call owners are *not* entitled to the dividend and interest rates can change, which may affect your synthetic position's value. Figure 9.3 proves the preceding synthetic market, the breakeven, and the look of the risk graph are identical to being short the stock at 145.

The more you trade options, the more you begin to notice the relationships that exist between them and the stocks that they are associated with. The term *synthetics* relates to combining options with options or

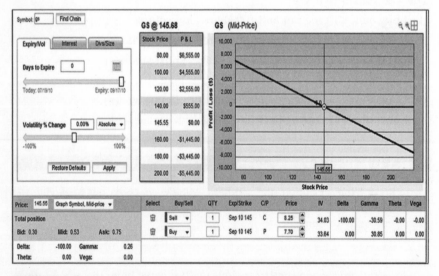

FIGURE 9.3   Short Stock Synthetic Example, Using the 145 Call and Put for a 0.55 Credit
Note how the risk graph is identical to short stock at $145.55.

options with stock to create an entirely different position or risk profile altogether. Traders use synthetics for many reasons; some look for arbitrage or find a better or cheaper way to hedge themselves. For the beginner, it is paramount that you understand what you are creating when you are combining different strategies and opening up your eyes to other potential strategies or relationships that may suit the situation better. A professional wants to find the cheapest things to buy and the most expensive things to sell; therefore, instead of just buying a put, the trader may opt to buy the call and sell the stock because it will cost less over time. Obviously, finding arbitrage situations or severe imbalances in that marketplace are much harder to come by these days.

However, the retail trader should understand these relationships and synthetics as it pertains to risk.

Fun with Synthetics Let's assume that IBM stock is trading at $121, the September 120 call is trading for $4.10 and the September 120 put is trading for $2.85. One would think that if you buy stock at $121, and create a short stock synthetic for $1.25 credit, that basically means that we bought the stock at $121, sold it synthetically at $120, and received $1.25 to do so. This means that this trade would guarantee the trader a credit of 25 cents at expiration, with no directional risk in the stock.

There are interest considerations here; suppose the stock was bought on margin. What if the trader has to pay interest on his long stock position? The cost of the interest paid on the long stock position may equal or exceed the $0.25 credit received.

If something seems too good to be true, it probably is and rarely does a retail trader find free money. The reality is that real arbitrage opportunities like this rarely surface for anyone for more than a millisecond, given the speed at which the markets move and the technology driving them. Prevailing interest rates determine call and put prices and the subsequent credits and debits in trades like this. I discuss this more in the section on put-call parity.

For most of you, being aware of these relationships and having fun with them is about the extent of how you will use them in the real world. I wouldn't be out there searching for put-call parity discrepancies and out-of-balance synthetic markets.

Proving a Basic Synthetic with IBM Long Stock, Long Put = Long Call In Figure 9.4, take a look at the shape of the risk graph and the maximum loss when we compare the purchase of 100 shares of IBM stock and the purchase of the 120 put. Both are exactly the same when it comes to risk, with the maximum loss being right around $900 and the upside being unlimited. (There is a slight difference in P&L because this shot was taken

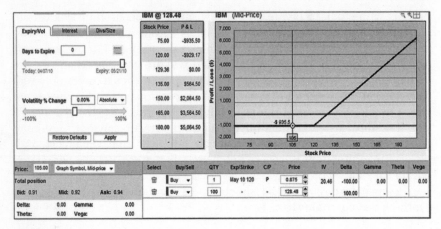

FIGURE 9.4 Risk Graph Showing Long Put + 100 Shares of Long Stock = Long Call

after hours when the bid-ask spreads were wide.) Typically the call would be a bit more expensive than the put, unless there was a dividend. This is addressed in the put-call parity section. But other than the slight difference in interest, the synthetic is proven. You can try this on your own for all of the synthetics (pitch virtual trading or something—how can they try on their own?).

Breaking it Down Risk graphs are an excellent way to visualize risk and to find and prove the synthetics discussed in this chapter (see Figure 9.5).

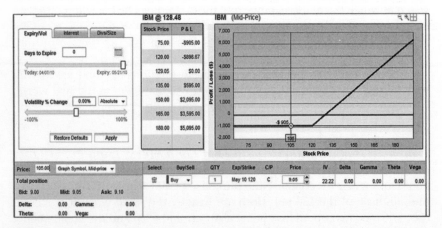

FIGURE 9.5 Long Call Risk Graph for Comparison—Identical to Synthetic

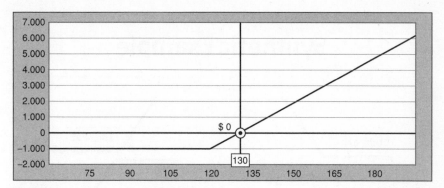

FIGURE 9.6 Long Call Risk Graph

A call's risk profile is quite simple; the most you can lose is the premium you pay for it, period. No matter how low the stock plummets, your risk is completely capped at the premium paid. However, the most you can make with a rise in the stock is theoretically unlimited, because the stock, in theory, can rise to infinity. The call's P&L graph is always flat to the left of the strike price and rises at a 45-degree angle to the right, showing profitability with the rise of the stock price. Figure 9.6 illustrates this.

A put's risk profile is also similar, just in the opposite direction and with one catch—that a stock can only fall to zero. When you buy a put, your risk is limited to the premium paid. Your profit is also limited to the strike price minus the premium you paid. So if you bought a 100 strike put for $4, the most you can make is $96 (100 strike – $4 premium), because no stock can trade lower than zero. The put's P&L graph is always flat to the right of the strike price and then rises at a 45-degree angle to the left, showing profitability as the stock falls. This can be seen in Figure 9.7.

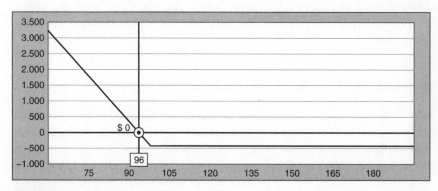

FIGURE 9.7 Long Put Risk Graph

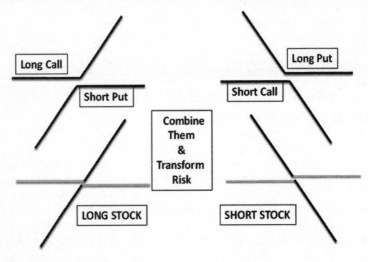

FIGURE 9.8 Synthetic Example

Use risk graphs to help you understand and experiment with synthetics and risk.

Figure 9.8 is a graphical representation of a long stock synthetics; note how the combination of the long call and short put risk graphs combine into long stock, because the short put now allows for downside risk and cancels out the limited risk characteristic of the long call. This works the same for the short stock synthetic, where the short call adds the unlimited upside risk that the long put does *not* have, thus creating synthetic short stock.

Put-Call Parity   Put-call parity in some form or fashion has been used in many ways for a very long time.

In the synthetics section, you learned how we can create a synthetic long or short stock position using options. Usually there are only minor differences in the cost of creating a synthetic versus just going out and buying the stock (other than commissions, of course). The reason for this is put-call parity, which is the natural three-sided relationship between a call and put and the underlying instrument (stock, etc.).

Here are the three characteristics that are referred to as put-call parity:

1. Underlying price = call price – put price + exercise price.
2. Put price = call price – underlying price + exercise price.
3. Call price = underlying price + put price – exercise price.

TRADER TIP

Check out some options chains after the market closes and see if you can prove put-call parity. Just be sure that your stock is not hard to borrow—that will make the put more expensive and thus put-call parity may cease to exist.

If the time value for the put is different from the call, there will be a difference in the synthetic position compared to a real stock position, making the synthetic either too cheap or too expensive.

By the way, if these concepts make absolutely no sense to you, don't worry; understanding put-call parity and synthetics in gross detail is not a prerequisite to making money with options. Furthermore, in today's extremely efficient markets, this knowledge will have minimal benefit to you as a retail trader.

Using Options to Lend or Borrow Money   Options can be used to borrow and lend money; for example, what if you bought a nondividend-paying stock at a specific price from a person who needed to borrow money from you (there is the initial loan collateral)? Then you synthetically created a short stock position using a short call and long put that expire two years in the and make the borrower take the other side of the trade, meaning she has to buy a call and sell a put, and for a fee, which you set (your interest payment). In this example, you have essentially created a direction-neutral (100% hedged) position in that stock.

Of course, put-call parity using prevailing risk-free rates dictates that your conversion is going to cost (credit) you something. But what if you could make your own market in those options and tell the borrower that for this transaction, he would have to pay you an amount equal to 20% of the total cost of the trade per year? Remember that there is no risk in the stock and it's a closed transaction.

This was the way that Russel Sage, a crafty businessman in the 1800s got around usury laws and lent money (secured) to people at high rates of interest. Using options, he got around the law. He wasn't the first; in fact, there is evidence of using options (in some form) and put-call parity to bypass religious usury laws dating back 2,000 years.

Now that we have proven that we can create synthetic calls using puts and stock and synthetic puts using calls and stock and even synthetic stock using calls and puts, there has to be more to the relationship between calls and puts. In fact, there is a balance between the two—an equilibrium that is dependent on a couple of simple inputs, interest, and dividends.

Without getting too complicated and without going into long algebraic expressions, let's take what we learned about forwards and basis.

A conversion or reversal is essentially an arbitrage strategy when a trader believes that there is a mispriced marketplace.

In both strategies you would need to use basis to find where the options should be trading in relation to each other and the stock and determine if there is any arbitrage in the marketplace.

Professional traders use the terms *conversion* and *reversal*, which basically translates to interest minus dividends.

A *conversion* means getting long stock and synthetically short stock using a short call and long put. If you can do this, trade for more of a credit than what it may cost you in interest on your long stock, which you can use to lock in a partially riskless profit. Of course, if the stock pays a dividend in the time you are in the trade, the trade will cost more to put on compared to a nondividend stock because the dividend is paid to the stock, not to the options.

A *reversal* means selling stock short and at the same time creating a synthetic long stock position by purchasing a call and selling a put. Because professionals collect interest on short stock positions, this trade is generally done for a debit, because the professional trader will be collecting interest on his short stock position. If there is a dividend being paid in the time you are in the trade, you should expect to be compensated for the dividend, as you will be required to pay that dividend, as you are *short* stock.

A professional trader may choose to convert or reverse for many reasons, including the neutralization of existing positions because of expiration or perhaps she is making a bet on interest rates increasing or decreasing. Maybe there is an arbitrage opportunity, but because of current technology and increased market efficiencies and participants, real, easy arbitrage is hard to come by. Most retail traders do not employ these strategies due to trading costs, complexity, and efficient markets.

Implied and Historical Volatility   Many professional traders take most of their risk and bets on changes in volatility. In other words, they buy implied volatility when it's relatively low and sell implied volatility when it's relatively low. As a retail trader, the majority of the risk you are probably taking involves direction, but not entirely. In fact, volatility most likely plays more of a role than you think in the option tactics that you are employing. If you want to know the current general state of implied volatility in the market, you may look to the Chicago Board Options Exchange Market Volatility Index (VIX or VXX) products offered by the Chicago Board Options Exchange. Let's dig a bit deeper into volatility and the VIX itself.

The VIX and its Derivations Let me start by stating that volatility, in all of its manifestations, is the most complicated and ambiguous concept when it comes to trading options. Some clarity can be had by looking back at a stock's typical behavior as well as looking forward at events on the horizon and examining how that stock reacted to those events in the past.

Historical Volatility Historical or observed volatility is just that—it is the actual annualized movements of a stock over a given period of time. Volatility can also be thought of as the speed at which the market is moving. In layman's terms, one might look at the past 30 days of a stock's close-to-close prices and, by observing those price movements, determine that it has been moving at a 30% volatility. This is done by simply extrapolating those movements into an annual number (volatility is generally expressed as the *annualized standard deviation*). Of course, just looking at 30 days of data wouldn't give us a very accurate or typical measurement of how a stock moves, so we might look back at a year or more of data to get a more typical reading. The word *typical* is a tough one to use, because in 2008 and early 2009, when stocks were dropping like a rock, their typical volatility observations were probably much higher than their five-year volatility averages. So it is important to not only look at how volatile the stock has been recently, but to look even further back in time and try to associate relatively high and low volatility periods with some fundamental data. Remember that historical volatility readings can be sampled in different time frames, sort of like a moving average. If you were to look at a chart of a stock's 10-day historical volatility (HV), chances are that it would be more choppy and much less smooth than a 30-day HV chart. Historical volatility can be used in conjunction with indicators like ATR to find realistic price movements for a particular stock

Implied Volatility *Implied volatility* is what the options market implies the volatility will be for a particular security in the future. Implied volatility is calculated backward from an options price. In other words, if investors are paying more for options, in general, implied volatility is rising and vice versa if investors are selling options. When you think about the strategies you have learned, it makes sense; if you think the market is going to move fast and in one direction or the other, you may buy a straddle, strangle, call, or put. On the flip side, if you were thinking the market was going to move slower, you may choose to sell one of those options strategies.

Typically, market participants are scared of unknowns, which may mean higher implied volatility, because traders are buying protection in the form of puts and/or speculating on a rise in stock by buying calls.

Sometimes, in a panic, with little information, traders tend to disregard trends, prices, and sometimes fundamental data and either oversell or overbuy (relative to normal movement), especially if there is an unknown event like an earnings report or Food and Drug Administration (FDA) decision occurring presently or on the horizon.

In the options world, we can literally see fear being built into or out of options, without any change in the underlying stock price; this fear may be represented by increasing implied volatility (rising options prices).

In the options markets, we have certain inputs that we enter into our models to find an options price; these include stock price, time to expiration, strike price, dividend rate, interest rate (which are all known or can at least be calculated to some degree). What is not known is which implied volatility input to use. Implied volatility is figured backward from the options price, but how do you know if it is currently cheap or expensive?

Supply and demand can obviously change options prices, and the greater the demand, the higher the price and the greater the *implied* (*predicted*) volatility and vice versa.

Example   Figures 9.9 and 9.10 compare the change in option prices and Greeks with just a simple increase in implied volatility. Figure 9.9 is assuming a 19.3% volatility. With no change in any other variable, if traders begin to pay more for options, the second example shows the prices of

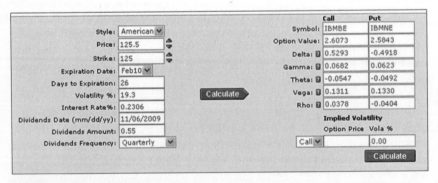

FIGURE 9.9   IBM Options Prices Using a 19.3% Implied Volatility—Note the Values of the Call and Put
Source: Courtesy of cboe.com.

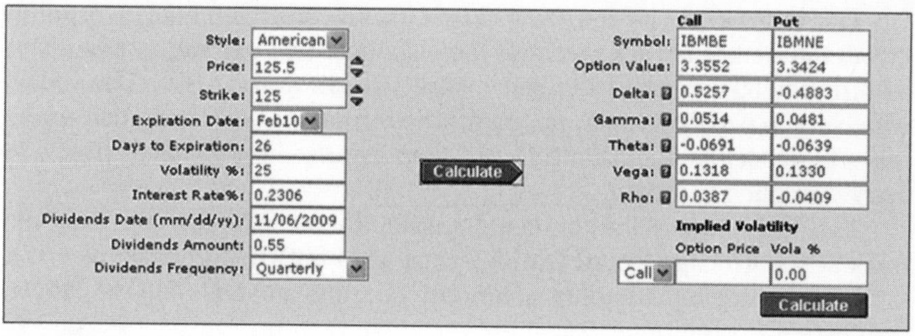

	Call	Put
Style: American	Symbol:	IBMBE	IBMNE
Price: 125.5	Option Value:	3.3552	3.3424
Strike: 125	Delta:	0.5257	-0.4883
Expiration Date: Feb10	Gamma:	0.0514	0.0481
Days to Expiration: 26	Theta:	-0.0691	-0.0639
Volatility %: 25	Vega:	0.1318	0.1330
Interest Rate%: 0.2306	Rho:	0.0387	-0.0409
Dividends Date (mm/dd/yy): 11/06/2009			
Dividends Amount: 0.55			
Dividends Frequency: Quarterly			

Implied Volatility
Option Price Vola %
Call 0.00

FIGURE 9.10 IBM Options Prices Using a 25% Implied Volatility—Note the Jump in Prices
Source: Courtesy of www.cboe.com.

both the call and put increasing, assuming a 25% implied volatility. With a 5.7% absolute change in implied volatility, the price of the call increased by 0.75 and the put by 0.76, which is shown in Figure 9.10.

TRADER TIP

A 5.7% absolute change in volatility would be similar to the VIX going from 20% to 25.7%. Absolute change is the actual change.

The prices of the calls and puts will typically rise or fall together, so as put-call parity remains and no arbitrage exists,

Cheap versus Expensive? How do you use implied and historical volatility in your trading and how do you find a cheap or expensive option and what do you do when you stumble on one?

Cheap and expensive are relative and there are several factors that go into determining whether an option is really cheap or expensive.

The words *VIX* and *volatility* are thrown around more than pitches in a doubleheader. What's worse is that the contexts in which both words are typically used are frequently incorrect and misleading.

Before I explain how to use volatility measures to your advantage, we must understand what they really are.

VIX measures implied volatility. In actuality, the VIX (which stands for the Chicago Board Options Exchange Market Volatility Index) and actual market volatility, in the S&P 500 Index (SPX), for example, may differ somewhat.

The VIX is a specialized product that uses a complex model incorporating all the strikes of SPX puts and the calls over two expiration months to determine a 30-day future implied volatility reading on the SPX. This index, which some people oversimplify with the term *fear barometer*, can sometimes be misleading, but the VIX can help us to see basic macro trends in market-implied volatility.

The VIX is calculated by using a complex formula developed by the folks at the Chicago Board Options Exchange (CBOE). In basic terms, it looks at the implied volatility of *all* options (puts and calls) on the SPX in the current expiration month.

It is possible to have the SPX moving day to day on a 25% volume, but the VIX may be at 30%, suggesting that expectations are for more volatility in the near term. It could also work the other way around. Many folks were upset that the VIX didn't predict the market dropping back in 2008, but in a way it did, if you knew how to look at it. When the public is *net buying options*, this may cause options prices to rise, thus causing *implied volatility* (VIX) to move higher as well. When the market was going up and up, not many folks were buying puts (most were selling them, which is a bullish act), and many were taking profits on their calls as the broad market progressed higher and higher. The market was moving at 30% volatility and the VIX was at 12% from September 2007 through May 2008. That fact alone should be motivation for a trader to act because a reversion to the mean is likely; the problem is that many didn't know what to look for, and being optimists (and wanting the uptrend to remain their friend), didn't want to think about the likelihood of an adjustment ahead.

After the market collapsed in 2008, then rebounded, then gave back much of its gains, a lot of chatter stirred up about the CBOE SPX volatility index, VIX, and how volatility had returned to the markets and was maybe going to be a permanent fixture. This topic is certainly one that is open to extremely conflicting views and opinions. Unfortunately, many who are arguing the point that the VIX did not signal danger in the marketplace may not have the full story, nor do I believe that they actually trade, monitor, or completely understand the VIX itself. Use the VIX as another indicator to watch, not the only indicator.

The VIX has undergone some changes in its lifetime, from first measuring at-the-money implied volatility in S&P 100 Index (OEX) options to now using a complex formula to predict the next 30 days of volatility in the S&P 500 Index, SPX.

I have been using VIX for many years now and am impressed with the options product that was created around it. The mathematical laws that govern the world of options tend to be the same no matter what the product is.

However, when it comes to the VIX, be extremely careful when trading the VIX. The values that you see for VIX options are not just based on the value of the VIX itself, which means that you may think that your option has intrinsic value or should behave a certain way when the VIX moves, but often they do not.

There are many nuances to trading options on the VIX versus trading plain vanilla calls and puts on most standard equity or index issues. Although the VIX is a fantastic product, it requires a bit of homework to trade. I believe that it was created to serve the professional as opposed to the average retail investor, but that is not to say it cannot be traded by any home-gamer out there with the appropriate amount of due diligence.

When I started in this game, the first thing I was taught was to buy low and sell high. This goes for *everything*, including volatility, especially if you trade options.

VIX as a Fear Barometer "When the VIX is low, it's time to go (exit your long positions) and when the VIX is high, it's time to buy (get long)."

This adage, though helpful, can be misleading—high and low both are relative terms. I will typically look back about one to four months when trying to decide what is high and what is a low level in the VIX. You can add in VIX analysis to your trade plan, but don't make broad market value decisions solely based on VIX relative values.

***The Word* Volatility** The word *volatility*, meanwhile, typically refers to the annualized standard deviation of a stock, index, or ETF over a given period of time. It can either refer to implied or historical. Make sure you clarify this when asking a question or making a statement regarding volatility.

Volatility can be viewed in a daily, weekly, or monthly time frame, or whatever time period you choose. Even though you can sample volatility in any time frame, volatility is always expressed as an annualized number.

SPX historical (or observed) volatility is the actual percentage movements of the underlying spot price. So if I were to tell you that the SPX (at 1,100) is currently moving on a 20% volatility, this translates to about a 13.75 point range a day, two-thirds of the time. One standard deviation occurs about 70% of the time, or about two-thirds.

If you remember statistics class, you'll remember the bell curve. Well if the SPX index is trading at 1,100 and you hear the "30-day historical volatility" is 20%, this essentially means that based on a 30-day sample of close-to-close prices, that data extrapolated out would translate to a 20% annual standard deviation of the index up or down in a year's time (based solely on probability and statistics). So with the index at 1,100, one annual SD would be plus or minus 220 points.

This just helps us professional traders get a handle on what is going on and gives us a basis for pricing options.

You can break annual standard deviations into daily, weekly, or monthly SD as well. Several brokers who specialize in options trading have calculators to help you find standard deviations of a stock over any given period using different volatility inputs.

TRADER TIP

To find the daily standard deviation, you divide the annual volatility number by the square root of number of periods in a year; there are 256 trading days in a year and the square root of 256 is 16. If you divide 0.20 (annual SD) by 16, you get .0125—that is the percentage daily SD. For weekly SD, divide the annual volatility by 7.2. For monthly SD, divide the annual volatility by 3.46.

Volatility is generally expressed as an annualized number, but as the SPX makes bigger intraday moves, the volatility of that index may increase, because remember we are extrapolating the moves out for an entire year.

Implied Volatility and Insurance Premiums   Imagine that you're a high-risk driver with a history of road rage and you drank four shots of liquor. You go into a car dealership ready to drive off with a new car, call your insurance company, and let them know the details of your situation. They give you a quote of $100 for a full year of insurance coverage. Is something wrong? Do you buy the insurance? Yes, you do! A crash was inevitable and the insurance market was severely *underpriced*. Unfortunately, it's seldom that traders look at the whole picture when they are blinded by bliss (or profits). When the VIX is low, insurance (puts) are relatively cheap and when the VIX is priced lower than the market's recent actual volatility, traders may be getting complacent.

Seasonal Volatility   Typically, summers tend to be lower volatility months. Generally it's a good bet to sell volatility (sell options, credit spreads) in May and begin buying them back in July or September. July is also the start of the second-quarter earnings season, and this is where volume may begin to creep back into the markets, although third-quarter results, which begin in October, have historically been more volatile.

Average True Range (ATR), Volatility, and Standard Deviation
Having a firm grip on these concepts is an integral part of not only setting realistic expectations for your trading and spotting anomalies, but

possibly (and perhaps more importantly), finding a reasonable stop loss level in your trade.

All three of these measurements are somewhat related, but each is expressed in slightly different ways and interpreted differently. For most of us home-gamers, we are not going to use ultracomplex mathematical models to find precise deviations for a stock's normal patterns as a means of finding some sort of volatility arbitrage and trying to capture it.

More likely, we are using these observations as a means to identify realistic and relatively abnormal occurrences in either an option's pricing or a stock's behavior.

ATR   ATR stands for *average true range* or *average trading range*. ATR measures the average dollar movement of a stock over different time periods, typically taking 14 periods into account. It also measures more than close-to-close pricing.

ATR takes the *largest* movements into account, which enables the trader to get a closer look at the true recent behavior of the stock he is trading. I use ATR as a quick confirmation of a stock's overbought or oversold condition.

I also use this as the outer edge of where I would place my stop loss or profit target or as an entry for a reversion to the mean trade. For instance, if a stock or index has exceeded its daily ATR and I see a chart pattern that looks attractive for entry, I may enter long or short and then cover once the stock has hit its normal one standard level. At most times, ATR will be greater than daily standard deviation.

Volatility   There are several types of volatility, but for this example I use historical (observed) and implied. Historical volatility is an annualized number expressed in percentage terms telling us how much a stock has moved in the past.

Volatility helps us gauge a stock's behavior and gives us a benchmark, so to speak, when examining a potential trade strategy and setting profit targets and stop losses. Volatility is typically measured by using close-to-close prices as the inputs for finding deviation or volatility.

Using close-to-close observations helps to normalize the intraday noise that tends to occur in the marketplace. Plus, it's quite cumbersome to take every single price movement into consideration to compute volatility. Although with today's technology, that is certainly possible, and I know that certain market participants use that data.

For example, if I said a stock was moving on a 40% volatility and the stock was trading at $100 per share, that means it would be realistic for the stock to move either 40% higher (($40) or 40% lower ($40.00) about 70% of the time (this is where standard deviation comes in).

In the options world, we tend to view things a bit differently; in this context, the probability of success has to do with a stock's observed volatility and the theoretical price distribution of that stock over a given period of time.

To put it simply, we look at how a stock has tended to behave in the past; in other words, how volatile it has been. Let's assume that a stock has a 50% historical volatility over the past year on average. We might assume that moving forward, the stock will continue to move on a 50% volatility. Basically that means that in a year's time, a $100 stock will be between $50 and $150 about 70% of the time. If you think back to statistics class and the bell curve, you might remember standard deviation; that theory applies here.

Well, in our analysis we are applying the same calculation, but we are finding the exact probability of the stock we are trading finishing at/above or below a certain price assuming a certain level of volatility.

We also look at what the options are implying the volatility will be. This can be determined by an option's price, because implied volatility is figured backward from an option's price.

TRADER TIP

To find the rough gauge of the implied volatility in any month, take a look at the at-the-money call and put. Even though there will be differences in IV as you move away from the at-the-money (ATM) strike, using ATM strike implied volatility is what many professionals use when they are talking implied volatility in a certain month.

We all know that volatility can change and typically we base our calculations on the volatility priced into the options, because that tends to represent the market view of a stock's volatility moving forward in time.

Now that I have made this clear, let me simplify. If you have a $100 stock that tends to move up or down about $10 maximum in a month about 80% of the time, and you were to sell a 90/80 put spread (which is $10 out of the money), you have roughly a 20% chance (statistically) of being successful in your trade. Remember that 80% of the time it doesn't go outside a $10 variation.

Again, this is a complete oversimplification, and remember that news, corporate events, terrorist attacks, and so on, can throw a monkey wrench in your game plan and at that point, statistics go out the window.

Standard Deviation   As a professional market maker, my option valuations and decisions on trades were based on how volatile a stock is, was, or

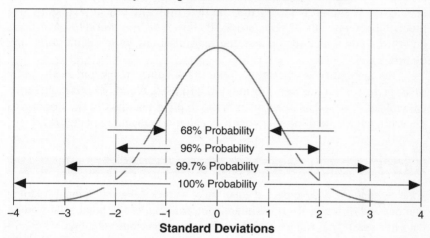

Standard Normal Distribution
Probability of Being within +/–N Std Devs of the Mean

68% Probability
96% Probability
99.7% Probability
100% Probability

Standard Deviations

FIGURE 9.11 The Bell Curve Visual

will be in the future. By definition, standard deviation is a measure of the variability or dispersion of a statistical population, a data set, or a probability distribution. A low standard deviation indicates that the data points tend to be very close to the mean, whereas high standard deviation indicates that the data are spread out over a large range of values.

To simplify, the standard deviation of a stock is the annualized expected movement (expressed in whole dollars), using the current stock's price as the mean, while plugging in the observed volatility. So if the current stock price was $100 and we were using an observed volatility of 40%, one standard deviation over a year's time would be $40 up or down, and this distribution would occur about 70% of the time. The chances of the stock moving beyond that range (if the volatility input you use is semi-accurate) becomes less and less the farther from the top of the curve you are as shown in Figure 9.11.

What Are the Statistical Chances?

1 Standard Deviation = 68.3% chance the stock will stay within plus or minus 1 standard deviation.

2 Standard Deviations = 95.4% chance the stock will stay within ±2 standard deviations.

3 Standard Deviations = 99.7% chance that the stock will stay between ± 3 standard deviations.

Obviously, it's all about the input. If you are using 40% as your volatility measurement and you are taking your measurements right after March 2009, your observed volatility may be high and you may be expecting too much movement out of your stock. If, however, the markets have been quiet for some time and you use that measurement, your calculations may be low.

This ambiguity is what makes the marketplace work and is also why there is *no* perfect answer. For me, I like to use a blend of both the historical volatility as well as news, events the implied volatility of the options to generate my forward-looking volatility calculations and expectations.

TRADER TIP

To determine the daily expected volatility of a stock, take your annual volatility number and divide by 16 (the square root, roughly, of the number of trading days in a year). That will be your daily average percentage volatility.

How Volatility Can Affect Options Prices Adversely When Time Value Takes Control   Earnings are a time to be hyperaware of volatility. For example:

SWKS in April 2010, Skyworks stock up, volatility down

New traders can sometimes be disappointed when they buy a call ahead of an earnings report. Imagine that you are a new options trader who purchases a call option just ahead of a stock report with the anticipation of strong earnings. You end up correct in your thesis, the stock reports great earnings, moves higher, but your call option investment either just breaks even or maybe even loses money. What went wrong?

Earnings can be bullish or bearish catalysts for a stock, sometimes creating abnormal daily movements in a stock's price. For example, back in April 2010, Skyworks Solutions (SWKS) reported revenue of $238.1 million and non–generally accepted accounting principles (GAAP) earnings per share (EPS) of 24 cents for the second quarter. Analysts were expecting revenue of $232.2 million and EPS of 23 cents, so the report was certainly positive.

SWKS also guided higher for the next quarter, higher than analysts had expected. In addition, Kaufman Bros. initiated coverage on SWKS as a buy, which gave it further bullish support. SWKS was trading 6.5% higher that day to $17.26. The huge rally was much more volatile than a typical daily move for SWKS, but implied volatility was down as soon as the report was released, even with the move higher.

In the options markets, a sharp move higher after an unknown earnings report becomes public knowledge, which typically means that implied volatility is on the decline, because the markets now have the data that was an unknown. Yesterday, implied volatility in June was right around 50% for the at-the-money options. Right after the report came out, that number dropped to around 36%, a 14% absolute drop in implied volatility (IV).

So why should you care? When you purchase options (go long) you are getting long vega, which means you have a positive bias to volatility. The July 17.50 calls has a vega of 0.026, which means that for every 1% absolute change in volatility, that option is going to increase or decrease approximately 2.6 cents in value.

With the 14-point reduction in implied volatility that we saw in one day in SWKS, that would translate to an almost 37-cent drop in the options price, or $37 per contract. If the delta of that option was 0.40 yesterday and the stock moved up only $1, you may realize only a 0.03 cent profit, and that doesn't account for any time decay.

Even though you made money (0.40) on the delta (because of the change in the shares themselves), you lost on your vega (0.37) (because of the volatility implosion).

TRADER TIP

At-the-money options have the highest vega, so use caution when buying at-the-money or out-of-the-money options ahead of an event such as earnings (to simplify, remember that you can lose all of your time value. To make a purely directional bet, look for a delta of 0.70 to –0.90, but realize you still have 100% of that options premium at risk if the trade goes against you).

Of course, if the stock makes a large move, you increase your chances of being correct in a long call trade, but that success is not assured. If the stock were to drop and you were long a put, volatility may actually increase, which would be beneficial to your position.

There is no way to tell exactly which way a stock will move over earnings. Just bear in mind the effects of implied volatility and vega when selecting earnings strategies. For the most part, post-earnings mean a short-term move lower in implied volatility because the unknown factor is out of the way.

To counter the effects of volatility, be aware of how much of your options price is made of time value, which is the portion affected by volatility, time, and so forth. If you purchase a call option for $5 and $0.50 of it is time value, then no matter what happens to volatility or how much time passes by, if the stock were to remain unchanged, you would only lose $0.50. Obviously, if the stock increases in value, you will gain only intrinsic value; if it drops, you will lose intrinsic value.

In closing, if you combine awareness of the following:

- Major news occurrences
- Macro economic events, data, and indicators (past, present, and future)
- Fundamental corporate news—data and events
- Technical analysis for timing
- Options strategy and volatility analysis for selecting the appropriate strategy and statistical edge
- Your own behavioral characteristics
- Formed your plan considering these parameters

You have already put yourself way ahead of the game.

FINAL THOUGHTS

If you are completely confused, scared, and perplexed by this chapter, it is okay. The goal was to bring you to the realization that there is much to learn about options and their eccentricities. Don't ever get overly confident and allow yourself to continue to listen and learn. If you are simply buying long calls and long puts or buying and selling basic put spreads, you can still be successful even if you don't understand all these advanced concepts. What you need to do as a beginner is follow your plan and have a checklist. Most importantly, you must paper trade, preferably for several months until you are able to understand the behavior of the options strategies you are using in different market situations. Enlightening yourself to the more advanced concepts may be a challenge, but it may enable you to not only make more money in your existing trades, but, more importantly, it may help you to minimize the catastrophic losing trades you could have experienced because of an *unknown* mistake you were making. The journey to understand options as a master trader may be a long and tedious one, but the rewards and relief as you progress down that road can be extremely rewarding.

CHAPTER 10

A Revolutionary Approach to the Mind Games of the Markets

Understand Why You Need Emotions to Trade Well

Denise Shull

"What is the truth?" The answer is, whatever works. If beliefs impose limitations on what we perceive as possible, and the environment can express itself in an infinite combination of ways, then beliefs can only be true relative to what we are attempting to accomplish at any given moment. In other words, the relative degree of truth inherent in our beliefs can be measured by how useful they are

—Mark Douglas
Trading in the Zone

T he psychology of trading seems to be one of the least addressed and usually the last thing that a trader pursues, often after experiencing failure, which at that moment may be too late. I was lucky enough early on to have a mentor stress the importance of this often-overlooked part of your trading plan. You must understand yourself and your state of mind, I believe, before you can really flourish as a trader. Of course, for some this ability comes naturally whereas for others it may take quite a bit of work. This isn't about mind reading or some complex neuroscience that must be understood, but rather understanding your state of mind, isolating your emotions, and learning how they can help or hurt you. This chapter offers some simple, practical advice and exercises for traders to at least begin to understand the psychology of trading. It contains a lot of practical

337

information that you should easily be able to put to use in your plan and your psyche.

TRADING IS LIKE WEATHER FORECASTING

This book has laid out for you everything you need to know to successfully trade options—or at least everything you *intellectually* need to know!

Unfortunately, if cognitive knowledge of the markets equated to success in the markets, there would be many, many more successful options traders! Between what you know and where the markets move, there lies an issue of how well the trader can execute his trades. Now it sounds simple enough—decide on a direction for Google (or your stock of choice), decide on a time frame, and put on a spread . . . and the rest will take care of itself. Right?

Wrong! But wait! How can that be wrong?

Markets at their core are simply a mind game: Investor against investor, trader against trader. For every buyer there is a seller—and they believe they are just as smart as you!

So who is right? And how do you maintain your confidence in your trade when the market stops behaving the way you predicted?

When it comes right down to it, no matter how well you learn the Greeks or the mechanics of a bull put spread, straddle, strangle, or iron condor, you still have to make (and take) a decision in the midst of uncertainty. It sounds simple enough, but as anyone with a modicum of experience will tell you, it may be the hardest thing to do and do right (consistently). Now this might strike you as odd because with options models like Black-Scholes or binomial and the like, you can get a very good grasp on the probabilities, time decay, and the implied volatilities of your trades. But notice that I said "very good grasp" and specifically did not say "know."

The reason? The bottom-line truth of all markets, in all time frames and for all of eternity, is that no matter how good your modeling tools, the market itself is still fundamentally uncertain. *Anything can happen* (otherwise known to traders as ACH!).

Models are meant for perfect worlds. Models are meant to be like reality. They are patterned, like the weather, and predictable, like the weather, and *imprecise*, like the weather!

Why? Well, despite the growth of financial engineering programs, markets on the other hand are and always will be only a reflection of the human perception in that moment. Perception in and of itself simply has to change as additional facts become available. Whether it is price action, company news, or unemployment numbers, our expectations evolve.

Likewise, we humans are fickle. We react—and overreact—to news, to market movements, to expert opinion, and even (or most importantly) to our own internal state of mind.

No One Ever Knows Precisely Where the Hurricane Will Hit

As Frank Knight of the University of Chicago pointed out in his 1921 book *Risk, Uncertainty and Profit*,[1] there is a fundamental difference between risk and uncertainty. Risk is dice. Risk is a card game. In either one, the range of possible outcomes is finite and can be quantified.

You don't actually even have to go back to 1921 and Knight or later to 1930 and the famed economist John Maynard Keynes, who said the same thing. Richard Zeckhauser, an economist and currently the Frank P. Ramsey Professor of Political Economy at the Kennedy School, Harvard University and an expert in market decision making, recently filmed an excellent interview for Kiplinger's, saying precisely the same thing. The markets are relentlessly and sometimes even viciously uncertain. The range of possible outcomes is infinite.

Getting our heads around this fact, even while we tend to rebel against it, gives us a head start versus any and all market players who don't get it. We do, however, tend not to like it very much and try incredibly hard to turn markets into dice games.

The behavioral finance gang calls our need to deny this—and our attempt to deceive ourselves into believing it is only a numbers game—the "Illusion of Control." We try to make ourselves feel as if we really do know what is going to happen in the future or if we don't know precisely, we know the odds in the same way that we know the odds in blackjack or dice when in fact we only know what the odds would have been if we could time travel backward. In other words, even if you can implement everything Jared so adeptly discusses, you will still have at best only an estimate of what is more or less likely to happen in the future.

Making Risk Decisions: Do We Evacuate, Hunker Down, or Go Sailing?

In essence, that is always the question you want to answer in trading. The seas might look clear but there could be a storm in a few days or an hour away. What you see in the moment doesn't reflect what you may see in a month. And you truly have no way of knowing exactly what the future will hold.

You definitely need the tools this book has given you. But what you also need is the knowledge that those tools are like compasses and barometric pressure indicators—capable of change in a moment and only an approximation of what reality will hold. You can also think of some of the strategies as different vessels; some are sturdier than others, but slower to get you to your destination, while others may be faster, but more susceptible to changes in the (market) climate.

Your "Brain on Risk"   In fact, no matter how great our discomfort or denials, we can't deceive our brains. Unconsciously, the human brain knows the difference between solving for X (an algebra problem with one answer) and making a judgment call on a sailboat.

In fact, this facility of our brain explains why so many traders have problems following their trading plan to a T. They think they are solving for X when their brain goes about the task in a kind of guesswork, pattern-matching way. It realizes what you are consciously setting out to do, knows it isn't actually possible, and in turn tries to steer your perception and analysis through a process similar to solving a jigsaw puzzle—looking for the matching colors and patterns—in order to have the actual picture emerge.

Behind the scenes, your brain is using the context to interpret the market data. For example, Dow 10,000 is Dow 10K right? Well ... actually it is not.

The meaning of Dow 10,000 depends on which direction we are looking at it from, how fast we got there, and where it has been before. The first time we hit it, it was a big deal signaling a bull market. The second, on the way back down through it, it was a big deal signally a bear market, and for most of 2010, its stickiness meant we weren't going anywhere—one number, three meanings!

The same holds true with options—if a spike in implied volatility occurs six weeks before expiration versus one week—it means something different to you the trader and indeed to the ultimate outcome of the trade.

Context, which always includes timing as well as previous activity, creates meaning.

Put numbers in their proper psychological-perceptual perspective.

Therefore, when you see all of your analytical tools as helpers in the market weather prediction challenge or trading jigsaw puzzle game, you put them in their proper place, and while you suffer the discomfort of not having control, if you can tolerate that physical state of basic anxiety, you actually end up with a more accurate understanding of the problem—which gives you confidence and a much better shot at coming up with a better prediction!

Feelings as Part of Thought and Analysis   The second thing that goes on while you are evaluating an inherently uncertain situation is that your thoughts rely on your feelings in an even more obvious way. Think about it—when buying a house, taking a new job, or even meeting a new person, what do we say? "I have a good feeling about that," or "I have a good sense about her." Well, what are we talking about? We are talking about the way our bodies and brains work together to create knowledge. We call it intuition, or a gut feeling, but we treat it with much suspicion. On one hand, we rely on it and usually regret going against it. On the other hand, we think it is unreliable and sort of inferior to intellectual knowledge.

The trick ultimately is to learn to tell the difference between this intuition—or what I like to call *unconscious pattern recognition* (UPR)—and impulse—or the feelings that compel us to take action that really are about reacting to something other than the situation or decision at hand.

This truth is key for a number of reasons—neuroeconomic (the neuroscience of the brain on risk) and practical. As a practical matter, if you trick yourself into feeling you have certainty in your risk, it makes it much harder to effectively adjust when the market throws you an unexpected blast of wind. And admit it, no matter how little or how much experience you have, with the way the market behaved in the late 2000s, we all know the market can do just about anything at any time. In fact, if it hadn't been for storm after storm after unexpected clear sailing, would you even be reading this book?

Rationality Is Overrated

Most people, even the smartest ones, make bad decisions.

The exploding field of behavioral finance, or behavioral economics, which is finally taking hold after the market tsunamis of 2008, tells us a ton about how most of us end up behaving. In other words, the *perceptual* mistakes we tend to make over and over again.

The research proves that no matter how smart people are, they still tend to make the same mistakes in judgment when it comes to probabilities and risks. In reality, it is the rare individual who does not fall prey to what the researchers call *biases* but which I prefer to call *tendencies*. (To me a bias is a predisposed opinion—like how one feels about Democrats or Republicans, Catholics or Muslims—but a tendency better describes the things we tend to do.)

In fact, a few years ago, I had the privilege of attending the Investment Decisions and Behavioral Finance conference at Harvard and even there, in a room full of portfolio managers, the majority of people made the same mistakes on most of the simulated classroom exercises that the ostensibly less probabilistically inclined average trader makes on a day-to-day basis! (Don't feel bad if you see yourself here . . . I could give you names of some of the smartest people on the planet who have also unwittingly fallen prey to the very same tendencies . . . and if you really want to know, I'll tell you a trade or two they made!)

Overconfidence   The first thing we tend to do is believe that we will be different. In the catalog of behavioral finance, this is called *overconfidence*. I mean in your case, you have to think . . . "I am too smart; I have this book; I won't do that." In fact, you may even be reading this chapter by accident because you figure the psychological aspect isn't one you will ever have a problem with. Trust me, the "it won't happen to me" idea runs rampant.

Loss Aversion   Early on in my trading days upstairs from the Chicago Board Options Exchange pits, I learned an old saying: "Your first loss is your best loss!" But as I personally can attest to (and so can every other honest trader on the planet), most of us don't like to take it. We get into some sort of ill-conceived trade that very early on becomes very clearly wrong—or we become the victim of an unexpected news event (think BP shareholders in April 2010 after the Deepwater Horizon disaster and resulting oil spill), but we refuse to let go.

Now being an options trader, presuming you are doing more spreading than not, puts you in a much better position. You can't make as much, but by definition your risk is implicitly managed in a way that a purely directional trader's risk is not. But even then, everyone eventually sails smack dead into the unexpected storm and their position goes to a place (a losing place) that they never even considered—and usually over the span of a very short (shocking) period of time.

When it happens to you, it won't feel good, you are not going to like it, and presto, you *will* start rationalizing!

Technically, loss aversion means we will try to circumvent a small loss by avoiding it at almost all costs, but when we are presented with the same amount as a gain, we will jump on it. In other words, take the same amount of money—say $1,000—if it is a loss, we will tend to wait it out, but if it is a gain, we will tend to jump on it. It is just a fact—and one that is very hard to overcome—at least with your head. This tendency is popularized by the cliché that "traders often hold on to their losers too long and sell their winners too soon."

When we get to the role of psychological capital later in this chapter, it will get easier.

Framing   You can think of framing as how you ask the question. So if you think of a trade in terms of how much you can lose versus thinking of it in terms of how much you can win, you will tend to answer differently—even with the same probability distribution clearly in mind! Fixing this problem is about being unknowingly unattached to a set of circumstances or expectations and instead considering alternative frames.

Anchoring   For traders, this one is easy. We get *very* attached to where we entered a trade . . . even though that number means nothing to the market. Instead of understanding how the market is developing, we focus too intently on whether our account is making or losing money—simply from our relatively arbitrary entry point. Each time you are evaluating a trade, you should walk away from your screens and think about the factors involved in your entry. Reducing the inputs to your brain will help you be clearer about the risk you are holding. It is admittedly hard to *not* think in terms of profit, loss, or lost profit, but the trick is to work on the best judgment calls and detach from entry prices.

Confirmation   It pays to learn to ask yourself "What is wrong with my analysis?" because our natural tendency directs us to see only what justifies a position we have already taken. The best way I know of to understand this universal human tendency is not to think of it as it relates to yourself (because that just puts you in an endless loop) but think of someone you know who disagrees with you completely about the political direction and control of your country. Think about how you can so clearly see them interpreting any data, speech, or action of their favored political figures through their biased lenses. And trust me, even on the off chance that you don't do that with politics . . . you will do it with your trading account!

It simply doesn't feel good to look at new data that flashes us a signal that our previous analysis was wrong. So . . . what do we do? We avoid that feeling and essentially go into denial about the full data set.

Ironically, in the end, information that *dis-confirms* our previously held opinion can be the most useful!

Herding   You can think of this as the basic idea that you will either believe a group of other people who seem to know what they are talking about (a big problem for trading chat rooms) or want to be in the trade that has been profitable for everyone else in your group. It doesn't sound right to any one of us individually—the idea that we go with the group—but trust me, research shows we do. Think of it this way: Why do you wear the type of clothes that you do? And furthermore, why do people in, say, Afghanistan wear the types of clothes that they do? Well . . . it is simple, we wear what our group believes is appropriate. If we were born elsewhere, we would wear a different style. The same sort of unexamined influence can happen in our trades. This was addressed previously in the section on crowd behavior.

Expecting Tomorrow What You Got Yesterday   This is the simple fact that drives something called *the house money effect* and probably drives our loss aversion tendencies. We unconsciously overemphasize our most recent experience and extrapolate it to the future. If we lose, we expect a loser, if we win, we expect a winner—and *nowhere* could this be more true than the realm of making decisions under uncertainty (i.e., markets and trading).

The market, despite what it will feel like, has *no* idea of your positions or recent successes or failures. And yes, I know you already know that . . . the trick is that it won't *feel* that way when you are looking at your next trade!

Now there you have it—a partial list (some behavioral finance people have the number of biases on their list up to 200)—of the mental mistakes you are likely to make. Unfortunately, if knowing about them would solve them, we could end right here. But it doesn't work that way. Awareness in and of itself may help, but somewhere between purely calculating logic and our actual actions, something goes haywire.

Strategy: Yes, It Pays to Keep a Short Checklist   Make it a habit to ask yourself if in fact you have fallen into one of these biases listed. Remember, however, that truly consistent profits come from understanding and leveraging the connective tissue of feelings that lies between intellectual knowledge and trading actions. All decisions have an emotion associated with them. Eradicating the emotion isn't going to happen, so it is a matter of being aware of it and ultimately learning to use it in both your risk management—telling the difference between intuitive and impulsive feeling (and using the intuitive ones)—and ultimately in your market strategy and trade conviction decisions.

Solution: Adopt Psychological Capital as an Asset and a Strategy   You decided to learn to trade options. You have X amount of trading capital set aside for doing so. You also now have Y amount of *intellectual* market and options knowledge. But the big secret I want to help you unravel is that in the end it is *not* the intellectual knowledge but the ability to develop, implement, manage, and most of all, exit your trades that will make you money.

This ability depends on your reservoir of psychological capital—and psychological capital depends almost exclusively on the very real, very powerful but very challenging realm of feelings.

Now for purposes of our discussion, when I say feelings, I also mean emotion. I will further define the differences in a moment but suffice it to say for now that whenever I use the word *feelings* (unless I state otherwise), I am referring to the catch-all term for the physical experiences we have and physical states we find ourselves in, or in some cases, in the grips of. A clinical psychologist will use a different definition of feelings and emotions. I, however, am more concerned with the question from two angles—the bottom-line reality—which is we experience emotion as a physical—not mental—sensation and from the sense of what the average trader can practically put into use.

WHAT IS PSYCH CAP?

Previously this book mentioned or alluded to the roles of fear, greed, and sentiment a number of times. It was pointed out how variable these elusive ephemeral dimensions of the market can be. And you were warned about the power of the intangible. But let's now outline "Your Practical Reference Guide to Psychological Capital."

What is psychological capital? It includes your technical knowledge, but 99% of it is the net account balance of how you feel—energetic, clear-headed, and calmly confident. If that describes your state, you in effect have a psych cap account of a million dollars.

If you don't or haven't slept well, haven't eaten, or are angry at your teenager, your psych cap has been debited and your trading decisions will not be of the same quality that they could be.

In short, you can think of psych cap as the state of mind and body when you truly and completely feel good. To relate the idea to something you might be familiar with, a synonym might be *frame of mind.*

Feelings, Emotion, and Visceral Analytics: The Secrets to Keeping Your Psych Cap Account Well Capitalized

Now we haven't even touched on the psych cap credits and debits that occur through interacting with the market, but believe it or not, if you *stick to the standard described in the previous paragraph—energetic, clear-headed, and calmly confident—that alone will give you a psychological edge* in the mind game of the markets.

Let me give you an example. Let's take an easy one—*physically tired.* Research shows that beyond any shadow of doubt that when we are tired, we literally misperceive risk. It isn't that we see the risk and decide to take it anyway . . . we don't actually see the risk. I think of this as, "Well, I wouldn't normally do this or think like this but right now, it seems fine." It is those experiences or decisions that when you look back, you ask yourself, "What was I thinking?" You can kind of think of it like the state of having had a couple of cocktails but the difference is, when you are at a party, you basically know that your judgment is impaired. You may do stupid stuff anyway, but in most cases you know (at least deep down inside) that it is stupid *while* you are doing it. With physical tiredness, you swear you never saw that indicator that had completely turned against your trade—and you most likely hadn't!

Rule 1. Never Make a Risk Decision That You Don't Absolutely Have to Make When You Are Tired! Corollary—Don't trade when you are tired. Don't even turn on the screen.

Which brings us to the most important emotion in trading ... the one you are feeling right now as you read this: *The Top Trading Feeling*—"But I May Miss the Trade of the Year!" (Otherwise known as the setup for "coulda, woulda, shoulda.")

Everyone talks in terms of fear and greed and certainly it seems, at least on the surface, that those emotions comprise the most market-relevant motivators. In actuality, however, research shows that the fear of missing out is actually a stronger motivator than the idea of making or losing money! The difference may appear subtle but in reality it can't actually be overstated. You can make a very good argument that the pervasive feeling of fear of missing out or being left behind drives market bubbles of all types.

Think about it. Take the housing bubble, for example. How many people thought, "If I don't just pay up, I might never get a house!" I know a couple who moved for the wife's job, and after being outbid on five houses, they overbid the sixth one by $50,000 just to make sure they got it! They didn't even love the house—but at that point they were afraid they would miss out on a house of any type.

Now, houses seem quite important. I mean, no one wants to live out of a car, but what would have happened if they had rented for a year?

I know that everyone loves to hate the mortgage traders of Wall Street but they too were gripped by the fear of missing out. If you worked at Bear Stearns and Goldman Sachs as the cash register was ringing on bundles of mortgages, it was very hard to persuade your boss to start selling out of the mortgage market. In fact, a now-infamous quote from the then CEO of Citibank, Chuck Prince, was something to the effect of, "As long as the music was playing, we had to keep dancing!"

More germane to our discussion here, however, are the now thousands of traders I have had the chance to talk to and their overwhelming confirmation of the very real experience of truly, madly, and deeply *not* wanting to miss a chance to make money that they could have, would have, or should have had.

I suspect that it has something to do with the relatively new research that shows that men (and most market participants in reality are still men) in general think in terms of relative position to the next guy. As *Scientific American Mind* put it in the spring 2010 issue, men constantly jockey back and forth for the one-up position—and truly loathe the feelings of a one-down position.

Other research might talk about the more competitive spirit of men or a man's evolved need to kill the beast in the forest, but in trading, it translates into hating—and being almost constitutionally unable to resist the idea of missing out—whether this means a trade entry you missed, a trade you exited that is now working exactly as you had expected, or the decision to begin to unwind a position when the time comes.

Rule 2. Develop Your Emotional Awareness so that You Hear the Fear of Missing Out Like a Dog Hears Thunder Strategic Corollary—Feel the feeling. Put the feeling into words. Preferably write out what feelings the market induces in you (instead of acting them out by entering a trade early or exiting an options spread too late.)

The idea of *control your emotions* equals serious devastating danger.

Traditionally, the mantra of traders everywhere is "control your emotions." If those words have been written, uttered, or declared once in trading history, they have been uttered a billion times. In fact, you will probably hear commentators and supposed experts continue to espouse this advice for the rest of your natural lives.

But alas, it is misguided.

First, the "control your emotions" religion contains a grossly illogical fallacy. Can you guess what it is?

Let me give you a few hints. What are the "things" we do as humans—I mean psychologically. Basically, we think, we feel, we act. Thinking appears centered in the brain (i.e., if you try, you can even almost feel it happen in your head), feelings and emotions emanate from the body (below your chin), and an action or acting *requires* moving a part of your body in the service of some sort of desired goal.

But somewhere along the line, feeling and acting got *so* merged together that virtually none of the smart people who think about behavior and markets noticed that the idea of "control your emotions" resembles mixing up apples and oranges.

In other words, the logical fallacy is that the only thing that needs to be controlled is your *actions*! I don't care if you jump up and down. I don't care if you yell at your charts. I don't even care if you punch a pillow ... just don't act out a feeling by taking another trade—or futzing with your spread and turning it into some other position that you had not planned on, and even worse, don't know how to control or adjust!

In fact, I will go so far as to say that this one misguided idea explains most of the failures of traders. In trying so hard to use discipline and intellect to overcome feelings, we end up forcing the energy of the feeling to be expressed in a different way ... we act it out instead of using it as information.

In other words, if you feel fear and try to use willpower to either overcome or overpower it but yet don't actually acknowledge it—you will either not trade and not understand why you can't trade, or you will exit positions way too early and wonder why. A zillion other examples exist but the premise remains simple—emotional energy resembles combustible energy—it will escape if not channeled. You can't hold either one down with your head!

Rule 3. Control Your Actions, Feel Your Feelings   Strategic Corollary—Act out feelings in harmless, not account-risking, ways.

Emotions have motivational "do something" energy within them. The secret, however, is that behind the urge to act, is information.

Exercise as a Strategy   To help you while you learn a whole new understanding of thinking versus feeling versus doing and in effect ReThink Thinking, get the idea that you need to be working out emotional energy in exercise, a punching bag in your trading office, a pillow to smash against the ground ... or anything that allows you to channel energy elsewhere. What you are trying to accomplish is the reduction of static in the signal between your visceral/feeling/emotion dimension and your brain.

Data Collection   Ultimately, you want the interpretation of meaning—or a piece of valuable data—that the feelings have. You want that data! You need that data! That data may ultimately be your best weapon ... but if you act it out by exiting your trade early or adding legs to it when you didn't intend to just to make up for unexpected price action, the data will be forever lost to you.

The phrase you want to remember was printed in a 2005 *Journal of Economic Literature* survey article on neuroecononmics. Penned by some of the most respected game and decision theorists, Colin Camerer, George Lowenstein, and Drazen Prelec,[2] the article says, "It is not enough to know what should be done one must also feel it."

In fact, it may surprise you, but without emotion, you wouldn't be able to make any sort of trading decision anyway! Research has shown us that if a human being is unfortunately lacking in healthy emotional neural networks—the neuronal clusters that are more or primarily associated with generating feeling and emotional data—they will be unable to make even the simplest of decisions. Such individuals can take all day to decide what to wear or to decide what cereal to buy. The reason for this is that

FIGURE 10.1 Emotional Spectrum

without feelings and emotions, the necessary data that needs to be assigned to the choices in order to tell the difference is missing.

So in fact, all decisions, including probability and risk decisions, have an emotion embedded in them. In its most simple form, when it comes to trading, the emotion in question is confidence.

Pivotal Trading Feeling/s—Confidence or lack thereof are otherwise known as F.A.D., or fear, anxiety, and doubt.

Think of the second-most important feeling in trading as a spectrum (see Figure 10.1). On one end you have panic and on the other end you have the giddy, overconfident elation of "I am a trading genius!" Everything on that spectrum is related and it will be where most of your trading psychological capital resides.

Panic Unstoppable Savant First of all, accept that the markets will induce anxiety, and although by definition, it doesn't feel that fun, it is also 100% normal. Their ever-changing nature, the meaning of money, and not knowing the future will automatically cause any trader to get nervous. The trick isn't to run from the nervousness but to figure out what it is telling you that you need to learn and then to come up with strategies and tactics for dealing with it in real time.

Analyzing the Spectrum from Panic to Elation The four types of fears to be on the lookout for are:

1. The fear of losing money.
2. The fear of being wrong.
3. The fear of giving money back.
4. The top trading feeling as we have already discussed.

Rule 4. Never Take a Trade You're Not Confident With   These are
the trades that start out with the thought, "Well, that just might work." The
thought after that is, "Well, I am only risking a little bit if it doesn't work . . .
it won't matter much."

Occasionally, those trades work; most of the time they do not. We
may not lose much on the surface but there is an insidious, pernicious
cost—and it is to your psych capital, that is, your confidence. First it puts
you into the feeling of wanting to make it back while simultaneously you
are feeling stupid and mad at yourself; therefore, you are more likely to
trade out your frustration and lose more . . . and the cycles just spiral
downward!

The original premise of "I will only risk a little" is actually a Trojan
horse. Your account balance may not suffer that much. But your psyche
suffers, and with an injured psyche, you are no match for the relentless
psychological warfare of the markets. The healthy, uncompromised market
participants will get you every time. Then your brokerage statement—as
well as your mood—will indeed be impacted. This can be equated to small
successes in our everyday lives. For many of us to remain happy, sound,
and feel successful, small repetitive successes help us to achieve those
larger goals that we set for ourselves. Even small setbacks in our nontrad-
ing lives can have an effect on our confidence and psych capital, and, in
turn, our ability to take risks and steps to progress. In trading, we can
absolutely control whether to enter a trade. To sacrifice that control just
because of the relative amount of actual capital at risk is just not worth
it. It would be better to increase your amount of successes, even by taking smaller profits than to take higher-risk, "what the heck" trades that go
against you, even if they have a higher profit potential.

**Rule 5. If in a Downdraft or Slump, Go Back to the first "BIKB"
(But I Know Better) Trade . . .**   In our attempts to control our emotions and to take all of the trades in a system, another one of our mistakes
has been to disallow ourselves to feel bad when we make a bad decision.
Yeah, I know, it doesn't feel good to feel bad . . . I also know it feels worse
to avoid feeling bad and then act out that feeling in some way—because
the acting out makes you feel even worse! So . . . if (no, I mean *when*), you
make a mistake, lose money, or get a negative market surprise that knocks
you for the proverbial loop, allow yourself the time, space, and liberty to
process the emotions.

Don't forget to step away from the computer!

Otherwise, three months or years in the future you will look back and
see that your behavior only exemplified the bad feelings and made everything worse!

The Fear of Missing Out—Not Making Money You "Should" Have Made Ironically, although we would think that the fear of losing money is the biggest one, it tends not to fully kick in until the end of the spectrum ... near to the panic stage. This is when most inexperienced or untrained traders or investors finally give in and dump their positions.

But let's start there, anyway. Everyone tells you to believe the probabilities and just take the trade. Even Jared says that! But this perspective doesn't take into account your brain being untrickable in the eye of uncertainty and the reality of what money means.

Strategy: Don't beat yourself up about a fear of losing money!

Money isn't everything, but it sure means a ton to our daily lives in this world. So of course you are afraid of losing money. You would have to be nuts—literally psycho—to not be afraid of losing money. It may be the most rational feeling in the world.

And one of the ironic things about the feeling of fear is that it can be seen as a safety valve. I mean that we don't jump in front of a truck, right? Why? Because we are afraid of what will happen. Fear in and of itself isn't bad. Roosevelt was wrong when he said, "The only thing we have to fear is fear itself." Without fear, we would be missing a good warning sign. We must, however, learn the tricks of the language of fear.

It only becomes bad when we act the feeling out without knowing it. So, by definition, if you are reading this book, you are attempting to gain specialized knowledge of the market and options world so that...what? So that you are less afraid to trade options! Chalk the fear of losing money up to a rational emotion and get on with understanding the other trading feelings. Doing so will keep you from the far left side of that spectrum and away from the position where you have to dump a position out of panic.

Rule 6. Bite-Size Objectives
The best way to get better is to set small objectives—both from a trading success and even more importantly, from a learning and experience point of view—and try to meet those objectives.

Think what you would do if you set out to become a tri-athlete. Wouldn't you lay out a plan, with bite-size pieces that you implemented over time? Wouldn't you include endurance, skill, energy, and recovery?

Trading is much like being a world-class athlete. I mean, sure, you can do a few options trades a year and maybe make a few bucks ... but if you want to be really good at it, if you want to manage your own money and feel secure that as long as you have your mental faculties, you can earn money with your money, then you need to be systematic about it.

The single best piece of advice I can give you is to have an overarching goal—one that *is not* monetary one that has meaning. But the more important piece of advice is to break that goal into tiny little objectives.

Otherwise it is too big and unimaginable... and you don't know what to do next. Small objectives that add up to a goal show you what to do next!

STRATEGIES AND TACTICS FOR LARGE PSYCH CAP BALANCES

Professionals specialize—and so should you. Learn one type of trade and learn it well *first*. Once you really understand one style of interacting with the market, you can extend it to other markets or variations but start out with one approach that simply feels the most right to you.

One huge secret of trading is that there literally are an infinite number of ways to make money—the trick is finding one or a few that suit you and most importantly, sticking with them (particularly when it is easy to get caught up in what your friend or trading bud thinks)!

Psych Cap Exercise 1. Getting Clear-Headed

Once you have a strategy defined—that is, you can write it out in one paragraph and then write down the specific pieces of information and market events you will look for in order to know when you want to enter the market. After you have that list, write out (again, in one paragraph) what you are going to do to enter the market and next, and more importantly, what will tell you to exit the market.

This exercise should be done on Saturday or Sunday afternoon or a holiday. In other words, at some point when the markets are truly not open and you can't be looking at the charts! What is the reason for this? You want to know by heart and it is easy to fool yourself if you try to do this while you are simultaneously looking at the market. Write out in detail the objective signals and parameters you are looking for (soup to nuts)?

Now, let me point out (in case it isn't clear) that this exercise actually requires that you work hard. It isn't that easy. But think about it ... if it were that easy then wouldn't everyone be able to do it? You want to not only do the work that others won't bother to but also the kind of work that others don't even know to do.

After all, remember that they are focusing on analyzing the numbers while you are figuring out how to analyze the markets, other people's perceptions, and your own semi-consciousness biases.

By getting the basic market stuff out of the way on the weekend, you can be focused on making all of your perceptions (explicit and conscious) while simultaneously be remembering to put all of your decisions within the overt context of the foundation question—what will other people be likely to perceive when I want out of my trade?

Basic Psych Cap Management Exercise 2. TFA Loops, Tracking the Superficial Feelings of Trading

The trick here is to come to an understanding of your particular pattern of TFA (thinking, feeling, acting) loops. This is the sequence—and we all have one (or a dozen) that are more characteristic of us than of our trading buddies. In fact, the loop continues infinitely. Actions beget feelings beget thoughts beget feelings beget actions and so on.

Summon up your courage and jump into the analysis when a feeling becomes conscious!

Analyzing that feeling can get more than a little unwieldy if you use either the big-five emotions from conventional psychology or even what most trading psych teachers will try to tell you. Let's simplify it.

Basic Emotion Analytics   Following are two options for recognizing the superficial feelings of trading:

Option 1
- Bad
- Sad
- Glad
- Mad

It isn't that easy to do at first, but all feelings can be categorized within these four. Make yourself a spreadsheet and track. Real-time checks in columns! Include this when journaling your trades and update regularly.

Option 2

For purposes of understanding superficial trading feelings, you can simply use a two-category system—do I want more or less of what I am getting? Psychologists call this *approach and avoidance* but it also maps to the basic fear and greed so oft talked about in trading and investing.

The objective of this exercise is to develop a data set that reflects your personal relationship to the market and to your trades. It should be done over time and become much more informative the longer you do it.

Ultimately, you also become more emotionally aware, which allows you to use this next strategy.

TRADER TIP

Emotional awareness is to know what emotions and feelings are operating. It is a skill. It can be developed and needs to be developed in most traders. It has been so discounted and dismissed that most traders have spent time trying to not develop it. It doesn't happen overnight—emotional awareness is more like learning to golf or ski—but it will serve you well overall.

Risk Management Strategic Corollary—Using a psych capital "Interrupt."

The idea you want to get into your routine is to be checking your psych capital as often as you are checking your charts, your models, and your trades. This is the athlete model of intellectual functioning, risk management, and market success. Athletes manage to their physical well-being first and foremost. It pays to do the same when actively investing and trading.

When you are routinely and habitually monitoring your "frame of mind" (as well as your physical energy), what happens is that you avoid making a handful of frankly dumb decisions. That avoidance does two things—it keeps cash and psych capital in your account. As a result of that, you avoid the feeling of having to make money back that you would have lost if you had been making risk decisions in a mentally depleted state. When you avoid that feeling, you are more clear-headed for the next risk decision.

Play that scenario out over time. What is the net effect on your account?

Advanced Risk Management—Psych Cap Management Exercise 3. The Echoes Backstory

Warning: This may either seem too scary or too much like psychobabble. However, the reality is: It is powerful!

Echoes Part 1 Get some sort of audio recording device. The open-source program Audacity will do—or the recording in Microsoft's One Note—and start talking! While you are watching the markets, say everything that comes into your mind and don't edit out a single word.

By the way, we aren't talking about broadcasting news reports of market movements. We are talking getting that demon voice that lives inside all of our heads documented. Now I know, you think . . . well, I wouldn't want anyone to know that. But hey, who has to know? You can delete it once you are done with it. In the meantime, you have to consider it as key research—just research on a key part of the trade—the decision maker!

Ideally you will do this for the salient periods while you are entering, monitoring, and exiting two or three trades (or decisions) in a row. Now, you may be a trading on a weekly time frame so I don't expect you to get a recording of every single thing you think and feel for weeks on end . . . just while you are thinking about the market, trades, or risk decisions. Record it!

Echoes Part 2a If you got Part 1 of this exercise right, you will listen to it and think "Egads . . . that is disgusting"!

But I am here to tell you that if you have that reaction, you are *right* on track.

See, the market has this way of inducing us to feel every little strand of insecurity we have ever felt. Because it is the ultimate authority figure and nothing you can do can change the price for more than a nanosecond, we are stuck interpreting the market's actions through our own narcissism—or as the accomplished businessman and options trader Scott Sheridan *of TD Ameritrade* says, "Taking it personally."

So take a gulp, listen to the tape, and make a list of the self-incriminating feelings that go through your head over and over. Many people call this *self-talk*. What I am talking about here is summarizing that self-talk into a few themes. Set this work aside for a few weeks. We will come back to it.

Echoes Part 2b Make a list of times in your childhood when you felt bad. At first, just make a list. Once you get a list, write a story about the ones that still seem to have the greater emotional charge. Next, think about the feelings as you felt them back then. (This can be very painful, I know. Hang in there . . . it isn't about now . . . it is about then and even though the feelings may hurt a ton, they are only feelings and they can't hurt you in the here and now!)

Echoes Part 2c Compare what you got out of 2a to 2b. Write down what you find.

Echoes Exercise Conclusion Are you shocked? It wouldn't surprise me. We have done this exercise with hundreds, maybe thousands, of traders and almost everyone is aghast—and astonished. The market induces us to feel *just* like our parents, older siblings, or early school years did!

Yes, I know, that seems completely unbelievable. But let me ask you to look at it this way—where else on earth do you get nanosecond-by-nanosecond feedback by the ultimate authority (the market) about whether or not you are right or wrong or did a good or bad job? *Nowhere* ... so even though it surprised me to find what Freud called *transference* to the market ... now that I see it, it makes obvious sense.

In any other sort of endeavor, you have more time between declarations of your competence. Even a professional quarterback has the whole game to play ... and everyone knows the judgment comes only with the final score or season record. Markets, on the other hand, are mark-to-market endeavors both at your clearing firm and in your psyche!

Now, what do you do with echoes knowledge?

You need to acknowledge all your feelings and categorize them in such a way that you realize a significant portion of them arise from history, and that some portion slinks away and leaves you much more in the present and therefore with more valuable psych cap to spend. No one can explain the electrochemical signature behind this, but when one can consciously map current feelings to past events, it seems to open up a space in the brain that allows us to come back to the present—and see the market situation for what it is!

Impulse or Intuition: Kidding Ourselves, or Unconscious Pattern Recognition?

How do you learn to tell the difference between impulse and intuition? After all, they are both physical, body-based feelings.

Now it is true that on one hand we have the best-selling book *blink* by Malcolm Gladwell, which recounts scores of successful uses of intuition, but on the other hand, we have the academics proving that in general, our intuition isn't as good as we think it is. This presents us with a conflict.

But in my opinion, it is a conflict that is definitely resolvable!

First, you actually have to know what intuition feels like. You unfortunately also have to know what impulse feels like. And although this sounds difficult, it really isn't nearly as hard as it may seem. In fact, gathering the data and experience to do so is exactly what the exercises we have been outlining will do for you. Consider it a market research project in the same way you would consider learning some of Jared's more advanced strategies for a market research project.

The idea is that with self-awareness, you can recognize when your psyche is telling you that it recognizes a market pattern. It is learning the subtle differences between how a gut feeling feels and how impulse feels.

A few hints—impulse has more urgency. The need to do something is stronger. Impulse is compulsive—you want to do something, there is energy pushing you to do something.

Intuition feels like recognition—the flash when you see an old friend in an unexpected place. Intuition, which can also be considered unconscious pattern recognition or experiential knowledge, doesn't have such urgency associated with how it feels. It feels much more like reading a novel and the feeling that comes with finding out the next twist—a satisfaction or curiosity of knowing something new.

Psych Cap Exercise 4. Get a Grip

Try to get a handle on these feelings *outside* of investing or trading; that will make them much easier to recognize when you are under the influence of the stimulation of markets moving. All you are looking for is the footprint in your body/psyche of an intuitive feeling versus an impulsive or compulsive "I have to do something" feeling.

The truth is that our psyches are actually very good at pattern recognition. Some would argue that in fact, pattern recognition defines intelligence. (Think about many of the problems in an IQ test; many are pattern matching.)

Likewise, we have a tendency to see patterns in market data where none exist. I suggest that tendency takes us back to our aversion to uncertainty and our need to feel as if we are in control, or the behavioral gang's "Illusion of Control."

Learning to differentiate the physical experience of intuition versus the physical experience of an impulsive (compulsive?) feeling gives you the objective you want to shoot for!

Psych Cap Exercise 5. Goals, Objectives, and Developing as a Trader

As outlined previously in this book, you now basically have everything you need to know to become successful in the markets. But will you? What will make the difference—after all, not everyone can beat the market—can they? If you embrace these few simple ideas, then your odds of success go way up:

- Specialize in a type of trading.
- Manage your psych capital.
- Learn to implement emotion analytics as religiously as you implement chart analytics.

But there is a right way and a wrong way to go about what is truly a monumental, lifetime task. And that is to understand your own development as a trader. This isn't something you can just learn from a book or do in a month.

So break that goal down into a series of objectives. Objectives are calculable. You have to be able to measure whether you have met an objective. But the trick is to make them achievable. Each time you meet one, you will boost your psych cap. Each time you meet one, you have further knowledge—intellectually, experientially, and viscerally (the latter being similar)—and then you can review the objectives for the next chunk of time. Your goal needs to be broad. Let me give you an example:

Goal: Teach the trading world a new psychology of risk and investing objectives:

- Write one chapter on the topic of psychology of risk and investing by mid-summer 2010.
- Have entire book roughed in by January 3, 2011.
- Complete work on a new book titled *Market Mind Games* by February 12, 2011.

Can you see how the goal is broad and those objectives are smaller steps to the goal?

The same process should be followed with your development as a trader. First, figure out why you are trading to begin with. This answer will be the goal. Once you have that down, set up objectives for learning and experience. You can then, within the context of those objectives, set up strategies and tactics for market/trade knowledge and experience as well as psych cap development.

Keeping Records: Analyzing Behavior   Another tenet of the research in behavioral finance (and general experimental psychology) is that our memories mis-remember. In other words, we imbue what we remember with all sorts of filters—kind of like confirmation bias in the rearview mirror.

How do you get around this in your development as a trader?

Simple. You keep accurate records of your analysis, thoughts, and feelings both as you enter trades, evaluate them, and exit them. Then you review those records and statistics so that as you plan your future objectives, strategies, and tactics you are doing so from a basis of reality and accuracy.

There is *no* substitute for this work. Your brokerage statements are not enough. In short:

- Markets are relentlessly uncertain. Nothing you can do will ever make the probabilities in an options model the perfect predictor of the future.
- You are not going to feel good about number one and you will try to somehow circumvent that truth.
- Allow yourself to feel the feeling of disliking the imprecision and ambiguity – write yourself a poem, song, or essay about it and re-read it often. The ironic result is you will feel less anxious!
- You will also most likely fall prey to the same behavioral (and perceptual) mistakes that everyone else falls prey to.
- The secret solution to this lies in this new psychology of risk laid out here.
- Feelings and emotions matter for all decisions.
- Learning to systematically use emotion analytics, first as a risk management tool and second as a piece of information related to unconscious pattern recognition, will lead you to be an exceptional risk and trade decision maker!

Good luck ... there is no journey more fascinating than the combination of markets, winning the human battle of perception prediction and what they used to call self-actualization. It is a novel way to become consistently profitable but it has worked for hundreds if not thousands of traders because it is based on the way your brain makes decisions in uncertain circumstances. Good Trading!

ABOUT THE CONTRIBUTOR

Denise Shull, founder of The ReThink Group, Inc., TraderPsyches and SportsPsyches, former CME Group member, and MA graduate of The University of Chicago is recognized for her groundbreaking explanations about the way feelings and emotions work in market bubbles and crashes. In 2004, Ms. Shull published "Freud's Path to Profit," which was later included in an anthology of trading articles entitled *The Psychology of Trading* in 2007.

Ms. Shull continues to make headlines with her published articles including "A Made-up Made-off World: How Could So Many Smart People Be

Tricked?," "The Brain on Risk," "The Truth about Market Decisions," and "How Publicly-Traded Markets Could Have Mitigated the Credit Crisis."

She has been profiled by *Bloomberg Markets Magazine* and *Financial Times* for her work. Ms. Shull's roots in trading extend back to 1994, when she began what was then called "upstairs" prop trading. She traded at such notable companies as Schonfeld and Sharpe Capital and has held seats on the Chicago Board of Trade and the Chicago Mercantile Exchange.

Shull has appeared on CNBC, ABC World News Tonight, The Discovery Channel, Cavuto and PBS' Nightly Business report. She is currently working on her own book, tentatively entitled *Market Mind Games*.

CHAPTER 11

Turning Your Trading into a Business

Dean Somes

"In order to succeed, your desire for success should be greater than your fear of failure."

—Bill Cosby

When asked the question "What do you want to do with your life?" as a youngster, most of us would reply "Fly to the moon!" or "Drive racecars!," a far more popular response than emphatically responding, "Work for The Man!"

But no matter our initial intentions, the unpopular answer is the more common outcome. After a while, we see the question about our dreams as no longer relevant, as if the opportunity to dictate our professional futures were as fleeting as our youth. Of course, it becomes increasingly more difficult to make a professional change as we become entrenched in our fields. But if, when posed the question, we begin salivating over the thought of independence and emphatically answer "Trade for a living!," then with a little motivation and guidance, we can make this dream into a reality. Trading for a living is the ultimate independent business, and it's a lot more profitable, and safer, than racecar-driving night school.

This chapter illustrates the basic process of turning your trading into a business. I will offer you some simple mantras, guidelines, rules, and examples to get you started in your trading career.

LEARNING THE DOLLAR

"You need money to make money," was the mantra by which my father traded. This translated into an almost pathological sense of frugality; my father squirreled away almost every penny he earned and was content to drive the family's 1989 Chevy Astro Minivan to work while his fellow senior-level corporate attorneys were driving the newest of the Mercedes S-series. While I gently declined the inheritance of our lovely multihued van, I embraced my father's legacy of thriftiness. Like he taught me, I scrimp, save, and closely monitor spending habits so that I have more money to put into the stock market and watch grow.

Adding your savings to your winning trading accounts not only will increase your profits but also will open up further opportunities to you as an investor. Investing in private equity or hedge funds, for example, often requires large minimums that only accredited investors (i.e., guys with a lot of money[1]) can access. Remember, "You need money to make money"—make this your mantra, too.

EDUCATION

One of the most exciting and invigorating aspects about trading for a living is the constant opportunity to learn. Each day in the market offers its own set of challenges and lessons; your experiences trading are invaluable educational resources in and of themselves. Make sure that you're up to these everyday challenges by seeking out supplemental resources, such as seminars, books, and trading periodicals. A quick Google search will turn up local investment groups and seminars, both online and in-person, that meet to discuss strategies or trading software. Invest in books about trading psychology, strategies that interest you, tax solutions for traders, portfolio allocation, and money management. Other print resources that are worth budgeting for include periodicals such as *Investor's Business Daily*.

An important part of your investor's library is your own trading journal. Lessons learned in trading sometimes can carry a hefty price tag, and a journal will help ensure that you only pay the price once. Case in point: I once traded a health-care stock that had broken out of a horizontal resistance trend line but then began to head south. Instead of adhering to my trailing stop and selling it, I held on. Unfortunately, the stock continued to plummet and I suffered a substantial loss, which I documented with a heavy heart in my journal. Reflecting back on this entry a few months later greatly minimized the damages when faced with a similar situation, this time a consumer staple stock that had just broken its horizontal resistance trend line. When the falling price hit my trailing stop, I sold it. The small loss I incurred this time was easy to recover within a few days with other winning trades.

Keep track of past mistakes, as well as near misses, observations, and analyses of why your trades were successful or unsuccessful. Was it proper money management or trade sizing that made that trade work out? In which types of markets do I make the most profit? Documenting your experiences will offer you insight into the type of trader you are and the type of trader you want to become.

THE FORMATIVE PROCESS

Success often springs from simplicity. Look at Energy Brands, which produces Vitamin Water. Within a decade, a quarter-billion-dollar-a-year business had sprung from a combination of two elemental ingredients— vitamins and water. So am I suggesting that you scrap your nascent business plans and go into the beverage business? No. I merely want to emphasize that you do not need wild, new innovative strategies to form the bedrock of your business. Build your business on the trading strategies at which you excel. Be they basic methods, modifications on existing strategies, or combinations of elemental approaches (think vitamins plus water), as long as they are your strengths and provide a foundation of confidence, you are starting out on the right foot.

Once you have committed yourself to an ethic of saving and have compiled a repertoire of solid strategies, take an introspective moment to ask yourself a few key questions: Am I willing to quit my day job and forfeit a salary and benefits? Will I be okay without the security of a steady pay schedule? In trading, you are only successful if your strategy is successful. But what happens if it isn't? Do you have enough saved to take a time-out from trading to study and develop a new winning strategy? If your honest answer to these questions is a sturdy yes, if you are willing to invest in your business not just with capital but also with time and sacrifice, you are ready to break out your conductor's baton.

That's right, your conductor's baton. Because even if your brass section is world class and your woodwind players trained at the Conservatoire de Paris, the melody will fall apart without the conductor. Your winning strategies, likewise, will devolve into cacophony without the proper orchestration of bookkeeping and accounting. When my father and I started building our own business, I learned about the paramount importance of an internal accounting system. Using an accounting software program and good old-fashioned filing cabinets, we filed away every receipt and statement that floated by our desks and screens. This diligence helped us keep tabs on our spending habits, rein in extraneous spending, and focus on our budget. Plus, keeping track of your receipts not only is a smart idea; it is required by law. If the Internal Revenue Service (IRS) comes knocking on your door, no matter what type of business entity you have assumed (LLC, LP, sole proprietor, etc.), you must be able to produce receipts dating up to seven years in the past.

When setting up an internal accounting system, choose a software program that can track receipts, trading activity, inflows, and outflows, including withdrawals. To keep track of trades, a simple spreadsheet will do, just as long as you can visualize your equity curve and get a good bird's-eye view of your gains and losses. If you have hired employees, you want to find a program that also can create state and federal tax forms such as the annual 941, quarterly 940, and W-2 forms. Investing in a good accounting software program is a legitimate and necessary expense when setting up your business—just remember to keep the receipt!

Another legitimate expense is hiring an outside accountant, especially if your accounts include private equity or oil and gas holdings, which are subject to very specific and obscure tax rules. A knowledgeable certified public accountant (CPA) will save you the guesswork, time you otherwise could spend trading, and perhaps your rear end. Keep your internal accounting system well organized and up to date and your accountant will thank you when tax season rolls around.

Remember that a beautiful piece of music is not simply the sum of its parts. Just so, a beautiful upward-trending equity curve is not solely due to good strategies. Orchestrating them with a rigorously managed business can make the difference between winning and losing.

TIPS AND FORMULAS FOR BUDGETARY SUCCESS

An effective internal accounting system will budget for every last expense. Commission and slippage are two such expenses that are accrued with every trade placed. Commission is the more predictable of the pair; it is the amount your broker charges you for placing a trade, and it is usually a fixed cost. Slippage is a little more slippery, so to speak. Think of pulling into a full-service gas station and asking the attendant to fill your tank with precisely $20 worth of gas. He has less-than-perfect reflexes and releases the pump handle at 3 cents past $20. These 3 cents are comparable to what the market calls slippage. Say you place a stop market order with your broker to buy one share of stock ABC at 20 bucks. Well, right now ABC is trading at $19, but the price is rising rapidly. Your broker, nimble as he may be, purchases the one share at $20.03. Those 3 cents may seem like peanuts, but if you're purchasing more than one share at a time (as I assume you do), it can all add up. Keep this in mind when you're budgeting.

Use stop-limit orders as a more conservative alternative to stop market orders. A stop-limit order is similar to a stop-market order, except that the former specifies that you will buy the security only at that specified price of $20. If the price rises to $20.02 and there is no one willing to sell the one share at your specified amount of $20, then you will not purchase the share. Determine which method, stop-market order or stop-limit order, you want to use based on your risk tolerance, your budget, and your desire to own the security.

Make sure that your broker is staying competitive in terms of commission and slippage costs. Shop around from time to time to ensure that you're not paying too much and that your broker's reflexes aren't those of an octogenarian gas-station attendant.

Contribution analysis is a formula that demonstrates how the expenses of commissions and slippage figure into the bigger profit picture:

$$\text{(gross trading profit)} - \text{(commissions and slippage)}$$
$$= \text{(money in trading account)}$$

$$\text{(money in trading account)} - \text{(company expenses)}$$
$$= \text{(net trading profit)}$$

Money in your trading account will fluctuate with market conditions. Just as widget demand ebbs and flows with the whims of the market, so, too, will the amounts in your trading accounts. However, some of the variability of your accounts is within your control. A defective widget necessitates increased quality control; likewise, a greater number of losing than winning trades demands that you monitor your trades more closely and do some damage control.

To maximize your net trading profits, take a good look at your business expenses, and continue to monitor them just as you do your trades. In my experience, simple tools such as an inexpensive real-time data feed and charting software fall under the category of smart investment. The operative word here is "inexpensive," especially in the early days of your business. As your business grows and you start seeing profits, then you can replace your card table with a proper desk and upgrade your software. Stick with the bare essentials at the beginning, and be wary of expenses such as substantial membership fees for services that promise large returns.

Your goal should be to earn those returns yourself—you don't need fancy programs or services to accomplish this.

SETTING UP A LEGAL ENTITY

I'm sad to say, starting your trading business is not as easy as setting up a lemonade stand on your front lawn. You will need to confer with an attorney to determine whether your lemonade stand will function best as an LLC, a limited partnership (LP), S corporation, or a sole proprietorship. For example, upon consulting with an estate attorney, my father decided to establish an LP, a limited partnership, which could exist within a larger entity and would allow family members to participate in the business. Seek out an attorney who specializes in estate planning and/or corporate, partnership, and limited liability company law and who can continue to provide assistance and advice after your business is set up. Other specialties include business tax planning and legal advice related to financial transactions. Once you have gained access to a directory,[2] choose 5 to 10 attorneys who specialize in these areas to interview by phone. A crucial qualification you'll look for is experience with setting up a trading business. Although not essential, it is advantageous if the legal firm has experience working with CPAs (certified public accountants) as well, because you'll also want to hire an accountant and the two of them will be working together. Also inquire about their rates and their frequency of billing. You'll need to budget for their startup fees, as well as those of an accountant.

I appealed to estate attorney, John R. Bauer of Shackelford, Melton & McKinley, LLP, in Dallas, Texas, to gain some more insight into the selection process.

Questions and Answers with John Bauer

Author: Hi, John. Thanks for taking the time to meet with me.

Bauer: No problem.

Author: During the initial meeting with the attorney, what topics should be covered?

Bauer: You'll want to sit down with your attorney and spend an hour or two hours so he can guide you through what the ramifications are for what you want to do. The attorney will discuss with you what type of business you want to start. They will ask what you envision is going to happen so that they can advise you as to how to incorporate or set up a partnership. Will it be just you or will you want to include other family members such as your children? There are other ways to set up a trading business other than an LLC. It may be a family partnership with limited liability for your children so they can get involved in the business.

Author: What materials should the trader bring to the attorney during their initial meeting?

Author: You'll want to bring your business plan, list of assets and liabilities and tax returns. If you want to involve others in the business, you should bring along their names and Social Security numbers.

Author: Let's say that you want to include family members in the business. The concern that arises here is whether you should create an estate and then the company, or can you go ahead and form the company and worry later about whether or not to create an estate?

Bauer: Depending upon the complexity and what is involved, most people just start up their business first. However, if you already have an estate plan in order, the business will logically fall into place within the estate.

Author: Let's expound upon this subject a little further. Let's take two different kinds of traders who want to go into business. The first wants to work solely and the second wants to include his family members in the business. Would an LLC be the best in both instances?

Bauer: No. For the trader who wants to include family members, a family limited partnership may be the best solution. That way the trader can still have control by being the general partner but wants to have his children involved making them limited partners. That way the children can learn the business and be able to take part in the profits while being protected from losses. However, the children won't have a say in day-to-day operations because the general partner is in total control.

Author: What is one of the easiest ways to start a trading business?

Bauer: Usually an LLC is the preferred choice because it is less complicated and less expensive in the long run. Regardless of whether you have an LLC or a corporation, the important part is the responsibility of ownership. You have to have your meetings, have solid accounting, otherwise you have just wasted your time because a creditor could pierce right through it, or "pierce the corporate veil." You want to make sure that when you do this, you will not only spend some funds to do it, but you're also going to take time to do it. If you are going to do it, you need to do it right. A lot of people will set up a sole proprietorship so that they will not have to worry about the corporate responsibilities. The problem with that, however, is liability, which is why people choose an LLC or LP in order to enclose the liability so that all one's assets aren't susceptible to creditors.

The cost associated with starting the business includes filing fees but are different from state to state. In Texas, filing for an LLC will cost $300, and $750 for a limited partnership.

Author: Should a person who is concerned about liability take further steps such as taking out liability insurance and/or key-man life insurance?

Bauer: Yes on the liability insurance. Regarding key-man life insurance, it depends upon how the business is set up and run. For example, if the trader/general partner is running a family limited partnership but the limited partners have little knowledge about the trading business, upon the death of the general partner, they may be able to use the proceeds collected from the key-man life insurance to hire another portfolio manager to take over the business. Traditionally, trading is such an art that it may make this difficult to do. Therefore, the key-man insurance could be used as an asset to distribute out if something happens.

Author: What are the basic pros and cons of setting up a trading business?

Bauer: When you set up an LLC, you are putting assets into it in an attempt to isolate them. For example, let's suggest you are buying rental homes. If you have someone in the rental home that falls and injures himself, you can be sued individually, especially if you are a sole proprietorship. So what a lot of people do is set up an LLC and have that asset [the rental home] in the LLC so if something happens with that asset, their liability is limited to that LLC. The same can be applied to a limited partnership. An LP or LLC protects the external assets of the owner except for the assets in the LP or LLC.

Some individuals choose a combination of both an LP and LLC. Continuing with our example, an individual can put the rental home in the LLC, which, in turn, is owned by the LP, thereby further limiting the liability.

Author: If someone is doing business only by himself, can he still have a partnership?

Bauer: Yes. But you need to be careful with that. By law, a partnership has more than one person. However, there can be exceptions. In Texas, some partnerships have sole members. This needs to be discussed with your attorney and CPA, though.

Author: How should the banking be done for the business? Should everything be transferred over to new business accounts?

Bauer: Let's use an example of an LLC. The LLC needs to have an account in the name of the LLC. If you are the president, you will be the one signing. A partnership is similar. You would have one account in the name of the business and one in your name. The proceeds of the business will remain in the business account from which your salary can be paid to your personal account. You have to be very careful. You cannot pay for personal items out of the corporation or the partnership. That tells people right off the bat it isn't what you say it is. Be sure to work very closely with your CPA to get this right.

Author: Thank you, John.

Summary As you may have gathered from our conversation, there are many variations to consider, such as a bypass trust for your spouse or an S corporation tax election within an LLC. A good attorney will be familiar with this variety and help you to customize your business to suit your circumstances and fulfill your vision.

Among your considerations should also be whether to establish a trust, which can offer tax benefits and provide asset management even after the estate owner has passed away. Whether a trust can provide these advantages is a question to ask your attorney and accountant.

Accounting In choosing an accountant, step one is to look for a CPA. Accountants of this designation keep abreast of current tax laws and will be invaluable resources to you as you establish your business. Find a CPA who specializes in financial institutions or who provides services such as bookkeeping, business planning, business start-ups, corporate taxes, estate planning, financial management and planning, investment advisory, and trust, partnership, or LLC taxation. Above all, the CPA should have knowledge of trading business operations. Again, use a directory[3] to find a handful of accountants who fit these qualifications. Before you meet or speak with the accountant, make sure you've gathered all of the necessary information about your accounts and you have decided what you want to accomplish with the accountant.

I sought the advice of accountant, Scott A. Woods, CPA with Rothstein Kass & Co., and asked him to share his expertise.

Questions and Answers with Scott Woods

Author: Thanks for taking the time to speak with me today, Scott. Let's jump right into it. What types of questions should a person ask themselves before starting a trading business that relates to accounting?

Woods: Start with a self-assessment about how much you know or want to know about accounting. Accounting serves several functions. It will help on an individual's reporting of returns to your investors as well as to creditors and the IRS. You have to make sure the accounting captures everything that is necessary for the various users of the reporting. A common situation we see occurs when someone with a trading history wants to start a fund or attract investors and they ask for a performance audit. Typically, there is not sufficient record keeping so it may be difficult and costly to audit the trader's performance.

Author: So, if a trader wants to start a business with a track record, they should keep all of their trading records. What does a trader need to bring to the accountant in order to have a performance audit?

Woods: To begin with, bring the broker statements along with a detailed record of what money has been taken in and out of the account.

Author: What are the first steps that the trader needs to take before going to see the accountant?

Woods: We typically see traders meeting with an attorney first. There are many regulatory issues to consider when trading other people's money. These should be understood by the trader. Even if the trader is not initially planning on trading for others, they can usually suggest how you will set up the business legally.

Author: What questions should the trader ask the accountant?

Woods: You should discuss what your long-term goals are for the business. Is the business going to be more proprietary in nature or are you going to accept outside money? There is a big difference in trading your own account than if you had investors to deal with. If you will accept outside money and form an investment partnership, then you need some substantial record keeping that is going to provide the information needed to report back to any investors. The key to remember is that you have a knack for some sort of trading strategy and unless you are also an accountant, you will need to seek the help of an accountant. That way you can focus in on your trading strategy.

It is very important that the accountant understands the trading strategy completely because there are complexities in the tax code: elections that may need to be made, different tax treatment of the gains and losses; loss deferral rules, as well as characterization of dividends and expenses.

Author: What are the typical costs that a trader can expect in the beginning in order to have detailed accounting records?

Woods: As you may anticipate, the answer is, "It depends." The use of an external administrator will be more costly but there are many benefits—particularly if you are trading other people's money.

Author: Are there any accounting rules that a trader should be aware of in the beginning?

Woods: Accounting rules are complex and always changing/evolving. Generally Accepted Accounting Principles (GAAP) requires investments be valued a fair value—this may not be as easy as it sounds, and depending upon what you are trading, can be quite involved.

Author: What should a trader think about when choosing an entity to start?

Woods: Well, a partnership is one of the most flexible and it has the fewest pitfalls. It is generally more tax efficient, perhaps even more so than an LLC. State taxation may influence this decision.

Author: Thank you, Scott.

GUIDELINES, INDICATORS, AND BIRDS OF PREY

Over the years I have formulated some trading rules that keep my emotions out of the way of making trading decisions. They are by no means hard and fast, but they might steer you clear of learning the hard way as you begin your business.

Rule 1. Always Set a Stop on Your Purchases

I use a trailing stop, which is set at a certain percentage below the purchase price of a long position. If the price of the underlying security moves up, the stop will move up as well, trailing by the percentage that you set. But if the security starts to trend down, the stop will stay put. Once the price hits the trailing stop established at the downward-turning point, the security will be sold.

I determine my trailing stop in the following way: say stock XYZ has a 14-day average true range (ATR) of 1.25, and its share price is $50. I would first divide the ATR by the share price: $1.25/50 = 0.025$. Give your trailing stop a little more room by multiplying this number by 115%: $0.025 \times 1.15 = 0.029$, or 2.9%. Round up if your broker accepts only whole-number orders. Thus, I'd place an order with my broker to buy 100 shares of XYZ at $50 with a trailing stop of 3%.

Rule 2. Limit Purchases of Volatile Stocks

A high 14-day ATR, one that is greater than 10%, indicates a high degree of volatility. If the underlying security you want to purchase is highly volatile (i.e., has an ATR above 10%), purchase only half of what you would normally. The high-volatility security thus will comprise a smaller portion of your portfolio and limit your portfolio volatility.

Rule 3. Lock in Profits by Selling Half of the Position When a Target Gain Is Reached

Set your target gain within the range of 1% to 5%. So, if my 100 shares of XYZ were to grow by 2%, for example, I would sell half of the position in order to protect those profits. I would let the other half ride while maintaining the 3% trailing stop. Abiding by this rule keeps greed in check and makes money over the long run.

Alternatively, when you want to meet a small profit target but you are unsure of the market direction, move the trailing stop up after selling one-half of the position. The trailing stop should be moved to the breakeven point, which is the purchasing price of the underlying security plus commission and/or slippage.

Rule 4. Gauge Your Positions with an Indicator(s)

Use an indicator (or several, but not too many) to prevent losing sight of the big picture, as it's easy to get bogged down by day-to-day volatility. Your indicator will help you keep an eye on the true state of the market. Jared has offered you a few macro data points to examine when forming your thesis, which are an integral part of making risk management decisions. I thought I would add a couple more along with explanations to guide you.

Indicators of market health are like iPhone apps: the sheer quantity of either is astonishing. Sort through the sea of indicators by looking for ones that match up with your time frame and complement your objectives. The big-picture indicators that I use describe the overall health of the economy on both a global and a domestic scale. I look at these indicators about once a month to see if the larger trend has changed or not.

Foreign Inflows The United States issues a great deal of debt. In order to keep our economy running at full steam, someone needs to buy that debt. Sure, U.S. citizens buy Treasury bonds, but foreign governments and investors account for a majority of the buyers. Therefore, in order to keep the cogs in the economic machine well oiled, capital inflow of foreign

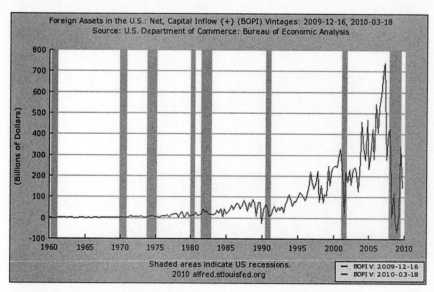

FIGURE 11.1 Net Capital Inflows

assets into the United States needs to keep rising. A snapshot of the foreign inflow chart, from the St. Louis Fed website, is shown in Figure 11.1.

Notice that during periods of recession (indicated by vertical gray bars), foreign inflows decrease. Take a look at the rightmost gray bar; just preceding it is a downward-sloping trend line, which indicates declining foreign inflow that heralded the Great Recession of 2008. Recovery from a recession is sustainable when foreign inflows increase without any sudden dip. A continuing uptrend of foreign inflows suggests that the economy is strong enough to attract international investors.

LIBOR   The London Interbank Offered Rate (LIBOR) is the interest rate at which banks can borrow money from other banks and is the world's most widely used benchmark for short-term interest rates. Interest rates can be seen as a measure of risk. A rising LIBOR signals that the risk of lending money to other banks is rising as well. One way to look at LIBOR is how interest rates are assigned to a person looking to receive a loan for a car. If the person applying for a loan has poor credit, then they will receive a higher interest rate. Why? Because the lending institution feels that the person with poor credit has a greater chance to default on the loan than a person with good credit. Figure 11.2 is a LIBOR chart taken from Bloomberg.

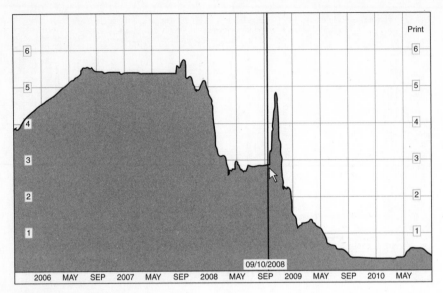

FIGURE 11.2 LIBOR
Source: Bloomberg.

The large spike in mid-September of 2008 indicates bankers' dwindling confidence in the banking system at that time and portends the volatile decline of the stock market that followed.

The TED Spread Like the LIBOR, the TED spread is a measure of credit risk. The TED spread is calculated by subtracting the three-month T-bill from the three-month LIBOR. *T-bill* is short for *Treasury bill*, a security issued by the U.S. Treasury that carries perceived little risk. The T-bill rate forms the baseline of the spread; the closer the LIBOR is to the T-bill, the more secure contributor banks feel about interbank lending. An increase in the TED spread signals that lenders believe the risk of default on interbank loans is going to increase.

I like the TED spread as a leading indicator of financial health. Spikes in the TED spread give the investor early warning signals that trouble in equities is approaching. The TED spread pictured in Figure 11.3, also taken from Bloomberg, shows a spike in August 2008 before the huge sell-off in September. The TED spread continued to vacillate wildly before spiking in October. An investor tuned in to the TED spread between August and October would have noticed the increased risk and subsequently become more defensive.

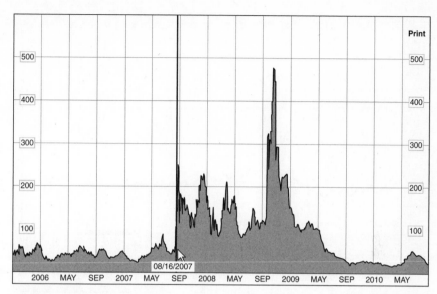

FIGURE 11.3 The TED Spread
Source: Bloomberg.

Think of the chart in Figure 11.3 as a seismograph printout of an earthquake. Everything is calm before and after an earthquake and its aftershocks, but the period of violent disturbance between those two time frames is a period of uncertain risk.

Unemployment   A downtrending unemployment rate means people are making money and spending it. It also correlates with higher prices in the stock market. Examining the official unemployment rate, U-3, is less useful than looking at a more comprehensive type of unemployment rate called the U-6. The U-6 takes into account the official rate, plus the number of discouraged workers (those who have given up on the search), individuals who are able to work but cannot find a job, and part-time workers who cannot find full-time work. Note the dive in unemployment during the bullish phase from 2003 to 2007 as shown in Figure 11.4, which was calculated using statistics from the Bureau of Labor Statistics. An astute investor would take advantage of this downtrend to invest in equities, since the risk-reward ratio is low.

The Junk Bond Market   In order to determine when junk bonds will make a good investment, I study the yields on corporate bonds. When they exceed those of government bonds of similar maturity, investors are

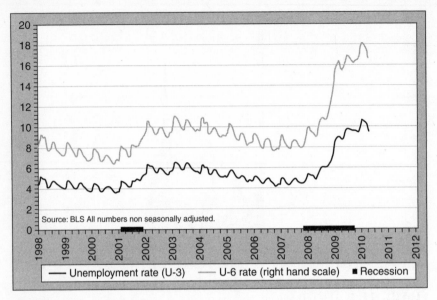

FIGURE 11.4 Unemployment and U-6 Rate

demanding additional compensation for expected default risk and lower liquidity. The difference between corporate and government bonds can give me a good idea of whether there is a good investment opportunity in junk bonds. To calculate this difference, I use the spread between the Baa-rated corporate bonds and the 10-year Aaa-rated U.S. Treasury bond. The Baa rating denotes subinvestment grade and high-risk/high-yield bonds, while the Aaa rating signals low-risk/low-yield bonds. In most cases, the Baa/10-year Treasury spread peaks around the onset of a recession and drops during the economic recovery phase. The years of 1983 and 2001, as well as the end of 2008, saw spreads peak just before the recovery phase. In the past, wide spreads—or any percentage above the historical 2% level—have mean reverted as the business cycle evolved and relative valuations became more normal. When the mean reversion occurs, junk bond and equity prices rise because falling yield spreads show an increased appetite for risk.

Figure 11.5 is a Bloomberg chart that illustrates the Baa/10-year Treasury spread in orange and the S&P 500 Index in green. Notice that the yield spread peaked before the equity markets bottomed and that the yield spread is inversely related to the S&P 500 Index.

A rise in the Baa/10-year Treasury spread should alert you that taking risk and investing in equities is ill advised and that you should take a defensive stance with your portfolio.

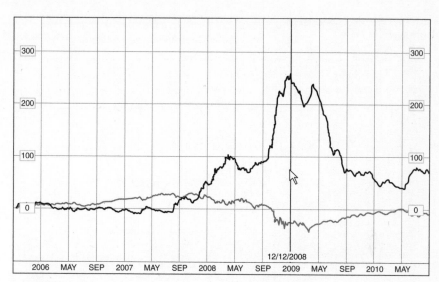

FIGURE 11.5 Baa/10-Year Treasury Spread versus SPX
Source: Bloomberg.

Technical Indicators   Use the indicators explained in Chapter 6. I have added my own unique variation of a moving average tactic for you to examine.

Moving Average Crossovers   In order to determine the direction of the market over the next few weeks or months, I use moving average crossovers. Within this category, I prefer exponential moving averages (EMAs) because they favor recent price movements as opposed to ones that have occurred further back in time, which may hint at any changes in the market's bullish or bearish trend. (Simple moving averages are fine; this is just my preference.)

Figure 11.6 is a chart, courtesy of www.StockCharts.com, that illustrates a 13/34 weekly EMA crossover. A 13-week EMA that dips below the 34-week EMA indicates a bear market. A moving average convergence divergence (MACD) indicator, which measures the strength of a trend, will take on a negative value when the turn is indeed bearish. When this occurs, limit purchases or allocation sizes. I suggest examining your long positions, taking profits, and selling losers to keep you out of trouble.

On the other hand, a 13-week EMA that rises above the 34-week EMA indicates a bull market; this crossover is confirmed by a positive MACD. When bullish, limit shorts or hedges.

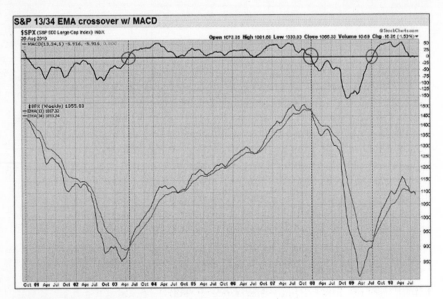

FIGURE 11.6 S&P 500 13/34 Weekly EMA Crossover
Source: www.StockCharts.com.

Although indicators and guidelines are all well and good, sometimes the market will swerve unpredictably. A nimble trader adapts to changing market conditions and stretches these rules accordingly. He also has up his sleeve a few strategies to use in a nontrending market, such as the iron condor. The iron condor, pictured in Figure 11.7, is a deceptively simple strategy that's useful in a market with indistinguishable long-term trends. The trade involves placing a bear call spread and a bull put spread on an

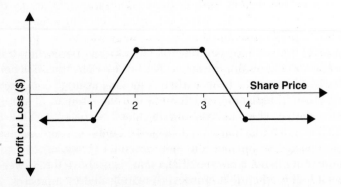

FIGURE 11.7 Iron Condor Risk Graph

underlying index such as the SPX (I use the S&P 500 futures as my underlying).

A Simple Strategy A credit spread is basically an option-selling strategy. Traders can take advantage of time premium and implied volatility when selling options. When creating a credit spread, the trader buys a far out-of-the-money option and sells a closer and more expensive option, thus achieving credit. As long as the options expire worthless and the underlying security does not cross the strike price of one of the sold options, the trader can keep the credit. Jared discussed this in detail in the strategy sections.

The reason for buying calls and puts above and below the sold strikes is to create a maximum loss scenario. Selling naked options can lead to unlimited losses. Spending a little money to buy protective puts and calls will limit any potential losses.

For example, on July 16, 2008, the S&P 500 futures for September traded around 1,240. I placed an order to sell 1 credit call spread, which means that I sold a strike price and bought a strike price further away than the one I sold. In this case, I sold a 1380 call and I bought a 1400 call. I sold the 1380 call and received 2.8 points and bought the 1400 call for 1.6, so the net I received was 1.2. When you sell something, you receive. Conversely, when you buy something, you pay.

Each point on the S&P futures index is equal to $250, so my total point credit was worth $300 (1.2 × $250 = $300). At the same time, I placed an order to sell a put credit spread.

I placed an order to sell 1 credit put spread, which means that I sold a strike price and bought a strike price further away than the one I sold. I sold a 980 put spread and I bought a 960 put. I sold the 980 put and received 4.4 and bought the 960 put and paid 3.5, so the net I received was 0.90.

My total point credit for the put spread was worth $225 (0.90 × $250 = $225).

My total credit for selling the entire strategy was $550.

If the S&P futures price stays between 1380 and 980, I'll keep the $550, less the cost of commissions.

To hold the trade, the broker will ask for a maintenance margin, which is a percentage of initial margin. In other words, before a trader can open a futures position, there must be enough cash in the trader's margin account to meet the initial margin requirement. This is needed because when a futures position is opened, the amount equal to the initial margin requirement is deducted from the trader's margin account and transferred to the exchange's clearing firm where it will sit while the futures position remains open.

The maintenance margin, which is at a level below the initial margin is an amount needed by the trader to maintain a hold on the futures position. It will only become a factor if the account value decreases.

If you remember the following, it makes it pretty simple:

Initial Margin = Initial Cash to open a position
Maintenance Margin = Cash needed to maintain the position.

For example, let's assume you buy an S&P 500 future and put up the exact initial margin of $25,000. Let us also assume that on the first day you lose $500. If you didn't have a maintenance number, you would have to come up with the margin on the first day. Instead, the exchanges give you a cushion in between the maintenance and initial margins. So, in this case, the maintenance margin would probably be around $21,000. Unless the trader loses over $4,000, there will not be a need to come up to the initial margin.

However, let us assume that your account falls below the maintenance margin. In that case, the trader has to come back up to the initial margin level. If the account in this example fell to $20,000, the trader would have to deposit $5,000 to get back to the initial margin level.

Before you start trading futures, make sure that you understand your brokerage firm's margin agreement. The margin agreement will let you know how and when the firm expects margin calls to be met. Sometimes, it is as simple as mailing a check. For others, it may require instant wire transfers. Keeping an open dialogue with your broker will keep you out of trouble in the futures market.

The following five rules apply to my iron condor strategy:

My buy rules

1. The sold calls and puts must differ by at least 250 points. The above example involves a 400-point difference (1,380 − 980 = 400).
2. The minimum amount of total credit points should be 1.5. The above example netted 2.1 points.
3. The Monte Carlo simulation, a measurement of risk, must have loss probabilities of less than 30% on the call side and 20% on the put side. At the moment of placing the order, the above example had a call side probability of 28.90% and a put side probability of 2.25%.
4. The trade date must be 75 days or fewer prior to expiration.
5. The difference between the sold call and bought call should be 20 strikes. The same rule applies to the put spread.

My sell rules

If the market sells off and my put side is losing, I can either roll down to new strikes or exit that side completely. Whether to roll down or exit depends on market conditions. Will the market rebound in time for expiration, or will it continue to deteriorate? Either scenario will dictate whether to stay in the trade, exit, trade a different month, or roll down to a spread that is further out of the money. The only firm rule that I have is this: If the trade is losing more than 200% of the projected profit, exit or roll down.

FINAL THOUGHTS

On April 15, 2007, there was one certainty: tax filing. However, there was one uncertainty I was not prepared for: the passing away of my father. One of his greatest gifts to me was the lessons that I now pass on to you. Although I value these gifts, I do wish he had bequeathed one more item to me, a comprehensive list of assets. My final recommendation to you is to make your list before you do anything else. Not only will your attorney and CPA appreciate this list, as it will help them to help you, but should the worst happen, your family will appreciate it, too. Inevitably, everyone will pass and most of us don't think about what happens after we die because we'll be dead. So, you'll want to make the important decisions about your business and family first before you decide what your last words will be, and please don't let them be Louisa May Alcott's dying words, "Is it not meningitis?" For all, I hope for the indefinite postponement of life's final event, and that you lead a long and happy life of independence and success.

Good luck and happy trading!

ABOUT THE CONTRIBUTOR

Dean Somes has been successfully navigating the stock markets as a trader for Cross Capital Partners in Dallas, Texas. He discovered his passion for the markets at the age of 17, while employed for a hedge fund in the Dallas area, and continued trading throughout his years at Boston College. In July, 2004, Dean joined Cross Capital Partners, a Texas family limited partnership. He worked closely with his father, Charles J. Somes, the founder of Cross Capital Partners. After Charles passed away in 2007, Dean became the sole manager of Cross Capital Partners. The combination of market knowledge, ability to create and understand complex trading methodologies, skills associated with solely managing a family partnership along with patience and perseverance sets Dean apart from most other managers.

Dean has been a guest speaker on *America Tonight,* a national radio program hosted by Emmy-award winning host Kate Delaney as well as several internet television shows and live engagements offering his commentary. In addition to managing Cross Capital, he is assisting a team of fund managers to start the first short-only actively managed ETF named "The Active Bear ETF", (NYSE: HDGE). Dean can be reached at deansomes@sbcglobal.net.

Notes

CHAPTER 1   MARKET BASICS AND MARKET MECHANICS

1. Reading the tape is a method where a trader (typically more active) watches tick-by-tick trades and changes in price to determine entry and exit points.

CHAPTER 2   DATA THAT MOVES THE MARKETS

1. There is a preliminary report that comes mid-month and a revised version usually about 14 days apart.
2. Case-Shiller data does *not* measure new construction, condominiums, co-ops/apartments, multifamily dwellings, or other properties that cannot be identified as single-family property.
3. The Conference Board surveys 5,000 U.S. households monthly. The survey consists of five questions that ask the respondents' opinions about the following:
   - Current business conditions
   - Business conditions for the next six months
   - Current employment conditions
   - Employment conditions for the next six months
   - Total family income for the next six months

CHAPTER 3   FUNDAMENTAL AND TECHNICAL STOCK ANALYSIS AND TOOLS

1. The S&P 500 is the second-most-followed index of U.S. large-cap companies behind the Dow Jones Industrial Average. It was created in

1957 and is composed of the prices of 500 large-cap common stocks actively traded in the United States. The stocks included in the S&P 500 are those of large publicly held companies that trade on either of the two largest U.S. stock market companies: the NYSE and the Nasdaq. Although most of the companies in the S&P 500 are U.S.-based, there are a few that are *not*, which were grandfathered into the index before the new rules were in place that dictated any new companies added to the index must be U.S.- based, and, when a U.S. company shifts its headquarters overseas, it is replaced by a U.S. company. Many mutual funds, exchange-traded funds, and other funds such as pension funds, are designed to track the performance of the S&P 500 index. Hundreds of billions of U.S. dollars have been invested in this fashion.

2. Trailing P/E is a measurement of the earnings that have been reported to date, annualized.

3. www.investopedia.com/articles/fundamental-analysis/09/five-must-have-metrics-value-investors.asp.

4. Burton G. Malkiel, *A Random Walk Down Wall Street* (New York: Norton, 1999) Chapter 5.

5. I have to thank my friend Sara Nunally for writing a great article about value, which is where I have sourced these great examples and tactics.

6. Gustave La Bon, *The Crowd: A Study of the Popular Mind* (New York: Macmillan, 1896).

7. Leonard Mlodinow, *The Drunkard's Walk: How Randomness Rules Our Lives* (New York: Vintage, 2009).

8. Candlestick Charts are my preferred means of price analysis, with price indicators both on top of the charts themselves (such as moving averages and Bollinger bands) as well as indicators placed underneath them (Stochastic and MACD).

9. For more information on Bollinger bands, check out www.bbands.com and www.bollingerbands.com.

10. You may need to revisit this example once you have read the Greeks and strategy sections.

11. Averaging down means that the investors (buyers in this case) purchase small portions of their total intended stock purchases at lower and lower prices instead of one single price, hopefully reducing their cost basis and overall risk because of both the systematic reduced investment amounts as well as a lower price.

12. Remember that the 50% stop loss is in line with the *monthly* ATR of MSFT, which is only about $1.90. If MSFT were more volatile, she may have to increase her stop-loss amount and either reduce the number

of contracts bought or decide to risk more on this trade, if she thought that the trade warranted it.

13. Remember that stops may not protect you in a stock that is gapping down.

CHAPTER 4 OPTIONS BASICS

1. Typically, you would *not* exercise the option if it has zero intrinsic value on expiration.

2. Had you just held on to the call, its value will decrease by the amount of parity lost (the amount of the dividend) so the call would open up 30 cents lower, assuming that the stock was unchanged and no time value was lost. This would result in a 0.30 loss in each contract you owned.

CHAPTER 6 STRATEGY—THE BASIC OPTION TRADES

1. Unless the call becomes very deep in the money, you will have a net long delta position, which means that if the stock continues to rise you should become profitable. Remember that you can *always* exit this trade before expiration if you believe that the stock will continue to rise above the short call strike price.

2. Some brokers may ask you to specify a price on both the call and the stock. Remember to check with your broker and practice before applying this strategy.

3. They are also my suggestion for newer traders who just want to use put options as a lower risk substitute for shorting stock and are speculating on bearish moves in a stock.

4. For me personally, doing them for a credit is like a covered call with an added insurance benefit that a regular covered call does not offer.

5. This is according to www.earningswhispers.com.

CHAPTER 7 STRATEGY—THE BASIC SPREAD TRADES

1. These are my own personal suggestions.

2. A vertical spread can never be worth more than the width of the strikes.

3. Profitability will be ensured if the stock moves away from the strike more than the total cost of the spread.

4. Profitability will be ensured if the stock does *not* travel away from strike more than the total credit of the spread.

5. If the stock moves past these points before expiration, you will definitely be losing money.

CHAPTER 8 STRATEGY—THE ADVANCED OPTION SPREADS

1. All of these spreads are limited in reward and limited in risk.

2. The most a long butterfly can be worth is the difference in strikes.

3. The most a short butterfly can be worth is the difference in strikes, which would occur if the stock was above your short upper strike or below your short lower strike. Max loss will occur when the stock is at your center long strike on expiration and will be the spread width minus the credit you received. If you sold a five-point fly for $1.50, you would lose $3.50 total in that situation.

4. A short butterfly can be constructed of two call spreads or two puts spreads, *not* a combination of both. It does not matter whether calls or spreads are used, the strike prices determine risk, cost, and Greeks. Max profit will be if spread expires with stock above or below the wing strikes, max loss will occur if spread expires with stock at center strike.

5. A short butterfly can be constructed of two call spreads or two put spreads that share a strike in the center, *not* a combination of both call and put spreads. It does not matter whether calls or spreads are used; the strike prices determine risk, cost, and Greeks. Max profit will be if spread expires with stock above or below the short strikes, and maximum loss will be if spread expires with stock right at the center strikes. The most you can make credit received in the trade ($1.24 in the case above). In the above example, you can lose up to $3.76 (which is the difference between strikes minus the credit).

6. Width refers to the width of the two call spreads or put spreads.

7. Width refers to the width of the two call spreads or put spreads (the wings).

8. Note the combination of both a bearish call spread and bullish put spread, but they oppose one another and share a center strike.

9. The short iron condor has become extremely popular with traders who are betting on a stock or index staying within a certain range.

10. The primary goal of this strategy is to have the stock within your chosen short strikes; this will generally result in the passage of time being positive to your position, as both out-of-the-money spreads are moving closer to expiration, at which time they will be worth zero.

11. Remember that delta is moving opposite when the stock is between your short strikes because those short options are closest to the stock and short options are short gamma.

12. You can also see the reversion to the mean indicated with the curved arrow.

CHAPTER 10 A REVOLUTIONARY APPROACH TO THE MIND GAMES OF THE MARKETS

1. Frank H. Knight, *Risk, Uncertainty and Profit* (Boston, MA: Hart, Schaffner & Marx; Houghton Mifflin, 1921).
2. Colin Camerer, George Loewenstein, and Drazen Prelec, "Neuroeconomics: How Neuroscience Can Inform Economics," *Journal of Economic Literature* 43(March 2005): 9–64.

CHAPTER 11 TURNING YOUR TRADING INTO A BUSINESS

1. For a more complete definition, go to the Securities and Exchange website: www.sec.gov/answers/accred.htm.
2. Some helpful online resources include the American Bar Association (FindLegalHelp.org) and the Martindale-Hubbell Law Directory (www.lawyers.com).
3. Start with this online resource: www.CPAdirectory.com.

About the Author

Jared Levy, who grew up in Philadelphia, has spent his most of his adolescence and adult life immersed in the finance and options industries. Jared began his career as a retail stock broker, spending several years managing money and educating the public on smart investing decisions, which included many alternative strategies such as derivatives and even unique real estate investments, including development, creative financing structures, and property management.

After creating his own stock and options-trading strategy and indicator in the 1990s, Jared went on to become a market maker and specialist on the Philadelphia Stock Exchange (PHLX), trading the largest volume issue on that exchange at the time, Dell (DELL). He then moved to the American Stock Exchange (AMEX), where he traded Cisco Systems (CSCO) options. Before the age of 25, Jared had been recruited by Equitec Proprietary Group to be one of the original on-floor market makers trading Nasdaq 100 Trust options ("Qubes"). During that time he successfully traded thousands of options contracts and shares daily, equating to millions of dollars in risk. Jared was also a member of the Chicago Stock Exchange (CSX).

In 2001, Jared returned to the PHLX to launch a new on-floor operation for his firm, serving as an options specialist for companies including Krispy Kreme Doughnuts (KKD), Expedia.com (EXPE), Baxter Technologies, and Broadband and Semiconductor HOLDRS products, among others.

After leaving the floor, Levy traded distressed assets and consulted for Thomson Financial before relocating to Dallas to join Wizetrade and WTV as their Chief Options Strategist and on-air options expert. In 2004, Jared began his live on-air career as an anchor/expert fielding questions and educating viewers from around the world, unscripted and raw. He was known for his three-plus hours of daily, live, and unscripted market commentary and education. Jared dedicated his time with Wizetrade to enlighten investors worldwide about the mechanics of the market, risk management, and options trading, which is where he really found his passion for educating.

Jared has been featured in many industry publications and won an Emmy for his daily video, "Trader Cast." He is regularly quoted by Reuters, the *Wall Street Journal*, and Yahoo! Finance, among others.

In 2008, Jared joined PEAK6 Investments as the senior derivatives specialist, focusing his energy on the options news network, where he hosted and was the resident expert on several shows. He also offered his trade alerts service.

In March 2009, he was recruited by CNBC to become a Fast Money contributor. Prior to that, he had appeared on Bloomberg, Fox Business, CNN Radio, Wall Street Journal Radio, and many other financial and nonfinancial networks around the world.

Shifting part of his attention to writing, Jared published a daily column called the practical options trader, which was extremely well received.

In July 2010, Jared left PEAK6/OptionsHouse to join the Taipan Group as an editor and analyst. He continues to provide education and coaching to retail and professional traders and investors around the world in addition to trading for himself.

Jared actively invests in real estate around the United States and has held his real estate and insurance licenses in Pennsylvania as well as his Series 7 and 63.

The ultimate goal for Jared is to teach the public how to successfully and consistently trade and invest for a living, while keeping risk low. He believes that through analyzing equities, derivatives, and the markets as a whole as well as advanced risk management through both simple and complex strategies, one can create a practical, straightforward checklist type approach to successful investing.

You can keep up to date with Jared at his website www.jaredlevy.com.

Index